FOUNDATIONS FOR EFFECTIVE
SCHOOL LIBRARY MEDIA PROGRAMS

FOUNDATIONS FOR EFFECTIVE SCHOOL LIBRARY MEDIA PROGRAMS

KEN HAYCOCK, EDITOR

School of Library, Archival, and Information Studies
The University of British Columbia

1999
LIBRARIES UNLIMITED, INC.
ENGLEWOOD, COLORADO

To Michele Farquharson and Karin Paul, exceptional leaders in depicting the foundations for integrated school library media programs through the professional literature.

LIBRARIES UNLIMITED, INC.
P.O. Box 6633
Englewood, CO 80155-6633
800-237-6124
www.lu.com

Library of Congress Cataloging-in-Publication Data

Haycock, Ken.
    Foundations for effective school library media programs / edited by Ken Haycock.
    xii, 331 p. 22×28 cm.
    Includes bibliographical references and index.
    ISBN 1-56308-720-0 (cloth)
    ISBN 1-56308-368-X (paper)
    1. School libraries--United States.   2. Library orientation for
school children--United States.   I. Title.
Z675.S3H39   1998
025.5'678--dc21   98-40343
                                                   CIP

Contents

Contributors

Bev Anderson was a teacher, teacher-librarian, coordinator of program resources and an elementary school principal with the Calgary (Alberta) Board of Education.

Liz Austrom was a teacher-librarian and district principal for curriculum resources with the Vancouver (British Columbia) School Board.

Mark Beasley is on the faculty of the Division of Administrative and Instructional Leadership at St. John's University in New York.

Martha Blake teaches in the division of Educational Leadership at the University of Houston-Clear Lake in Houston, Texas.

Paul Brandt is coordinator of the University of Iowa College of Education Curriculum Laboratory where she consults with faculty on the integration of trade books and other resources into K-12 curriculum.

Kathy Brock is curriculum director for Douglas County Schools in Douglasville, Georgia, and adjunct faculty for the Department of Research, Media and Technology at the State University of West Georgia in Carrollton, Georgia.

Jean Brown is associate professor at Memorial University of Newfoundland in St. John's, where she teaches courses in educational leadership, including teacher-librarianship.

Karen Buchanan is in the Division of Administrative and Instructional Leadership at St. John's University in New York.

Susan Casey is teacher-librarian with the Calgary (Alberta) Board of Education.

Ray Doiron is assistant professor on the Faculty of Education at the University of Prince Edward Island. He also teaches in the pre-service teacher education program and coordinates the Diploma in School Librarianship Program.

Christina Doyle is director of learning technologies with the Kern County Superintendent of Schools Office in Bakersfield, California.

Rita Dunn is professor in the Division of Administrative and Instructional Leadership and director of the Center for the Study of Learning and Teaching Styles at St. John's University in New York.

Mary Tarasoff Egan is principal at Prospect Lake School in Saanich School District in Victoria, British Columbia.

Mike Eisenberg is professor at the School of Information Studies at Syracuse University, director of the ERIC Clearinghouse on Information & Technology and the AskERIC Project, and coordinator of LM_NET.

Sonya Emperingham is teacher-librarian at Saanichton Elementary School in Saanich School District, British Columbia; she is also trained as a cooperative learning and instructional theory resource teacher.

Doris Epler was director of school library media services for the state of Pennsylvania.

Mary Ann Fitzgerald is an assistant professor in the Department of Instructional Technology at The University of Georgia, where she teaches school library media courses. Prior to earning her doctorate in 1998, she taught and worked as a media specialist in Georgia public schools for 11 years.

Ken Haycock is professor at the graduate School of Library, Archival, and Information Studies at The University of British Columbia; he is a former teacher, teacher-librarian, district coordinator, school principal and senior education official.

Barbara Howlett is a secondary school teacher-librarian in Langley, British Columbia.

Doug Johnson is district media supervisor for Mankato Area Public Schools in Minnesota and an adjunct faculty member of Mankato State University.

Ruth Law is past teacher-librarian at George Kennedy School in Georgetown, Ontario.

David Loertscher is a professor at San Jose State University in California in the School of Library and Information Studies.

Josette Lyders is a writer, owns an antiquarian book business, and serves as a library consultant and trustee in Peacham, Vermont.

Michael Marland was headmaster at the North Westminster Community School in the Inner London Education Authority in the United Kingdom.

Mary Megee is director of the Media Education Laboratory at Rutgers University-Newark College of Arts and Sciences and executive producer of the On Television Project Documentaries for the Public Broadcasting System.

Antoinette Oberg is associate professor in the Faculty of Education at the University of Victoria in British Columbia.

Dianne Oberg is associate professor at the University of Alberta where she holds a cross-appointment in Elementary Education and the School of Library and Information Studies; she is also vice-president of the International Association of School Librarianship and editor of *School Libraries Worldwide*.

Carol-Ann Page was a teacher, teacher-librarian and district administrator and is now president of the HRD (Human Resources Development) Group, a consulting and staff training firm in Vancouver.

Patti Hurren Plotell was the English-as-a-second-language staff development specialist with the Vancouver (British Columbia) School Board for four years. She is currently working as an elementary vice-principal.

Linda Rafuse is past teacher-librarian and an administrator with the Halton Board of Education in Burlington, Ontario.

Bruce Sheppard is associate dean of the Graduate Programs and Research in the Faculty of Education, Memorial University of Newfoundland.

Debra Simmons is teacher-librarian at Tupper Secondary School in Vancouver, British Columbia.

Sharon Straathof has been a teacher, teacher-librarian and staff development specialist with the Vancouver (British Columbia) School Board.

Julie Tallman is associate professor in the Department on Instructional Technology in the College of Education at the University of Georgia.

Jean Donham van Deusen is on the faculty at the University of Iowa School of Library and Information Science, where she teaches courses in school librarianship, materials for children, and multimedia.

Patricia Wilson is associate professor in the School of Education at the University of Houston-Clear Lake in Houston, Texas.

Introduction

Effective school library media programs have a positive impact on student achievement, in both the student's ability to process and use information effectively and in knowledge development in subject content areas, on motivation and ability to read, and on the quality of experiences that teachers and students have in our schools (see, for example, Clyde, 1996; Haycock, 1992; Krashen, 1993; Woolls, 1990).

The mere presence of staff, facility and resources, however, are not sufficient in and of themselves to bring substantial gains, although there is evidence for improvement in achievement even at this level of development.

Quality programs exemplify specific foundations or prerequisites for success:

- a stated aim for the program,
- a clear definition of the role of the qualified "teacher-librarian" as well as the other partners in program development and delivery—the district, school administrators, classroom teachers,
- a priority on collaborative program planning and team teaching between the teacher-librarian and classroom colleagues,
- a systematic approach to teaching the information process based on a school-based continuum of information skills and strategies,
- flexible scheduling of classes and groups, and

- appropriate and effective program and personnel evaluation by administrators.

Studies indicate that the development of student competence in information skills is most effective when integrated with classroom instruction through collaborative program planning and team teaching by two equal teaching partners—the classroom teacher and teacher-librarian—in a flexibly scheduled library resource center. A program such as this requires strong administrative leadership and support and effective staff development and training.

Much has been written on school library media management but considerably less on these foundations for effective school library media programs.

This collection of readings brings together thirty-nine papers on critical elements of program development and implementation. They are organized by seven distinctive areas: the foundations; the school context; role clarification; information literacy; collaborative program planning and teaching; program development; accountability. The papers are written by recognized leaders in the field who blend a strong research base with practical suggestions for improving student learning.

Taken together, this collection provides both an overview of the critical attributes of successful programs and a design for developing and implementing a strong, integrated program that will have a positive effect on student achievement. All of the thirty-nine papers originally appeared in the journal *Emergency Librarian* (now called *TeacherLibrarian*); one-third also appeared previously in *The School Library Program in the Curriculum* (Libraries Unlimited, 1992); two thirds of the papers have been published since 1990 and one third since 1995. Each paper stands on its own and is as relevant today as when it was first published.

While there has been dramatic change in the resources and delivery systems for information in schools, particularly through newer technologies, the fundamental ingredients of well-planned and integrated programs, team taught by teachers and teacher-librarians in a thoughtful and systematic way, adjusting to student needs and monitoring learning throughout the process, remain unchanged. There has been considerable attention given to emerging technologies and their integration in school library media programs, there has been much written and promulgated regarding student research processes as well, but unless these are taught collaboratively by teacher and teacher-librarian together in flexible programs, the results will not be as significant.

All of the papers reflect sound professional practice. Taken together they should serve the needs of both the novice and experienced teacher-librarian. They also have much to offer to instructional partnerships in a variety of other academic settings, including at the post-secondary level.

References

Clyde, L. A. (Ed.). (1996). *Sustaining the vision: A collection of articles and papers on research in school librarianship.* San Jose, CA: Hi Willow Research and Publishing for the International Association of School Librarianship.

Haycock, K. (1992). *What works: Research about teaching and learning through the school's library resource center.* Seattle, WA: Rockland Press.

Krashen, S. (1993). *The power of reading: Insights from the research.* Englewood, CO: Libraries Unlimited.

Lance, K., Welborn, L. & Hamilton-Pennell, C. (1993). *The impact of school library media centers on academic achievement.* San Jose, CA: Hi Willow Research and Publishing.

Woolls, B. (1990). *The research of school library media centers.* Papers of the Treasure Mountain Research Retreat, Park City, Utah, October 17–18, 1989. San Jose, CA: Hi Willow Research and Publishing.

PART ONE

THE FOUNDATIONS

In setting the foundation for the elaboration of critical elements of program development and implementation, it is essential that one articulate and specify those elements and provide the research evidence for their importance.

If the program is to have meaning it must have a stated aim or mission statement that is clear and well-understood by those engaged in the educational enterprise. The American Association of School Librarians, for example, suggests that the mission of the program is to ensure that every student and teacher is an effective user of information and ideas. Based on a stated purpose, whether articulated at the district or school level, it is easier to clarify the roles and responsibilities of the various partners. That the school library media program is a partnership, if it is to be effective, is beyond question but who those partners are and what their roles and responsibilities might be is less clear. An effort is made to clarify those roles here for the school district, the school principal, the classroom teacher and the teacher-librarian. Similarly, student achievement is best improved when the teacher-librarian

places a premium on collaborative program planning and teaching with classroom colleagues. Units of study are developed together, based on the school's continuum of information skills and strategies, with goals and objectives, authentic assessment of achievement and joint responsibilities set out; going so far as to record these units provides a foundation for continued improvement and extension into other areas.

Studies tell us that teacher-librarians who have education and training in collaborative planning and teaching with classroom teachers tend to engage in it more frequently and with greater success than do those without, providing clear direction for programs that educate teacher-librarians. We also know that in the 1990s and beyond, if teacher-librarians are unable to market themselves and their programs, as well as to advocate for necessary support, the program will be in jeopardy in tight financial times. Advocacy here is not lobbying or public relations, but rather a planned, deliberate and sustained effort to develop understanding and support incrementally over time.

The paper "Strengthening the Foundations for Teacher-Librarianship" was first delivered at a conference of the International Association of School Librarianship and subsequently reprinted in more than a dozen state and national journals. It was referenced in national guidelines and standards as "an important contribution." It is as relevant today as when it was first delivered.

The research base for teacher-librarianship provides credibility and evidence for advancing the school library media agenda. Effective programs do have an impact on student achievement, on reading, and on the school's culture. What is becoming more evident is that the effect is not only on the development of information skills and strategies but also on improved learning in subject content areas. We need to become more familiar with this body of research and to use it effectively in program planning and in advocacy.

Research in curriculum implementation and staff development and training likewise provides teacher-librarians with guidelines for effective programs. Rather than being disappointed when a single workshop does not transform our faculties or lead to changed behaviors, we need to be more conversant with what approaches will make a difference and ensure that these are considered by our colleagues when moving to improve the school library media program.

CHAPTER ONE

Strengthening the Foundations for Teacher-Librarianship

Ken Haycock

As we consider the issues of library media program development, it is critical that we also consider the means by which the profession of teacher-librarianship itself might be strengthened and even enhanced. I use the term "teacher-librarian" purposely here, for the signs are clear that there is relatively little danger to the continued existence of school libraries. The issue is the continued existence of school librarians. We have been successful in building facilities and collecting and organizing materials, but we have been less successful in developing an awareness and understanding of the role of the school librarian as a professional teacher, as an equal partner in the educational enterprise, and in developing strong support for that position.

There have been a number of studies that show that the concept of the library as part of an instructional system responding to teacher and student needs, and even creating needs within that system, is perceived by relatively few school librarians and only dimly by most teachers and administrators. We are left with the fact that our school library resource centers are "beauty spots on the body politic."

Now it would be all too common for us to bemoan the lack of understanding of our roles and our many contributions, and wonder why the intrinsic value of our goods and services is not well-regarded and well-supported. But I would submit that while we know the answers to these questions, we just too often prefer to wring our hands, or reject difficult answers to easy questions. In the words of James Baldwin: "Not everything that is faced can be changed, but nothing can be changed unless it is faced."

There are clear and straightforward approaches that can be taken to ensure strong programs and their continued development. School resource centers, and teacher-librarians, can be educationally essential and economically justifiable. There are many school districts where teacher-librarians are not "the first to go," even in times of dire economic restraint.

The Mission Statement

Millions and millions of dollars are invested in school library resource centers each year by individual school districts. It would seem logical that the funding agency, whether the state or each school district, would have a clear stated aim or purpose for the library program. Surely, school board members and officials, together with administrators and teachers, should know what the purpose of a program is before it is funded. This provides both a basic level of understanding and a general framework for the program and its evaluation.

Strangely, however, few school districts have a written statement of purpose for the program, or a "mission statement" if you will, thus leaving it in the never-never land of the extra, the educational frill, good to have when you can afford it, but hard to justify when no one really knows what it is for; this mission statement must be clear, concise, and stated in educational terms. It is just not significant or defensible to state this aim as simply fostering a love of reading and libraries.

One common mission statement reads: The aim of the library media program is to assist students to develop a commitment to informed decision-making and the skills of lifelong learning.

We know that to achieve this stated aim, teachers and teacher-librarians cooperate to plan and implement units of study as teaching partners; these units integrate those skills necessary to locate, evaluate, organize and present information from a variety of sources. Through such planning and cooperative teaching, students develop, master and extend information skills and strategies in different subject contexts and at varying levels of difficulty. A secondary emphasis is placed on language improvement and enjoyment, and the promotion of voluntary reading through collaboratively developed programs.

Partnerships

The library media program is a partnership involving the school district, the principal, the classroom teacher, and the teacher-librarian.

The school district is the public agency accountable to the community for the educational program. It has a specific responsibility to provide leadership in a number of areas, most of which cost little or no money. The school district, for example, should approve a stated aim for the program that is clear to everyone; after all, if public funds are to be invested in this area, doesn't the educational community as well as the community at large have a right to know its purpose? If teacher-librarians are to be engaged, there should be a clear, written role description which stresses professional functions as well as minimum qualifications for that position.

The district should also have procedures in place to entrench or infuse information skills and strategies in the school curriculum.

The district provides leadership by insisting on flexibly scheduled library resource centers, after planning between the teacher and teacher-librarian. The success of the program rests on planning: If teacher-librarians are providing teachers with spare or relief periods, planning becomes impossible and the program doomed to failure, thus squandering public funds. Also, only the school district is in a position to organize support services, such as central cataloguing and processing and central collections of expensive and unique resource materials.

Some districts virtually set up teacher-librarians and resource-based programs for failure due to benign neglect in the policy and support areas. This leadership does not necessarily cost money; it does require a commitment from the teacher-librarian, however, to work individually and through associations to advocate change and necessary improvements.

As with the school district, the principal, as the professional responsible for the implementation of school district policies and procedures, is accountable for the school program and has a responsibility to see that all school resources, including the teacher-librarian and learning resources, are used as fully and effectively as possible.

There are a large number of things that the principal can do to support and enhance the program, from querying prospective new teachers on how they would involve the teacher-librarian in their programs to attending orientation and inservice programs put on by the teacher-librarian for staff members, through to including questions about the ways in which the resource center and teacher-librarian were used in instructional programs when evaluating teachers for written reports. The research on the role of the principal is quite clear: the principal is the single most important factor in the development of a strong library program; teachers respond to the principal's expectations. This points to a critical need for effective communication with administrators at all levels.

From research we know that certain factors affect teacher use of the school resource center and teacher-librarian. We also know that the more that teachers make use of the resource center and the teacher-librarian, the better the program and the stronger the support. Those factors which affect teacher use are involvement in program planning by the teacher-librarian and team teaching, inservice programs organized or led by the teacher-librarian, administrative support for the program, and the behaviors and qualifications of the teacher-librarian.

The classroom teacher bears considerable responsibility for the effectiveness of resource-based learning. Effectiveness is severely impaired if we simply transfer thirty youngsters from one teacher to another, from classroom teacher to teacher-librarian. The strength of the teacher-librarian lies in providing the classroom teacher with an opportunity to share not only planning but also preparation and implementation of programs. The teacher who chooses not to use the services of the resource center or teacher-librarian is surely accountable for the development of information skills and strategies, especially as they have been outlined in the mandated curriculum guides.

It is becoming increasingly possible to evaluate the teacher-librarian as but one component of the resource center program, and the more that we can recognize and reinforce this, the better that things will be for us. There are a great many factors which affect the quality of the program but for which the district, the principal or the teacher, the other partners, are responsible and should be accountable. For example, the teacher-librarian does not determine the quantitative aspects of the program such as the size of the facility, the size of the budget, the amount of time and clerical support available, and so on. Qualitatively, the district must provide some leadership in providing a framework for the implementation of quality programs—by stating the aim of the program, the role of the teacher-librarian, principal and teacher, the continuum of information skills and strategies to be developed, and by providing policies, procedures and services to support the implementation of the program. The principal is the key player in seeing that a program is developed, supported and enhanced. The principal selects and evaluates the staff; the principal is accountable for the implementation of school district policy; the principal can create the necessary collaborative environment to enable the teacher and teacher-librarian to work towards effective programs for resource-based learning. The teacher, of course, is responsible for the development of independent learning skills within the context of state, district and school guidelines and for seeing that all school resources are used effectively for student learning. If the program is a partnership, then the teacher has some responsibility to plan and work closely with the teacher-librarian.

If we can begin to evaluate the resource programs, rather than simply teacher-librarians, if we can spell out each player's responsibility, there will be better understanding of the program as a joint effort and there will also be more commitment to it.

Clarification of the Role of the Teacher-Librarian

This leads to some determination of the role of the teacher-librarian. Many studies on the perceptions of educators of the role of the teacher-librarian have found that principals are amazingly consistent in their view of the teacher-librarian as having a strong role in the curriculum affairs of the school. Teachers are also consistent in their view of the teacher-librarian, but as responsible for clerical and technical tasks, rather than teaching tasks, unless they have experience in working with a teacher-librarian, while teacher-librarians themselves are terribly confused. The conclusion that these studies reach, of course, is that unless teacher-librarians start to speak with a unified voice about what the purpose of the program is and why they are in the school there is never going to be a basic level of understanding and support for that program and its continuation.

In order to develop the necessary program elements to implement this stated aim requires a strong and close partnership with colleagues. Thus, we would do well to establish common bonds and eliminate unnecessary barriers. Let's start by eliminating unnecessary jargon from our vocabulary. We use terms like library skills when we could talk about information skills which are outlined in a large number of curriculum guides as each and every teacher's responsibility. The term library skills simply denotes something that is taught in the library, by a librarian. Other educators have moved through library skills, primarily physical and locational in nature, to research and study skills, incorporating the research process, to information skills and strategies, the ability to use information effectively, especially to solve problems and to make decisions. Instead of a library program, we could focus on resource-based learning, a viable and educationally sound approach. The catalogue, print or electronic, which we insist on shrouding in mystique, is simply an index to the school's collection of curriculum materials, and beyond to the resources of the community. A vertical file is simply vertical, why not information file or pamphlet file? And why periodicals for what teachers, students and the rest of the world call magazines? If we could break down some of these walls and establish common educational bonds, we could go a long way to entering the mainstream of educational thinking and decision-making.

Similarly, everyone has a personal vision of the purpose of the library because of personal experience in a public library or university library. I would submit that this is irrelevant. The school resource center serves quite a different function from other types of libraries, due to an emphasis on teaching young people how to process and use information. Even the subtle move to the term teacher-librarian designates the school librarian more clearly as a teacher and member of the teaching staff. And, of course,

most school librarians are not professional librarians at all but are teachers, professional teachers, and should be proud of it.

The very nature of the role of the teacher-librarian is that of initiator and change agent. We talk of getting teachers to use the library when this is not the issue—what we are talking about is getting teachers to change the way that they teach and to adopt team teaching, resource-based strategies. This is why the job is so difficult and so challenging.

The library media program rests on teacher contact. The teacher-librarian must take the initiative to plan with colleagues. It isn't a matter of time, it's a matter of priorities. It isn't a matter of territory, it's a matter of commitment to student learning. The involvement of teachers is critical for successful, educationally viable program implementation.

I have asked the same question of hundreds of classroom teachers: "How many of you have been approached by a teacher-librarian, even informally, to plan and teach a unit of study together?" The results are always the same. In every group of forty to fifty teachers there will only ever be three or four who have been so approached. We presume rejection and too often never even make the initial overture. We presume that teachers will view cooperation as interference. Perhaps we should extend to classroom teachers the right to reject us themselves—rather than doing it for them!

Then there are those who hold the view that we must start "where the teachers are at." Consequently, we tolerate programs determined by teachers who often see us in that subservient position of clerk or technician and allow our roles and responsibilities to be determined by a colleague—something no one else would allow. Where is our professional commitment and integrity? "The meek may indeed inherit the earth, but I can guarantee that news of it will never get out!"

The teacher-librarian's major task is to work with classroom teachers to plan, develop, and implement units of study which integrate information skills—not the only task, not the most time-consuming task, but, yes, major task—and if this isn't the major task, what is? Teaching involves primarily three professional functions—the ability to diagnose learning needs, to design programs to meet those needs, and to assess the degree to which the program has been successful and thus maintain or revise it. For the teacher-librarian to be successful, these are done in conjunction and consultation with the classroom teacher. Instead of having one teacher and thirty youngsters, we now have two teachers, the classroom teacher and the teacher-librarian, a range of carefully selected materials, and those same thirty youngsters. Research indicates that this is by far the most effective way of developing information skills in young people. In fact, if you believe in the class size issue at all, it stands to reason that two teachers working with the same group of youngsters are going to have a much higher level of success than one teacher.

We can no longer afford to waffle on this issue. The link that is missing from many of our programs is that clarity of communication that comes through working together with the classroom teacher to plan and teach resource-based programs. Indeed, staffing reductions have occurred primarily in school districts where there is no stated aim for the program, where the role of the teacher-librarian is not understood, too often even by teacher-librarians, and where the teacher-librarian has traditionally provided spare periods for classroom teachers.

What has been eliminated, however, is not the teacher-librarian position at all, since it never really existed; what has been eliminated is the position of "prep time" or relief teacher. In secondary schools, the same is true of the reference librarian who answers questions and helps kids individually but has not planned programs and is certainly not viewed as a teaching partner. Too many teacher-librarians still seem to think that they are language arts teachers working in an enriched language arts classroom, or that they are a children's or reference librarian simply providing public library services for students in schools.

If the program is a partnership, then we have to determine not only objectives for the program, but also who is best at implementing them. For example, one objective for the program may be

that youngsters in the primary grades have a regular storytelling and story reading experience in the library resource center. However, there is no indication that it is necessary that this be done by the teacher-librarian. In fact, if the teacher-librarian is part-time, it may be much more appropriate that the classroom teacher provide that experience in the resource center during the time that the teacher-librarian is absent, if the activity requires only one teacher and involves an entire class.

We know too that the promotion of voluntary reading can be done best through the classroom teacher. Youngsters will accept recommendations for recreational reading from their peers and then their classroom teacher before the school librarian. This is indisputable; thus, if we put one-tenth of the energy that we now put into preparing book talks and literature appreciation programs on our own into working with classroom teachers to promote voluntary reading in the classroom, our objective might be better realized, while we may not necessarily be the active participant with the students. All teacher-librarians are not trained storytellers, expert in children's literature and literary appreciation; in fact, many teacher-librarians have no more specialized training in these areas than most primary teachers. And besides, that expertise and knowledge of the resources should be shared with teachers, not jealously guarded.

In the school there are many factors affecting the development and extension of a program, even at a most basic level. Obviously, there must not only be an understanding of the role of the teacher-librarian, but also a strong commitment by the teacher-librarian to that role. The teacher-librarian must place a premium on planning. Emphasis on day-to-day operations almost always pushes planning into the background: putting out today's fire takes priority over planning. The conclusion one reaches here is that fire fighting interferes with fire prevention. There is no question that planning takes time. There is also no question, however, that answering the same question 30 times from 30 different youngsters takes a lot more time, and is far less effective, and it certainly does not typically require the professional teacher's expertise.

Collaborative Program Planning and Teaching

In planning a program of study, a teacher goes through a number of steps. Objectives are established for the unit. There are some teachers who carefully think through their objectives and write them down. There are even more teachers who don't stop to think about objectives but know in the back of their minds what it is that they want to accomplish with the youngsters; content or subject matter to be taught is then determined and put into sequence. The content can be organized in a large number of ways quite aside from what the textbook publisher has determined.

As professional teachers, we have a whole range of instructional strategies at our disposal in order to accomplish the objectives we have identified. We may set up activity centers in the classroom. Perhaps a Socratic question-and-answer approach is most useful for our purpose. It may be that we are going to use library resources and team teach with the teacher-librarian. Activities are planned for the youngsters, and we evaluate student performance and occasionally take the time to look at the effectiveness of the unit itself.

The major weakness in teacher-librarianship is that we have tended to plug in at the learning activities phase of program planning. By the time the eighth youngster has asked the same question, it dawns on us that someone has given an assignment somewhere. We then simply reinforce our stereotype as handmaiden, run around and help the kids, and complain about not getting advance warning. Rarely do we pursue discussion with the teacher to prevent a recurrence. It is foolhardy, if not downright dishonest, however, to claim that we are helping teachers to accomplish their objectives if we do not even know what they are, let alone have any role in helping to plan them.

We all know how well a 10-year-old can interpret the directions given her by another adult and yet teacher-librarians persist in using the youngster as the link with the classroom teacher to determine objectives and the parameters of the assignment or project. We have to move our involvement back to planning with the teacher so

that we have that clarity of communication and each knows what is expected, and where we are going. Only in this way can everyone work effectively toward accomplishment of the objectives. Stated another way, discussion with teachers should focus less on what we want the students to do and more on what we want them to learn, and only then on how we are going to organize for that learning.

By putting time into planning, there will be that clarity of communication about what the students are to learn, what previous skills and activities they are involved in, what resources are appropriate, and how they are to be used; there will be determination of how student competence in these skills and strategies is going to be measured, and there will be some assessment as to the effectiveness of the unit itself.

If we believe that information skills and strategies, whatever we call them, are important then there must be a systematic approach to their development. They have to be specified and included in school district goals. We can no longer simply react to teachers and take a gentle, hodgepodge approach. We are wasting our time teaching skills that are not going to be followed up and extended in succeeding years. We are also saying that these skills are not really important for all youngsters because some students can be taught how to make effective notes five years in a row, while other students are never taught it.

Consequently, tied in with collaborative program planning and teaching, there must be a school-based, staff developed continuum for information skills development. At the elementary level this is relatively easy to develop, and at the secondary level it is relatively easy to develop with different subject departments, beginning simply with what is being done now and making some sense of it and moving to a degree of coordination. The process of involving teachers in articulating specific information skills at different grade levels provides part of the framework or reference points for effective collaborative planning. For example, in planning a unit at the third grade level in science or at the tenth grade level in social studies, it is much easier to refer with the teacher to the school's continuum of skills to determine which skills or strategies should be introduced or reinforced during that unit so that there is a systematic and developmental approach to teaching information skills.

The continuum overcomes many of the problems of a haphazard approach and implicates the staff in the success of the program. With the information skills continuum, it is easier to develop different units of study with classroom teachers at each grade level; all students at the grade level are taught specific information processes incorporated with classroom instruction. In this way the program becomes entrenched in the school and provides a foundation for continuing growth and development.

It is critical that the teacher-librarian write down the unit as it was developed with the classroom teacher, noting such things as the objectives, how the program was organized and scheduled, what activities were developed, what specialized resources were used, which materials were better for slower students and which were better for youngsters who needed more challenge, and what the two partners thought the strengths and weaknesses of the unit were and how it might be changed if it was undertaken again.

This provides an important support system. When working with the teacher again on the same unit in a succeeding year, or with different teachers on that unit, it is easier to revise and adapt to new students and circumstances than to start from scratch. In this way, the resource center also develops a large collection of resource-based units which integrate information skills and strategies for demonstration to teachers and for revision to meet emerging program needs.

What happens too often is that when the teacher-librarian leaves the school, the program essentially leaves with her. The new teacher-librarian goes through all the same processes of getting to know the staff, making overtures, starting to plan with one person, and so on. How much better if would be if the new teacher-librarian found that there had been a large number of units developed and filed in the school and could work with teachers to revise, adapt, and then build on them rather than starting over.

Similarly, when the classroom teacher leaves, these collaboratively developed units can be presented to a new teacher-librarian in a new situation, again revised and adapted, but forming a component of a program that is ongoing. Without this foundation for resource-based learning we are really no farther ahead than we were years ago. Each September we virtually start all over again. What an incredible waste and what a loss of easily obtained commitment from teaching colleagues.

The prescription for survival and even growth is relatively simple—a stated aim for the program, acknowledgment of the partnership of district, principal, teacher and teacher-librarian, a clearly defined role for the teacher-librarian, commitment by the teacher-librarian to that role, collaborative program planning and teaching as a philosophical framework, a school-based continuum of information skills and strategies, and units of study which are not only jointly planned and taught but also recorded for future use and improvement.

Guidelines for these can be established both at the district and the school levels. There must be guidelines for flexible scheduling, for example, and guidelines for collaborative planning. The district has a responsibility to define these guidelines, but this is increasingly a school-based decision. With flexible scheduling it is not unusual for teacher and student use to increase and for the circulation of materials to increase. And, if the purpose of the program is simply to provide spare periods for teachers, there are many cheaper and better ways of accomplishing that goal.

Education for School Librarianship

The question that comes to mind is "How did we get to this position?" Where we are badly let down is in the institutions training teacher-librarians. Obviously, there is a critical need for minimum qualifications for teacher-librarians. You cannot simply transfer a teacher from the classroom to the library resource center and presume that the knowledge of information skills and strategies, collaborative planning, team teaching, resource-based learning and the evaluation, selection and organization of materials is all intuitive. These are specialized skills that have to be developed in addition to teacher education and classroom experience. But there is no stated objective for the program in most faculties of education and of library and information studies, there is no outline of competencies to be developed, there is no cohesive statement on the role of the teacher-librarian, and yet this is where it all begins. Teacher-librarians are graduating from these programs having been convinced that every component of the resource center, from curricular leadership to on-site cataloguing, is equally important. They have not been provided with a context of collaborative program planning and teaching and they have not been provided with the important skills to set priorities within that context, or to advocate strong support for the program with decision-makers.

Not only is there need for a stated aim, clarified role, and context for the program, but just the number of units assigned to each area of work is message enough for the prospective teacher-librarian. Ample time is often given over to cataloguing and organizing resources, for example, while collaborative planning and teaching is buried in general courses on services, which include not only storytelling, story reading and book talks, but often facilities management as well. Prospective teacher-librarians must have opportunities to learn the skills necessary to plan with colleagues and team teach and to provide leadership in program advocacy.

Program Advocacy

If teacher-librarians do not have a clear understanding of their role, if they cannot speak with a unified voice, how do we expect principals and teachers to understand what we are doing, work closely with us, and speak on our behalf? Until we develop an understanding of who we are and what we are about, the essential component of program advocacy becomes very difficult to implement with confidence. We are not both teachers and librarians; this is not a dual role—we are teachers who specialize in the effective use of learning resources, teachers who know what information skills and strategies are and how they might best be integrated in instructional programs.

We must become advocates for our programs, there is no question of this. We must also speak in the language of the audience, namely in terms of education. We must speak with a clear, cohesive and unified voice.

Strong programs in schools are not so very difficult to develop. But strong programs must rest on strong philosophical foundations with stated goals and objectives if they are to be both valid and sustaining. This means that the programs must operate within a framework of collaborative program planning and teaching and a well-understood and supported role for the teacher-librarian, with many referral points for entering the curriculum, such as through a continuum of information skills. A so-called strong program which takes place within the framework of scheduled library skills classes, or scheduled literature appreciation classes, or at the secondary level within the context of English classes only, is not a strong program at all. The resource center may be busy and the kids seem productive, but the research is clear that these youngsters are not going to retain those skills of processing and using information and apply them in different contexts in their school careers and beyond.

We might begin with our sense of professionalism. Some believe they are professional simply because they are teachers or librarians. In other words, professionalism is defined by the level of academic achievement. Others define professionalism by the long hours they work, and not being a puncher of clocks in order to collect a check. Professionalism may involve both of these things. There is indeed a body of knowledge that is necessary for one to master to be an effective teacher-librarian. There is also a framework or understanding of where the program is going and how one is going to get there that is essential. These are developed through academic achievement and long hours of work.

But there is also the question of commitment—the commitment of the teacher-librarian to teacher-librarianship. Professionalism is also, after all, an attribute. Too many teacher-librarians are not concerned about program erosion because they know they will always have some kind of position. There is no commitment to the program, there is no commitment to the profession, there is only a commitment to continued employment regardless of where that might be within the school or system. I would submit that advocacy and commitment are what we will be looking for over the next few years if we expect the program to expand and survive.

We are indeed living in a world that is information rich, a cliché for sure, but also a world which may be knowledge poor. The reason for this is that citizens will not be able to handle information effectively. Surely this is what teacher-librarianship is all about. Helping youngsters to develop a commitment to informed decision-making, through the ability to locate, process and use information effectively, is going to be critical to the continuation of democratic societies and to technological achievement.

Teacher-librarians have a central role to play in this, as an integral component of schooling. Teacher-librarians are essential to educational achievement. With role clarification, a strong commitment to collaborative planning and teaching, a framework for success through flexible scheduling and a school-based continuum of information skills, units jointly planned and recorded with teachers, teacher-librarians will be in the forefront in the resolution of educational problems in schools in the information age.

Graduates of our schools will be able to define important problems, locate pertinent information, extract it, analyze it, organize it, and use it effectively, whether from books or databases. They will be well-prepared for the society of today and tomorrow. This is our potential. I would urge you, through your professional and personal commitment, to make it your promise.

CHAPTER TWO

Research in Teacher-Librarianship and the Institutionalization of Change

Ken Haycock

One often hears the refrain that there is no research in teacher-librarianship, no proof of effect on student achievement, no concrete evidence of value for money: if only there was some strong justification for school libraries and school librarians, there would be no need to lobby for adequate staff, collections and facilities. However, there is a strong research base for teacher-librarianship, there is evidence of effect on student achievement and there is ample justification for the presence and effective use of teacher-librarians and school library resource centers. Why then are there ongoing problems of support?

First, the research is not as well known to the profession as it should be and researchers and practitioners alike criticize when it took place, where it took place and with whom it took place. If we accepted our own research and built on it we would progress far beyond the generalization of a single experience and the intuition alone of the principal, teacher and teacher-librarian. Nothing is ever certain in a complex world but research which is reliable, valid and replicated has value and worth.

Second, even with what we do know about effective library media programs and services, we find it difficult to put them in place. Principals and teachers can be convinced of the value of the teacher-librarian and school resource center and hold an image of the appropriate and effective role of the principal, teacher and teacher-librarian as partners in the educational enterprise but implementation still does not occur, and does not reach a stage of institutionalization, of becoming an integral, essential part of the fabric of the school. In this case the research in curriculum implementation and staff development can provide guidance for the successful initiation, implementation and institutionalization of library media programs.

The terms "teacher-librarian" and "resource center" are used here as these are common in many parts of the world. A teacher-librarian is a qualified teacher with successful classroom teaching experience and additional post-baccalaureate education in teacher-librarianship. The teacher-librarian performs a unified role, uniquely combining teacher and librarian, and may work full-time or part-time in the school resource center. The term resource center is similarly used for consistency; the resource center houses the school's collection of curriculum resources, including information books and other media and electronic resources and imaginative literature, and access to off-site resources; these are coherently and consistently organized for ease of physical access and the teacher-librarian plans with classroom teachers to develop and implement programs which assure intellectual access by increasingly independent student learners.

Research in Teacher-Librarianship

The research in teacher-librarianship is rich and diverse and recent publications provide useful guides to the research and scholarly literature (see, for example, Clyde, 1996; Haycock, 1992; Krashen, 1993; Lance, Welborn & Hamilton-Pennell, 1993; Woolls, 1990). This review is delimited to the characteristics of effective programs which affect student achievement in a significant way and which have the support of educational decision-makers like school principals and superintendents. It therefore does not include factors related to the selection and management of resources, to facilities or to general school and classroom practice.

The Impact on Student Achievement

There is a positive relationship between the level of resource center service and student scholastic achievement. In schools with good resource centers and the services of a teacher-librarian (TL), students perform significantly better on tests for basic research skills, including locational skills, outlining and note-taking, and the knowledge and use of reference materials, including the use of a dictionary and an encyclopedia (Becker, 1970; Callison, 1979; Greve, 1974; McMillen, 1965; Nolan, 1989; Yarling, 1968); they also perform significantly better in the area of reading comprehension and in their ability to express ideas effectively concerning their readings (Yarling, 1968).

More recent studies corroborate that students learn more, and produce better research products, following planned, integrated information

skills instruction by the teacher and teacher-librarian together (Bland, 1995; Cole, 1996; Friel, 1995; Hara, 1996). During the research process students move through different stages, with predictable thoughts, feelings and actions; these thoughts progress from general to more specific to focused, and confidence increases from initiation of the search through to closure; this knowledge base enables teachers and teacher-librarians to plan appropriate intervention strategies. For example, students typically lack a clear research focus at the beginning of the process and need better search strategies, and the appropriate skills and strategies can be planned, integrated with classroom content and taught together to ensure student learning and success.

Students are positive about resource-based research assignments but are often not given sufficient instruction or time to produce quality work. Students are more successful when whole class, full period instruction occurs in the classroom with brief reminders at the beginning of the process in the library resource center than when information skills are taught for a full period solely in the library. Frequent interventions by the teacher-librarian, especially one-on-one conferencing, helps to bridge the gap between the student's actual and potential developmental level.

At the secondary level one often hears the plaint that teachers need to "cover the curriculum" and that process issues, as embodied in resource-based learning, cannot be incorporated with classroom instruction. However, students learn best when units of study emphasize both subject matter and information seeking and use, and these units are best planned and implemented by teacher and teacher-librarian together (Pitts, 1994a, 1994b; Pitts et al., 1995a, 1995b).

Several domains or learning strands influence the decisions a student makes about information seeking and use: for example, the subject–matter domain (e.g., science), the life skills domain (e.g., problem solving, planning, interpersonal communication) and the production domain (e.g., the required product or output). Students make most of their decisions based on prior learning. As they work in a domain their ideas become more connected. The domains then act as learning strands and together support student activity during a unit of study; in other words, prior learning in each domain—for example, subject matter and information skills and strategies—support or interfere with overall student learning.

Problems occur regularly for students without these connections; to illustrate:

- if the student does not understand the subject matter, the student cannot recognize or state information needs to guide searches; however, if the student has useful prior learning in information seeking, projects can be started by finding a general overview to expand subject matter understanding;

- if the student has limited prior learning of information sources, decisions about the usefulness of the school resource center are made after one limited search;

- if the student does not have strong understanding of organizing information, the information will be left essentially as originally recorded.

Student learning in the subject area is impaired by lack of knowledge of appropriate and effective information seeking and use behaviors and skills. The teacher-librarian's intervention and support of student learning is impaired as student knowledge of subject matter is often overestimated and the student's inability to clarify the information need is not recognized. The teacher's intervention and support of student learning is impaired as teacher knowledge of information seeking, especially in libraries, is limited. Students cannot overcome these adult barriers alone.

Units of study which emphasize one strand only, that is, subject matter or information seeking and use, limit learning on all strands. Clearly, specialists in the domains, teacher and teacher-librarian, should collaborate in planning and implementing the unit of study for the benefit of student learning and academic achievement.

In what is commonly referred to as the "Colorado study" (Lance, Welborn and Hamilton-Pennell, 1993) the Colorado Department of Education determined that among school and community predictors of academic achievement, the size of the resource center staff and collection is second only to the absence of at-risk conditions, particularly poverty and low educational attainment among adults. Students who score higher on norm-referenced tests tend to come from schools that have more library resource staff and more books, periodicals and videos, and where the instructional role of the teacher-librarian and involvement in collaborative program planning and teaching is more prominent.

The researchers concluded that the school resource center should be staffed by a certified teacher-librarian who is involved not only in identifying materials suitable for school curricula, but also in collaborating with teachers and others in developing curricula. These activities require that the teacher-librarian have adequate support staff. The degree of collaboration between the teacher-librarian and classroom teachers is also affected by the ratio of teachers to students. Collaboration of this type then depends on the availability of both the teacher-librarian and teacher (it thus cannot be the role of the teacher-librarian to provide the teacher's preparation time); teacher-librarians who play an instructional role tend to have teacher colleagues whose workloads permit such collaboration. This involvement in the instructional process helps to shape a larger—and presumably more appropriate—local collection of resources. School expenditures affect resource center staff and collection size and, in turn, academic achievement. This also reinforces earlier studies (Greve, 1974) finding a correlation between collection size and achievement.

The Impact on Reading

The evidence is similarly clear that more reading is done where there is a school library and a teacher-librarian; children also read more where they live close to a public library (Krashen, 1993). Students in schools with centralized resource centers and teacher-librarians not only read more, they enjoy reading more (Lowe, 1984). A print-rich environment, including larger library collections, and a good reading environment, including comfort and quiet, affect reading, literacy development and reading scores (Krashen, 1993). Further, providing time for free voluntary reading in schools has a positive impact on reading comprehension, vocabulary development, spelling, written style, oral/aural language and control of grammar (Krashen, 1993).

Krashen (1996), a linguistics professor, went on to contend that to improve reading scores and motivation to read, schools and school districts need to improve school library staffing and collections. If reading is a priority, then every school must improve its library through more accessible reading material and qualified staff. In addition, to encourage free voluntary reading, schools need to provide time for students to read self-selected material.

Long-term development of reading interest and grade level achievement are more assured through print-rich environments, quality literature programs, reduced pressure to achieve on tests and opportunities to read for pleasure and interest. These learning effects and results are even more pronounced for English as a second language learners.

Accuracy in writing comes from reading; reading ability comes from reading—skills need to be taught specifically to make texts more comprehensible and to edit writing. For some educational decision-makers Krashen may go too far in suggesting that literacy-related technology should be de-emphasized until school libraries are adequate and that language testing should be reduced, with the savings in time invested in worthwhile literacy activities and the savings in funding invested in school libraries; nevertheless, the evidence appears to support his case.

School resource centers with full-time teacher-librarians even contribute to the development of positive self-concepts (McAfee, 1981).

Foundations for Success

Why are these gains not realized in all situations and circumstances? First, the role of the teacher-librarian requires clarification if there is to be any improvement in existing resource center programs (Charter, 1982). Principals, teachers and teacher-librarians themselves have many misconceptions about the role of the TL in the instructional program (Bias, 1979; Burcham, 1989; Hambleton,

1980; Hodson, 1978; Jones, 1977; Kerr, 1973; Kim, 1981; Olson, 1966) such that states and school districts need to provide a clearer definition of the role expected of the TL (Markle, 1982). TLs need to take an active part in defining their role, particularly in cooperative program planning and teaching, and need to communicate their role more effectively to principals and teachers, through inservice programs and through an emphasis on work with people more than management and production processes (Bechtel, 1975; Bias, 1979; Pichette, 1975; Sullivan, 1979). In fact, TLs who place a higher priority on personal relations offer more services to teachers and students; TLs who rate personal relations as a lower priority spend more time on circulation and related tasks (Adams, 1973).

Teacher-librarians require teaching qualifications and classroom experience prior to further education and training as a TL in order to be effective. Prior successful teaching experience is necessary for TLs to perceive and solve instructional problems (Van Dreser, 1971). Exemplary teacher-librarians, as identified in the professional literature and by exemplary principals, display the traits of exemplary teachers—as well, they plan with teachers, use flexible and innovative teaching and public relations approaches, teach well, provide continuous access, design flexible policies, and develop collections which support the curriculum (Alexander, 1992). More years of classroom teaching experience and more preparation in curriculum development and implementation are needed than is currently the case, however (Corr, 1979). Superintendents, principals and teachers consistently point to the need for teacher-librarians to have more classroom teaching experience if programs are to develop in a credible and successful way (Wilson, 1972).

The development of student competence is most effective when integrated with classroom instruction through cooperative program planning and team teaching by two equal teaching partners—the classroom teacher and the teacher-librarian—in a flexibly scheduled resource center (see, most recently, Barlup, 1991; Bishop, 1992; Bishop & Blazek, 1994; Kreiser, 1991; Tallman & Van Deusen, 1994a, 1994b, 1995; van Deusen,

1991, 1993; van Deusen & Tallman, 1994). The teacher-librarian plays important roles as information specialist, teacher and instructional consultant; the most significant change in roles occurs when the school moves to flexible scheduling and curriculum-integrated instruction, and greater curriculum involvement by the TL occurs when flexible scheduling is combined with team planning. Increased interest in books and more enjoyment in reading is also more apparent with reading integration throughout the curriculum, and flexible scheduling. Even student attitudes toward the resource center and reading are more positive in flexibly scheduled programs.

Minimal gains in research and study skills can be achieved through instruction by the classroom teacher alone or the teacher-librarian alone (Nolan, 1989). Effective instruction depends on the cooperative effort of both teacher and TL; stated another way, scheduled library skills classes taught solely by the TL are not as effective as integrated, cooperatively planned and taught programs (Smith, 1978). Indeed, not only do flexibly scheduled resource centers provide greater academic benefits, but students themselves believe that the resource center is more useful in their school work than students in scheduled schools (Hodson, 1978; Nolan, 1989). When flexibly scheduled, the TL and resource center can have a significant effect on student achievement in information handling and use and in content areas. Indeed, the most significant changes in library programs occur when the teacher-librarian moves to flexible scheduling and curriculum-integrated instruction; positive cooperative relations with teachers, administrators and students contribute to this success (Bishop, 1992).

Although collaboration between teacher and teacher-librarian can be difficult to achieve, the result is improved student learning (Bingham, 1994; Jones, 1994; Lumley, 1994). These partnerships occur in three ways—purposeful, springboard and accidental. In order to survive, partnerships must evidence support, maintenance and reward. These partnerships are facilitated by communication, and maintained by consideration, cooperation, compromise and commitment. Also, formal planning, even if brief, is more productive than informal planning. Although teacher/teacher-librarian partners maintain team building relationships and form strong networks, school contextual constraints do exist, which impede collaboration.

It is difficult to imagine why teacher-librarians are not involved in cooperative program planning and team teaching with classroom colleagues as equal teaching partners to the extent that principals, teachers and teacher-librarians themselves believe that they should be (Corr, 1979; Johnson, 1975; Kerr, 1975; Stanwich, 1982). If the teacher uses the resource center and consults with the TL about planning student work, then the use of the resource center is greater (Hartley, 1980). In fact, students rate schools more highly when there is agreement and communication among principals, teachers and TLs regarding program objectives, and where there is planned, consistent and integrated instruction in resource center use (Scott, 1982).

Important factors which affect TL involvement in curricular issues include the principal's attitude towards the TL's role, teacher preference for TLs with successful classroom teaching experience and a teacher's frame of reference, the number of support staff, and degree of teacher understanding of the role of the TL and the potential of the resource center (Corr, 1979). Perhaps most importantly, teacher-librarians require extensive training in cooperative program planning and team teaching which builds on prior successful classroom teaching experience. Programs which educate teacher-librarians would do well to structure programs around cooperative program planning and teaching and the skills necessary to convince educators that TLs are vital partners in instruction (Royal, 1981). These competencies, however, tend not to be supervised in practica to the extent that other competencies are.

Cooperative program planning and teaching as an instructional development activity requires more social interaction with other teachers than is required of other roles of the TL, yet there is a low level of communication between teachers and TLs (Urbanik, 1984). Teacher-librarians may also need education and training in social interaction skills. Teacher-librarians in exemplary resource centers are extroverted and independent: as leaders they have "tough poise" (Charter, 1982). Teacher-librarians who are less cautious and more extroverted than their colleagues tend to be more successful; indeed, the best pair of predictors of high circulation of materials in the resource center is high extroversion and a high degree of curriculum involvement by the TL (Madaus, 1974).

Since principals, teachers and teacher-librarians all agree on the importance of cooperative program planning and teaching, all three should be involved in resolving issues mitigating against substantial involvement. TLs need to organize more in-service training for colleagues (Callison, 1979; Hartley, 1980), and educators of TLs need to revise programs to include courses which foster cooperation and understanding between teachers and TLs (Royal, 1981).

Studies also place the school library and teacher-librarian firmly in the context of the school's culture. Where the school fosters and supports collaborative work environments the role of the teacher-librarian is more easily achieved. Where this collaboration leads to greater cohesion around instruction, there are greater gains in academic achievement (Bell, 1990; see also Bell & Totten, 1991a, 1991b, 1992).

Research in the Implementation of Change

The research literature provides considerable evidence and guidance as to what constitutes effectiveness in the implementation of any desired change (Fullan & Stiegelbauer, 1991). While this overview cannot do justice to the extent of research in this field sufficient conclusions can be drawn which can impact on the effective implementation of cooperative program planning and teaching, and flexible scheduling, across a school district.

The Implementation Plan

The content of effective staff development must be research-based (Cawelti, 1989; Griffin, 1987; Howey & Vaughan, 1983), proven effective (Hunter, 1986), practical (Guskey, 1986; Hunter, 1986; Nevi, 1986), and relevant to identified needs and problems faced in the classroom (Daresh, 1987; Elam, Cramer & Brodinsky, 1986; Howey & Vaughan, 1983; Orlich, 1989; Paquette, 1987; Rubin, 1987); these are all evident in the effective use of the teacher-librarian through cooperative program planning and teaching and flexible scheduling.

Successful implementation also requires that this new program have clear goals (Cato, 1990), that the nature of the change be explicit and realistic (British Columbia Ministry of Education, 1989b; Pratt, 1980) and pay particular attention to the contexts, the schools and classrooms, in which teachers work (Griffin, 1987).

An effective implementation plan is based on an understanding of the developmental aspects of change (Fullan, 1985; Fullan et al., 1986), sets clear expectations and manageable objectives (Ornstein & Hunkins, 1988), incorporates realistic time lines (British Columbia Ministry of Education, 1989a; Dow, Whitehead, & Wright, 1984; Loucks & Lieberman, 1983; Pratt, 1980), allocation of resources and monitoring and feedback procedures (Fullan & Park, 1981), and incorporates the professional development of consultants, principals and resource teachers as well as classroom teachers (British Columbia Ministry of Education, 1982; British Columbia Ministry of Education, 1989b; Fullan et al., 1986). In other words, change is a process, not an event like one workshop, and requires the understanding of all "stakeholders."

The Role of the District

A district policy to guide and support implementation and a district plan for a structured implementation process will prove helpful (British Columbia Ministry of Education, 1989b; Dow, Whitehead, & Wright, 1984; Fullan & Park, 1981; Lee & Wong, 1985; Mooradian, 1985; Ornstein & Hunkins, 1988). Priorities will need to be established among competing demands if a state or school district is facing several curricula changes at once (British Columbia Ministry of Education, 1989b; Dow, Whitehead, & Wright, 1984); too often a district library media coordinator will lead a change effort in library media programs while other district and school administrators are leading changes in other areas which are competing for the same time, attention and resources of the school— the response of the school is, understandably, to set its own priorities or to ignore them all.

The importance of the new approach, expectations for its use (British Columbia Ministry of Education, 1982; Fullan & Park, 1981; Loucks & Lieberman, 1983), and implementation plans should be communicated widely throughout the system (Lee & Wong, 1985; Romberg & Price, 1983). Significant changes in behavior, roles and responsibilities expected of teachers need to be described in detail, clarifying both the similarities and differences with what they are already doing (Fullan et al., 1986), and teachers need the opportunity to discuss the implications and adaptation with colleagues (British Columbia Ministry of Education, 1989b).

Effective change procedures also require some pressure to change (Fullan, 1990) as well as a support system (British Columbia Ministry of Education, 1989a); this is often done by working with a school staff rather than through cross-district workshops in order to encourage both peer pressure and peer support to change.

Teacher-librarians and their advocates will need to work more effectively with senior education staff. School superintendents support the need for professional teacher-librarians and generally understand the potential impact of a teacher-librarian but they nevertheless often set other priorities (Lowden, 1980). Many superintendents believe that a teacher-librarian is an absolute necessity and few would staff a resource center with only an aide, but a sizable minority still see the TL as a luxury (Connors, 1984). While sometimes skeptical about the TL's and resource center's influence on teaching in the school, superintendents nevertheless believe that teachers would notice if the resource center was closed and teachers would have to teach differently (Connors, 1984). Superintendents also believe that the teaching background and experience of the TL may be too limited to support a significant impact

on the school (Connors, 1984). Clearly, TLs and their superintendents need to communicate more often and more effectively if successful implementation is to take place (Payne, 1967).

Implementation requires the involvement and support of the right people and groups within the district at the right time; both educational and political criteria should be used to select a district planning committee to ensure the quality of any implementation plan and its acceptability (British Columbia Ministry of Education, 1989b). One goal is the creation of a well-informed group of teachers and administrators with a clear sense of mission and the confidence that can bring about change (Ornstein & Hunkins, 1988); an internal advocacy group improves the chances for change by putting pressure on the people and the organization (Ornstein & Hunkins, 1988).

As we know, the implementation of change requires persistent advocacy and continual leadership and school support (British Columbia Ministry of Education, 1989b). Program leaders, like district coordinators, need to anticipate initial resistance to change, need to deal with how people feel about change, need to deal with conflicts, need to know what can be done to lessen anxiety and need to know how to facilitate the change process (Ornstein & Hunkins, 1988). The school library media coordinator can have a positive effect on school resource center program development in the school district (Coleman, 1982); even the existence of a coordinator seems to result in significantly higher implementation of guiding principles for personnel, budget, purchasing, production, access and delivery systems, program evaluation, collections and facilities (Coleman, 1982), and the higher the coordinator's position is placed in the hierarchy, the wider the range of activities that can be performed in the development and regulation of school resource center programs and services (Carter, 1971). The coordinator must be more involved in curriculum and public relations work, however.

The Role of the Principal

Above all else, the role of the principal is the key factor in the development of an effective school resource center program. The principal is the single most important player in the change process and plays a direct and active role in leading any process of change by becoming familiar with the nature of the change and by working with staff to develop, execute and monitor a school implementation plan (British Columbia Ministry of Education, 1982; Fullan & Park, 1981). Principals are in the strongest position to conduct personal advocacy of innovations in the schools (Pratt, 1980)—through visible and clear support the principal can significantly affect the implementation and institutionalization of educational change (Gersten, Carnine & Green, 1989). The district needs to provide training and follow-up for principals to take responsibility for facilitating implementation in their schools (Fullan & Park, 1981).

Successful implementation requires principal support both substantively (by ensuring resources are available and schedules are accommodating) and psychologically (by encouraging teachers, acknowledging their concerns, providing personal time and assistance, rewarding their efforts, and communicating that the implementation is a school priority) (Cato, 1990; Cox, 1989; Fullan & Park, 1981; Hord & Huling-Austin, 1986; Loucks & Lieberman, 1983; Virgilio & Virgilio, 1984). Successful implementation requires that principals create the climate (e.g., collegiality, communication and trust) (Fullan et al., 1986) and the mechanisms (e.g., time and opportunity, interaction, technical sharing and assistance, and ongoing staff development) to support the implementation of innovation (Cox, 1989; Fullan, 1985; Fullan et al., 1986; Pratt, 1980).

Even the attitude of the principal toward the role of the teacher-librarian affects the TL's involvement in curricular issues (Corr, 1979). Indeed, exemplary school resource centers are characterized by strong administrative support (Charter, 1982; Shields, 1977). Principals in schools with exemplary resource center programs integrate the resource center in instructional programs, encourage student and teacher use and provide flexible scheduling (Hellene, 1973).

Effective Staff Development

Plans for effective staff development recognize that change is a gradual and difficult process (Guskey, 1986), provide sufficient time to produce demonstrable results (Hunter, 1986; Rubin, 1987) and demonstrate that the strategies will bring about short- and long-term benefits to students (Rubin, 1987). Short presentations can be valuable as awareness sessions and in helping people to make decisions about those areas where extended workshops would be beneficial (Nevi, 1986) but they will not result in changed practice.

The steps in effective staff development include the presentation of information or theory, modeling or demonstration of the change, an opportunity to practise, feedback (British Columbia Ministry of Education, 1985; British Columbia Ministry of Education, 1989), and on-site assistance to staff in the form of technical assistance, coaching and peer support (Cawelti, 1989; Hunter, 1986; Kent, 1985; Rubin, 1987; Showers, Joyce, & Bennett, 1987; Sparks & Bruder, 1987; Van Sant, 1988). This is particularly effective through a collegial support system that values growth activities, provides moral support and facilitates small group interaction (McGiffin, 1990; Paquette, 1987).

Building on the research in teacher-librarianship—through role clarification, cooperative program planning and teaching and flexible scheduling—and in curriculum implementation and staff development—through careful planning, effective leadership, credible in-service and coaching, with both pressure and support—teacher-librarians and other educators can implement the major changes required for TLs and resource centers to become effective agents for student achievement. Too often we believe so much in the value of our programs that we think that a "one-shot" workshop will change the way principals schedule, the way teachers teach and the way teacher-librarians plan with colleagues, and then we are disappointed when these changes do not occur. The implementation of a change as significant as cooperative program planning and team teaching and flexible scheduling, however, requires the involvement of all the partners and systematic and ongoing training, pressure and support.

With successful programs in place, teacher-librarians can then assume more responsibility for writing about their role and about collaboratively planned programs for professional journals read by teachers and administrators (Mack, 1957). This accepted means of communication is not being used to its fullest potential in communicating the contribution of teacher-librarians and school resource centers and the curricular role of the TL (Van Orden, 1970), and this can be done effectively only by TLs themselves (Holzberlein, 1971). It is critical that principals and teachers read about exciting approaches such as resource-based teaching and learning in the journals that they read since they are not going to read ours. The successes of cooperatively planned and taught units of study need to be celebrated not only in our publications but also in the publications of our teacher partners and in the publications of principal leaders.

For an information profession, we need only learn from our research and build on its precepts in order to become that force for excellence that is within our grasp. We have the evidence that we can make a difference through cooperative program planning and team teaching and flexible scheduling; we have the principles for the effective initiation, implementation and institutionalization of change.

Now we need only do it.

References

Adams, E. (1973). *An analysis of the relationship of certain personality factors to the amount of time allotted to specified public service tasks by selected school librarians.* Unpublished doctoral dissertation, University of Southern California.

Alexander, K. (1992). *Profiles of four exemplary elementary school media specialists.* Unpublished doctoral dissertation, University of Miami.

Barlup, J. H. (1991). *Whole language, the librarian, and children's literature beyond the basal reader: A case study of the attitudes of students, teachers, and librarians with literature-based reading.* Unpublished doctoral dissertation, University of Pittsburgh.

Bechtel, D. (1975). *Media specialist competency and inservice evaluation preferences in the junior high and middle schools of South Dakota.* Unpublished doctoral dissertation, University of South Dakota.

Becker, D. (1970). *Social studies achievement of pupils in schools with libraries and schools without libraries.* Unpublished doctoral dissertation, University of Pennsylvania.

Bell, M. D. (1990). *Elementary school climate factors and personality and status variables associated with school library media specialists chosen by classroom teachers for cooperation on instructional problems.* Unpublished doctoral dissertation, University of North Texas.

Bell, M. D. & Totten, H. L. (1991a). School climate factors related to degrees of cooperation between public elementary school teachers and school library media specialists. *Library Quarterly, 61,* 293–310.

Bell, M. D. & Totten, H. L. (1991b). Interactional patterns of school media specialists with school instructional staff. *Library and Information Science Research, 13,* 367–384.

Bell, M. D. & Totten, H. L. (1992). Cooperation in instruction between classroom teachers and school library media specialists: A look at teacher characteristics in Texas elementary schools. *School Library Media Quarterly, 20,* 79–85.

Bias, L. (1979). *The role and function of the media specialist as perceived by principals, teachers, and media specialists in elementary schools in Montgomery County, Maryland.* Unpublished doctoral dissertation, University of Maryland.

Bingham, J. E. M. (1994). *A comparative study of curriculum integrated and traditional school library media programs: Achievement outcomes of sixth grade research papers.* Unpublished doctoral dissertation, Kansas State University.

Bishop, K. (1992). *The roles of the school library media specialist in an elementary school using a literature-based reading program: An ethnographic case study.* Unpublished doctoral dissertation, The Florida State University.

Bishop, K. & Blazek, R. (1994). The role of the elementary school library media specialist in a literature-based reading program. *School Library Media Quarterly, 22,* 146–150.

Bland, K. (1995). *CD–ROM utilization in the high school student research process.* Unpublished doctoral dissertation, University of Memphis.

British Columbia Ministry of Education. (1982). *Guidelines for planning program implementation.* Victoria, BC: British Columbia Ministry of Education.

British Columbia Ministry of Education. (1985). *Research update: Effective staff development.* Victoria, BC: British Columbia Ministry of Education.

British Columbia Ministry of Education. (1989a). *The principal as instructional leader: Facilitating Ministry of Education program changes* [workshop booklet]. Victoria, BC: British Columbia Ministry of Education.

British Columbia Ministry of Education. (1989b). *School district planning of curriculum implementation.* Victoria, BC: British Columbia Ministry of Education.

Burcham, C. (1989). *The perceptions and beliefs of principals, teachers, and media specialists regarding the role of media specialists in the public schools of Georgia.* Unpublished doctoral dissertation, University of Georgia.

Callison, H. (1979). *The impact of the school media specialist on curriculum design and implementation.* Unpublished doctoral dissertation, University of South Carolina.

Carter, E. (1971). *The organizational structure for state school library supervision and the functions, duties, and activities of state school library supervisors.* Unpublished doctoral dissertation, Indiana University.

Cato, J. (1990). Principals: Key in school improvement. *Educational Leader, 3(10),* 1, 16.

Cawelti, G. (1989). Designing high schools for the future. *Educational Leadership, 17(1),* 30–35.

Charter, J. (1982). *Case study profiles of six exemplary public high school library media programs.* Unpublished doctoral dissertation, Florida State University.

Cole, P. G. (1996). *Self-regulation and the secondary school library media center: A development project.* Unpublished doctoral dissertation, University of Southern California.

Coleman, J., Jr. (1982). *Perceptions of "guiding principles" in "Media programs: District and school."* Unpublished doctoral dissertation, University of Virginia.

Connors, M. (1984). *The superintendent's perception of the school library media center.* Unpublished doctoral dissertation, Boston University.

Corr, G. (1979). *Factors that affect the school library media specialist's involvement in curriculum planning and implementation in small high schools in Oregon.* Unpublished doctoral dissertation, University of Oregon.

Cox, P. (1989). Complementary roles in successful change. In R. Brandt (Ed.), *Effective schools and school improvement: Readings from Educational Leadership* (pp. 131–134). Alexandria, VA: Association for Supervision and Curriculum Development.

Daresh, J. (1987). Staff development—guidelines for the principal. *NASSP Bulletin, 71(497),* 20–23.

Dow, I., Whitehead, R. Y. & Wright, R. L. (1984). *Curriculum implementation: A framework for action.* Toronto: Ontario Public School Teachers' Federation.

Dyer, E. (1976). *Cooperation in library services to children: A fifteen year forecast of alternatives using the Delphi technique.* Unpublished doctoral dissertation, Columbia University.

Ekechukwu, M. (1972). *Characteristics of users and nonusers of elementary school library services and public library services for children.* Unpublished doctoral dissertation, University of Washington.

Elam, S., Cramer, J. & Brodinsky, B. (1986). *Staff development: Problems and solutions.* Arlington, VA: American Association of School Administrators.

Friel, L. D. (1995). *The information research process with low-achieving freshmen using Kuhlthau's six-stage model and the interventions that facilitate the process.* Unpublished doctoral dissertation, University of Lowell.

Fullan, M. (1985). Change processes and strategies at the local level. *The Elementary School Journal, 85(3),* 391–420.

Fullan, M., Anderson, S. & Newton, E. (1986). *Support systems for implementing curriculum in school boards.* Toronto: OISE Press and Ontario Government Bookstore.

Fullan, M. & Park, P. (1981). *Curriculum implementation: A resource booklet.* Toronto: Ontario Ministry of Education.

Fullan, M. & Stiegelbauer, S. (1991). *The new meaning of educational change* (2nd ed.). New York: Teachers College Press.

Gersten, R., Carnine, D. & Green, S. (1989). The principal as instructional leader: A second look. In R. Brandt (Ed.), *Effective schools and school improvement: Readings from Educational Leadership* (pp. 127–130). Alexandria, VA: Association for Supervision and Curriculum Development.

Greve, C. (1974). *The relationship between the availability of libraries to the academic achievement of Iowa high school seniors.* Unpublished doctoral dissertation, University of Denver.

Griffin, G. (1987). The school in society and social organization of the school. In M. F. Wideen & I. Andrews (Eds.), *Staff development for school improvement* (pp. 16–37). Philadelphia: Falmer.

Guskey, T. (1986). Staff development and the process of teacher change. *Educational Researcher, 15(5),* 5–12.

Hambleton, A. (1980). *The elementary school librarian in Ontario: A study of role perception, role conflict and effectiveness.* Unpublished doctoral dissertation, University of Toronto.

Hara, K. (1996). *A study of information skills instruction in elementary school: Effectiveness and teachers' attitudes.* Unpublished doctoral dissertation, University of Toronto.

Hartley, N. (1980). *Faculty utilization of the high school library.* Unpublished doctoral dissertation, George Peabody College for Teachers of Vanderbilt University.

Haycock, K. (1992). *What works: Research about teaching and learning through the school's library resource center.* Seattle, WA: Rockland Press.

Hellene, D. (1973). *The relationships of the behaviors of principals in the state of Washington to the development of school library media programs.* Unpublished doctoral dissertation, University of Washington.

Hodson, Y. (1978). *Values and functions of the school media center as perceived by fourth and sixth grade students and their teachers in compared school settings.* Unpublished doctoral dissertation, State University of New York at Buffalo.

Holzberlein, D. (1971). *The contribution of school media programs to elementary and secondary education as portrayed in professional journals available to school administrators from 1960 to 1969.* Unpublished doctoral dissertation, University of Michigan.

Hord, S. & Huling-Austin, L. (1986). Effective curriculum implementation: Some promising new insights. *The Elementary School Journal, 87(1),* 97–115.

Howey, K. & Vaughan, J. (1983). Current patterns of staff development. In G. Griffin (Ed.), *Staff development* (82nd Yearbook of the National Society for the Study of Education, pp. 92–117). Chicago: University of Chicago Press.

Hunter, S. (1986). *The school makes the difference: What the research says about—staff development* (Bulletin Number 5). Vancouver, BC: Vancouver School Board.

Johnson, H. (1975). *Teacher utilization of libraries in the secondary schools of Tucson District No. 1.* Unpublished doctoral dissertation, University of Arizona.

Jones, C. (1977). *The Georgia public school library media program, 1965–1975.* Unpublished doctoral dissertation, University of Georgia.

Jones, J. (1994). *The teacher-librarian partnership in a literature-based approach.* Unpublished doctoral dissertation, Arizona State University.

Kelley, I. (1992). *Cooperation between public libraries and public school library/media centers in Massachusetts.* Unpublished doctoral dissertation, Boston University.

Kent, K. (1985). A successful program of teachers assisting teachers. *Educational Leadership, 43(3),* 30–33.

Kerr, S. (1975). *The diffusion and implementation of an instructional-developmental function for learning resources specialists in public schools: A study in role consensus.* Unpublished doctoral dissertation, University of Washington.

Kim, J. (1981). *The role of the library media specialist in curriculum development and instructional design.* Unpublished doctoral dissertation, George Peabody College for Teachers of Vanderbilt University.

Krashen, S. (1993). *The power of reading: Insights from the research.* Englewood, CO: Libraries Unlimited.

Krashen, S. (1996). *Every person a reader: An alternative to the California Task Force on Reading.* Culver City, CA: Language Education Associates (P. O. Box 7416, Culver City, CA 90233).

Kreiser, J. L. C. (1991). *A comparative study of curriculum-integrated and traditional school library media programs: Fifth-grade students' reading and media program attitude and utilization.* Unpublished doctoral dissertation, Kansas State University.

Lance, K., Welborn, L. & Hamilton-Pennell, C. (1993). *The impact of school library media centers on academic achievement.* Castle Rock, CO: Hi Willow Research and Publishing.

Lee, L. & Wong, K. (1985). *Curriculum implementation: Results, issues, and strategies* (Research report 84-03a). Winnipeg, MB: Manitoba Education, Planning and Research Branch.

Loucks, S. & Lieberman, A. (1983). Curriculum implementation. In F. W. English (Ed.), *Fundamental curriculum decisions* (pp. 126–141). Alexandria, VA: Association for Supervision and Curriculum Development.

Lowden, E. (1980). *Level of sophistication of instructional media/learning resource center programs in area vocational-technical schools in the state of Oklahoma as perceived by superintendents and instructors as compared to their preferences for these programs.* Unpublished doctoral dissertation, Oklahoma State University.

Lowe, J. (1984). *A comparative analysis of reading habits and abilities of students in selected elementary schools in North Louisiana with and without centralized libraries.* Unpublished doctoral dissertation, North Texas State University.

Lumley, A. M. (1994). *The change process and the change outcomes in the development of an innovative elementary school library media program.* Unpublished doctoral dissertation, Kansas State University.

Mack, E. (1957). *The school library's contribution to the total educational program of the school: A content analysis of selected periodicals in the field of education.* Unpublished doctoral dissertation, University of Michigan.

Madaus, J. (1974). *Curriculum involvement: Teacher structures, and personality factors of librarians in school media programs.* Unpublished doctoral dissertation, University of Texas.

Markle, A. (1982). *Defining the roles of library/media personnel in a large school district.* Unpublished doctoral dissertation, George Peabody College for Teachers of Vanderbilt University.

McAfee, D. (1981). *A study to determine the presence of observable conditions of positive self-concept in elementary school media centers.* Unpublished doctoral dissertation, University of Wisconsin—Madison.

McGiffin, P. (1990). *The school library media specialist as a resource person: A descriptive study.* Unpublished doctoral dissertation, University of Massachusetts.

McMillen, R. (1965). *An analysis of library programs and a determination of educational justification of these programs in selected elementary schools of Ohio.* Unpublished doctoral dissertation, Western Reserve University.

Mooradian, E. (1985). *Curriculum planning in a selected school district that lacks curriculum staff workers.* Unpublished doctoral dissertation, State University of New York at Buffalo.

Nevi, C. (1986). Against the grain: Half truths that hinder staff development. *Principal, 65(3),* 44–46.

Nolan, J. (1989). *A comparison of two methods of instruction in library research skills for elementary school students.* Unpublished doctoral dissertation, Temple University.

Olson, L. (1966). *Teachers', principals', and librarians' perceptions of the school librarian's role.* Unpublished doctoral dissertation, University of Minnesota.

Orlich, D. (1989). *Staff development: Enhancing human potential.* Boston: Allyn and Bacon.

Ornstein, A. & Hunkins, F. (1988). Implementing curriculum changes: Guidelines for principals. *NASSP Bulletin, 72(511),* 67–72.

Paquette, M. (1987). Voluntary collegial support groups for teachers. *Educational Leadership, 45(3),* 36–39.

Payne, D. (1967). *The superintendent's perception of selected library practices in the public schools of the state of Mississippi.* Unpublished doctoral dissertation, University of Southern Mississippi.

Pichette, W. (1975). *The role of the IMC director in two types of elementary school organizational structures.* Unpublished doctoral dissertation, University of Wisconsin-Madison.

Pitts, J. (1994a). *Personal understandings and mental models of information: A qualitative study of factors associated with the information seeking and use of adolescents.* Unpublished doctoral dissertation, Florida State University.

Pitts, J. (1994b). Personal understandings and mental models of information: A qualitative study of factors associated with adolescents' information seeking and use; 1993 AASL Research Grant Award interim report. *School Library Media Annual, 12,* 200–202.

Pitts, J. (1995). The 1993–94 AASL/Highsmith Research Award study: Mental models of information. *School Library Media Annual, 13,* 187–200.

Pitts, J. (1995). Mental models of information: The 1993–94 AASL/Highsmith Research Award study. *School Library Media Quarterly, 23,* 177–184.

Pratt, D. (1980). *Curriculum: Design and development.* New York: Harcourt Brace Jovanovich.

Romberg, T. & Price, G. (1983). Curriculum implementation and staff development as cultural change. In G. Griffin (Ed.), *Staff development* (82nd Yearbook of the National Society for the Study of Education, pp. 154–184). Chicago: University of Chicago Press.

Royal, S. (1981). *An investigation of the relationships between the educational level of school library media personnel and perceived competencies needed to develop instructional activities.* Unpublished doctoral dissertation, Florida State University.

Rubin, L. (1987). Curriculum and staff development. In M. F. Wideen & I. Andrews (Eds.), *Staff development for school improvement* (pp. 172–181). Philadelphia: Falmer.

Scott, M. (1982). *School library media center programs: Student perceptions as criteria for library media program funding.* Unpublished doctoral dissertation, University of Southern California.

Shields, D. (1977). *A fault tree approach to analyzing school library media services.* Unpublished doctoral dissertation, Brigham Young University.

Showers, B., Joyce, B. & Bennett, B. (1987). Synthesis of research on staff development: A framework for future study and a state-of-the-art analysis. *Educational Leadership, 45(3),* 77–87.

Smith, J. (1978). *An exploratory study of the effectiveness of an innovative process designed to integrate library skills into the curriculum.* Unpublished doctoral dissertation, George Peabody College for Teachers of Vanderbilt University.

Sparks, G. & Bruder, S. (1987). Before and after peer coaching. *Educational Leadership, 45(3),* 54–57.

Stanwich, E. (1982). *School library media specialist's involvement in curriculum planning.* Unpublished doctoral dissertation, State University of New York at Buffalo.

Sullivan, J. (1977). *The role of the elementary school media director as viewed by media center directors and principals.* Unpublished doctoral dissertation, Northern Illinois University.

Tallman, J. & van Deusen, J. (1994a). External conditions as they relate to curriculum consultation and information skills instruction by school library media specialists: The 1993–94 AASL Highsmith Research Award study part two. *School Library Media Quarterly, 23,* 27–31.

Tallman, J. & van Deusen, J. (1994b). Collaborative unit planning—Schedule, time and participants: The 1993–94 AASL/Highsmith Research Award study part three. *School Library Media Quarterly, 23,* 33–37.

Tallman, J. & van Deusen, J. (1995). Is flexible scheduling always the answer? Some surprising results from a national study. *School Library Media Annual, 13,* 201–205.

van Deusen, J. (1991). *Effects of fixed versus flexible scheduling on curriculum involvement and skills integration in elementary school library media centers.* Unpublished doctoral dissertation, University of Iowa.

van Deusen, J. (1993). The effects of fixed versus flexible scheduling on curriculum involvement and skills integration in elementary school library media programs. *School Library Media Quarterly, 21,* 173–182

van Deusen, J. & Tallman, J. (1994). The effect of scheduling on curriculum consultation and information skills instruction: The 1993–94 AASL/Highsmith Research Award study part one. *School Library Media Quarterly, 23,* 17–25.

Van Dreser, R. (1971). *A survey related to job competencies of the instructional media specialist.* Unpublished doctoral dissertation, University of Nebraska.

Van Orden, P. (1970). *Use of media and the media center, as reflected in professional journals for elementary school teachers.* Unpublished doctoral dissertation, Wayne State University.

Van Sant, R. (1988). Staff development in the 1980s. *Wingspan, 4(1),* 11–13.

Virgilio, S. & Virgilio, I. (1984) The role of the principal in curriculum implementation. *Education, 104(4),* 346–350.

Wilson, L. (1972). *The role of the media specialist as perceived by public elementary school media specialists and principals in North Carolina.* Unpublished doctoral dissertation, George Washington University.

Woolls, E. B. (1973). *Cooperative library services to children in public libraries and public school systems in selected communities in Indiana.* Unpublished doctoral dissertation, Indiana University.

Woolls, B. (1990). *The research of school library media centers.* Papers of the Treasure Mountain Research Retreat, Park City, Utah, October 17–18, 1989. San Jose, CA: Hi Willow Research and Publishing.

Yarling, J. (1968). *Children's understandings and use of selected library-related skills in two elementary schools, one with and one without a centralized library.* Unpublished doctoral dissertation, Ball State University.

PART TWO

THE SCHOOL CONTEXT

While each school is a unique social and professional culture we are only recently learning that the school library media program is a reflection of that culture and that it is indeed much easier to develop programs in some school cultures than in others. Where there is a collaborative work environment, for example, and where the principal expects teachers to plan and work together, it is more common that the teacher-librarian collaborates with classroom colleagues on a regular basis.

In examining leadership for school improvement, Jean Brown notes that schools are not rational, predictable, well-controlled settings where we can apply the management styles of the last century or even the last decade to the complex issues facing us today. Dr. Brown reviews the changing views of leadership in organizations and makes a strong cases for transformational leadership, where we tie our agendas together and support and lead each other toward a commonly agreed upon purpose; and transformational leaders support and elevate followers who then become active leaders themselves. Of course the school's organizational culture and leadership approaches have enormous implications for our work. The basic assumptions that have been accepted and that have worked in the schools in the past tend to get passed on to new staff members as the "correct" way to think and act. Transformational leadership does provide us with some mechanisms, however, to develop problem-solving cultures that can support innovation and change.

Dianne Oberg places the school library media program firmly in its school's culture. Dr. Oberg examines the school as a workplace and the implications for the teacher-librarian as an agent of change. Teachers are individualistic, conservative, and rooted in the present, making school improvement that much more challenging. Some teachers are more classroom-oriented while others are more school-oriented, resulting in differences in perception and in practice. Implementation of a school library media program will likely require changes in a school's culture. The implications for the program and possible approaches for change are outlined in order to foster a collaborative environment that encourages and supports school improvement.

While Jean Brown and Dianne Oberg are researchers, Michael Marland is a secondary school principal. In examining actual instructional practice in schools Marland sees major problems in the common approach to "departmentalize" and thus "compartmentalize" school programs. The aggregate of courses, the emphasis on content knowledge, the use of worksheets and the underestimation of the complexity of the intellectual tasks involved in information literacy, all contribute to poorly designed and implemented programs. If teacher-librarians could emphasize curriculum more than resources and develop their role as teachers they could be more successful; similarly, if schools emphasized curriculum planning, coordinated approaches to information skills development and the characteristics of a collaborative culture, teacher-librarians could be more successful. Marland's article is more than ten years old and based on his experience in the United Kingdom: is the situation here, today, that different?

This section provides the school context, pinpoints the overarching issues and makes several suggestions for improving programs.

CHAPTER THREE

Leadership for School Improvement

Jean Brown

We are living in an era of change. Vaill (1989) refers to current conditions as living in a world of "permanent white water" (p. 2), suggesting that we are caught up in turbulent movements, being subjected to strong currents and pressures without the security of being in total control. There are other labels: the "post-industrial society" (Krantz, 1990; Schlechty, 1990); "postmodernity" (Hargreaves, 1991); "post-business" (Drucker, 1989), "post-entrepreneurial" (Kanter, 1989); but as Hargreaves (1991) comments, "As the prefix 'post' itself suggests, there is more clarity about what we are moving beyond than what we are moving towards" (p. 14). He would agree with Drucker (1989), however, that we are currently in the midst of "new realities," that we are not talking about the future as much as the present.

What are the new realities? Drucker (1989) speaks of new political realities—the loss of faith in "the belief in salvation by society, whether communism or any other ism" (p. 11); the loss of faith in simple solutions to social problems: "We now know that social situations, social behavior, social problems are much too complex to admit a simple 'right answer'. If they can be solved at all,

they always have several solutions—and none is quite right" (Drucker, 1989, p. 13).

Explanations for such loss of faith vary, but there is agreement that it is partly due to the globalization of information and communication. Governments can no longer limit what people hear and see as satellite dishes and computer technology allow an easy flow of information without regard for national boundaries. Not unrelated to this reality of a world linked tightly together in a communications network is another reality which Drucker (1989) refers to as "transnational economy" and "transnational ecology": a reality in which the world economy is controlled by stock market prices around the world rather than by national economies based on trade in goods and services; and a world in which "the environment no more knows national boundaries than does money or information" (Drucker, 1989, p. 116).

The impact of such changes on our political, economic and social lives cannot be overestimated and the future implications are but dimly perceived and poorly understood. Hargreaves (1991), however, singles out one important response, which is the attempt to find personal meanings and to reconstruct national identities (p. 15). Lacking an overriding belief system, the result in most nations, he claims, has been "the resurgence of ethnic, religious and linguistic identities of a more localized nature," a "quest to reconstruct meaningful identities and attachments in the face of globalization" (p. 15). Postmodernity, then, has had profound effects on society, leading to a need for new types of organizations and new approaches to leadership.

Kanter (1983) refers to the 1960s–1980s as "a transforming era" in the design of organizations, and compares the factors influencing the design of organizations in that period with those that influenced the design of organizations in the 1890s–1920s, a period she sees as "the formative era for the traditional industrial corporation," (p. 42). She found:

> The turn-of-the-century labor force was largely uneducated (in the formal sense), less skilled, often immigrant, with high turnover and high labor conflict. The distinction between workers and managers was one not only of task but also often of language and social class. Production tasks were quite straightforward: moving objects, assembling mechanical devices, adjusting machinery, and using sheer physical energy. (p. 42)

By contrast, in the 1960s–1980s she found: "Educated, sophisticated career employees; complex and intellectual tasks; electronic and biological technologies; organic views, multiple causes and effects; fluid markets and supplies; overlap between workers and managers" (pp. 42–43). She concludes that, "we cannot use the organization of the 1890s to solve the problems of the 1980s" (p. 43). Five years later, she writes, "Clearly, the bureaucratic pattern has to go. But what do we replace it with?" (Kanter, 1989, p. 309).

The eighties has seen numerous works which propose new forms of organization (see, for example, Bennis, 1989; Bennis & Nanus, 1985; Hickman & Silva, 1984; Kanter, 1983, 1989; Ouchi, 1981; Peters & Austin, 1985; Peters & Waterman, 1982; Vaill, 1989). Such works have created a great deal of interest, for they are accounts of some of the largest, most successful international companies, such as General Motors, Chrysler, and IBM.

There is little doubt, then, that as Louis and Miles (1990) point out, "there is uneasiness in the general administration and management literature with the dominant models of how to organize," and "most organizations—and particularly schools—do not look like the rational, predictable, well-controlled settings that the textbooks on planning and administration tell us they should be" (p. 19). They conclude that "those that are now emerging as most effective and adaptive organizations are designed very differently from the norm of even the recent past" (p. 19).

As Louis and Miles (1990) comment, "If we believe that new ways of organizing will work better, we can also predict that tried-and-true administrative practices probably won't lead to effectiveness in the 1990s, much less in the twenty-first century" (p. 19). Educators are having to cope with new terminology and new concepts of leadership: "institutional renewal," "school culture," "empowerment of teachers," "restructuring," "site-based management," and the "collaborative leader." The problem, however, is that few "have discussed how these new ideas relate to school systems," or how they may affect the roles of school leaders (Louis and Miles, 1990, p. 19).

The work that has been done has mostly concentrated on the elementary school. Particularly noteworthy are studies by Judith Little and Susan Rosenholtz. However, despite the emphasis placed on more "organic" forms of management, which involves "supportive forms of administrative leadership, participative forms of organizational decision-making, and increased teamwork" (Rowan, Raudenbush, and Kang, 1991, p. 239), little is actually known about the conditions that support such forms in schools, particularly high schools. The NASSP report on high school leaders notes: "The high school principalship has been linked in recent years to school effectiveness and collaborative leadership approaches in the educational literature. Little research exists, however, on the formative processes of effective leadership" (Pellicer et al., 1990, p. 52).

These new leadership ideas, if implemented, will dramatically affect the role of the principal, other administrators, specialists, librarians and teachers. It will mean wide use of administrative teams and advisory committees, yet, "There is no standard version of the administrative team concept," and what little literature does exist is "largely composed of single school efforts or of conceptual treatments discussing how schools might employ teams" (Pellicer et al., 1990, p. 18). What is needed is more clarity on "the nature of the social interactions between leaders and other members of the school organization, in particular, which build commitment and enhance capacities for change" (Leithwood, Jantzi, & Dart, 1991, p. 34).

We in teacher-librarianship have been at the forefront in restructuring, in changing our profession in order to meet the challenges of an Information Age. Yet, in the major efforts at educational reform and restructuring, the school's learning resource center and the role of teacher-librarians appear to be overlooked (Keegan & Westeberg, 1991, p. 10). The problem, I believe, relates to leadership, with leaders both in teacher-librarianship and leaders in curriculum areas not making the links or the connections with each other that we require if we are to meet the needs of today's students. Teacher-librarians have done an admirable job in connecting with each other. The problem emerges when we consider connecting outside our own group, to education in general. The developing theory of transformational leadership in education is an attempt to clarify these interactions. It begins by looking to the research already accumulated in the social sciences and business administration literature to see if there are things that we can bring to the study of leadership for change in the school system.

Changing Views of Leadership in Organizations

Kanter (1983, 1989) after extensive examination of the major corporations in North America, describes them as taking on a different shape: they are flatter and leaner organizations that have trimmed away the layers of middle management; they are more specialized, "focused on doing only those things in which it has competence" (p. 115); they have a more "horizontal" organization, in which there is cooperation, collaboration, and communication between divisions, departments and units. Kanter (1989) views the change as the "triumph of process over structure" in that "relationships and communication and the flexibility to temporarily combine resources are more important than the 'formal' channels and reporting relationships represented on an organizational chart" (p. 116). New world conditions require these newer organizations to respond quickly and with flexibility so "what is important is not how responsibilities are divided but how people can pull together to pursue new opportunities" (Kanter, 1989, p. 116). To survive, organizations have to "develop the capacity to change, learn, and adapt quickly and decisively" (Krantz, 1990, p. 53). This requires new forms of leadership.

For Bennis and Nanus (1985), leadership is "the pivotal force" (p. 3) behind the creation and survival of organizations, necessary "to help organizations develop a new vision of what they can be, then mobilize the organization to change toward the new vision" (p. 3). This, however, will require a new type of leader:

> The new leader…is one who commits people to action, who converts followers into leaders, and who may convert leaders into agents of change. We refer to this as "transformative leadership." (p. 3)

"Transformative leadership," or transformational leadership as it is more commonly called, is a form of leadership needed for change.

Like most other writers on transformational leadership, Bennis and Nanus (1985) based their work on the earlier writing of James MacGregor Burns. Burns (1978) defines transformational leadership as:

> The transforming leader recognizes and exploits an existing need or demand of a potential follower. But, beyond that, the transforming leader looks for potential motives in followers, seeks to satisfy higher needs, and engages the full person of the follower. The result of transforming leadership is a relationship of mutual stimulation and elevation that converts followers into leaders and may convert leaders into moral agents. (p. 4)

The central idea behind Burns' view of transforming leadership is the idea that the purposes of leaders and followers, or in education it makes better sense to talk of leaders and teachers—that the purposes of leaders and teachers become a common purpose. They may have started out as separate but "related," but they become "fused," as "power bases are linked not as counterweights but as mutual support for a common purpose" (Burns, 1984, p. 20). Transformational leadership, then, is not linked to formal leadership positions, but may be demonstrated by anyone. It may involve two or more teachers in a partnership or collegial relationship, or it may involve teachers influencing principals as well as principals influencing teachers. It can occur in the daily activities of people who may be regarded as ordinary, although the result may be far from ordinary.

There are various views of transformational leadership (see, for example, Avolio & Bass, 1988; Bass & Avolio, 1989; Bass, Waldman, Avolio & Bebb, 1987; Burns, 1978; Podsakoff, Mackenzie, Moorman, & Fetter, 1990; Tierney, 1990; Yammarino & Bass, 1990; Yukl, 1989), which raises the question of who is a transformational leader. I have already said that it is leadership for change. Hitler was responsible for tremendous change. Would he be a transformational leader? There are those who argue yes, that it is the process of being a leader and bringing about change that is important, and Hitler certainly did that. I disagree. Transformational leadership, as I and many others use it, carries with it definite moral implications. I agree with Burns, that the result of such leadership is to raise "the level of human conduct and ethical aspirations of both leader and led, and thus it has a transforming effect on both" (Burns, 1978, p. 20). In the way that I perceive transformational leadership, it is "dynamic leadership in the sense that the leaders throw themselves into a relationship with followers who feel 'elevated' by it and often become more active themselves, thereby creating new cadres of leaders" (p. 20).

This is viewing leadership as a process rather than a set of discrete steps. Burns (1978) describes it as "a stream of evolving interrelationships in which leaders are continuously evoking motivational responses from followers and modifying their behavior as they meet responsiveness or resistance, in a ceaseless process of flow and counterflow" (p. 440).

It may be useful here to pause and compare transformational leadership with another form of leadership, which Burns (1978) referred to as transactional leadership. The latter, transactional leadership, is characterized by appeals to the follower's interest. For example, a principal asks a teacher-librarian to serve on a committee. The teacher-librarian agrees, knowing that such a request is within the principal's right and that it may lead to a good evaluation at the end of the year. A leadership act took place, but there is no "enduring purpose," there was nothing that unites the principal and teacher-librarian together in a "mutual and continuing pursuit of a higher purpose" (Burns, 1978, p. 20).

Transformational leadership has become popular because the times require us to go beyond thinking of leadership in transactional terms. If the status quo was satisfactory, transactional leadership would suffice. But when we want leadership for change, we require more than merely doing the job. What is required is performance beyond expectations. What we need is extra energy, extra involvement, more than ordinary commitment and dedication, in order to bring about change. Bass (1985), a leading researcher in transformational leadership, makes the point that: "To achieve follower performance beyond the ordinary limits, leadership must be transformational. Followers' attitudes, beliefs, motives, and confidence need to be transformed from a lower to a higher plane of arousal and maturity" (p. xiii). This calls for "an accelerated increase in effort and/or a change in the rate at which a group's speed and accuracy are improving" (p. 4), and "may involve large changes in attitudes, beliefs, values, and needs" (p. 4). These are the changes which lead to "quantum leaps in performance" (p. 4), new paradigms, new contextual frameworks. The old models of transactional leadership do not suffice here, "The higher order of change calls for something distinguishable from such an exchange relationship—transformational leadership" (p. 4).

The question, then, is to try and explain why some schools are more open to change and improvement than others, to describe the type of leadership which is found in these schools. Susan Rosenholtz's book, *Teachers' workplace* (1989), describes "stuck" schools and "moving" schools. She defined "stuck" and "moving":

> The stuck feel no sense of progress, growth, or development and so tend to lower their aspirations and appear less motivated to achieve. They shy away from risks in the workplace and proceed in cautious, conservative ways. The moving, by contrast, tend to recognize and use more of their skills and aim still higher. Their sense of progress and future gain encourages them to look forward, to take risks, and to grow. (p. 149)

How do we explain the difference between "stuck" and "moving" schools? What happens in "moving" schools? Are there leadership practices which might explain what is happening? Who are the leaders?

I have been searching for answers to these questions for the past three years with a group at the Ontario Institute for Studies in Education. Under the direction of Ken Leithwood, a group of us, two research officers and three doctoral students, have been examining different aspects of leadership in schools which are successfully involved in multiple changes. Our search has led to certain conclusions and findings about the nature of leadership for educational change, or, as we prefer to call it, transformational leadership.

Key Practices Associated with Transformational Leadership

All theorists see transformational leadership as multidimensional. Six practices currently accepted as being associated with transformational leadership are:

- *Identifying and Articulating a Vision*—Practices on the part of leaders aimed at identifying new opportunities for the school, and developing, articulating, and inspiring others with a vision of the future.
- *Providing an Appropriate Model*—Practices on the part of leaders that set an example for others

to follow that is consistent with the values the leaders espouse.

- *Fostering the Acceptance of Group Goals*—Practices on the part of leaders aimed at promoting cooperation among teachers and assisting them to work together toward a common goal.
- *High Performance Expectations*—Practices that demonstrate the leaders' expectations for excellence, quality, and/or high performance on the part of others.
- *Providing Individualized Support*—Practices on the part of leaders that indicate that they respect others and are concerned about their personal feelings and needs.
- *Intellectual Stimulation*—Practices on the part of leaders that challenge others to re-examine some of their assumptions about their work and rethink how it can be performed.
                (Leithwood and Jantzi, 1990, p. 9)

This description makes it clear that transformational leadership is concerned with values, beliefs, norms, goals, feelings. This leads us into the field of organizational culture.

Organizational Culture and Leadership

There are many definitions for organizational culture. There are informal and simple definitions, such as: "The way we do things around here" (Deal & Kennedy, 1982, p. 4); or "the way things are" (Corbett, Firestone & Rossman, 1987, p. 37). However, the formal definition provided by Schein (1985) provides the most comprehensive definition:

> A pattern of basic assumptions—invented, discovered, or developed by a given group as it learns to cope with its problems of external adaptation and internal integration—that has worked well enough to be considered valid and, therefore, to be taught to new members as the correct way to perceive, think, and feel in relation to these problems. (p. 9)

Due to the popularity of the work by Deal and Kennedy (1982), elements to analyze the content of a culture, what people think, say and do, have become well known. These elements include values, norms, assumptions as well as heroes (heroes are defined as "pivotal figures in a strong culture" p. 37), rites and rituals. Their work also introduced a cultural network composed of "spies, storytellers, priests, and whisperers" (p. 86). But in discussing school culture, there is also a need to examine the form of the culture, the relationships between individuals and groups within the school. Two common forms of culture are collaborative cultures, where people work together and share, and isolated settings, where people work alone in an individualistic manner. Hargreaves (1990) and Little (1990) discuss other forms of school culture, particularly one which Hargreaves (1990) called "contrived collegiality" which, although it might appear to be truly collaborative, is, at its best, "a useful phase in the move towards more collaborative relationships between teachers"; at its worse it may be "little more than a quick, slick administrative surrogate for more genuinely collaborative teacher cultures" (Hargreaves, 1990, p. 19).

Little's work reveals how an understanding of the culture of an organization is necessary in analyzing leadership. In her study of norms of collegiality in teaching (1982), for example, she identifies norms within a school's culture which indicate collaboration amongst teachers: "teachers engage in frequent, continuous, and increasingly concrete and precise talk about teaching practice"; "teachers are frequently observed and provided with useful (if potentially frightening) critiques of their teaching"; "teachers plan, design, research, evaluate, and prepare teaching materials together"; and "teachers teach each other the practice of teaching" (p. 331). Using Little's indicators of collaboration and indicators of transformational leadership from previous leadership research, Leithwood and his associates at OISE conducted a number of studies to examine how school leaders changed the culture of their schools. In a 1990 study of nine elementary and three secondary schools in Ontario, they identified six strategies used by school leaders. I will use these six strategies as a framework, drawing on Leithwood's work but also including the work of others, as well as my own observations, in the discussion of each strategy. The purpose is to show

how leadership strategies can influence and change the culture of a school.

1. *Strengthening the school's culture.*

A number of researchers have written about the weakness of the school culture (see, for example, Fullan & Hargreaves, 1991; Leithwood & Jantzi, 1990; Rosenholtz, 1989). By that, it is generally meant that in many schools teachers work in self-contained classrooms, isolated from one another and from administrators. Goals in such situations tend to be ambiguous and vague. The staff tend to work on their individual problems rather than adopting a school focus. A first step in reforming the culture of the school was an attempt to strengthen the culture of what Fullan and Hargreaves (1991) call the "total school." A process was used to help teachers clarify and prioritize a set of shared goals, and to break down the isolation of the classroom by creating a shared, technical culture. The following quotation, taken from Leithwood and Jantzi (1990), gives one example of a process used for that purpose:

> Initially the SIT [School Improvement Team] got together to talk about goals for the SIP [School Improvement Project] and then we decided to take everything back to the staff to see what kind of general direction they wanted. We (the whole staff) brainstormed what we needed to do with resource based learning in the school. We broke into groups and decided on a variety of very tight recommendations and after discussion were able to reduce all our ideas to the six subgoals under RBL. We then took on the commitment of working each of these through until we were comfortable they had been achieved.

To reduce teacher isolation, a variety of methods were used to create opportunities for teachers to talk to each other about their work. Examples include: creating time for joint planning, holding staff retreats, providing opportunities and a structure so that teachers teach other teachers, encouraging teachers to visit other teachers' classrooms. In my own work in secondary schools, an excellent example of this was found in one secondary school which held breakfasts on Thursday mornings so that the teachers involved with the Junior High Grades could meet and share teaching strategies and personal solutions to instructional problems.

2. *Use of bureaucratic mechanisms.*

The schools in these studies used a number of bureaucratic mechanisms to foster the implementation of school improvement goals and to create more collaborative cultures. These bureaucratic mechanisms facilitated the introduction of changes within the school culture, making them easier to accomplish, and recognized the constraints and opportunities within the school. The reallocation of money or the finding of new money for the intended changes is one such mechanism, but there are others that are equally or perhaps even more important. Two that I found to be particularly important are:

Evaluation mechanisms: Rosenholtz (1989) found that evaluation criteria were very significant in teachers' commitment to shared school goals. However, evaluation criteria needed to be seen by teachers as "important, central to their work, applied frequently, and capable of being influenced by their own efforts" (p. 27). In my work in Ontario last year, I became aware of the influence of one board's evaluation plan, called "Supervision for Growth" (S4G). Teachers I spoke to were positive about this approach to evaluation, which emphasized their personal growth as professional teachers. An example of how it worked: some teachers might decide that using computers in the classroom as an integral part of their instruction was one of their goals for the coming year. This would be recorded as an objective for the year in their S4G plan. Colleagues who already use computers in instruction might be approached and asked to coach the teachers in this new strategy. At the end of the year, this objective would be part of the teachers' evaluation. The colleagues who coached would also have their coaching role considered in their evaluation, and knew that such activities might be useful for promotion in the future.

Planning and scheduling: Another bureaucratic mechanism involved facilitating the planning of purposed changes and revising scheduling procedures within the school. A common example was the provision of time for collaborative planning during the workday. Other examples include making timetable adjustments so that teachers can plan and work together, and using staff meetings and other meetings (such as department head meetings) to ensure that school improvement initiatives are not overlooked.

3. *Staff development.*

Fullan (1990) writes, "It has been well known for at least 15 years that staff development and successful innovation or improvement are intimately related" (p. 3). He defined staff development as "any activity or process intended to improve skills, attitudes, understandings, or performance in present or future roles" (p. 3), and used the term interchangeably with "professional development" and "inservice."

We are only beginning to understand the complexities of what makes staff development effective. Recent work by Little (1982, 1990), Hargreaves (1990), and others, link staff development and increased collaboration, and show that when teachers have access to "others' knowledge and experience, and to shared work and discussion, teachers are likely to favor some participation in staff development," and that "Staff development appears to have the greatest prospects for influence where there is a prevailing norm of collegiality" (p. 339).

Staff development, then, which creates opportunities for teachers to learn from one another, both fosters and nurtures a collaborative culture. The evaluation example I used earlier, the Supervision for Growth model in which teachers taught other teachers, is an example of staff development as a mechanism for changing the culture of the school. It recognizes the teacher as a lifelong learner, it provides the support and resources needed for learning to take place, and it reflects a coherence in the whole system, from the determination of personal objectives to the year-end evaluation of teacher performance. This is not to suggest, however, that teachers only learn from each other. Studies have shown many different kinds of staff development activities that changed the culture of the school, from the sending of staff to relevant conferences (followed by their sharing of their experiences with colleagues when they return), to the inviting of "experts" into the school. The key to the success of this strategy seems to be collegial support that makes it meaningful to the aims of the school. Rather than isolated professional development activities of an individualistic nature, there appears to be a concern for the total school and for collaborative problem solving by groups of teachers utilizing whatever means are possible. Interview data collected by Leithwood and his associates in their study of the Year 2000 Project in British Columbia reveal the collegial relationship existing in one school: several classroom teachers became leaders in new teaching practices (having to do with whole language) and were very influential in helping other teachers; they made a practice of sharing new knowledge with their colleagues; when one teacher attended a meeting or conference where new ideas were circulated, she came back to the school and shared it with others; they learned together, attending inservice sessions as a group. In one case, where only one of the teachers was not slated to attend a conference, the other teachers arranged "to drag her along." They truly regarded each other as resources and learned from and with each other. (Notes from personal interview data, 1991).

4. Direct and frequent communication.

Leithwood's work in the Ontario study clearly showed the importance of the principal having direct and frequent communication with teachers, as this quote from a principal in the Ontario study illustrates:

> In actual planning in half day sessions I was actively involved with a planning team working with consultants. It's important to work through with the teacher to understand each unique classroom setting and the problems that may arise...I think the thing I've learned (in this process) is that a principal needs to learn as much as she can about a teacher. You need to know your staff thoroughly, listen and show people you truly care about them. When they realize you are

ready to help them realize their goals, you will find a positive and favorable response. (Leithwood and Jantzi, 1990, p. 27)

The evidence is overwhelming for the administrator's role in communicating with teachers, but my own research interest has taken me into investigating the communication within the entire school that is required for changing the school culture. The example I used earlier, of the junior high teachers meeting for the Thursday morning breakfasts so that they could share teaching strategies, is an example of new structures for communication which may emerge as traditional school cultures move towards collaboration.

Last winter I visited a large secondary school in order to interview school leaders about their role in bringing about change. It became clear to me as I spoke to different people in that school that communication was essential since it was the involvement of a large number of people that allowed the change to evolve and happen. Let me illustrate. A traditional Ontario school is involved with implementing *The transition years* document from the Ministry of Education. As one of the vice-principals explained it, for this school that meant "moving towards a student centered approach, a holistic approach which requires a totally different way of looking at delivery of program." To achieve this, the school began by inviting teachers to volunteer to act on a working committee to examine the grade nine program. Twenty-six people volunteered immediately, others were added later as subcommittees were formed. The vice-principal described what happened:

> And so the key idea that we went with was that we would continue to evolve and develop programs using the resources of the individual teachers, trying to establish with them confidence in their own experience and in their own knowledge, in their ability to carry this through, and so we set up meetings to have a chance to explore things together, and make sure that we were addressing concerns and make sure that there was a support basis there for staff to feel they weren't out on their own, on the edge of a cliff or out on a limb. (Personal interview data, 1991)

The mention of evolution of programs brings to mind the concept of "evolutionary planning" as discussed by Louis and Miles (1990). As used by them, "the evolutionary perspective rests on the assumption that the environment both inside and outside organizations is often chaotic" (p. 193). Specific plans are often outmoded by events that cannot often be anticipated, what Collingridge (1980) refers to as decisions made under "conditions of ignorance" rather than conditions of certainty. To bring about change and improvement, this perspective sees the planning as evolving, and maintains that "Getting there is half the fun" (Louis and Miles, 1990):

> The organization can cycle back and forth between efforts to gain normative consensus about what it may become, to plan strategies for getting there, and to carry out decentralized, incremental experimentation that harnesses the creativity of all members to the change effort.

> This approach is evolutionary in the sense that, although the mission and image of the organization's ideal future may be based on a top-level analysis of the environment and its demands, strategies for achieving the mission are frequently reviewed and refined based on internal scanning for opportunities and successes. Strategy is viewed as a flexible tool, rather than as a semi-permanent extension of the mission: If rational planning is like blueprinting, evolutionary planning is more like taking a journey. There is a general destination, but many twists and turns as unexpected events occur along the way. (p. 193)

Based on the approximately two hundred schools in which they worked, Louis and Miles (1990) concluded, "the evolutionary model may be the best for schools undertaking a major renewal and change effort" (p. 194). My own observations support this finding. The vice-principal I referred to earlier who saw this process as evolutionary emphasized that planned change came about because people worked together. She saw her own role as administrator as a facilitating one:

> The role of the vice-principal, I really feel, is to make sure that students really achieve success, that they have the opportunity, the equality of access, opportunity outcome, and that through my assisting staff I believe that I can facilitate that to happen for students. But that to me is the bottom line, so I am here to work with staff and students in achieving those outcomes for students.

The whole process becomes that of communicating what the school is about:

> To make sure that we do empower students to be as successful as they can and to provide the kinds of quality experiences that would facilitate that success, and so I see my role as a facilitating one, I feel that I have to have a sense of the big picture, what it's all about, and see where things have to go in terms of being able to achieve that result. And I don't feel for one minute that I paint that big picture and I think that it's through the involvement and participation of staff that you get the sense of that big picture and you help—for those people often who work in departments and in the nature of a high school setup, often is one that's working from isolation or from a very small area so they don't have that sense of what the big picture is all about, and I think that once that's there, then staff begin to unfold that big picture as well for you. And so, I'm here to do that as well as to assist in directing the kinds of things we want to achieve for students. (Personal interview data, 1991)

That leads to the fifth strategy used to change school culture:

5. Share power and responsibility with others.

It should be obvious from the examples used so far that the concept of a collaborative culture involves the sharing of decision-making within the school. The vice-principal quoted above had no hesitation in affirming that she did not paint the picture alone, that maybe she facilitated the process, but then, as she stated it, the "staff begin to unfold that big picture as well for you."

Another common way to share power and responsibility is through the setting up of School Improvement Teams. Working with the administration of the school, these teams shared the responsibility for implementing the project, and more importantly perhaps, bridged the gap between administrators and classroom teachers, as this quote from an administrator shows:

> The SIT [School Improvement Team] was involved in planning where we are going, looking to the future and getting input from staff in terms of where we think we need to change. (Quoted in Leithwood and Jantzi, 1990, p. 28)

Whatever the name, whether it's a school improvement team, or a committee, there is evidence of teachers (whether classroom teachers or department heads) being involved in serious decision making in the school. Often they also acted as role models, coaches and on-site experts, trying out new ideas, sharing information with their fellow teachers, and clarifying the school improvement effort for those who were less involved.

For those teachers who are not used to collaborating, to using different resources, to creating units with the teacher-librarian, a movement towards resource-based learning and cooperative planning and teaching is threatening. If we want professional teachers to share their fears, to take risks and try new teaching strategies, then we too must be willing to be vulnerable and to take risks, and let others know of our own uncertainties.

6.   Use symbols and rituals to express cultural values.

The isolation of many teachers has been well documented over the years, by researchers such as Lortie in 1975 to a current book by Fullan and Hargreaves in 1991. Last year I visited a classroom where an enthusiastic newly graduated grade one teacher reflected on the loneliness of her teaching experiences. She had nobody to plan with, nobody to celebrate with when things worked. Schools that are reforming the traditional school culture and moving towards collaborative cultures need to demonstrate by words and actions the new cultural values and norms. The studies show various ways that schools do that.

One important way is by some variation of show and tell. In schools I visited, department head meetings began with a session called "Sharing

the good news," where Heads reported on successful happenings. The "Thursday Morning Shares" referred to earlier is a variation of this, allowing teachers to share experiences with their colleagues while at the same time receiving recognition and feedback. Staff meetings and school assemblies are also used to recognize and celebrate successes. Not only does this recognize the individuals involved, it also alerts the rest of the school to the new practices, values and norms, and invites others to share in similar events.

On a more personal level, school leaders tended to place an emphasis on writing of personal notes to people expressing appreciation for special efforts, and ensured that they praised individuals when praise was due. These school leaders came from different levels of the school system: committee chairs, department heads, administrative team, board office personnel.

In summary, then, studies reveal six strategies used by school leaders to reform the culture of the school: strengthening the culture; use of bureaucratic mechanisms, such as money, evaluation criteria, and planning and scheduling; staff development; direct and frequent communication; and the use of symbols and rituals to express cultural values.

Questions About Transformational Leadership

If changing the culture of the school is necessary for school improvement and change, several important questions need to be addressed about such leadership.

Whose Vision Is It?

Nothing is more central to transformational leadership than vision. The question is, however, whose vision? And how is vision created? Sheive and Schoenheit's (1987) definition of vision is a clear, concise one: "A vision is a blueprint of a desired state. It is an image of a preferred condition that we work to achieve in the future" (p. 94). But whose blueprint? Whose images? There appears to be primarily two perspectives to this question. The first is the business management view of vision: "it is assumed that a vision of the future is presented to the chief executive of the organization as revealed truth"; and "the spread of the leader's vision is often assumed to be, in large measure, a function of a mystical charisma" (Louis and Miles, 1990, p. 217). Conger (1989) sees it essential that such leaders be able to "communicate and persuade—especially on the emotional level" (pp. 68–69).

Hargreaves (1991) is one of many researchers who question this perspective, viewing it as having the potential for "manipulation" and "co-optation" (p. 18). Fullan (1992) sees such people as "blinded by their own vision when they feel they must manipulate the teachers and the school culture to conform to it" (p. 19).

The problem with vision is that all too often vision is individual, or else it reflects only the vision of a particular group, leading to what Andy Hargreaves (1990) refers to as "balkanization." Fullan (1992) refers to "visions that blind" (p. 19). There are the strong advocates for a particular change, whether it's resource-based learning, computers across the curriculum, or whole language, who pursue it in such "narrow and self-defeating ways that key teachers will resist the idea" (p. 19).

An alternative perspective sees vision as "rarely one person's dream"; rather it is "a complex collage" (Tichy & Devanna, 1986, p. 128). This sees vision as process, as a "synthesizing vision," which requires selecting, organizing, structuring, and interpreting information about the future "in an attempt to construct a viable and credible vision" (Bennis & Nanus, 1985, p. 101). Instead, then, of one person, there are many, and the vision is not one person's dream but it is a collective vision.

For teacher-librarians, only the latter perspective makes any sense at all. We are, as we have stated in all our guidelines and standards, partners in the action of the school. Our role is a collegial, collaborative one, and although we have our visions, we must realize that we work in a particular school culture; that others have their visions as well; that other teachers' visions may be as valid as our own; that vision-building takes time as it is a learning process; and that we can all learn from one another. As teachers, as administrators, as university professors, we all can connect at one level, for regardless of the songs that we may sing in the privacy of our dreams, the song we must sing together is one that will lead to us working together for the good of our students.

Leadership: Of People or with People?

Bennis and Nanus (1985) set out to dispel what they saw as "perhaps the most damaging myth of all" about leadership—that is, that "the leader controls, directs, prods, manipulates" (p. 224). The truth of the matter, they argue, is that transformational leadership "is not so much the exercise of power itself as the empowerment of others. Leaders are able to translate intentions into reality by aligning the energies of the organization behind an attractive goal" (pp. 224–225). Roueche, Baker & Rose (1989) support this view with their description of the transformational leader:

> This transformation—or change—is accomplished, in part, through the development of a leadership team—a cohesive group of people working and moving together in the same direction. The cohesion of these teams is due to the acceptance of the CEO's influence. Through this acceptance, followers are transformed into leaders, infusing the shared vision into all parts of the college. This vision is then made real by using the skills of competent managers, faculty, and support staff. (p. 11)

There are two quite different interpretations to what transformational leadership means in these descriptions. For some it means that there is an elite group of leaders who are enlightened and another group of followers who require alignment. This is not the meaning that Burns (1978) had in mind when he spoke of mutual support and mutual stimulation between leader and follower. It is also quite different from the more egalitarian leadership of Barth's (1990) school which he describes as "a community of leaders, where students, teachers, parents, and administrators share the opportunities and responsibilities for making decisions that affect all the occupants of the schoolhouse" (p. 9). Barth's view is that:

Committees and coordinators thus help to break down the isolation of teachers' lives and of the principal's life as well. This blurring of roles between "teacher" and "administrator" solved some problems and created some new ones, enabling all members of the school community to contribute their strengths and share the power and the satisfaction—as well as the price—of influence. (p. 61)

Barth's view of leadership is similar to Roberts' (1985) view of transformational leadership. Her definition captures Burns' (1978) original meaning of transforming leadership:

This type of leadership offers a vision of what could be and gives a sense of purpose and meaning to those who would share that vision. It builds commitment, enthusiasm, and excitement. It creates a hope in the future and a belief that the world is knowable, understandable, and manageable. The collective action that transforming leadership generates, empowers those who participate in the process. There is hope, there is optimism, there is energy. In essence, transforming leadership is a leadership that facilitates the redefinition of a people's mission and vision, a renewal of their commitment, and the restructuring of their systems for goal accomplishment. It is a collective process involving heightened activity in response to a crisis. (Roberts, 1985, p. 1024)

In this latter perspective, formal leaders within the organization "see themselves less as soloists than as collaborators" (Bennis, 1989, p. 139), as part of a team, as a "leader of leaders" (Schlechty, 1990, p. 241). It is a perspective that places trust and faith in people. It is the view popularized by Peters and Austin (1985):

To achieve distinction on either of these dimensions, then, requires not sleight of hand by geniuses but the commitment to excellence (quality, service, make it better/innovation) by everyone. In short, people are the unmistakable base.... Make no mistake about it. "Techniques" don't produce quality products, educate children, or pick up the garbage on time: people do, people who care, people who are treated as creatively contributing adults. (p. 235)

Transformational Leadership as Problem-Solving

Leithwood, Begley and Cousins (1992) see the enhancement of individual and collective problem-solving capacities of members within the organization as central to the concept of transformational leadership. The centrality of problem-solving is based on a view of leadership as involving: the development of "a widely shared, defensible vision" assisting members of the organization "overcome obstacles they encounter in striving for vision"; and "increasing the capacity" of individuals within the organization to overcome obstacles (Leithwood, Begley and Cousins, 1992). This perspective recognizes the need for leadership to go beyond instructional leadership by encompassing what Fullan (1991) refers to as "institutional renewal," leading to the creation of new working cultures.

Conclusion

Transformational leadership, then, is about vision, and working with others. It is about respect for people, and allowing, encouraging the growth of others. It is concerned with influencing people to work willingly for group goals. It is not as much concerned with the power of the leader as it is with empowering others; it is concerned with growth rather than control. It is shared leadership, where school leaders, with or without formal leadership roles, use various strategies to change the culture of the school in school improvement efforts.

Roland Barth (1988) doesn't use the term "transformational leadership"; instead he talks of schools as being "a community of leaders," insisting that "all teachers can lead" (p. 131). He maintains that "there is plenty of leadership to go around" (p. 132), that "Leadership is not a zero-sum game in which one person gets some only when another loses some."

Max DePree (1989) defines leadership as "Liberating people to do what is required of them in the most effective and humane way possible" (p. 1). Isn't that what we all want as we seek to connect with others? But if we are to succeed, we need to see ourselves as transformational leaders who respect others, who provide opportunities for others to grow, to be the best that they can be. It requires us to see beyond our own narrow specialties, whether it be teacher-librarianship or administration or a curriculum area; to adopt a focus on the total school, and to see ourselves as part of a community of educational leaders who together can accomplish a lot for the learners entrusted to our care.

Barth used a song by R. D. Stromberg to illustrate what he meant by his community of leaders. He makes the point that the goose can't fly "from way up North to way down South and back again" alone, that "it's something he can only do in community" (cited in Barth, p. 145). The research on transformational leadership and school improvement supports the need for educational leaders to work within the community, to be leaders by working with others to achieve the goals they seek. It might indeed appeal to some to see themselves as "on the eagle's side, solitary, self-sufficient, strong," but like Stromberg, the evidence suggest that "God made us more like the goose."

References

Avolio, B. & Bass, B. (1988). Transformational leadership, charisma, & beyond. In J. Hunt, B. Galiga, H. Dachler & C. Schriesheim (Eds.), *Emerging leadership vistas* (pp. 29–50). Lexington: Lexington Books.

Barth, R. (1990). *Improving schools from within: Teachers, parents, and principals can make the difference.* San Francisco, CA: Jossey-Bass.

Bass, B. (1985). *Leadership and performance beyond expectations.* New York: The Free Press.

Bass, B. & Avolio, B. (1989). Potential biases in leadership measures: How prototypes, leniency, and general satisfaction relate to ratings and rankings on transformational and transactional leadership constructs. *Educational and Psychological Measurement, 49,* 509–527.

Bass, B., Waldman, D., Avolio, B. & Bebb, M. (1987). Transformational leadership and the falling dominoes effect. *Group and Organization Studies, 12(1),* 73–87.

Bennis, W. (1989). *On becoming a leader.* Reading, MA: Addison-Wesley.

Bennis, W. & Nanus, B. (1985). *Leaders.* New York: Harper & Row.

Burns, J. (1978). *Leadership.* New York: Harper & Row.

Burns, J. (1984). Foreword. In B. Kellerman (Ed.), *Leadership: Multi-disciplinary perspectives.* Englewood Cliffs, NJ: Prentice-Hall.

Collingridge, D. (1980). *The social control of technology.* New York: St. Martin's Press.

Conger, J. (1989). *The charismatic leader: Behind the mystique of exceptional leadership.* San Francisco, CA: Jossey-Bass.

Corbett, H., Firestone, W. & Rossman, G. (1987). Resistance to planned change and the sacred in school cultures. *Educational Administration Quarterly, 23(4),* 36–59.

Deal, T. & Kennedy, A. (1982). *Corporate cultures: The rites and rituals of corporate life.* Reading, MA: Addison-Wesley.

Drucker, P. (1989). *The new realities.* New York: Harper & Row.

Fullan, M. (1991). *The new meaning of educational change.* (2nd ed.). Toronto: OISE Press & Teachers College Press.

Fullan, M. (1992). Visions that blind. *Educational Leadership (5),* 19–20.

Fullan, M. & Hargreaves, A. (1991). *What's worth fighting for? Working together for your school.* Toronto: Ontario Public School Teachers' Federation.

Hargreaves, A. (1990). Cultures of teaching. In I. Goodson (Ed.), *Studying teachers' lives.* London: Kegan Paul.

Hargreaves, A. (1991, April). *Restructuring restructuring: Postmodernity and the prospects for educational change.* Paper presented at the annual conference of American Educational Research Association, Chicago.

Hickman, C. & Silva, M. (1984). *Creating excellence: Managing corporate culture, strategy, & change in the new age.* Markham, ON: New American Library.

Kanter, R. (1983). *The change masters: Innovations and entrepreneurship in the American corporations.* New York: Simon & Schuster.

Kanter, R. (1989). *When giants learn to dance: Mastering the challenge of strategy, management, and careers in the 1990s.* New York: Simon & Schuster.

Keegan, B. & Westerberg, T. (1991). Restructuring and the school library: Partners in an information age. *NASSP Bulletin, 75(535),* 9–14.

Krantz, J. (1990). Lessons from the field: An essay on the crisis of leadership in contemporary organizations. *Journal of Applied Behavioral Science, 26(1),* 49–64.

Leithwood, K., Begley, P., & Cousins, J. (1992). *Developing expert leadership for future schools.* Washington, DC: Falmer Press.

Leithwood, K., Dart, B., Jantzi, D., & Steinbach, R. (1990). *Interim report. Policy implementation processes: Understanding the school administrator's role.* Report submitted to the British Columbia Ministry of Education.

Leithwood, K. & Jantzi, D. (1990, June). *Transformational leadership: How principals can help reform school cultures.* Paper presented at the annual meeting of the Canadian Society for the Study of Education, Victoria, BC.

Leithwood, K., Jantzi, D., & Dart, B. (1991, January). *Toward a multi-level conception of policy implementation processes based on commitment strategies.* Paper presented at the 4th International Congress on School Effectiveness, Cardiff, Wales.

Leithwood, K. & Steinbach, R. (1989, June). *A comparison of processes used by principals in solving problems individually and in groups.* Paper presented at the annual meeting of the Canadian Society for the Study of Education, Quebec City.

Little, J. (1982). Norms of collegiality and experimentation: Workplace conditions of school success. *American Educational Research Journal, 19(3),* 325–340.

Little, J. (1990). The persistence of privacy: Autonomy and initiative in teachers' professional relations. *Teachers College Record, 91(4),* 509–536.

Louis, K. & Miles, M. (1990). *Improving the urban high school: What works and why.* New York: Teachers College.

Ouchi, W. (1981). *Theory Z.* Reading, MA: Addison-Wesley.

Pellicer, L., Anderson, L., Keefe, J., Kelley, E., & McCleary, L. (1990). *High school leaders and their schools. Vol. II: Profiles of excellence.* Reston, VA: National Association of Secondary School Principals.

Peters, T. & Austin, N. (1985). *A passion for excellence.* New York: Warner.

Peters, T. & Waterman, R. (1982). *In search of excellence: Lessons from America's best-run companies.* New York: Warner.

Podsakoff, P., Mackenzie, S., Moorman, R. & Fetter, R. (1990). Transformational leader behaviors and their effects on followers' trust in leader satisfaction and organizational citizenship behaviors. *Leadership Quarterly, 1(2),* 107–142.

Roberts, N. (1985). Transforming leadership: A process of collective action. *Human Relations, 38(11),* 1023–1046.

Rosenholtz, S. (1989). *Teachers' workplace: The social organization of schools.* New York: Longman.

Roueche, J., Baker, G., & Rose, R. (1989). *Shared vision: Transformational leadership in American community colleges.* Washington DC: National Center for Higher Education.

Rowan, B., Raudenbush, S., & Kang, S. (1991, January). Organizational design in high schools: A multi-level analysis. *American Journal of Education,* 238–265.

Schein, E. (1985). *Organizational culture and leadership.* San Francisco, CA: Jossey-Bass.

Schlechty, P. (1990). Schools for the 21st century: The conditions for invention. In A. Lieberman (Ed.), *Schools as collaborative cultures: Creating the future now* (pp. 233–256). New York: Falmer.

Sergiovanni, T. (1984). Leadership as cultural expression. In T. Sergiovanni and J. Corbally (Eds.), *Leadership and organizational culture* (pp. 105–114). Urbana: University of Illinois Press.

Sheive, L. & Schoenheit, M. (1987). Vision and the work life of educational leaders. In L. Sheive & M. Schoenheit (Eds.), *Leadership: Examining the elusive* (pp. 93–104). 1987 Yearbook of the Association for Supervision and Curriculum Development. Alexandria, VA: Association for Supervision and Curriculum Development.

Tichy, N. & Devanna, M. (1990). *The transformational leader.* New York: Wiley.

Tierney, W. G. (1990, April). *Advancing democracy: A critical interpretation of leadership.* Paper presented at American Educational Research Association, Boston.

Vaill, P. (1984). The purposing of high-performing systems. In T. Sergiovanni and J. Corbally (Eds.), *Leadership and organizational culture* (pp. 85–104). Urbana: University of Illinois Press.

Vaill, P. (1989). *Managing as a performing art: New ideas for a world of chaotic change.* San Francisco, CA: Jossey-Bass.

Yammarino, F. & Bass, B. (1990). Transformational leadership and multiple levels of analysis. *Human Relations, 43(10),* 975–995.

Yukl, G. (1989). *Leadership in organizations.* (2nd ed). Englewood Cliffs, NJ: Prentice-Hall.

CHAPTER FOUR

The School Library Program and the Culture of the School

Dianne Oberg

Understanding the nature of change is essential to every teacher-librarian. The implementation of a school library program through cooperative planning and teaching involves major changes, both in the teachers who participate in the program and in the organization within which the program is developed. Over the past decade, there has been a growing awareness in the field of school librarianship of the teacher-librarian's role as change agent, of the steps in the change process, and of the factors that facilitate or impede change.

Teacher-librarians are involved in the process of change whether they are implementing a program for the first time, making changes to an established program, or participating in some aspects of ongoing school improvement. The magnitude and depth of the changes involved in these activities has been underestimated at times because we have not looked closely enough at the context within which these changes are being made. However, there appears to be a growing awareness of the importance of considering this context, or recognizing that the work of the teacher-librarian involves changes in the very nature of the school. When we initiate a cooperative integrated library program, we are initiating changes in the culture of the school, in its important artifacts and regular activities, in the roles that its members play, and in the norms or values that shape the behavior of its members.

The literature of school librarianship advocates the implementation of school library programs through the cooperative work of classroom teachers and teacher-librarians. Learning activities are designed that support, that integrate classroom curriculum content and information skills. The library program is not developed in isolation from the school's curriculum. Research, study and appreciation skills are taught through resource-based activities based on the content of subject area curricula. When teacher-librarians work together to develop learning activities for their students, they are likely to be negotiating a change in the cultural norms of their school, from privacy and self-reliance to collegiality and experimentation. The implementation of a cooperative integrated school library program requires major changes in the way classroom teachers traditionally have organized and thought about their work in school.

The School as a Workplace

In the area of school improvement research has increasingly been focusing on the school as a workplace that shapes and is shaped by the members of that workplace. One researcher who examined the nature of classroom teaching as an occupation found that, through the way that its members are recruited, socialized and rewarded, the occupation of classroom teacher has developed orientations of conservatism, individualism and "presentism."

Teaching is an occupation marked by ease of entry: candidates may enter early or late in their working life; training is accessible; and entry requirements are sometimes made less demanding when teacher shortages occur. Strong attractors to teaching are contact with young people, service to society, continuation of school life, material benefits and working schedules that allow time for other obligations and pursuits. These factors tend to attract candidates who are positively disposed towards schools and who are not likely to see a need for change in the schools. As well, these types of candidates who are attracted by the possibility of limited time demands, are not likely to want to invest the time and energy needed to make major changes in the school system.

The individualism of teachers is related to ways that individuals are inducted into teaching. It is an occupation where neophytes are given full responsibility at the beginning of their careers and there is rarely opportunity to observe and learn from more skilled, experienced teachers. Teachers generally learn their skills by trial and error, in isolation in the classroom. For this reason, teaching skills generally are viewed as personal and idiosyncratic. Because teachers work in isolation, they face a great deal of uncertainty in their work and often take the problems of teaching personally. They also rely heavily upon the experiences they had when they were students in

the classroom regardless of the amount and degree of formal training they have had.

The presentism of teachers is related to the ways in which the rewards of teaching are organized. Entry level salaries are high in relation to career maximums. When this happens, there is less incentive to remain in a career. Nor does this encourage high involvement since increases in salary are not tied to effort but to years of training and experience. Teachers focus then on psychic rewards, particularly those related to the classroom and their students.

The orientations of conservatism, individualism, and presentism affect the teachers and school system in circular and self-perpetuating ways. The traditional practices of schooling and the traditional teacher ethos are very pervasive in North American schools and they appear to have remained stable over many decades. This makes change difficult.

Yet, change does occur; some schools and school systems are clearly different from and better than others. Lortie in 1975 speculated that an erosion of the traditional culture of the school might occur as teachers increasingly faced pressure for more adaptability, for more effective collegial relationships, and for more sharing in issues of knowledge and expertise. This pressure might come from researchers and theorists in education, from district administrators, from educational reformers and from parents and society in general.

There is evidence indicating that because of differing expectations and pressures, changes in practice have and will continue to occur. In a one year study of six urban schools in the United States, Little (1982) found that certain types of teaching practices characterized successful schools, that is, schools where students were doing well (defined by SAT scores and by nomination by district administrators and staff development personnel) and where teachers were highly involved in development activities. Four types of teaching practices clearly differentiated the more successful schools from the less successful ones: discussion of classroom practice, mutual observation and critique, shared efforts to design and prepare curriculum, and shared participation in instructional improvement. In the successful schools, the traditional norms of privacy and self-reliance had been altered. The new norms of collegiality and experimentation, which involve teachers working together for continuous improvement, had become part of the culture of these schools.

LaRocque (1986) also discovered these contrasting sets of norms in her study of policy implementation in a school district. Instead of one universal teacher ethos, she found two: school-oriented and classroom-oriented. Although both groups of teachers emphasized the importance of the student-teacher relationship, the groups differed markedly in their view of the relationships between the classroom and the school and of the relationships between teachers and other members of the school community. The classroom-oriented teachers saw their efforts in the classroom as the major significant factor in students' learning; the school-oriented teachers saw the whole school as being important to their success and to their students' success. The LaRocque study focused on the implementation of two policies: a district community relations policy and a school self-assessment policy. The two groups of teachers responded quite differently in interviews about the policies. In relation to the community relations policy, the classroom-oriented teachers favored infrequent parent involvement in the school, with parents taking a supportive but subordinate role; the school-oriented teachers favored regular parent involvement with parents acting in a cooperative partnership with teachers. In relation to the school self-assessment policy, the classroom-oriented teachers focused on obstacles and regarded school policies as unnecessary and restrictive; the school-oriented teachers focused on benefits and regarded school policies as necessary and unifying. Schools with a higher proportion of school-oriented teachers were more successful in implementing the policies.

Rosenholtz (1989) found, in her study of 78 elementary schools, that school-oriented ways of thinking and acting characterized the teachers in successful elementary schools. Four measures of school success were used in Rosenholtz's study: (1) student learning outcomes, measured by SAT scores; (2) school problem-solving and renewal capabilities; (3) teachers' certainty about instructional

practice; and (4) teachers' motivation and commitment to the values of the school. Rosenholtz found five themes especially significant in differentiating the best or 'moving' schools from the worst or 'stuck' schools: shared school goals, teacher collaboration, teacher learning, teacher certainty and teacher commitment.

School effectiveness appears to be multidimensional (Rosenholtz, 1985); the workplace conditions that support effectiveness are also multidimensional and strongly interrelated. Rosenholtz found that teacher perceptions of workplace conditions were generally consistent within each school and where commitment was high, so was teacher certainty, teacher collaboration and so on.

One theme found in successful schools was that of shared school goals. These shared goals defined what teachers should emphasize in their instruction and how they should gauge their success. Teachers in these schools worked with the principal to establish the goals of the school and the means by which they would best be achieved.

Consensus on school goals was related to teacher collaboration, the second pattern evident in successful schools. Where goals are vague and a common purpose is lacking, instructional uncertainty is greater and teachers are left to define and pursue their own goals. Teachers who feel uncertain about their instructional practice are unlikely to risk sharing problems or successes.

Teachers' opportunities to learn increased when there was useful evaluation of teacher performance and school support for improving performance. Evaluation and continuing education activities are most effective when there is a clear definition of what excellence in teaching means, when there is a consensus in relation to instructional goals and practices.

The fifth theme identified by Rosenholtz (1989) was that of teachers' workplace commitment. This variable was found to be related to three workplace conditions: teachers' task autonomy and discretion; their learning opportunities; and their psychic rewards. Teacher commitment appears to increase when teachers have the opportunity to make the decisions that are necessary to ensure that their instruction has a direct impact on student growth and development, when they can see their work in terms of ongoing challenge and continuous growth, and when they feel positive about what they are accomplishing in their work.

Rosenholtz's study (1989) supported two major theoretical assumptions. The first is that teachers' definition of their work is guided by context and communications, that is, by the culture of the school within which they work. The individual biographies and beliefs of teachers within a school may be quite diverse but the practices and values of the workplace appear to override individual differences in the daily work of the teachers in a school. It appears that the school as a workplace encourages and facilitates certain teacher orientations. Conditions within the workplace may reinforce a classroom orientation and discourage a school orientation, for example. Teachers coming into such a school may be expected to work alone and to avoid talking about instructional matters. These expectations are powerful and subtle shapers of teacher behavior, especially for beginning teachers.

The second theoretical assumption supported by the study is that uncertainty about the technology of teaching works against rational planning and action. When teaching technique is viewed as personal and idiosyncratic, there is little reason to search for school-wide approaches, to share strategies, or to learn from others.

Thinking about the school as a workplace gives us a new way to think about the implementation of change in schools. Change has often failed because the complexity of change was underestimated and because the change agents relied on a model of change that addressed only one group of factors, e.g., a technocratic model.

Successful change must involve different aspects of the change process: personal, political and organizational. In other words, we must look at the school as a culture, as an ecological whole. Changing the personal, i.e., the beliefs and commitment of individuals, is not enough to change the whole. A culture works to stability and equilibrium. For a culture to change in a significant and enduring way, many aspects of that culture must change.

The School Library Program Within the School as Workplace

Implementing a cooperative school library program involves changes in many aspects of school culture. One way of understanding how the school library program fits into the culture of the school is to compare the nature of classroom teaching in the traditional school culture with the expectations that are assumed as part of the cooperative school library program. This program assumes, as do many other programs in our schools, that teachers act in quite different ways from the traditional norms of classroom teaching.

Brown (1988), in her analysis of the changing expectations for teaching, outlines some of these differences. The traditional features of classroom teaching include isolated planning, teacher autonomy, vague goals, group instruction, reliance on textbooks, teacher control, teacher as central to the learning process and self-contained classrooms. The implementation of a school library program assumes different teaching norms: cooperative planning, team teaching, precisely defined goals and objectives, individualized instruction, variety in resources, maximum freedom for the learner, teacher as facilitator for independent learning, and different locations for learning. These, of course, are the norms that are appropriate to curriculum and to school organization advocated by departments of education, teacher educators and by educational reformers.

The traditional ethos of classroom teachers, marked by conservatism, individualism, and presentism, does not facilitate teachers' involvement in cooperative integrated school library programs. Conservatism means a preference for time-honored approaches. The new school library program requires that teachers work in a partnership with the teacher-librarian, sharing the planning, teaching and evaluation of students. This means that the classroom teacher must share some of the decision-making with another professional, must take the risk of teaching in front of another teacher and must give up some of the control over the class of students. The integrated nature of the program means that the classroom teacher must reveal the nature of the classroom program to another teacher. This transgresses the norms of privacy and self-reliance that are a powerful part of the traditional ethos of the classroom teacher. The presentism of teachers means that they value the rewards that can be gained now and are likely to be reluctant to agree to short-term disruptions and difficulties for possible but uncertain long-term improvements. Teaching is an inherently difficult activity; the routines of the classroom have generally been established over time and with difficulty. Teachers may be reluctant to try new approaches to the library program, particularly if they can see no short-term rewards.

The traditional norms of teaching appear to be less evident in effective schools. Little (1982) discovered in her study of the norms of teaching, that effective schools were marked by "critical practices of success and adaptability" (p. 330). These critical practices, in fact, are the kinds of teacher interactions that routinely and necessarily occur when a classroom teacher and a teacher-librarian are involved in cooperative planning and teaching. For example, in Little's inventory of teacher interactions, we find such practices as: designing curriculum; writing curriculum; preparing lesson plans; reviewing or discussing existing lesson plans; designing and preparing materials; persuading others to try another idea or approach; observing other teachers; and analyzing practices and effects. All of these practices are aspects of the work that teachers and teacher-librarians do together in implementing an integrated school library program.

LaRocque (1986) also found evidence of a change in teacher ethos, particularly in those schools that were most successful in implementing policy. She terms the difference in teacher ethos as a classroom orientation or a school orientation. School-oriented teachers are more open to implementation of policy and are more likely to be supportive of the implementation of the policies that underlie school library programs. School-oriented teachers view policy as a unifying force that benefits the school; they should therefore view a school library program (which advocates a school-wide approach to research and study skills for example) positively. In LaRocque's study (1986), the school-oriented teachers saw the school self-assessment policy as "a means of coordinating programs grade to grade, of developing consistent, school-wide practices, and most important, of assessing what it is they as a staff, are trying to do and how well they are doing it" (p. 10).

Classroom-oriented teachers, on the other hand, were less open to policy implementation and saw policy as unnecessary and restrictive. Perhaps this comes from their belief in teacher autonomy and from their view that collaborative activities represent encroachment on their territory, especially in terms of available instructional time and of established teacher-student relationships.

Schools with a high number of school-oriented teachers were more successful in policy implementation. It should follow that, when school library programs are being implemented, schools with a high number of school-oriented teachers are more likely to be successful. Teacher orientation or ethos is only one of the factors involved, of course. Teachers have to believe in the worth of the policy or innovation if they are to work for it. In addition, the political and organizational context must be congruent with the demands of the innovation.

School-oriented teachers focused on the professional competence of their principal and colleagues. They expected the principal "to be familiar with school programs, to know what is happening in each classroom, to assist teachers implement new programs, to encourage teachers to innovate and to support teacher initiatives" (LaRocque, 1986, p. 11). Their expectations of the principal are consistent with the recommended role of the principal in implementing school library programs. Their expectations of their teaching colleagues are also consistent with the recommended role of the teacher-librarian. School-oriented teachers valued team teaching and planning and believed that working with the principal and their colleagues would assist them in improving their own teaching performance.

The aspects that identified the effective schools in Rosenholtz's study (1989) are also concepts that have significance in the implementation of effective school library programs. The school library program should be a school-wide program where the staff is involved in setting the goals of the program. Principal involvement and support sends the message that the program is important. Development of a skills continuum or statements of student learning outcomes ensures that everyone on staff is aware of the purpose of the program and the criteria for student success in the program.

Developing goal consensus for the program requires and reinforces teacher collaboration. This collaboration also involves talking about the goals and the means to achieve them, thereby increasing "conceptual clarity," which is critical to successful implementation (McLaughlin, 1979). Teachers must understand the innovation in a specific and concrete way in order to implement it. Teacher and teacher-librarian collaboration breaks down the isolation of teaching, and is essential to the development of a cooperative integrated program.

When teachers give and get assistance, effective teaching behaviors increase and teacher performance improves. As classroom teachers and teacher-librarians work together to provide learning experiences for their students, they teach each other about teaching, They must reach agreement about instructional goals and practices, which in turn increases teacher certainty. This collaborative process demands that teachers and teacher-librarians define more precisely their instructional purposes and teaching strategies. The collaborative process challenges teachers and teacher-librarians to design learning experiences that meet the needs of the students, to vary materials and approaches to meet individual needs. This is a demanding professional task but it carries with it considerable potential for student success and the important psychic rewards that it entails.

Implications for Implementing School Library Programs

Lortie (1975), Little (1982), LaRocque (1986) and Rosenholtz (1989) each make the point that the components of teacher ethos and of school climate are interrelated and that they reinforce each other. Those undertaking the implementation of policy and practice related to the cooperative integrated school library program need to recognize that they are embarking on a complex and demanding task. What they are attempting is no less than a change in the culture of the school. The excitement of this challenge is highlighted by the knowledge that the change in the culture of the school that they are advocating is consistent with and essential to the success and effectiveness of education for our young people (Rosenholtz, 1985).

Commitment to this idea and advocacy of this point is essential for the implementation of the program (with colleagues and the school community). The best schools are places where teachers regularly collaborate in setting school goals and in defining, developing and improving school policy, programs and practice. School improvement is not and cannot be simply a change in teacher training, or the implementation of a new program (not even the implementation of a library program!). This means that teacher-librarians must continue to play advocacy and leadership roles in the improvement of their schools. As Goodlad (1983) comments, improving schools does not mean improving the quality of individual elements of the school, it means improving them together.

Teacher-librarians and other educators implementing change need to examine their own thinking about the process through which change can occur. The initial work in developing a theory and practice of change was influenced by an industrial model which was very appropriate for the teaching of clearly defined skills, to be applied in specific circumstances, e.g., learning to use a new technology. It was also influenced by models of personal decision-making, e.g., consumer buying behavior. Change in education, however, is much more complex and needs to be thought about in a variety of different ways (Smith, Prunty, Dwyer, & Kleine 1986).

The work that has been done in relation to teachers as professionals suggests some guidelines for the teacher-librarian implementing a program. Teachers are generally inducted very briefly into the profession and there is rarely the opportunity for new teachers to gradually take on increasing responsibilities or to work under the careful tutelage of a skilled professional. Teacher education programs generally include very short practicum or inservice experiences and the models of teaching presented by the sponsor teachers vary widely. In terms of exposure to a school library model, many student teachers see only book exchanges and isolated library lessons. Few will be placed in schools that have trained teacher-librarians and even fewer have the opportunity to work with a teacher-librarian during their practicum. The focus of the practicum, as in many of their teacher education courses, is the classroom. The traditional or classroom-oriented ethos of teaching is being reinforced powerfully in teacher training.

This means that the task of the teacher-librarian in introducing new teachers to the potential of the school library program will continue to be a necessary and critical aspect of the teacher-librarian's role. Teacher-librarians must make every effort to work with the student teachers in their schools and must ensure that much effort is put into supporting and working with new teachers. Rosenholtz states that "nowhere is the contrast between ineffective and effective schools more profound than in the process of learning how to teach" (1985, p. 375).

Where induction into teaching means learning to teach in isolation, there appears to be a ceiling effect on teachers' capacity for professional growth, with teacher effectiveness beginning to decline after five years. Teacher-librarians who support and participate in collaborative relationships with new teachers are performing a professional task with implications far beyond the development of students' research and study skills. They are building the professional resources of the school.

Implications for Future Research

Teacher-librarians need to examine their practice in light of the training and induction that they and their classroom teacher colleagues have received. The question arises of whether teacher-librarians are conscious of how the ways in which they became classroom teachers and then teacher-librarians are enhancing or constraining their work with colleagues in the school. A deeper understanding of how we have learned to teach will guide our efforts to work with other teachers, both neophyte and experienced, in ways that enhance opportunities for all of us to learn from others and continue to learn throughout our professional lives.

The concept of school culture helps to explain why implementing an innovation such as the cooperative integrated school library program is a complex and demanding endeavor. Our understanding of how best to accomplish such a task is limited at present by the lack of research on the implementation of school library programs. However, research on implementation of other programs and policies have significance for the school library program and provides a useful base for designing and conducting research on this topic.

References

Brown, J. (1988). Changing teaching practice to meet current expectation: implications for teacher-librarians. *Emergency Librarian, 16(2),* 9–14.

Fullan, M. (1982). *The meaning of educational change.* Toronto: OISE Press.

Goodlad, J. (1983). The school as workplace. In G. Griffin (Ed.), *Staff development* (82nd yearbook of the National Society for the Study of Education, Part II). Chicago: University of Chicago Press.

Houston, H. (1988). Restructuring secondary schools. In A. Lieberman (Ed.), *Building a professional culture in schools.* New York: Teachers College Press.

LaRocque, L. (1983). *Policy implementation in a school district: A matter of chance?* Unpublished doctoral dissertation. Simon Fraser University.

LaRocque, L. (1986). *Teacher ethos: School-oriented and classroom-oriented teachers.* Unpublished manuscript.

Lieberman, A. & Miller, L. (1984). *Teachers, their world, their work: Implications for school improvement.* Alexandria, VA: Association for Curriculum and Staff Development.

Little, J. (1982). Norms of collegiality and experimentation. *American Educational Research Journal, 19,* 325–340.

Lortie, D. (1975). *School teacher: A sociological study.* Chicago: University of Chicago Press.

McLaughlin, M. & Marsh, D. (1979). Staff development and school change. In A. Lieberman & L. Miller (Eds.), *Staff development: New demands, new realities, new perspectives.* New York: Teachers College Press.

Rosenholtz, S. (1985). Effective schools: interpreting the evidence. *American Journal of Education, 93,* 352–389.

Rosenholtz, S. (1989). *Teachers' workplace: The social organization of schools.* New York: Longman.

Smith, L., Prunty, J., Dwyer, D. & Kleine p. (1986). Reconstruing education innovation. In A. Lieberman (Ed.), *Rethinking school improvement: Research, craft and concept.* New York: Teachers College Press.

CHAPTER FIVE

Libraries, Learning and the Whole School

Michael Marland

The school library resource center has generally appeared uncontroversial; the only issue has been "more"—more money, more space, more staff— but a greater pedagogical rigor is required, particularly with regard to the relationship of libraries to learning in the context of the whole school, and especially the planned curriculum.

The Current Situation

What is the present situation? Individuals have an increasing need to be able to find things out; never before have lives depended so much on the ability to handle information successfully. We all, therefore, need to search out what we require, to assess it critically, to examine the ideas and facts offered and then to make use of the findings. This "learning to learn" which begins at school, continues throughout adult lives, and yet the paradox is that schools, concerned with learning about all else, seem to find it very difficult to teach students how to learn. Although some students are able to use the full range of resources, most are not; and yet it is the central responsibility to of the school to help its students cope with

learning. There has been a growth in the "project method," a love affair with projects which starts when children are about seven and are told to find a topic, to find out something about it and write it up. It goes on every year until they are about 17, with no noticeable increase in skill apart from the cover pages, which are rather more carefully done by the 17-year-olds.

This learning to learn is rarely stated as a specific overall aim. It seems to be presumed by those planning school curricula that the process will be assimilated while subjects are being studied; while you are being taught math, you will learn "learning." As students meet the middle years of secondary school the burden placed on them by the sheer quantity of facts and concepts increases, then the emphasis moves from the process to the product and hard-pressed teachers start short-circuiting this by just getting over the information in the quickest possible way. All the evidence suggests that when "how to write a paper" is taught, it is taught separately, without conceptualized lessons on the use of the index or use of reference sources and it is not put in context. In many schools it is not even taught at all.

Most research shows, what is painfully obvious to all teacher-librarians, that the use of books and other materials at all levels is disappointingly inefficient. And new demands that schools should plan their curriculum as a whole give no hint as to how this should be done nor do they as much as mention the fact that learning how to learn, study skills, and information handling, are among the most important "whole school" curriculum issues.

There is often too much stress on charisma in the teacher-librarian's role. There are, instead, five conditions for any educational activity to flourish. First, there must be a fair definition of aims; second, an expectation of its value; third, specific teaching—research has shown that when you teach, students may not learn everything but they do learn more than if you did not teach it; fourth, a suitable range of materials; and fifth, opportunities to practice. Even in those schools where there are good facilities and a reasonable budget many of those five conditions are not present. There is not a fair definition of the aims of information handling skills; there is not an expectation of their value on the part of the teaching staff; there is little teaching and precious few opportunities for practice. Of course in many other schools there is not a suitable range of materials either.

Do resource centers deserve more money? Do they have a right to go to government for more money when in many schools there are shelves of books, but they constitute some of the most expensive wallpaper known, because they are ineffectively used? If you were to go into a school and ask a 14- or 15-year-old to find a resource in the library, the youngster could very well say, "I'd ask Miss, Sir," because asking "Miss" is the main information strategy that we have managed to teach.

The Causes

That is the situation, so what are the causes? Even when the resources are available, programs are still not doing very well. Ten rather dismal causes follow, for only by looking at why there are problems can any solutions be developed.

The first is a disparity of specialists. One can study the teaching of reading, the teaching of the less able, the teaching of English, even how to be a teacher-librarian. But on the whole, library schools don't teach about the teaching of reading, because that is someone else's job. And indeed, the specialist in the teaching of the less able, is not taught about libraries or how to make effective use of the resource center.

Second, education is seen as an aggregate of courses. A well-educated person has added math to history to social studies to something else. That additive method of curriculum planning is at the heart of the problem because it does one of two things. It either leaves library "user education" out completely, or makes it yet another subject on its own, struggling forcefully to try and be a separate subject but not, in fact, illuminating all other activities.

The third problem is the perversion of the recent emphasis on learning methods. The stress on practical work is fine until it produces science lessons in which looking quizzically at fuming test tubes is regarded as the only thing that real scientists ever do; until it produces craft design and technology lessons in which drawing and making is assumed to be the only thing a technologist does. Another aspect of this perversion of modern teaching methods is the idea that a textbook is some fiendish invention of commercial authors who do not understand children and it is used only by teachers who want to dominate children. This was a convenient belief when it became obvious that many students could not read the textbooks. This was presumed to be the author's fault and the publisher's fault and part of the capitalist plot for bringing the wrong kind of writing into schools. Probably there is some truth in this for many of the books placed before children in this way were not suitable, but it totally ignored an alternative hypothesis that students had not been taught how to read these books and as a solution to this the allegedly child-centered worksheet arrived.

The worksheet is something that a teacher has typed out somewhat inaccurately late at night; it is presumed the student can read it more easily because the teacher typed it. This worksheet simply extracts a paragraph and gives it to a student—it is the most teacher-centered learning material there is, because the student has been denied the opportunity to select from the book, never mind select the book itself. It is relevant that there is no way that students brought up on pre-selected paragraphs will ever be able to use a library properly.

Some learning approaches in themselves are good—more practical work, more individualized work, but it is too easy to lose some important central skills.

The fourth problem is simply to stress that the non-fiction book is a complex tool and the practice in many secondary schools of teaching reading only through the study of literature is not a preparation for the utilization of the book as a learning tool.

A fifth problem is that surface detail becomes more important than underlying intellectual problems. For example, in a ninth grade English or language arts lesson which is concentrating on the research paper, the teacher may be teaching footnoting. Now that's fine, but footnoting (to take the small example) is a surface detail of a much deeper and fundamentally more difficult problem—when do you require support for a point you are making? That is not taught. When you are in fact having information searches and need to write up your findings, you have to work out that which is obvious, that which requires support and that which is contentious and the whole paraphernalia of bibliographic reference is really only the surface detail to that. While the teaching of the surface detail has its place, this fifth problem is that we do not teach the fundamentals on which this detail lies, and you cannot teach these fundamentals in a library lesson or a language arts lesson because they are not library issues, and they are not language arts issues. They are intellectual issues that have to be taught in the specific subject area.

The sixth problem is teacher training, which is particularly weak in the use of studies, resources, and personnel.

Seventh is the lack of quality resource-based programs as examples.

Eighth is the inadequate resources in many parts of the world. Many UK secondary schools for example do not have libraries that are retained as resource centers throughout the week. They are often timetabled for teaching for any subject that has to be jammed in there.

And the ninth problem is the inherent intellectual difficulty of what we are really concerned with, which is the intellectual task of deciding what it is that you want to know. That is the most difficult thing. We are facing a great problem because of the wastage of public money on Ph.D.s that never get completed. If you read the study of uncompleted Ph.D.s or talk to people who have given up on their Ph.D.s the usual reason is the same reason that a 15-year-old fails with a research paper—they find that the question they set out to investigate is too vague to pin down, or impossible to research. The inherent intellectual difficulty in the task of information searching is too easily glossed over.

The tenth and final problem is the difficulty about the role of the teacher-librarian in the educational system. Just check out where "the librarian" is listed in the faculty list. Many schools provide a list of teachers, office staff, janitor and librarian. Few have thought out why there is a teacher-librarian in a school. Is the librarian there to select materials, to maintain the collection, to teach library skills, to be a general propaganda guru—or be part of curriculum planning and team teaching? That is the final problem because the school library movement is foundering on this failure to define the role of the school librarian. In other words, problems are not primarily involved with resources, with staff, with persuading "those damn teachers," but with something much more fundamental. It is a failure to produce a coherent school policy which defines the role of the teacher-librarian. (My favorite definition is that a librarian is a teacher whose subject is learning itself.) And the feelings described here are not limited to poor schools, to the lazy, or the ill-trained. They are endemic even where professionals are working very hard indeed.

The Teacher and the Teacher-Librarian

Two relationships become critical: that between the teacher and the teacher-librarian, and that between the curriculum and the library resources.

First—get the school library out of the area of resources and under the label of curriculum. Resources are secondary as a problem; the key problem is relating the resource center to the curriculum.

Second, develop the concept of the teacher-librarian's role. We need a close working relationship between the teacher-librarian and other teachers. With a clear definition of why there are teacher-librarians and what the job is, the gap could be closed. The teacher-librarian is part of the curriculum planning team. (This is less difficult in those countries where the school librarian is qualified as a teacher, but more difficult in the UK where few professional school librarians are qualified teachers.)

The teacher-librarian should be a leader of teachers, an adviser and guide to teachers, rather than one who is primarily looking after materials or even working directly with students. One cannot generalize the expertise of the "librarian" throughout the entire student body. If teacher-librarians expect to work on a one-to-one basis with the whole student body, they will never complete the job. Nor will this produce "library impelling instructors." The second aim then would be to reconstruct the concept of the teacher-librarian's role as a primarily in-service training and curriculum planning person.

The third aim is to actually have curriculum planning in our schools. That's easy to say and difficult to pull off. Even where there are small curriculum planning teams, they are still working in pre-determined divisions and those matters which go across the divisions are still difficult to plan. Start with the overall curriculum aims first, within which the separate segments, sectors, or focuses are planned. Fourthly, there should be a reading curriculum so that there is continuity in reading development. I would wish there to be, fifthly, a research and study skills continuum. Labels are less important—study skills or information handling skills—the important thing is that there has to be a continuum and a framework.

The sixth aim deals with the setting of assignments. Hard work in the resource center counts for little if teachers are setting impossible assignments or assignments for which there are no resources. Similarly, there is a lack of communication between the teacher and the teacher-librarian over the preparation of reading lists. The specification of reading lists in lessons needs very great care.

Seventh, the functions of the resource center require different sections for studying, teaching, searching. These are incompatible tasks. Yet in many schools the same geographical space and architecture is being used for all these different tasks.

The selection policy too often seems to cover the entire field of human knowledge at every level possible. Now there will never be enough resources for that, so the result is that most students learn most of the time when they go into the resource center to find a book that they will not be able to find it. We all need experience of success, but we have such experience of non-success in school resource centers because of our selection policy. There may be whole sectors of human knowledge not stocked in the school; for these, refer students to the public library because the school cannot do everything. Eighth, then: there should be good material on key topics, at all ability levels, all reading levels, in the resource center rather that an unsuccessful attempt to cover the whole of human knowledge.

Ninth, there must be a good relationship between book and non-book material.

Tenth, the catalogue should be a focus, but really thought out from the student's point of view. There are too many schools where the jargon of teachers is not compatible with the jargon of the catalogue. There should be access to reasonable on-line bibliographical searches available in schools. It is fatuous to teach children about the computer revolution and not provide this experience.

Eleventh, there should be a close relationship between the resource center in the school and bookshops and other libraries outside. It is a peculiar thing that we take children on visits to the theater, exhibitions, and sports events but rarely to the public library or bookshops. There should be a very close liaison, advertising each other's services, having displays of each other's wares. Perhaps in some schools there should not even be a library— one high school is so near the public library that they don't have their own resource center but still have their own teacher-librarian.

Twelfth, the library could assist teachers with bibliographical control and ordering.

And thirteenth, there must be more in-service training for teachers in this whole area.

The Major Issues

These fall within the context of some major issues:

Curriculum planning. The main difficulty of teaching information handling is to relate this to different subjects. Time is precious in schools; therefore, programs have to be a vehicle for carrying the subject content and at least one, if not several, skills. This requires good curriculum planning. It also requires whole school policies. Just ask: what does each student by the age of such and such need to know in terms of facts, concepts, and skills and attitudes on this facet of the curriculum?

Now one facet of the curriculum will be concerned with information handling and study skills for which there needs to be a school outline. This should start at a high level of generality working down to quite small details. This is not something taught and left, because there are important things which keep coming up again as we get older. Within this overall curriculum, one can begin to divide out the aspects.

All teachers have responsibility here, but this can mean that no one is doing it. Without adequate planning, some students are taught how to use indexes all day, while others go through five years without having been exposed to indexes at all.

Then a good teacher of history could be a good teacher of library use in history. A good teacher of science could be a good teacher of information handling skills in science. Then ensure that any assignment in those areas has the double payload of the skills and the content simultaneously.

Overall resources policy. This is very difficult. It means at its least the putting right of the problems mentioned earlier—the mismatch between books recommended in the classroom and the books available in the resource center. There should be a policy for all resources in a school to ensure that they relate one to another, they relate book to non-book media, they are balanced from

the point of view of having a world view and not a locally centered view of the world, that they relate clippings and journals to bound books. Now this requires leadership and control which is very difficult to achieve.

Underlying skills. One of the problems is teaching the surface and not the underlying foundation. When teaching "library use," we have started too late—intellectually too late. We have started with how the resource center is laid out—the orientation. However, a technological design problem or a historical research problem basically have similar intellectual stages and, as an educational institution, the school has to help students to analyze those stages and to see that they are in fact analogous to one another. An information search is like a design problem.

Every single assignment, from the short piece of written work that the six-year-old does, to the major piece of research, has to proceed through the same kind of sequence and teaching should ensure that specific skills are taught.

Reading curriculum. Not only should there be practice in vocabulary building, in essential structured reading, in the analysis of paragraphs, in selection of material, in the pace of reading—knowing where to pause, where to go back, where to focus—there should also be time for reading.

Recent research findings have shown that for:

- science teaching in high schools, only 9% of students' time was spent reading, and

- in humanities for fifteen-year-olds, the amount of time spent reading was in bursts of forty seconds.

So, a reading curriculum should be planned and integrated as a sequence up the years.

Information skills program. This could be a kind of index to the curriculum, a check list that could be drawn on by all other subject teachers. It would have in it the start of topic definition, which of course is the most difficult part. Students are lost in most school resource centers because they have not defined what is being searched for. It would go on to search strategies, to selection, and rejection. We give students a whole battery of books and say to choose the right one, but we rarely give them an extract sheet with paragraphs, one of which is totally irrelevant and all they have got to do is strike it out—easy exercises seeing the irrelevance, but of course as you get to higher levels, seeing the irrelevance is a very hard part of the study. Then one could go on to the apparatus of a book, how to judge whether it is covering the field or not. The simple details of bibliographic data aren't taught often enough. Then it is important to teach how to go through and judge the parts of the book and decide how to get out of it what you want. Even that great human invention, the index, is too often taught at the level of surface skills. It is critical to understand the function of an index, which literally disorganizes a book, and by disorganizing it makes it available for the reader to reorganize it. The index needs to be taught at all levels of the curriculum using more and more difficult examples. It cannot be left entirely to chance nor can it be left entirely to exercise. It has to be a mixture of the specific and the disseminated.

Then there are all the other study skills of note-making and references. When is the student allowed to copy? What about the use of visual evidence? How many schools teach the reading of a photograph? A photograph is too often regarded as an artifact that is totally unproblematic. It is evidence, just straight evidence. But if the student is going to use a photograph as evidence, there is a need to know how to judge, to see how it came to be, and the effect the photographer had on it.

This curriculum is a two-way flow as skills feed back into the subject curriculum to provide context for the items in the research and study continuum.

Assignments. The most important part of a resource center is neither the resources nor the staff, but the assignments set by teachers. One thread of a student's schooling is a series of things to do. From short tasks to complex ones—"look it up," "find out"—are frequent injunctions we throw to students. But very often these apparently easy assignments prove to have unexpected snags, as many a parent has found out.

Perhaps more than that are the massive assignments which are so huge that when the teacher reads the ultimate report and is unhappy about it, it is difficult to know where the student has gone

wrong. Was it in the first stage of defining the topic; or finding the resources; or having found them, understanding them; or having selected from them, making their notes; or whether having made their notes writing it up?

Too often teachers give "unmodulated assignments." We start by giving mechanical assignments—look up the date of someone or some event. When we have given two or three weeks of exercises, we then say, "right, you've now learned how to find things out. Now here is a library of 3,500 volumes and you can choose anything that interests you or which you feel is important to write about and you've got three weeks to do it. If you have any problems, come see me." That is an unmodulated assignment. We go straight from the small mechanized, to the huge amorphous, and then when we get an unhappy result, we can't pin down where they have gone wrong.

The key to study skills is the setting of assignments and we have to break down these assignments into stages so that everything is not thrown at students simultaneously. Sometimes they might be concerned only with the search—accept a pile of books as the end of the assignment. They don't have to read them or make notes. Other times they would be given all the references collected together for them. They might be given the specific pages. At that point, their task is the end only—the note-making and writing.

Teachers need to be taught to set assignments. First they must work out the purpose and context of the assignment. Sadly, assignments are too often just time fillers.

Relate assignments to the skills program. Don't throw in too many skills at once. Ensure an adequate range of material, otherwise students use the same information source year after year after year. Make sure they have to use different types of sources. Finally, the teacher has to know the point of assignment reinforcement, that is to say that they absolutely have to make sure that in setting the assignment, they give the crucial advice at that particular time. One of the snags of having lots of good teacher-librarian time in a school is that the teachers clear off. I have sat in an American school staffed with three teacher-librarians—therefore, divide the class in three and what does the teacher do, go off to read *Beautiful Homes and Gardens* in the corner. In the UK, the school librarian often complains that when the teacher brings the class to the resource center, he or she slips off to the staff room to do a bit of marking. What we have to ensure is that when the teacher sets the assignment, the teacher gives the specific piece of advice that will be helpful for that assignment. Essentially, we need to pull the whole issue from resources and staffing to the curriculum.

For the Future

For the school, requirements include an adequate definition of the role of the teacher-librarian, emphasis on the planning of the curriculum as a whole, a reading and research and study continuum, with more trained student assistance. Resources must match specific curriculum needs, and other libraries and bookshops be promoted. Material must be more accessible through student-oriented catalogues or indexes.

Close collaborations between teacher and teacher-librarian of an equal status provide the best approach to effective library use and resource-based learning.

PART THREE

ROLE CLARIFICATION

Studies tell us that principals are generally agreed on the role of the school librarian, teachers are generally agreed on the role of the school librarian (and their perception improves after collaborating with a teacher-librarian) but that teacher-librarians themselves are confused about their role, not individually of course but as a profession. Until and unless we can speak with one unified voice about our role and our contributions to student learning, and how that occurs, administrators will continue to base decisions affecting school library media programs and personnel on individual experiences, intuition and financial expediency.

We also know from our research that teachers prefer to work with teacher-librarians who have classroom experience since they can more easily perceive and solve instructional problems and understand the teacher's world, yet we have not made a strong case for the role of the school librarian as a professional teacher. While my position paper was written almost twenty years ago and is the oldest paper in this collection, it still speaks to the need for professional teaching qualifications as well as school library media certification and credentials and helps to explain why we are educated, hired, paid and evaluated as teachers.

Jean Brown adds the essential component of change agent to the skill set of the teacher-librarian. Her discussion of educational change and the impact of effective instructional leadership is important reading for anyone looking to effect change in schools. Building on the previous section on school context and school culture, Brown points out that schools that are collaborative settings are more conducive to change and to school library media programs than those that are "isolated settings." With strong values and a vision, leadership skills and a view of change as problem-solving, teacher-librarians can lead schools in improvement "just for the kids."

Of course, working with teachers and students in information-based problem-solving is a fundamental part of the role of the teacher-librarian and Kathy Brock outlines her research-based model in developing information literacy through the information intermediary process. Her six-step search and use process involves the teacher-librarian and teacher in instructing, coaching and facilitating.

In a recent study, Jean Brown and Bruce Sheppard, researchers and colleagues in educational leadership, reached the conclusion that teacher-librarians need to reflect the traits of exemplary teachers, a conclusion reached by other researchers, but that exemplary teacher-librarians exhibit a "mirror image plus" or value-added contribution to the school. Through case studies and observation, the researchers note the new work of the teacher and the teacher-librarian (mirror image) and of the teacher-librarian alone (mirror image plus). These value-added differences are in the knowledge base and technical skills (resource-based learning), personal, interpersonal and team skills, and values and beliefs. They conclude by making clear the importance of the "mirror image" in gaining the principal's support.

A few years ago Canada's two national associations for teacher-librarians, the Association for Teacher-librarianship in Canada and the Canadian School Library Association, a division of the Canadian Library Association, collaborated to define the competencies necessary for teacher-librarians to thrive into the twenty-first century. The draft documents were reviewed by principals and school superintendents before final completion. In a role clarification document, the competent teacher-librarian is committed to

- the principles outlined in the Student's Bill of Information Rights;
- implementing curriculum with colleagues;
- initiating collaboratively planned and taught programs to integrate information literacy in the context of the curriculum; and
- the effective use of information technologies.

The professional competencies of the teacher-librarian relate to knowledge and skill in the areas of collaboration and leadership, curriculum and instruction, collaborative program planning and teaching, information resources, information access, technology, management and research, and the ability to apply these abilities as a basis for providing library and information services. The teacher-librarian's personal competencies represent a set of skills, attitudes and values that enable teacher-librarians to work efficiently and effectively, be good communicators, focus on continuing learning throughout their careers, demonstrate the value-added nature of their contributions and thrive in the new world of education.

If we can articulate our abilities and contributions, and model these in schools, our effect on student achievement will be that much more significant and our future that much more assured.

CHAPTER SIX

The School Librarian as a Professional Teacher

Ken Haycock

In the last fifteen years changes in education have been rapid and decisive. The traditional lock-step methods of teaching in small, enclosed classrooms using limited instructional resources—mainly textbooks—have developed into more innovative approaches based on research related to children, teaching and learning. Due to changing environments and the information explosion, instruction now centers more on the process of learning itself than on subject content. It is becoming far more important that the student understands factors which contribute to a given situation than to memorize data describing it. The method of the subject specialist is of concern but specific knowledge of the field is less necessary. Discovery and inquiry methods of teaching are becoming increasingly common and contribute to the development of independent, disciplined learners who can recognize problems, formulate hypotheses, ask important questions, locate, analyze and evaluate information and reach valid conclusions.

Students are treated on a more individual basis as it is finally accepted that everyone does not learn in the same way or at the same rate. Each child is not necessarily following an individual program but efforts are made to correlate expected performance with individual ability levels to ensure realistic goals. Grouping of students is used to an increasing extent to match what is to be taught to those who need to learn it, whether it is a large group lecture to introduce facts or a small group work session to reinforce skills. These trends have also led to more independent study programs at all levels of education. The three R's (reading, writing, arithmetic) are still among the basic skills of schooling but the three I's (inquiry, individualization, independent study) represent an improved approach to teaching and learning.

School library resource centers have been a vital part of these changes in education. Indeed, many innovations would not be possible without the services of a resource center. As a reflection of these changes, emphasis has shifted from the traditional library base of selecting, organizing, and circulating materials to the more pronounced educational and teaching services of planning for the effective use of book and non-book media through collaborative program planning and teaching. If the resource center has any validity whatever in the school it must be on this firm theoretical and educational foundation. Libraries *per se* are not seen as particularly significant in a formal education context: the planned use of learning resources is, however. The development of the school library to a resource center then represents more of a change in function than a change in name. The implications of educational research and the implementation of new programs have led to a need for a vital integral resource center. With a strong movement towards more effective team work, professionals in schools need a common base of concern and understanding to exploit the full potential of instructional methods.

The Teacher-Librarian

Traditionally, the person in charge of the school library has been called the school librarian; today, however, since all roles in education are being redefined in light of new trends and priorities and since the term "librarian" should include professional library qualifications, school "librarian" is less acceptable to many. The school librarian is usually not a professional librarian in education, training or outlook; indeed, perhaps it was a mistake to ever use the terms "school library" and "school librarian." The school librarian is, or should be, an outstanding or master teacher with specialized advanced education in the selection, organization, management and use of learning resources, and the school library, a resource center inseparable from the instructional program. For the sake of clarity and simplicity the terms the "teacher-librarian" and "resource center" are used here. "Teacher-librarian" clearly denotes a teaching role with a library-related specialization. A teacher-librarian is not an unqualified or "under-qualified" librarian but a professional learning resources teacher who may also be a professional librarian. The term refers to a single unified teaching/librarianship role and not to the amount of time spent in the classroom or the resource center.

Teacher-librarians are increasingly involved in curriculum development and in collaborative teaching situations where each teacher—classroom and resource center—prepares for instructional responsibilities based on areas of expertise. Teachers accept teacher-librarians as equal partners in the school when they witness competence in the planning and implementation of curricula. With increased attention to the needs of individual students communication must be particularly effective between the classroom teacher and the teacher-librarian; the same professional language and education as well as the same core of experience—classroom teaching—go a long way towards reaching this goal.

Collaborative Program Planning

In the development of any specific unit of study in a school certain factors predominate. Societal needs and influences determine the direction mandated by government, the curriculum followed by a local school board and the program implemented by a school within its community. The curriculum designer brings to the task a theoretical knowledge of teaching and learning supplemented by subject content, tested with practical classroom experience. The foundations of society and of education, in conjunction with the implications of individual differences, group relations, growth, motivation, teaching methods, learning processes and evaluation, are examined and considered. Although it is far to narrow to categorize youngsters by specific characteristics at definite ages it is recognized that mental and physical development generally proceeds on a continuum. The characteristics of varying levels of this development can be identified and do have significant implications for appropriate teaching methods and the resulting use of the resource center.

In order for learning resources to have validity in the instructional program, their use must be carefully planned through integration with this curriculum. As a specialist in the selection, organization, management, and most important, the utilization of all manner of media, the teacher-librarian is most concerned with the quality of use of reference and research tools and learning materials. The subject specialist has an intimate knowledge of an academic discipline or content whereas the teacher-librarian's "subject" is learning itself. There is no teaching content to a library or resource center, only the process of unlocking knowledge and critical thinking, the process of learning. As a learning resources teacher, the teacher-librarian is concerned with those skills which are necessary to the development of motivated independent learners who can locate, analyze and evaluate information in all media formats.

The following principles were identified by the National Council for the Social Studies [in 1963, hence the male gender only] as essential for undergirding a developmental skills program:

1. The skill should be taught functionally, in the context of a topic study, rather than as a separate exercise.

2. The learner must understand the meaning and purpose of the skill, and have motivation for developing it.

3. The learner must be carefully supervised in his [or her] first attempts to apply the skill, so that he will form correct habits from the beginning.

4. The learner needs repeated opportunities to practice the skill, with immediate evaluation so that he knows where he has succeeded and/or failed in his performance.

5. The learner needs individual help, through diagnostic measures and follow up exercises, since not all members of any group learn at exactly the same rate or retain equal amounts of what they have learned.

6. Skill instruction should be presented at increasing levels of difficulty, moving from the simple to the more complex; the resulting growth in skills should be cumulative as the learner moves through school, with each level of instruction building on and reinforcing what has been taught previously.

7. Students should be helped, at each stage, to generalize the skills, by applying them in many and varied situations; in this way, maximum transfer of learning can be achieved.

8. The program of instruction should be sufficiently flexible to allow skills to be taught as they are needed by the learner; many skills should be developed concurrently.

In planning for the implementation of a program based on these principles the teacher-librarian joins with the classroom teacher to form a horizontal team of two equals working toward established objectives. This dyad collaboratively plans what is to be done and the most effective way to accomplish the task. The classroom teacher and the teacher-librarian each bring different backgrounds and strengths in teaching but they do understand the potential of various approaches to learning and recognize common goals. Through planning with other teachers the teacher-librarian also becomes a source of ideas for program development.

If the use of learning resources is intended, the teacher-librarian is involved in pre-planning before a unit of study begins. In this way the teacher can at least ensure that appropriate materials are available. Since the teacher-librarian will be working with a class, group or individuals, it is important to know what the preliminary objectives of the teacher are. The teacher decides on a unit of work and outlines its scope. General teaching strategies which may be conducive to resource center use are considered. The teacher meets with the teacher-librarian to select and plan the use of materials and services. The teacher and the teacher-librarian determine the sequence of content on the basis of availability of materials and necessary personnel.

The dyad or teaching team redefines objectives and determines the skills to be stressed in relationship to local curricula, student needs and available learning resources. These may be subject skills, study and critical thinking skills, reference and research skills or listening and viewing skills. The teacher and teacher-librarian then set up a series of learning experiences involving individual students, small and large groups, or whole classes. Selected materials may be kept in the resource center or moved elsewhere, whichever is most appropriate. At this point the unit is introduced by a team member. The students work on the unit in the resource center and the classroom with the classroom teacher and teacher-librarian stressing skills related especially to the program unit. The teacher-librarian may teach a short integrated skill lesson, develop a series of related lessons, offer an enrichment lesson or give a book talk on the theme.

When planning with one teacher, a group or committee of teachers, or a teaching team, the teacher-librarian *collaboratively*:

- determines the contribution that the resource center is to make to the overall teaching plan;
- determines specific teaching objectives to be accomplished through the use of learning resources and guidance;
- identifies basic concepts, skills and strategies to be introduced, reinforced or extended;
- structures learning guides; reading, viewing, listening checklists; summary forms; reaction charts; critical evaluation cards;
- determines appropriateness of proposed assignments and the availability of suitable materials;
- sets target dates for each phase of the resource center role in the program;
- designs specific teaching strategies requiring resource center support;
- designs specific learning experiences and activities requiring learning resources;
- designs specific unit and support activities;
- designs strategies for meeting student needs, interests, goals, abilities, progress rate, concerns and potential;
- identifies specific media uniquely appropriate for each of the teaching and learning activities;
- designs programs for the most logical use of media in progressive, sequential order;
- designs appropriate culminating teaching and learning activities;
- designs appropriate assessment devices for gauging student performance;
- designs appropriate evaluating activities to determine the effectiveness of the resource center role (adapted from Davies, 1979).

Collaborative Teaching

In this collaborative teaching situation the teacher-librarian may work with a group of students over an extended period of time while the classroom teacher works with another group in the classroom. The contribution of the teacher-librarian extends to the specific needs of the student. This means that the teacher-librarian may be offering remedial teaching, leading novel study, managing behavior or teaching in other ways suitable to the particular level, subject, unit and objectives related to resource center use as determined collaboratively by the team. Throughout the project, the teacher and teacher-librarian evaluate the growth made by students in planned skills, the effectiveness of the materials as well as the effectiveness of the unit itself.

With the movement from an insular school library to an integrated resource center the skills for using libraries effectively have been better integrated with the curriculum. Scheduled library classes are inappropriate and no longer offered where effective programs predominate. These classes were not based on the principles of learning and psychology outlined. They were not seen as relevant by the learner, were not necessarily given when needed and were generally ineffective in terms of impact on student achievement. Scheduled classes on a regular timetable persist only where the principal has little notion of the educational foundation of the resource center, where the classes provide spare periods for teachers—misnamed a library program—or where the teacher-librarian is not prepared to become actively involved in program development and curriculum implementation.

Collection of Materials

Although a professional librarian, given a knowledge of curriculum content, can obviously select materials to support units of study from appropriate evaluation tools, the criteria for previewing and reviewing learning resources involve additional factors not often included in selection for a general or public library audience. The teacher-librarian needs to know not only the community and users, the nature of the existing collection, general and specific criteria for different types of subject material and sources of bibliographic and review information, but also needs to have a professional knowledge of other teachers, of instructional strategies used for specific units of study, of the instructional design of products examined, of the intended audience in grade and ability levels, of curriculum relationships and of the principal and potential uses of the material. Learning resources must have a planned purpose or at least the possibility of such and this means a more complete integration with teaching/learning processes.

The balanced collection found in many public libraries is a mistake in a school resource center. To select material on all topics, a financial impossibility at best, is to neglect the context of the service. If one country is studied using Socratic approaches, while another country is studied using inquiry approaches and learning resources, then little material about the former country should be purchased because the teaching method does not require many materials, but a great deal more material about the latter country should be purchased, because the teaching method used for it requires support for a specific number of users (usually at least each student in a class). Similarly, when organizing resource center information the nature of the users and elements of the school curricula are taken into account. The subjectivity of the selection and organization of materials can become more precisely defined in the school setting.

Interagency Cooperation

With increasing demands on learning resources, coupled with decreasing tax dollars, there should be improved cooperation among schools and among schools and other libraries. Such cooperation is based on a clear understanding of the role of each agency and a commitment to sharing materials and services where mutually beneficial. Each agency serves a quite different purpose based on institutional goals and the nature of the client group. Librarians must recognize the unique expertise of the teacher-librarian and be knowledgeable about the role of the resource center. The development of the resource center as an integrated learning center to provide the skills of self-realization means that public library use will increase, not decrease; if the public library is relatively untapped by students as a community

resource, this can be overcome through cooperation. The school must also be aware of the services of the public library and actively promote its use with both staff and students.

Design and Production of Materials

Should suitable material not be available in the resource center, not available on loan from another school or agency, and not available from commercial sources, the teacher-librarian has the ability as a media specialist to determine the instructional need and design a product based on theories of learning and educational technology. The appropriate medium is matched to instructional purpose and message to be conveyed. The teacher-librarian then produces or supervises the local production of needed learning resources. Too often the production of materials is seen as a purely technical matter but in the resource center the instructional design function is an important factor in the development of media. The unique characteristics of a filmstrip, for example, with its fixed sequence and visual qualities might be much more justifiable for the intended purpose and audience than a sound recording which can require a higher level of motivation and improved listening skills.

Promotion of Reading

Reading continues to be of prime importance to the teacher-librarian and numerous methods of motivating voluntary reading are common in resource centers. In conjunction with teacher colleagues, the teacher-librarian works toward broadening horizons, increasing language proficiency and resolving student problems through storytelling and book talks as well as improved reading guidance (which can approach bibliotherapy), creative dramatics, puppetry and related programs.

Information Services

Information services are offered to students and teachers, with the reference interview becoming a professional teaching situation in many cases. Since the teacher-librarian is familiar with individual units through advance planning the student may receive precise information immediately or have skills introduced or reinforced depending on defined objectives. Teachers gain the ability to ask questions at a variety of levels, from the recall of information to the evaluation of abstract concepts, through professional education and classroom experience. These techniques are necessary in the resource center to gauge the precise information needs of the student and the level of specific skill attainment at the time. Reference and research skills are taught as an integral part of the instructional program in each subject on a continuing sequential basis. Where desirable and valid, however, some skills may also be reinforced and extended as a short unit themselves. For example, a collaborative unit may be planned for a senior commerce class where the student will need to know a variety of specific skills such as how to use a dictionary and thesaurus for business composition, how to locate quotations for speeches, the correct form of address to be used in given circumstances and how to file information for easy retrieval in order to function effectively and efficiently in a business office. Evaluation of learning always takes place in the context of classroom teaching and its extensions.

Media Skills

The teacher-librarian is also actively engaged in teaching students the effective use of media and equipment; this includes the skills necessary to report research in many and varied ways other than the traditional essay format. The student must be knowledgeable about print, audio-visual and electronic environments inside and outside the school. We know that by the time a student completes secondary school more time has been spent watching television than has been spent in school—it would be gross negligence to overlook the skills necessary to evaluate this and other commercial sources of information or to relegate these learning skills to a single separate course in media education. Graphic analysis and visual and aural literacy are necessary components of a student's education; as a media specialist, the teacher-librarian works with other teachers to integrate these learning skills with appropriate areas of the curriculum.

Professional Development Services

Two of the most important areas of competence in teacher-librarianship are professional development services to teachers and strategies for change, both of which necessitate teacher education for maximum effect. Educational information services for staff members are necessary and useful if the teacher-librarian considers the specific interest, time and energy of the user. An even more fundamental professional development service is in-service education. As a curriculum developer and educational leader the teacher-librarian has a professional obligation and responsibility to lead seminars and workshops on the effective use of the center and its resources. Topics range from the operation of equipment to the implementation of effective resource-based teaching and learning strategies. In-service education is carefully planned and pursued. It demands a critical analysis of need based on relevant educational principles, a real reason for teachers to attend, effective teaching by the teacher-librarian and involvement by participants. Evaluation of the session itself and how well it met the need originally identified provides guidance for future workshops. Only through increased knowledge of resource center services as necessary components of teaching methodology will the potential of teacher-librarians and resource centers be realized.

A parallel consideration is the area of strategies for change in which in-service education programs are one part. Through perspective as a teacher plus an intimate knowledge and understanding of the institutional framework within which the resource center operates, the teacher-librarian can identify areas of potential support and hindrance more easily. By exploiting political realities and building on aspirations of administrators and the goals of teachers, the teacher-librarian can not only integrate services better but also develop a well-supported program.

The debate over faculty status for community college and university librarians has continued for years but is not a concern in schools. The teacher-librarian has full faculty status and is recognized as an equal partner in education in terms of salary, working conditions and leave. This status was gained by the most obvious means possible—the same basic qualification to be in the school in the first place followed by specialization in resource based learning. Indeed, many school districts have defined the role and expectations of the teacher-librarian as a master teacher and have granted additional responsibility allowances for department headships and educational leadership.

Collegiality is a strong characteristic of the teaching profession that cannot be ignored; just as the professional with a Master of Arts or Master of Science degree has a teaching certificate so too does the professional with a Master of Library Science degree. Professional roles in a school, other than peripheral or support positions, begin with teacher education and classroom experience followed by additional qualification for specialization. Whether one agrees or not, it is a fact of life in a school that teachers do not extend their privileges, rights and status to noncertified personnel, regardless of position or qualification. Familiarity with curriculum design and successful experience in the classroom provide a respectability that cannot be achieved by academic qualifications alone.

Standards

Comparison of libraries is often done by examining quantitative data but in a school the number of personnel, book and nonbook materials, equipment and square feet per student are relatively meaningless for determining the level of development and value of resource center services. Numbers are significant only when establishing new resource centers to equalize tangible products and potential. Much more useful but more difficult to measure are qualitative considerations. The resource center can be distinguished from a library by its specialized curriculum implementation (that is, collaborative program development and teaching) services; the teacher-librarian and resource center represent the implementation of a variety of teaching strategies found to be educationally effective. The school which practices inquiry-centered approaches to learning requires much more personnel, resources and space for the same number of students than a school which stresses textbook-oriented Socratic methods. The resource center must be essential to the instructional process if it is to have significance, or even to survive. With budgetary restraints the resource center is using money that could mean smaller classes, more counselors or more remedial assistance. Unlike an integrated resource center, a children's or young adult library added to the school could not and would not outlast financial cutbacks and the setting of priorities. Perhaps a more reasonable method of informal evaluation would be to close the resource center for a month to see if teaching and learning continue as before. If a teacher can teach and if the student can learn without the resource center and the teacher-librarian, the service as it exists in that situation is merely a "beauty spot on the body politic," an expensive and doomed educational frill.

The following problems have traditionally prevented the full implementation of a planned program for facilitating independent learning using the resource center:

1. lack of a school district K through 12 developmental study skills program that mandates the integration of independent learning skills with all aspects of the program;

2. limitation of instruction in the use of the resource center to a brief orientation session;

3. failure to include in courses of study, specific learning experiences requiring resource center support and specific reference to the necessity of integrating instruction in the use of information within the framework of the teaching-learning program;

4. isolation of the teacher-librarian from curriculum study and revision activities;

5. failure of teacher education institutions to include in basic programs an adequate understanding of the function of the resource center as a learning laboratory and the role of the teacher-librarian as a teacher colleague;

6. failure of the teacher to expand class knowledge beyond textbook content and classroom confines;

7. reluctance of the teacher to pre-plan with the teacher-librarian for the effective use of resource center media, facilities, and services before a unit is introduced to the class (or,

unfortunately, the reluctance of the teacher-librarian to pre-plan with the teacher);

8. lack of sufficient staff—both professional and para-professional—to support adequately a comprehensive, diversified instructional program in the processing and use of information and the use of the resource center—methods which will effectively utilize resource center personnel and services (adapted from Davies, 1979).

The resource center will never be really necessary until students are unable to do satisfactory work without access to the professional teaching and library media services that it provides.

Education for Teacher-Librarians

Although it is possible to define the role of the teacher-librarian as a teacher and as a librarian it is unwise to do so. Indeed, this is a common mistake made by educators of teacher-librarians. There are essential competencies necessary from teacher education, classroom experience, and library and media education but it is the fusion of these that leads to excellence, not dual qualifications in themselves. Until programs which educate teacher-librarians, whether faculties of education or library science, recognize, require and develop these areas of competence, there will continue to be a chronic shortage of teacher-librarians who understand this specialized teaching role and have the necessary skills to implement it. The time is long overdue for instructors in school librarianship to examine the basic research and get on with the job of developing the necessary course components. A specialized Master of Education degree in school librarianship would provide sufficient scope at the appropriate level to build on a teacher's background and experience. It would also provide a suitable framework for the components which are too often missing: instructional design, collaborative program planning, team teaching, human relations, selection of learning resources in all formats, the institutional setting, design and production of media, developmental reading. For

too long lip service has been paid to a specialized teaching role and translated it into courses in administration, cataloguing and literature.

Conclusion

The school must examine its own program in order to determine the type of service that it requires from the resource center. If the only concern is the circulation of materials, then parent volunteers or a clerical assistant may be sufficient. If selection and organization warrant increased attention as well as children's and young adult services and programs then a library technician or librarian should be employed depending on the scope and quality of service preferred. If the utilization of learning resources through valid, planned experiences leading to independent learning is of prime importance then a master teacher with advance education and training in teacher-librarianship is required.

Teacher-librarians have progressed from the days when it was all too common for refugees from the classroom to be placed in charge of school libraries to a time when outstanding specialist teachers head vital integrated resource centers. School libraries have moved from their position outside the mainstream of education to resource centers at the physical and philosophical heart of the school. This development is a direct result of changes in education and, more specifically, changes in teaching strategies. Instruction in learning skills is integrated with all aspects of the curriculum and taught together by the classroom teacher and teacher-librarian. The direction of teaching and learning focuses increasingly on learning how to learn so that students will have the necessary motivation and the skills to examine their own environment, evaluate it and perhaps even reform it.

References

Davies, R. A. (1979). *The school library media program: Instructional force for excellence.* (3rd ed.). New York: Bowker.

CHAPTER SEVEN

Navigating the '90s— The Teacher-Librarian as Change Agent

Jean Brown

Expectations have never been higher. One is reminded of John Goodlad's observation (1984), "When it comes to education, it appears that most parents want their children to have it all." (p. 99) Our situation today is no different. We are bombarded by pressure groups. Whatever ills there are in society, it seems to be the school's job to cure them.

The vision of society as post-industrial is an attractive one, and one with which most of us would probably agree. Education is seen as a key element, essential in the development of this kind of society, and again there are affirmations today on the importance of education which sound like music to the ears of all of us who are concerned with education. It is reassuring to hear such statements and we would even agree, I think, that current expectations are not unrealistic, that schools should have strong goals, and that given proper support, schools may indeed endeavor to produce a highly educated society.

All of us are aware that we could be doing better, and in fact all of us have a wish to change current practices so we can better meet the needs of our students. But we also know that it is becoming increasingly difficult to teach, that far too much is expected of teachers today, and that often there is little or no support where support is desperately needed.

There was a time, not long ago, when we felt immune to the problems of society, but that's not the case any more.

There have been those, of course, over the years who have expressed concern over placing excessive demands on schools, who recommend that schools make hard choices and figure out what they are uniquely equipped to teach, and then focus on that.

Despite these voices calling for restraint on expectations for the schools, one cannot be optimistic that such a reduction will occur. At present, it seems that the voices demanding more and more be included in the school's curriculum are much louder and having much greater effect. There is no indication that social problems will decrease: in fact, they seem to be escalating. As we approach the '90s, teachers and teaching appear to be heading for turbulent times. Teachers will indeed need to be talented, energetic, and committed professionals if they are to cope successfully with the challenges that are facing them.

If we wish to navigate the '90s, then we are charting a course on a tempestuous sea. If teacher-librarians are to chart a course that will enable them to act effectively as change agents, what do they need to do? What do they need to keep in mind? What do they need to know?

We have become accustomed to a new world, where information is available as never before: television brings the world's events into our homes nightly, with even a 24-hour news network available; documents are faxed from one part of the country to another; instant tellers provide not only cash but an update on your bank balance, even when you're thousands of miles from home. Some of us delight in this, seeing it as convenient and indeed marvelous. Others despair, seeing an old world disappear and a new, uncertain world emerging.

Whether it's the best of times or the worst depends on your perspective, and we don't need to be futurists projecting into the '90s to know that technology is drastically changing our world. We need only look around us to know that our world is indeed changing:

- In remote schools, some students are studying advanced mathematics through distance education. Each site has an IBM microcomputer, a telewriter, a facsimile machine, and an audio-teleconference convenor kit. The student engages in weekly tutorials with a "remote" teacher.

- Many remote homes have satellite dishes in their backyards. Some of them pick up 40 or more channels. To students in such homes, the Bermuda weather report is as commonplace as "Here and Now."

- Videocassette players are common in schools and homes, with video outlets found in even the smallest communities.

- The vinyl phonograph album is disappearing, being replaced by compact discs and audio cassettes.

Whether we consider it "the best of times" or the "worst of times," the "age of wisdom" or "the age of foolishness" will depend on our backgrounds, our philosophies, our values, our experiences. But regardless of how we view it, we must all realize that we are, indeed, in an era of change.

These changes have been mainly brought about by the introduction of information technologies and their expansion into all facets of society. There has never been a time in our history when so much information has been available to the general public and never before have our lives depended so much on our ability to use information successfully.

To make effective use of the information, all of us will need to be able to search out what we require, assess critically the ideas and facts presented to us, and make effective use of our findings. More than ever before, we will need to be critical readers and viewers. How are we to do this? How will the school teach students to think about and manage information? Information will be available, but will our students, and indeed will we, have the ability to use it and be more knowledgeable? We do not know into what forms the information technologies will evolve in another ten years (although we have some serious projections) but we need to be concerned now with the implications of these technologies.

The transformation to an information society is still in its early stages, and to prepare students for it is a formidable challenge. Although we in learning resources are concerned with it, we are, of course, far from alone in this concern, All of us in education, whatever our area of concentration, wrestle with these problems. Society in general is also struggling with these problems. There are important questions which we need to answer. What should children learn? What are the "basics" needed in the '90s and beyond? We all know that information is not the same as knowledge, but what is the relationship between the two? What are the skills students need in order to cope with future needs? Are there generic skills that can be transferred to new learning environments? What kinds of environments will the new information technologies create? Is there difference in using and understanding electronic and print data? How is information received?

Coupled with these questions are other questions which strike at the very heart of teaching. Who sets the pace for learning—the student or the teacher? This raises the whole question of curriculum orientations: do we view curriculum as mainly transmission of content to be presented and mastered? Or are we moving towards a transactional orientation, where there is emphasis on the learner as well as on the content? We are beginning to focus on the latter, viewing education as a process in which teachers attempt to create learning experiences which will best meet learners' needs as well as fulfill curriculum objectives. Lately, we have been using the terms "resource-based learning" to refer to this philosophy.

This is not new of course, the limitations of total dependency on a single text have been discussed for years. However, the educational system is now more committed to this approach but finds itself handicapped by the need for more resources during a period of restricted budgets.

For those of us in learning resources, this is cause for celebration, for we have long recommended this approach, and see this as an important step in providing students with the kind of education they need. I think that most teachers are aware of this philosophy and many accept it. However, our knowledge of change tells us that intellect acceptance (or adoption) of an idea is far from implementing it. Work done by Joyce and Showers (1982) in particular shows that even after teachers are aware of new ideas and have gained intellectual understanding of them and how they can be used in the classroom, they still need help in actually acquiring the skills to integrate these ideas into their classroom work. The role of the teacher-librarian is very important in providing that type of assistance. As a professional group, our emphasis needs to shift from the strong advocacy role which characterized us in the '80s to a more active teaching role in the '90s. The problem facing us today will not be as much *introducing* the concept of resource-based learning, as much as it is figuring out, in partnership with classroom teachers, curriculum consultants, other specialists and administrators, how we can do it.

That is where we, as teacher-librarians, can play an important role as change agents

Educational Change

During the '80s we have learned a great deal about educational change. Many are familiar with Michael Fullan's book *The meaning of educational change* (1982) and realize that any kind of change is a process, involving people and taking time, rather than an event. We know that there are distinct phases to planned change, and most refer to them as adoption, implementation and continuation. We know that different individuals are involved in different phases, that the administrators are key players in phases one and three, but that classroom teachers control phase two. Fullan's work is a comprehensive coverage of the research in this area and is an excellent beginning point for those wishing to read in this area. The greatest area of interest is the second phase, curriculum implementation, the phase concerned with actually translating theories into practice.

We know a great deal about change in the implementation phase. We know that an educational innovation, such as cooperative program planning and teaching, is a complex process, which will require teachers to learn how to do their work differently, To implement it will require some classroom teachers to learn how to use a wide range of resources effectively, to plan and team teach with a teacher-librarian, to allow students more control over learning than perhaps they had before. Change is personal, and for teachers to make such a move, there must be support as they struggle through the first attempt.

We know that people are at the heart of planned change and that these people are part of a complex setting. Implementing a change will not occur in a vacuum. Schools are social settings with values, norms, accepted ways of doing things. To introduce any change into that setting requires an understanding of how things are naturally done in that school. Susan Rosenholtz's book, *Teachers' workplace* (1989) provides new insights into how school organization influences instructional practice. Using quantitative and qualitative research strategies, she examined 78 elementary schools and 1,213 teachers in eight Tennessee districts. Her book describes how school practices influence school improvement efforts. Some schools were what Rosenholtz refers to as "high consensus schools," in which teachers "have a common purpose and work openly and cooperatively" (Rosenholtz, 1989, p. xi). Other schools were referred to as "low consensus schools," where teachers "did not enjoy a sense of community," where teachers worked alone in isolation.

The type of school, whether high or low consensus, greatly affected the chances of successfully bringing about any school improvement. In high-consensus schools, teachers were united in their view of what schooling should be, they believed that teaching was important, they looked for alternative instructional practices that might improve their efforts, they were open to comments about their teaching and to suggestions and alternative practices that might improve their practice. Other teachers were seen as valuable resource people and the teachers had a sense of community. Rosenholtz concludes: "High-consensus and forward-moving schools were enriched by a marked spirit of continuous improvement in which no teacher ever stopped learning how to teach" (Rosenholtz, 1989, p. xi).

The norm of teacher collaboration governed what happened in these schools. Rosenholtz's study found that "teachers' certainty about a technical culture and their instructional practice is one of the most powerful predictors of collaboration" (Rosenholtz, 1989, p. 46). Technical culture refers to "the processes designed to accomplish an organization's goals" (Rosenholtz, 1989, p. 4), and for teachers, "technical knowledge encompasses the skills, procedures, and methods that help pupils progress academically" (Rosenholtz, 1989, p. 4). A technical culture is labeled *uncertain* if there is no one way to do it, if there are few well-established techniques. When teachers feel uncertain about teaching skills, procedures and methods, is it not to be expected that they would shy away from collaboration? This is a second point that Rosenholtz makes: that uncertainty about the technical culture and one's ability to help students leads teachers to be on the defensive because their self-esteem is threatened. None of us want to appear incompetent. We want to look

our best in front of others. It stands to reason then, we would "avoid situations where our performance adequacy, and thus our sense of self-esteem, may conceivably be called into question" (Rosenholtz, 1989, p. 5). As Rosenholtz points out, it is more than saving face, "it also involves our need to maintain control, of our work and our lives."

Rosenholtz analyzed the schools' norms for teachers helping each other, and used the terms "collaborative settings" and "isolated settings" to describe the difference between those where help was given and those in which teachers worked alone (Rosenholtz, 1989, p. 49). As teacher-librarians, committed to a philosophy of partnership with the classroom teacher and administrators, we advocate and need a collaborative setting if we are to be successful. However, the problem in most of our schools is that we are working in isolated settings.

To move from a low-consensus to a high-consensus school, from an isolated to a collaborative setting, is no easy task. It will involve the whole staff and require strong leadership, especially from the principal. However, leaders will be needed at all levels, and we can perform an important role as instructional leaders within the school, helping to bring this change about. For the teacher-librarian, being a change agent means being an instructional leader.

Instructional Leadership

What indeed is educational change but instructional leadership? However, to speak of instructional leadership may only serve to confuse the issue. Greenfield (1987) defines instructional leadership as "actions undertaken to develop a productive and satisfying work environment for teachers and desirable learning conditions and outcomes for children" (p. 46). Even given that definition, the meaning can be ambiguous and convey multiple meanings. To see it in concrete terms is difficult. What exactly does instructional leadership look like? Is it the same in secondary schools as it is in elementary schools? Who are the instructional leaders? In answering these questions, it will be important to get at the very essence of instructional leadership, which is, I would suggest, providing the means "to bring about or preserve changes needed to improve schooling"

(Greenfield, 1987, p. 57). Viewed in this way, are not instructional leadership and planned educational change flip sides of the same coin?

To provide the means to bring about desired change requires strong leadership. But again we need to ask ourselves what we mean by "leadership." Burns (1978) reported that a recent study had "turned up 130 definitions of the word" (p. 2). The one that I would like to use defines leadership as: "the process of moving a group (or groups) in some direction through mostly noncoercive means" (Kotter, 1988, p. 5), with effective leadership defined as "leadership that produces movement in the long-term best interests of the group(s)" (p. 5). This definition "is generally consistent with those used by…thoughtful writers on the topic" (Kotter, 1988, p. 5). Burns describes the production of movement as being "the reciprocal process of mobilizing" people, in order to reach goals "mutually held by both leaders and followers" (p. 425). The simplest definition is the one provided by Peters and Austin (1985) in which they see it as "unleashing energy, freeing, and growing" (p. xix). In all these definitions, there is a movement from current practices to desired outcomes or goals.

In order to be an effective leader, then, it is necessary to have strong values and a vision of what can be. In order to make decisions, to decide on one course of action rather than another, one needs to make judgments, to assign values. This leads to what Greenfield (1987) calls "moral imagination" (p. 64), to be able "to see the discrepancy between how things are and how they might be—not in terms of the ideal, but in terms of what is possible given a particular individual, group, or school situation" (p. 64). Effective or strong leadership will require "a vision of what is desirable and possible in that school's context" and the ability to inspire or "mobilize" others to work towards that vision (p. 64). It is "moral" because "the discrepancy, the possibility envisioned, is rooted in an awareness of and a commitment to the standards of good practice, of effective schools, and good teaching" (p. 61–62). It is moral because it is "the application of some standard of goodness that illuminates the discrepancy between the present and what is possible, and better" (p. 62).

If we are to have vision that will allow us to be effective leaders, then we will need to understand the school and the curriculum well. We will need to make sound judgments on whether the current state is satisfactory or not. Some standard of excellence must be used, whether it's found in provincial/state documents, national guidelines, or writings from leaders in the field. The decision must be made whether to leave things as they are, or to try and change them. Success may depend on the soundness of the vision, whether what you aspire to might be both possible and better in your particular school district.

This analysis is very close to the approach taken by Ken Leithwood (1987) who views educational change as problem-solving. Like Greenfield, Leithwood suggests that we first analyze the current state of affairs, then identify the desired state (requiring the vision), and that we see planned change as reducing the gap between them. This is a simplified explanation of Leithwood's framework, but it is useful for any who are attempting to implement change. A central concept in Leithwood's problem-solving orientation to change is the concept of stages of growth. In order to make the change more concrete and achievable, Leithwood suggests that we first identify the critical dimensions of practice that will need to change; then, that we describe what full implementation looks like; and that we then define, as concretely as we can, manageable stages through which to "grow" in order to move towards the goals for change. Lack of clarity about what we are attempting to do is a major problem experienced by anyone involved in implementing changes in the school system. Leithwood's innovation profile is one procedure that can help in clarifying the vision for all those involved.

This only scratches the surface of much which could be said about educational change and about leadership. Much of what we need to learn comes from our own field, education, but we have a lot to learn about leadership from the world of business. In comparing excellent businesses and outstanding schools, Peters and Austin (1985) found many common characteristics which together help describe the outstanding leader:

Clear philosophy or vision. All the best companies and schools "are imbued with philosophies," with "a crystal clear and simple vision." The best school philosophies were "simple and to the point," sometimes no more profound than "I believe in kids" but that "philosophy or vision was quickly turned into symbols by the best school leaders."

Use of symbols. Outstanding leaders are masters at using symbols to set a tone and reinforce the philosophy. Creating heroes or myths makes the vision visible. Whether it's insistence on school attendance, or an obsession with keeping floors and walls clean, actions symbolized the values held by the leaders. School assemblies, daily activities, all provided opportunities for the symbolism and showmanship. While talking to a learning resources coordinator last week, she remarked that when a school moved, she spent two days in the school, helping them move. She wore her jeans, and went prepared to work. I would suggest that she achieved more by doing that than she could ever imagine. Her presence, her attitude, her attire, all symbolized to the teacher-librarian and to the staff that she was one of them and that they were important.

Thinking in pictures. Related to vision and symbols, leaders tended to think in pictures. Business leaders spoke of "dramatizing the vision" or "seeing the glory." A school principal reported that he thought "in pictures." Once a picture seemed right, he wanted to "keep it that way." Most of the leaders seemed intuitively to use visualization: "Within their head is a picture of what a positive outcome would look like, and of what the individual components of it are. They attempt to set the picture and, as leaders, to paint it for others."

Being in touch. Leaders, in business and in schools, need to be in touch with their people, to be informed. This requires listening to your people. John Couch developed Apple's Lisa computer (which led to the Macintosh), a computer noted for its user friendliness. When asked about his success, John explained that he had bought his father a computer outlet, and then worked in it himself for the first two years. He worked on weekends, on the floor, incognito. In that way, he explained, he learned "about the fears and frustrations of the average first-time user." He saw this listening to the user as "the single most significant source of what we came up with."

Keeping in touch means different things to different leaders, but Peters and Austin see it as "wandering around, staying in touch, keeping out of the office." They see it as one of the main differences between the superb leader and the not-so-good. Keeping in touch centers on an intense involvement and empathy with your people, whether they are customers, students, or teachers.

Just for the kids. Good companies put their customers first, with key words being courtesy, listening, perception. They stress the importance of "cherishing the customer." In schools, Peters and Austin see the exact parallel in "for the kids." I would add that for teacher-librarians it might be "for the kids and the teachers." It means treating people (whether they're students or teachers) with dignity and respect. It means having high standards of service and quality, treating people with common courtesy, or as Peters and Austin refer to it "uncommon courtesy." In business or education, this is a key element in good leadership: "treat your people as adults, and they will respond as adults, conscientiously and creatively."

Leadership means vision, values, enthusiasm, trust. It means listening, coaching, effectively wandering around. It means caring for your people (both students and teachers) and treating them with dignity and respect. It means a million little things, done with consistency and care.

Why Bother?

Why do this? Why bother with being leaders? Being a change agent or an instructional leader means not being content with the status quo, it requires personal commitment and hard work, it goes far beyond the requirements for the job. For most of us the answer to that question is that we have no choice, that we want to provide students with the kind of education we feel they need. We have a dream or vision of what can be, perhaps a passion for excellence, and we have acted upon it. For some, that passion led to subject specialization or administration, for us it led to learning resources.

The current state of education isn't a pretty or a bright picture. Teachers are caught in a world of social problems, overburdened with expectations. The situation probably won't improve, the problems we now see will be with us in the '90s.

We can be optimistic, however, about the role that teacher-librarians can play in the schools of today and the '90s. We are in a unique position to offer individualized and ongoing assistance to teachers. Whether we call it "coaching," or "partnership," or "cooperative program planning and teaching," or simply caring and working with our fellow teachers, the process involves "providing personalized information for specific teachers' needs and facilitating each teacher's use of the new program by clarifying meaning and solving individual problems" (Hord & Huling-Austin, 1986, p. 106). Successful implementation requires a large amount of consultation, reinforcement, practice and support, particularly in the first two years. You, as the school's teacher-librarian, have first-hand knowledge of the school, the teachers, the principal, the community. You also should be totally familiar with the curriculum and the school's collection of learning resources, both what's available and how best to use them. Add to this knowledge of instructional development, and you have the potential to provide on-site assistance to classroom teachers as they are faced with a changing technology and curriculum.

Classroom teachers have so many demands placed upon them that to expect them to locate resources, acquire them, organize them, independently learn how to use them effectively as an integral part of their classroom work, to expect them to do all this in addition to meeting their classroom responsibilities is expecting too much. Teacher-librarians have an important role to play in helping schools meet the challenge of the '90s. Since we have already discussed the need for visualization of a vision, I suggest that you see yourself not as a prima donna, but rather as a workhorse; not as the icing on the cake but as one of the main ingredients.

If you want to fulfill this leadership role, you will need to be lifelong learners, to constantly seek new answers and solutions to educational problems, to stay in touch with the public, the students, and your fellow teachers. You will need to keep faith in what you are doing, never losing sight of the value of what you have to offer. You will need to keep your vision simple, and you will need to learn to work with your fellow teachers in true partnership, treating them with a sense of dignity and respect.

Reader's Digest often provides insightful and revealing glimpses into the personal lives of the rich and famous. A short incident related in the August, 1989 issue serves to remind us of what successful leadership is all about:

Estee Lauder, billionaire baroness of the beauty industry, was the daughter of immigrants. She sold her uncle's skin cream concoction during the Depression. "I was single-minded in the pursuit of my dream," Lauder says, referring to her goal of owning a beauty-products company. She worked her way out of beauty parlors and into department stores, manning counters with unforgettable flair.

"Never say, 'May I help you?'" she states, "say, 'Madam, won't you please let me show you how this finest of creams, created from only pure ingredients, can make your complexion glow with youth and radiance?'" Then she would touch the woman's face, look into her eyes and press a sample into her hand. (p. 60)

We, too, have a quality product, and we, too, have a vision. As we enter the '90s, I hope we will learn how to put that vision into practice, how to act as a catalyst for change. But as we do that, I hope we retain the human touch. Change, after all, is about people.

References

Burns, J. (1978). *Leadership*. New York: Harper & Row.

Fullan, M. (1982). *The meaning of educational change*. Toronto: OISE Press.

Goodlad, J. (1984). *A place called school*. New York: McGraw-Hill.

Greenfield, W. (1987). Moral imagination and interpersonal competence: antecedents to instructional leadership. In *Instructional leadership: concepts, issues and controversies* (pp. 46–64). New York: Allyn and Bacon.

Hord, S. and Holding-Austin, L. (1986). Effective curriculum implementation: some promising new insights. *The Elementary School Journal, 87 (1)*, 97–115.

Joyce, B. and Showers, B. (1982). The coaching of teaching. *Educational Leadership, 40(1),* 4–11.

Kotter, J. (1988). *The leadership factor.* New York: The Free Press.

Leithwood, K. & Montgomery, D. (1987). *Improving classroom practice using innovation profiles.* Toronto: OISE Press.

Peters, T. & Austin, N. (1985). *A passion for excellence: The leadership difference.* New York: Random House.

Rosenholtz, S. (1989). *Teachers' workplace: The social organization of schools.* New York: Longman.

CHAPTER EIGHT

Developing Information Literacy Through the Information Intermediary Process: A Model for Teacher-Librarians and Others

Kathy Thomas Brock

Current goals for restructuring public education include giving students a whole list of new basic competencies such as information literacy and technological literacy (Caissey, 1990; "Critical reform," 1990). In the United States, professional groups are focusing on these new competencies as they work to develop voluntary national content and performance standards in seven curriculum areas ("Creating standards," 1993). Objectives associated with information and technological literacy are very much in evidence as new student standards documents appear.

The library literature echoes this emphasis, defining information literacy as the ability to recognize an information need and to locate, understand, evaluate and use the needed information effectively (American Library Association, 1989). *Information power* charges teacher-librarians with the responsibility for helping students become information literate. It calls them information intermediaries—professionals who help "students,

teachers and parents learn how to cope with the information explosion and how to exploit the possibilities of an extraordinarily rich information world" (American Association of School Librarians & Association for Educational Communications and Technology, 1988, p. 15).

The process involved in being an information intermediary, however, has not been so clearly defined. Typically, there are nonspecific references to the teacher as content specialist and the teacher-librarian as information specialist who plan cooperatively and "help" or "assist" students using information sources. In the new curriculum-area documents, on the other hand, an attempt is made not only to describe content and performance standards, but to identify specific "powerful" teaching strategies designed to help students achieve.

The purpose of this study was to formulate a literature-based model describing the information intermediary process. The model was intended to depict what teacher-librarians do as they help students involved in the information search and use (ISU) process. The study was also designed to determine whether teacher-librarians work with students in all phases of the ISU process and the extent to which their intermediary activities can be related to categories imported from other current instructional models.

The study involved the following phases—collection of data from the literature, development of a preliminary model describing the information intermediary process, review of the preliminary model by a panel of experts and synthesis of review data resulting in a final model revision.

Data for the preliminary process model were obtained by searching the library and education literature published since 1985 for resources addressing what students do in the ISU process and what teacher-librarians or other intermediaries do to help them. A total of 170 documents were identified as potentially relevant, and data from 80 were actually incorporated into the model.

The library literature consisted of ISU process models, including those developed by Kuhlthau (1989), Irving (1985), Stripling and Pitts (1988) and Eisenberg and Berkowitz (1990), as well as monographs and articles from other individuals and education agencies. In all, 20 ISU process models were examined.

The education literature included references on critical thinking, learning theory, instructional design and staff development. Relevant information focused on the cognitive skills used by students in various phases of the ISU process and the instructional activities and strategies associated with teaching those skills. A number of recently published conceptual models and discussions were found to have implications for the study and are included in the References list at the end of this paper.

Model Development

Based on analysis of the literature, a list was made of specific skills used by students in the ISU process. Additional lists identified instructional content and strategies or methodologies used by teacher-librarians or others working with students. Of particular interest were instructional strategies used in the kinds of activities typically characterized as resource-based, problem-solving, or student-centered. A process model framework within which this information could be organized was then devised, using adaptations of a number of common model components.

A second framework based on components from current instructional concept models and discussions was added to overlay the process model and provide an additional layer of descriptive data. This part of the model uses a continuum to portray the relationship of the teaching strategies to each other and to the learning objectives.

A survey was conducted to obtain formative data on the preliminary model from a panel of 15 contributors to the literature on which it was based. The panel consisted of library educators, bibliographic instruction and/or reference librarians in academic settings, or teacher-librarians working in school library resource centers or as district or state coordinators/supervisors. Along with a brief explanation and a copy of the model, panel members received a questionnaire asking for information about their experience, the perceived accuracy and utility of the model and open-ended feedback regarding the model.

Eleven responses were received during the allotted time period, resulting in a return rate of 73 percent. Information from the questionnaires was analyzed and reported in summary form in the study. It resulted in additions being made to three phases of the preliminary information intermediary process model.

Results

The Information Intermediary Process Model (Figure 8.1) was the primary outcome of the study. It consists of a grid formed by overlaying a representation of the generic ISU process with a three-phase instructional model adapted from current education literature. Instructing, coaching and facilitating phases of instruction are portrayed on a continuum ranging from intermediary-directed to student-directed. Within the grid, content and teaching strategies characterizing a wide range of information intermediary activities are described.

Figure 8.1   Information Intermediary Process Model

		Intermediary-Directed ⟶ Student-Directed		
		Instructing	**Coaching**	**Facilitating**
Information Search and Use Process	**Phase 1** **Defining the problem**	☐ Build awareness of ISU Process ☐ Introduce and model strategies for selecting, developing, and refining topic and for formulating research questions	☐ Monitor and provide feedback as students practice brainstorming, clustering, and webbing techniques in cooperative learning settings	☐ Help students select topics independently ☐ Suggest sources for overview ☐ Consult as students develop authentic topics and research questions
	Phase 2 **Developing information-seeking strategies**	☐ Introduce information sources ☐ Model development of search strategy	☐ Provide practice in selecting appropriate sources ☐ Provide guidance as students identify, expand, limit, and combine terms to develop search strategies in practice settings	☐ Suggest specific resources for student topics ☐ Help students develop individual search strategies
	Phase 3 **Locating information**	☐ Demonstrate retrieval of citations from indexes and databases, location of sources in media center, and location of information in sources ☐ Discuss access to sources outside media center	☐ Give directions as students practice retrieving citations, locating sources, and using scanning and skimming techniques to find information in a controlled setting	☐ Assist as students locate information independently ☐ Provide access to outside resources
	Phase 4 **Gathering and assessing information**	☐ Discuss criteria for evaluating relevance, reliability, and adequacy of information ☐ Demonstrate strategies for taking notes ☐ Explain rights and responsibilities of information use	☐ Monitor and provide feedback as students apply criteria for evaluating and selecting or rejecting information using practice data in cooperative learning settings	☐ Consult as students assimilate, evaluate, select or reject, and record information independently ☐ Help students determine copyright compliance and obtain clearances as needed
	Phase 5 **Synthesizing information**	☐ Introduce and model strategies for organizing information, identifying relationships, and drawing conclusions ☐ Describe format options for communicating results	☐ Give guidance as students practice strategies for organizing and synthesizing information in cooperative settings	☐ Help students organize and synthesize information independently ☐ Consult as students plan presentation of results ☐ Help students access appropriate production formats
	Phase 6 **Evaluating and refining results**	☐ Discuss criteria for evaluating product and process ☐ Discuss how evaluation may suggest revisions	☐ Provide direction as students apply criteria and suggest revisions using practice data in cooperative learning settings	☐ Provide feedback as students evaluate process and products ☐ Consult as they make revisions

The study found that the information intermediary process can be described by portraying how teacher-librarians or others interact with users in all phases of information searching and use. Teacher-librarians do help students to define information-based problems, to develop information-seeking strategies, to locate information, to gather and assess information, to synthesize information and to present, evaluate and refine results. These phases provide a framework for describing the information intermediary role. They mirror the current emphasis on helping students obtain intellectual as well as physical access to information by teaching a generic information-handling process that includes, rather than focuses solely on, teaching about particular data sources.

The model is not an attempt to provide a comprehensive list of specific information skills or to suggest subject area correlations or grade levels at which skills should be introduced, reinforced and mastered. This information is readily available in recently produced skills documents, many of which are cited here. Rather, the model establishes the broad parameters of the body of skills with which teacher-librarians or others work in the information intermediary role.

In addition to describing the content of the information intermediary process, the model also portrays how that content is addressed. It suggests an array of instructional activities (i.e., cooperative learning, modeling of cognitive processes, use of graphic organizers) widely discussed in the current literature for their applicability to development of the new literacies—especially those involving the ability to use complex processes independently. Teacher-librarians have instinctively used these strategies in their formal and informal interactions with students.

The continuum device used in the model as an organizational framework for these activities also mirrors an informal pattern followed instinctively by teacher-librarians. They provide initial information about processes and resources to individuals and to small and large groups of students. They plan and implement activities that give students an opportunity to use these processes and resources in a practice setting. Finally, they are available to provide individual help in response to the needs of students working independently.

Traditionally, location of information was the point in the ISU process at which teacher-librarian involvement was most obvious. Today, there is increased recognition that the training and experience of teacher-librarians in working with information systems and technologies make them valuable resources in all phases of information searching and use. When a student begins work on an information-based problem, teacher-librarians provide data about content and process essential to topic selection, development and refinement. Panel members identified developing information-seeking strategies as a phase where teacher-librarian involvement is vital—particularly in the electronic information environment. The assistance teacher-librarians can provide in evaluating and synthesizing data is more important than ever, due to the current glut of information. Finally, because of their expertise with a variety of media, teacher-librarians play an important role in helping students prepare to communicate findings or results.

Findings of the study indicate, however, that the information intermediary model is applicable to the role of both teacher and teacher-librarian. The literature and expert feedback emphasize the importance of cooperative efforts involving both professionals in the intermediation process. The distinct delineation of responsibilities between the two partners now seems to be less important than previously thought and more dependent on factors inherent in the working situation.

Implications

This study represents an initial exploration of the content and methodologies making up the information intermediary role. Findings are based solely on data obtained from the literature and from surveying a panel of experts. As a result, additional studies are needed to verify these preliminary findings and to explore related questions. These activities might include surveys and observational studies focusing on beliefs, actual practices and student needs. Attention should be given to the relationship between information intermediation and such variables as technology, teacher and teacher-librarian collaboration, adherence to an information skills continuum and student achievement.

As the resources and expectations associated with information use continue to change, there is a need for constant reexamination of the teacher-librarian role. These findings should be considered by those responsible for developing or revising teacher-librarian role definitions to determine whether current documents adequately address participation in the entire information intermediary process.

Since role documents form the basis of professional education, certification and performance evaluation programs, the study has implications for these programs as well. Library educators, as well as those responsible for teacher certification programs, should consider whether academic courses of study prepare professionals to work with the content and methodologies described in the Information Intermediary Process Model. Those responsible for developing performance evaluation programs should determine whether these programs recognize and assess the teacher-librarian's performance of the information intermediary role to the same extent that administrative duties are recognized and assessed.

There is evidence of renewed interest at school, district and state levels in developing or revising information skills programs, and increased recognition throughout the education establishment of the strengths of resource-based and collaborative teaching models. At the same time, lack of familiarity with certain resources and methodologies causes reluctance on the part of some teachers and teacher-librarians to experiment with these models. When a process-centered information skills program is implemented across the curriculum by collaborating teachers and teacher-librarians, the optimum environment for exploring these models results. The Information Intermediary Process Model can provide an implementation framework for resource-based units and a sampler of activities to be cooperatively planned by teachers and teacher-librarians.

Parents, administrators, teachers, teacher-librarians and students are intrigued by technology and the instant access to the massive amounts of data it brings. In the push to fund and implement technology, lower pupil-teacher ratios and provide other improvements designed to raise student achievement, the importance of the information intermediary has often been overlooked. It is easy to focus on teaching the mechanics of using technology and forget about helping students learn how to use the information that technology provides. The instructing, coaching and facilitating that must take place if students are to become information literate requires time and expertise. Some teacher-librarians may feel they lack the time and maybe even the expertise to participate in activities portrayed by the Information Intermediary Process Model. Assuming and raising awareness

of the information intermediary role, however, are crucial if teacher-librarians are to solidify their positions within today's volatile education environment.

References

American Association of School Librarians & Association for Educational Communications and Technology. (1988). *Information power: Guidelines for school library media programs.* Chicago: American Library Association.

American Library Association Presidential Committee on Information Literacy. (1989). *Final report.* Chicago: American Library Association.

Anderson, M., & Alley, C. (1989). *Matrix for curriculum planning in library media and information skills education.* Madison: Wisconsin Department of Public Instruction.

Arizona Guidelines Steering Committee. (1990). *Information strategy model.* Phoenix: Arizona Department of Education.

Baker, B., Huston, M., & Pastine, M. (1991). Making connections: Teaching information retrieval. *Library Trends, 39(3),* 210–222.

Beyer, B. (1992). Teaching thinking: An integrated approach. In J. Keefe & H. Walberg (Eds.), *Teaching for thinking* (pp. 93–109). Reston, VA: National Association of Secondary School Principals.

Boyvey, M. (1988). Thinking skills and high school libraries. In Texas Education Agency (Ed.), *REACH: Realistic educational achievement can happen* (pp. 33–34). Austin: Texas Education Agency.

Breivik, P. (1991). Literacy in an information age: A signal for the need to restructure the learning process. *NASSP Bulletin, 75*(535), 1–7.

Caissey, G. (1990). Research, thinking, decision making, problem solving: Skills for the information age. *Education Digest, LV(6),* 51–53.

Collins, A., Brown, J., & Newman, S. (1989). Cognitive apprenticeship: Teaching the crafts of reading, writing, and arithmetic. In L. Resnick (Ed.), *Knowing, learning and instruction: Essays in honor of Robert Glasser* (pp. 453–494). Hillsdale, NJ: Lawrence Erlbaum.

Costa, A., Hanson, R., Silver, H., & Strong, R. (1985). Building a repertoire of strategies. In A. Costa (Ed.), *Developing minds: A resource book for teaching thinking* (pp. 141–143). Alexandria, VA: Association for Supervision and Curriculum Development.

Craver, K. (1989). Critical thinking: Implications for research. *School Library Media Quarterly, 18(1),* 13–18.

Creating standards and building frameworks. (1993, Fall). *OERI Bulletin, 3,* 4.

Critical reform issues must be addressed by public school administrators, ASCD told. (1990). *Education USA, 33(7),* 47.

Cutlip, G. (1988). *Learning and information: Skills for the secondary classroom and library media program*. Englewood, CO: Libraries Unlimited.

Duffy, G. (1992). Let's free teachers to be inspired. *Phi Delta Kappan, 73(6)*, 442–447.

Eisenberg, M. & Berkowitz, R. (1990). *Information problem-solving: The big six skills approach to library and information skills instruction*. Norwood, NJ: Ablex.

Fitzpatrick, K. (1991). Restructuring to achieve outcomes of significance for all students. *Educational Leadership, 48(8)*, 18–22.

Haycock, K. (1990). The role of the school librarian as a professional teacher: A position paper. In K. Haycock (Ed.), *The school library program in the curriculum* (pp. 19–24). Englewood, CO: Libraries Unlimited.

Hughes, C. (1986). Teaching strategies for developing student thinking: Strategies for teachers and for library media specialists. *School Library Media Quarterly, 15(1)*, 33–36.

Irving, A. (1985). *Study and information skills across the curriculum*. London: Heinemann.

Kneedler, P. (1985). California assesses critical thinking. In A. Costa (Ed.), *Developing minds: A resource book for teaching thinking* (pp. 276–280). Alexandria, VA: Association for Supervision and Curriculum Development.

Kuhlthau, C. (1989). Information search process: A summary of research and implications for school library media programs. *School Library Media Quarterly, 18(1)*, 19–25.

Loertscher, D. (1988). *Taxonomies of the school library media program*. Englewood, CO: Libraries Unlimited.

Marzano, R. (1992). A rationale and framework for teaching thinking tactics. In J. Keefe & H. Walberg (Eds.), *Teaching for thinking* (pp. 15–25). Reston, VA: National Association of Secondary School Principals.

Miller, R. & Spanjer, A. (1985). The library media specialist as change maker: Implications from research. In S. Aaron & P. Scales (Eds.), *School library media annual: Volume 3* (pp. 323–335). Littleton, CO: Libraries Unlimited.

Oklahoma State Department of Education. (1987). *Suggested learner outcomes grades K–12*. Oklahoma City: Oklahoma State Department of Education.

Oregon Department of Education. (1987). *Library information skills guide for Oregon schools K–12*. Salem: Oregon Department of Education.

Rosenshine, B. & Guenther, J. (1992). Using scaffolds for teaching higher level cognitive strategies. In J. Keefe & H. Walberg (Eds.), *Teaching for thinking* (pp. 35–47). Reston, VA: National Association of Secondary School Principals.

Rosenshine, B. & Meister, C. (1992). The use of scaffolds for teaching higher-level cognitive strategies. *Educational Leadership, 49(7)*, 26–33.

Stripling, B. & Pitts, J. (1988). *Brainstorms and blueprints: Teaching library research as a thinking process*. Englewood, CO: Libraries Unlimited.

Swindle, D. & Craft, A. (1987). *A process approach to curriculum-based research skills instruction: Developing a Gwinnett County K–5 research continuum*. Unpublished education specialist study, Georgia State University.

Tabberer, R. (1987). *Study and information skills in schools*. (British Library R & D report 5870.) Philadelphia: NFER–Nelson.

Teger, N. (1992). CD-ROM: Meeting educational challenges. *Media & Methods, 28(4)*, 26–28.

Tenopir, C. & Neufang, R. (1992). The impact of electronic reference on reference librarians. *Online, 16(3)*, 54–60.

Walisser, S. (1990). Developing a school-based research strategy, K–7. In K. Haycock (Ed.), *The school library program in the curriculum* (pp. 93–100). Englewood, CO: Libraries Unlimited.

Washington Library Media Association. (1987). *Information skills curriculum guide: Process, scope, and sequence*. Olympia, WA: Superintendent of Public Instruction.

Wilson, B. & Cole, P. (1991). A review of cognitive teaching models. *Educational Technology Research and Development, 39(4)*, 47–64.

CHAPTER NINE

Teacher-Librarians:
Mirror Images and the Spark

Jean Brown and Bruce Sheppard

The demands placed on schools today are intensified by globalization, declining resources, greater calls for accountability, and the impact of information technology. The roles of teachers and administrators are in transition, as all must be leaders and effective users of information technology. Like other teachers and educational leaders, teacher-librarians also need to be leaders in this new environment, and they must develop a specialized expertise to facilitate organizational learning within their schools by placing a priority on staff development and school-wide improvement initiatives. The research reported here will show how some principals, teachers and teacher-librarians are facing this challenge.

For the past three years we have been building a research program investigating leadership for change in schools and districts. Working within the conceptual framework of the Senge learning organization, we have been engaged in four different but related studies.

Study One, now in its second year, is a five year study. It began with eight schools, 139 teachers,

and 2,623 students from one school district in Newfoundland, but it has since been extended to include a total of four districts, 12 schools, 254 teachers, and 4,566 students. The 12 schools are located in both rural and urban centers and range in size from 50 to 870 students.

Study Two is a case study of two large secondary schools, in two different school districts. Both have been recognized provincially and nationally for outstanding leadership in dealing with change. Both schools have business partners, and both are involved with implementing leading edge technology throughout the curriculum. In both these studies, data were collected using survey instruments, interviews, document analysis (curriculum documents, departmental guidelines and policy documents, school profile information, committee papers and records), observations and teacher journals.

Study Three was conducted in seven schools from Study One and one of the schools in Study Two, and focused on the role of and expectations for the teacher-librarian. The schools were visited and interviews were conducted with the principal and the teacher-librarians in each school during November, 1996 and January, 1997. As part of the interview, each person was asked to sketch a diagram illustrating how leadership occurred in his or her school.

Study Four (in which we are two of four investigators) focused on research for a special project on school improvement for the Newfoundland Department of Education (1995–1997). Qualitative data for this latter study were collected in eight districts and 19 schools, while insights were also gained from survey data obtained from 19 districts, 155 principals, 279 teachers, 223 parents, and 69 students.

Our data for this paper draws on the holistic view of school leadership which we have formed from Studies One, Two, and Three. It also is informed by the findings from Study Four. Our analysis followed the steps outlined by Woods (1986). These are: 1. speculative analysis consisting of "tentative reflection, perhaps revealing major insights, that is done throughout the data collection" (p. 121); 2. classifying and categorizing, or the creation of major categories within the data; 3. concept formation, which Woods sees as involving the creation of models, typographies and theory. We see this as the beginning of theory development regarding teacher-librarianship in schools as learning organizations.

Teacher-Librarians as Mirror-Images of Teachers and Mirror-Images Plus

Our findings confirm the validity of what Fullan (1993) describes as the "new work of the teacher." In this "new work" teachers must: have a moral purpose—making a difference in the lives of children; have a deepened knowledge of pedagogy; recognize the links between their work and societal development; have purpose and vision and be "highly interactive and collaborative"; be able to work in new structures (teams of teachers, networks of learning); be lifelong learners; and be change agents (see Table 9.1).

All staff (administrators, teachers and teacher-librarians) in the schools in our studies are driven by a moral commitment to help students. Their talk and interests reveal their practice of and interest in pedagogy. They are knowledgeable of the changing economic times, the movement towards a new post-industrial society, and the impact that has on the skills and knowledge students need. Although individuals emerge as strong leaders in their own right, they are also aware of the need for staffs to work together, of the expectation for partnerships with parents, community members and other professionals. For example, in one district (in Study One), 54 percent of the 122 staff members in seven schools identified the whole staff as providing leadership for school improvement.

Table 9.1   The New Work of the Teacher and the Teacher-Librarian

Teacher and Teacher-Librarian: Mirror Images of Each Other	Teacher-Librarian: Mirror Image Plus
The new work of the teacher (Fullan, 1993) □ Be committed to a moral purpose—making a difference in the lives of children □ Deepen their knowledge of pedagogy □ Be cognizant of the links between their moral purpose and educational policy and societal development □ Be their own person vis-à-vis purpose and vision, and at the same time be highly interactive and collaborative □ Work in new structures—clusters of students, teams of teachers, common planning time, links to home and community, participate in wider networks of learning □ Develop the habits and skills of continuous inquiry and learning □ Immerse themselves in the change process (pp. 80–81)	*The new work of the teacher-librarian* □ Design training programs as needed, for groups and individuals, students, teachers and others □ Assume a leadership role in school improvement and staff development □ Be a model of lifelong, independent learning □ Create a learning environment that fosters the new work of the teacher

Although all those we surveyed and interviewed were highly qualified as teachers, they realized that they needed to be lifelong learners if they were to meet the needs of their students. Teacher-librarians were mirror-images of teachers, in that they exhibited the same characteristics as the teachers. In fact, in the research it was difficult to distinguish the unique role of the teacher-librarian. Instead of a sharp division between the roles of the teacher and the teacher-librarian, we found an overlap. Table 9.2, which provides examples of the qualifications and work assignments of the teacher-librarians studied, readily reveals this overlap in roles. For example, all four of the teacher-librarians in Table 9.2 have extensive experience as classroom teachers, and three are currently assigned classroom teaching responsibilities in addition to their role as teacher-librarian.

This paper focuses on two major findings of our studies. The first is that, within schools as learning organizations, teacher-librarians must not only possess the expertise required of teacher-librarians, but they must also be mirror-images of other teachers if they are to have credibility with them. The discussion of this finding is developed through an analysis of four categories of essential characteristics of the work performed by both teachers and teacher-librarians. These are: knowledge base; technical skills; personal, interpersonal and team skills; and values and beliefs (see Table 9.3). The second finding is that principals are extremely influential in school-wide leadership, and teacher-librarians will only have credibility with them if they are mirror-images of teachers. Without that credibility, they cannot successfully perform their specialist role—that of the mirror-images plus.

Table 9.2   Teacher-Librarians: Examples of Qualifications and Work Assignments

Sue

She is a full-time teacher-librarian, in her 20th year of teaching, in an urban school which has a French Immersion stream. She is responsible also for the school's computer lab which adjoins the learning resource center. She has a Bachelor of Music degree and a B.Ed. (Elementary Education). In addition, she has completed the undergraduate Diploma in School Resource Services. She is bilingual, and provides all services in English and French. She is self-taught in computers, and although she does not see herself as having an aptitude for the technical side of computers, she has learned to install software and be the main troubleshooter for technical problems in the school.

Ruth

Over 20 years teaching experience. Currently teaching in a rural school. Her teaching assignment for the current year is: 25 percent teacher-librarian, 50 percent kindergarten, 25 percent grade six classroom teacher. She has a B.Ed degree in primary education, a second B.Ed degree in special education, and has completed six of the ten courses for her undergraduate Diploma in School Resource Services. Although she has not completed formal courses in computers in education, she is self-taught with a computer with Internet access at home. She shares responsibility with another teacher for the school's computer facilities.

May

Fifteen years teaching experience as a high school teacher, twelve of which was as a guidance counselor. Currently she is one of two full-time teacher-librarians in an urban secondary school which is on the leading edge of technology. She has a B.Ed, a M.Ed. in School Counseling, and a second M.Ed. in Learning Resources (teacher-librarianship). She and the second teacher-librarian work as a team and are responsible for a compulsory language course which focuses on the research process, taken in the second year of high school (equivalent of grade eleven). This course ensures that all students are taught research skills in a curricular context, including the skills of Internet searching for information. Of her role in a dynamic learning environment, she stated, "I couldn't tell you what my role is because it changes every day." She sees herself as a lifelong learner and commented: "I have never felt so ignorant and yet I never felt so accomplished in learning. I have never felt more of a problem solver than since I have taken this [job] on." She concluded: "You can never master it [all the skills you need as a teacher-librarian]; you are only going to evolve to the next level. You are not going to master everything."

Jim

A high school science teacher with 16 years experience, Jim is currently in his first year as a teacher-librarian. Jim has completed all course requirements for his M.Ed in School Resource Services except for his final project (which is near completion). Jim has developed considerable expertise in cooperative learning and is a school leader in working collaboratively with others using cooperative learning strategies. He became interested in becoming a teacher-librarian after working cooperatively with the school's teacher-librarian. Although he has assumed a major role in teaching colleagues to use new technology in the classroom, and is responsible for much of the school's computer resources, he admits that "I am mainly self-taught." He adds, however, that "I want to know it" and that has motivated him to keep ahead of the technology.

Knowledge Base and Technical Skills (Resource-Based Learning)

As can be seen from Table 9.3, two major areas of the work of teachers and teacher-librarians, the knowledge base and technical skills, are grounded in resource-based learning. It is apparent in all schools in our studies that this resource-based learning philosophy is desirable and endorsed in current curriculum documents and guidelines from the provincial Department of Education. The definition of resource-based learning in this context is based on the one from *Learning to learn* (Newfoundland Department of Education, 1991). It is a broad philosophical approach to learning which (a) actively involves the student in the center of all learning activities, (b) is dependent on the articulation of process and content objectives, and (c) requires deliberate teacher planning so that multiple resources and varied teaching strategies are incorporated in all plans. Inherent in this definition is an understanding of child development and learning theory, knowledge of the curriculum and instructional development, and a repertoire of instructional strategies which will allow the teacher to design instruction to meet the needs of learners. Since the focus is on the use of a wide range of resources, all teachers are expected to be familiar with the learning resources appropriate for their grade levels and subject areas. Although resource-based learning does not necessarily require collaborative work, our work on schools as learning organizations reveals that the best work occurs when there is collaborative planning and when teachers engage in planning and teaching together. This is consistent with Fullan's findings regarding "the new work of the teacher" (Table 9.1), which requires teachers to be highly interactive and collaborative.

To be successful, teacher-librarians must be mirror-images of the teachers described above, or, in other words, have credibility as a teacher committed to a resource-based learning philosophy and competent in all aspects of implementing such a program. Currently, all teachers and school administrators (not only the teacher-librarian) are expected to keep up to date and integrate new ideas (including new information

technologies) into instruction. On the "plus" side, however, teacher-librarians need to be knowledgeable about recent research and developments in teacher-librarianship, have advanced skills in instructional development and information technology, and in accessing information and learning resources. They also need an understanding of staff development and adult learning and training so that they can be school leaders in providing training to their colleagues in this area.

However, teacher-librarians need to be sensitive to the priorities and skills of their mirror-images (other teachers) and the school administration. Principals and teachers don't need to be persuaded that students need to be taught how to access and effectively use information that is available in many formats, from the World Wide Web to traditional print sources. Neither do they need to be convinced that resource-based learning, with its emphasis on the student being actively involved, is appropriate and preferred in today's schools. In our research on classroom practices, 146 teachers in seven schools across four districts were asked to indicate the extent to which (rare, occasionally, frequently) they employed resource-based learning in their teaching. In their responses, 79 percent responded that they employed it frequently (the range was 54 percent in one school to 100 percent in another).

For anyone to assume the role of "expert" and approach administrators or teachers with the intent of persuading them to adopt such priorities would be ill-advised since the underlying assumptions of ignorance would be quite rightfully resented. Yet, it is true that neither resource-based learning nor the teaching of the necessary information skills are found in all classrooms. The problem is that school staffs have few images of successful implementation. For example, teachers want professional development in how to integrate computer technology, particularly new information technology, into their classroom practices. In Study Four, the provincial study of school improvement, of all initiatives that promoted school improvement, technology was noted as the most significant by all respondents (administrators in schools and district offices, teachers, students, department of education personnel).

Table 9.3   Mirror Images and Mirror Images Plus of the Work of the Teacher and Teacher-Librarian

Teacher and Teacher-Librarian: Mirror Images of Each Other	Teacher-Librarian: Mirror Images Plus
Knowledge Base *(Resource-Based Learning)*	
□ The practice of pedagogy	□ National & Provincial Standards and Guidelines for Teacher-Librarianship
□ Instructional strategies	
□ Child development	□ Advanced training in instructional development
□ Learning theory	□ The teaching of independent learning skills
□ Instructional development	□ Access to information/Information networks
□ Curriculum knowledge (Theory and Practice)	□ Validation of appropriate learning resources to meet learning objectives
□ Learning resources—access and use	
□ Children's literature (Primary/Elementary)	□ Broad range of instructional strategies
□ Educational change process	□ General overview of the school-wide curriculum and grade levels
□ Interactive professionalism	
□ Action research	□ Leadership and change theory
⊔ Leadership (not management)	□ Staff development and adult learning principles
□ School and society	
	"Credibility as a good teacher plus added value as a teacher-librarian"
"Model of good teaching practices"	
Technical Skills *(Resource-Based Learning)*	
□ Use of appropriate technology (including current and traditional technology and computer technology)	□ Trainer of technical skills
	□ Selection and operation of automated library systems, technical hardware and software
□ Up-to-date knowledge of current technologies	□ Advanced skills in information technology
□ Library user and basic technical skills	□ Awareness of emerging technologies
	□ Operation of a learning resources center
"Integrating current technology in the curriculum"	
	"Learn it—then give it away and move on!"
Personal, Interpersonal and Team Skills	
□ Likes working with kids	□ Risk taker
□ Leadership skills	□ Group facilitator and trainer
⊓ Collaborative team player	□ Instructional leader
□ Flexible and open to ideas of others	□ Creator of a collaborative culture
□ Pleasant, friendly personality	□ High tolerance for change & innovation
□ Assertive but not threatening	□ Entrepreneurial/business skills
□ Approachable and collegial	□ Advanced presentation skills
□ Coach and peer tutor	□ Transformational leader/leader as servant
□ Good communicator	□ Delegation and time management skills
□ Good presentation skills	□ Management skills
"A spark in the eye for kids and teaching"	*"A spark in the eye for independent lifelong learning"*
Values and Beliefs	
□ Equality of educational opportunity	□ The value of the research process and systematic instruction integrated into curriculum for all
□ Moral commitment to improving children's learning experiences and meeting students' needs	□ The right of all students to be taught to access, retrieve and use information technology
□ Resource-based learning philosophy	
□ Commitment to collaborative school cultures	□ Commitment to independent, lifelong learning
□ A love of learning and the value of education	□ A commitment to the intellectual and physical access to information for all
"Preparing students for a new age"	*"Building a fire truck as opposed to putting out fires"*

Teachers and principals need to observe and be engaged in concrete examples of such integration. For example, teachers generally agree that students should have access to the Internet, that skills surrounding such use should be integrated into the curriculum, but they need to see what it looks like in practice. That is why the image of Ruth (one of the teacher-librarians in Table 9.2) introducing third grade students in a rural and remote school to a whale expert, located hundreds of miles away at the provincial university, through the use of a computer network, is a powerful example of how technology can be integrated into a science unit:

> We got Dr. John Lien online one day on Stem-net [school computer network] and we brought all the grade three students to the computer laboratory and everyone posed a question to him...they were there when I typed it in...he responded to every student so when it came in I took off a hard copy for everybody; he also sent everybody a new resource information booklet on the whale they had asked information on...they were tickled to death.

This example demonstrates that knowing that there is information on the Web about whales is quite a different matter from developing a unit for third grade students which will integrate such information into meaningful instruction. The online interaction with the whale expert was carefully researched and planned, and there was total curriculum integration and follow-up.

Although, in the schools we studied, we were told that the greatest needs for professional development was integration of new information technology in the curriculum, it was clear that school staffs also need examples of how the teacher-librarian can be directly engaged in other forms of resource-based learning. For example, one principal admitted that he had an incorrect perception of the role of a teacher-librarian, that he saw the role as clerical and managerial, until he was "trained" by the teacher-librarian who joined his staff, that through her actions he realized what the role ought to be:

> I walked in and saw the goals and objectives of the unit were all set up and there were two or three teachers working together and the students in about five or six different centers and every day they would just rotate. And I said, "Hey, this is working...you can see learning here."

If teacher-librarians are to survive, we were told, this is where there is a need to show the value of their contributions. They have to show that their work is directly or indirectly related to students' learning outcomes. They may be working with other teachers in the implementation of large, ambitious resource-based units, but, we were also told, this method of connecting the teaching of the skills and the curriculum creates problems. First, the units are too time-consuming, and even worse, they can be intimidating for some teachers who are not involved in them. We were told of cases where the school's learning resources center and the time of the teacher-librarian was completely scheduled for implementing such units, and the only contact between the teacher-librarian and the classroom for the school year was limited to this intensive three or four week unit. Our understanding of changing school leadership, the needs of students and teachers, and the role of the teacher-librarian has convinced us of the seriousness of this situation. Even a teacher-librarian like Ruth (Table 9.2), trained in, committed to, and successful with this model, admitted that she has stopped developing new units and has chosen instead to work directly with classroom teachers to integrate skills into the classroom instruction on a day-by-day basis (such as in the whale unit reported above). Instead of working in the larger units, more time is being spent supporting teachers and providing the professional support so that the total integration of skills throughout the school can take place. One teacher-librarian saw the task as "building a fire truck as opposed to putting out the fire," and that the aim was to share expertise with the classroom teachers, so that, in some respects, "every single teacher in the school is becoming a learning resources teacher." This teacher-librarian has made staff training and development a priority. His school was a national leader in piloting new information technology throughout the curriculum, and most classroom teachers were using computers in their classrooms. As he explained, his role is to learn the new ways of accessing resources, and then train teachers so that they are comfortable using them in the classroom. The teacher-librarian is then free to investigate other emerging technologies which can help teachers teach and students learn. At the time of the interview, this particular teacher-librarian was just beginning to investigate the potential of satellite technology in the senior level geography course. Questions he was considering included: Was satellite technology available to the school? What would it cost? What hardware and software would it require? Would it help the teachers in the social studies department better meet the objectives of the geography course? Further along was the work with a group of teachers on the use of Java software and the development of a multimedia laboratory.

It is through total curriculum integration that students will learn the skills they need, and it is to that end that teacher-librarians must work. This will mean a greater emphasis on their role as staff developers and trainers.

Personal, Interpersonal and Team Skills

The "new work of the teacher" requires all teachers to have strong interpersonal and team skills. They are expected to relate well to students, to be collaborative team players, to be flexible and open to new ideas. Principals want teachers with friendly and pleasant personalities, who are approachable and collegial. Current curriculum guidelines stress that teachers be facilitators rather than lecturers, that they be strong communicators and school leaders. This is the mirror-image that all teacher-librarians are expected to have. However, as one principal observed, teacher-librarians are expected to have that, and also the "plus":

> A learning resource teacher has to be a good teacher. Do they have to have something above the regular teacher? Well, if I'm a regular classroom teacher and I'm responsible for 150 students that come in my classroom during the year, all I

have to do is deliver a good program to them so that they get their money's worth. [But] if you are a learning resource teacher, you have to be able to do that and you also have to be able to work with 25 other professionals.

As difficult as it may be for some to accept, principals, when looking for a teacher-librarian, place much more emphasis on personal, interpersonal and team skills than they do on specialized knowledge or technical skills. One principal commented:

> We all have knowledge of the library, we've all used books all our lives and in our training, so that's the narrow-based part. It is the leadership and drive you have that makes the library program work or not. I've had people know about the resources but if they can't make people and the children want to go there, then they're useless to me.

Teacher-librarians themselves saw this area as critical for success. One observed that he worked with other teachers 100 percent of his time. Another commented:

> I have to be approachable; I have to be flexible enough to drop whatever I am doing and listen to somebody; I have to be a good listener. You have to be a super communicator…and test the waters before you change things…You also have to be well organized with your time because it gets busy.

One teacher-librarian related that the need for interpersonal skills is even greater when it involves training teachers to use new information technology:

> If you don't have these skills, your job will become very uncomfortable…. We are talking [about] training teachers to do things which they never had to do and for the most part they are scared to death of it, and you just have to make them feel so comfortable in doing these new things…Skills in getting along with people is what will help you to train these people. The team effort is what will keep you from going insane.

Teacher-librarians need to understand people (whether teachers or students) and know how to treat them differently depending on their personality:

You can't approach every one...the same way...Some...you have to joke along with...others...You have to feel it out...and get a sense of what's the best way to approach them so they are going to be most comfortable...

Personal attributes of the teacher-librarian also set them apart from their mirror-images. In the interview with one teacher-librarian, it was observed that teacher-librarians need to be risk-takers. It was observed that living life on the edge of new and emerging technologies meant that there was a need to take chances; occasionally you will fall, and "if you fall, you have to jump up and go for it," but you don't give up. Classroom teachers may have a choice in the level of involvement they have in leading edge information technology. The teacher-librarian does not. The position itself requires a commitment to lifelong learning, to constantly upgrading one's skills, to keeping current. Teacher-librarians, therefore, as mirror-images plus, must exhibit a high tolerance for change and innovation.

Values and Beliefs

Teacher-librarians, first and foremost, are teachers. This was apparent in an examination of the values and beliefs they held. As teachers, the most deeply held values are connected to the work of helping children learn. We found that there is no distinction between teachers and teacher-librarians in their primary motivation in teaching—the love of children—illustrated by this comment made by Ruth (Table 9.2), a primary teacher-librarian who responded to the love and trust of small children, and the joy of helping them learn:

We were doing an activity today and a little boy, it was the first day he wrote down a sentence by himself. Well that made my day! He was so excited and pleased with his work. It's just this kind of everyday thing that I value.

This caring for students exists, but in different manner, in high schools as well, as revealed in this comment from Jim, a high school teacher-librarian (Table 9.2):

I believe in people, and helping people. I believe in showing them the way and holding their hand until they get so far and then letting them go. There is an extreme satisfaction already in this position from watching somebody light up when they see the information they are looking for.

Teacher-librarians like Ruth and Jim have a moral commitment to improving children's learning opportunities and they tend to be passionate in their belief in equality of educational opportunity. In this, teacher-librarians are mirror-images of teachers.

Principals recognize and appreciate this unique contribution of values and beliefs, and it is reflected in their view of what makes a good teacher-librarian—a combination of being a good teacher (the mirror-image of all good teachers on staff) and someone who provides the extra (the mirror-image plus). It is what one principal referred to as "the spark in the eye." One principal combines love for children and knowledge of technology as the primary characteristics of teacher-librarians:

The most important thing for a teacher-librarian is to like kids. That is the first step. The next thing is to have the latest technical skills to turn a kid on. Teaching isn't what it was like 20 years ago...they should be committed to their job, committed to kids, they must be willing to go the extra mile.

More and more teachers are able to meet this expectation as they become comfortable in using modern technology. Teacher-librarians need to reflect this mirror-image and also bring essential values and beliefs to their roles.

To value the love of lifelong learning for oneself and others, and to hold a passionate belief in providing equal opportunity for all in this quest, is the "mirror-image" of values and beliefs held by teachers and teacher-librarians. However, creating a collaborative learning environment, commitment to independent lifelong learning, and commitment to "building the fire truck as opposed to putting out fires," that is the real "plus" of the teacher-librarian.

The Importance of the Mirror-Image in Gaining the Principal's Support

In the four studies used in our analysis, we found school principals to be extremely influential as educational leaders. In fact, the main problem that the teacher-librarian encountered was lack of credibility as a high school teacher (the mirror-image of the other high school teachers). This was based mainly on the fact that her initial teacher training was in elementary education (so she was not expected to be a good secondary teacher) and she also made it clear to everyone, including the principal, that her experience and preference was in elementary school teaching. To command the respect and the support of the principal, this teacher-librarian needs to do two things: first, show that she is capable of teaching high school students; and second, that she has the competencies that the principal wants.

The importance of credibility as a teacher was reinforced in observations and data from other schools as well. Another teacher-librarian, who is a full time teacher-librarian shared between an elementary and a junior high school, is trained as a secondary teacher with most of his experience in the junior high grades. He is an acknowledged leader in his school district (described as "one of the best" by an assistant superintendent) and running successful programs in both schools. Yet, even he reflected on the problem of establishing credibility in the elementary school. He attributed his success at the junior high school partially to his training and background experience:

> I came into this as a junior high school teacher where I knew the curriculum well and I could make connections where even people in the subject areas never saw them.

He has progressed in this school to the stage where teachers initiate activities with him and there is joint planning and teaching. However, in the elementary schools, it has been a greater struggle to obtain the same degree of acceptance with teachers:

> There is more reticence. I don't know if it was because I was a junior high school teacher, and they knew it. I certainly had to take some time to get to know the curriculum, to figure out how elementary school worked and how people worked together.

He concluded that the elementary school and the junior high school are "two distinctly different cultures," and that as a teacher-librarian he needed to become part of both.

Teachers (including teacher-librarians) and principals can and do move from the levels where they were initially trained and become teachers or administrators at other levels. However, they all have to prove themselves as teachers within the particular school setting in which they are working before they can hope to establish credibility and contribute in a mirror-images plus role. Successful movement across different levels of the school system requires what the teacher-librarian above did: taking time to understand the school, its curriculum, and its special needs. Only then can teacher-librarians have the credibility that will allow them to assume a leadership role and influence what is happening in schools. Their relationship with the principal must be built on an understanding of the importance of credibility. Only if the teacher-librarian is perceived to be credible by colleagues in the school will he or she receive the support of the school principal. Without that credibility and support, as one principal commented, "The teacher-librarian is dead in the water!"

Conclusion

Teacher-librarians in a learning organization must function both as members of teams engaged in organizational learning and as leaders of leaders. Images of how to do this are lacking since schools are currently involved in a major paradigm shift in perceptions of school leadership and teachers' work. The images that we have developed from our research are based on teacher-librarians as mirror-images of other teachers and, as well, contributing to the school as a learning organization by being mirror-images plus. In examining the characteristics of the work of teachers and teacher-librarians, we used four major categories: knowledge base; technical skills; personal, interpersonal, and team skills; and values and beliefs. The knowledge base and technical skills provide new mental models for all teachers. The acceptance of resource-based learning, with its emphasis on lifelong learning is consistent with personal mastery, a key discipline of the learning organization. New information technology also challenges the mental models of all teachers. Our research clearly indicates that teacher-librarians should lead this endeavor. If they are to assume this leadership role, however, they will have to remain on the cutting edge and must be exemplars of personal mastery. In addition, they will need strong personal, interpersonal, and team skills, if they are to engage in and lead the team learning required in a learning school. They will succeed in meeting this challenge only if they are motivated by deeply held values and beliefs regarding the development of a shared vision, one that includes the right of all to develop a love of lifelong learning and the skills to make that possible. This right extends not only to students but also to their teachers, for teacher-librarians must increasingly assume a leadership role in staff development and training.

Our findings suggest that if teacher-librarians are to successfully fulfill this role, they must have the credibility that comes from being the mirror-image of other teachers. Only then will they be able to contribute in their "plus" role of the mirror-images plus. Teacher-librarians also need the mirror-image of other teachers in order to gain the respect and support of the school's most influential leader, the principal. Teacher-librarians who recognize their role as a mirror-images of other teachers and as mirror-images plus, and who recognize the need to work with the principal and others toward meeting the needs of students, are beginning to think systematically. We contend that those teacher-librarians who are able to function in this manner are poised to be "pioneering voyagers, reshaping library information centers by engaging future technologies with critical expertise and imaginative joy."

References

Fullan, M. (1993). *Change forces: Probing the depths of educational reform.* New York: Falmer Press.

Newfoundland Department of Education. (1991). *Learning to learn: Policy and guidelines for the implementation of resource-based learning.* St. John's: Queen's Printer.

Woods, P. (1986). *Inside schools: Ethnography in educational research.* London: Routledge and Kegan Paul.

CHAPTER TEN

Students' Information Literacy Needs: Competencies for Teacher-Librarians in the Twenty-First Century

*Association for Teacher-librarianship in Canada
and the Canadian School Library Association*

Students in Canada today need to be able to think rationally and logically. With more and more sources of information, both print and electronic, and the increasing difficulty of ensuring that students can derive meaning from this information, the role of the teacher-librarian becomes central. Teacher-librarians are skilled in accessing and evaluating information regardless of delivery system, book or computer, and providing leadership in the appropriate use of newer information technologies.

There is a significant body of research that demonstrates that a qualified teacher-librarian has a positive impact on school culture and student achievement. Indeed, several studies have established that teachers collaborate more in schools with a teacher-librarian and students read more, enjoy reading more, write better, access and use information more effectively and excel in academic content areas. This does not happen by chance, however.

In these schools information literacy is incorporated into school and classrooms programs because:

- the program is recognized as a partnership of the principal, teacher and teacher-librarian, supported by the school district and community;

- the district insists on flexible scheduling (the teacher-librarian is not the preparation time or "relief" for classroom colleagues);

- the principal encourages collaboration and team teaching through this flexible schedule;

- teachers acknowledge that the processing and use of information is a school-wide concern, for integration with classroom content instruction;

- the teacher-librarian takes the initiative, places a priority on cooperative program planning and teaching with colleagues and encourages team planning.

The teacher-librarian is a highly skilled teacher, with competencies provided by a combination of teacher education, classroom experience and courses in teacher-librarianship and information studies. The teacher-librarian should be in the forefront of curriculum and staff development, familiar with the full range of instructional strategies and learning styles, able to organize time and resources, and active in professional concerns within the school and the district.

In approving this document, school boards, agencies and professional associations affirm the research evidence that indicates that integrated library programs impact positively on collaboration, leadership and student achievement when the teacher-librarian has experience as a classroom teacher, qualifications in teacher-librarianship and information studies and learning resources management, preferably at the graduate level, and works collaboratively with teachers in flexibly scheduled programs to integrate information problem-solving skills and strategies in the ongoing instructional program.

The Competent Teacher-Librarian

The competent teacher-librarian is committed to

- the principles outlined in the Student's Bill of Information Rights;
- implementing curriculum with colleagues;
- initiating collaboratively planned and taught programs to integrate information literacy in the context of the curriculum; and
- the effective use of information technologies.

Professional competencies relate to the teacher-librarian's knowledge and skill in the areas of collaboration and leadership, curriculum and instruction, collaborative program planning and teaching, information resources, information access, technology, management and research, and the ability to apply these abilities as a basis for providing library and information services.

Personal competencies represent a set of skills, attitudes and values that enable teacher-librarians to work efficiently and effectively, be good communicators, focus on continuing learning throughout their careers, demonstrate the value-added nature of their contributions and thrive in the new world of education.

The following sections highlight the major professional and personal competencies of teacher-librarians and provide practical examples of the multitude of roles and tasks that teacher-librarians can perform. The examples are illustrative and are tempered by critical factors such as the nature of school leadership and culture, the climate for collaboration and innovation in the work environment, flexible scheduling, the time allocation of professional and support staff and the specific education and training of the teacher-librarian to do the job.

Professional Competencies

The teacher-librarian:

1.1.   places a priority on staff relationships and leadership in the implementation of change.

Examples: Establishes rapport with school staff, students and the community. Develops a collaborative approach with the principal, teachers and other staff. Provides an environment conducive to learning. Keeps abreast of and communicates developments in curriculum, instructional strategies, and newer information technologies. Participates in the school's governance by serving on advisory and decision-making bodies.

1.2.   provides leadership in collaborative program planning and teaching to ensure both physical and intellectual access to information and commitment to voluntary reading.

Examples: Advocates the integration of information skills and strategies in classroom programs through collaborative program planning and team teaching with colleagues. Develops with teachers a coordinated approach to information literacy, including decision-making, problem-solving and research strategies, integrated with classroom instruction. Understands and distinguishes between physical and intellectual access to information. Provides leadership for reading and research programs, incorporating both informational and imaginative literature. Plans and teaches with teachers from establishing objectives through to student assessment and unit evaluation.

1.3.   knows curriculum programs mandated by the province, district and school.

Examples: Is aware of new curricula and implications for implementation. Provides support for teachers through training and implementation. Understands the appropriate integration of resources and technologies with specific curriculum areas. Promotes congruence of stated learning outcomes, delivered curriculum, assessment and supporting resources and technologies.

1.4.   understands students and their social, emotional, and intellectual needs.

Examples: Understands child and adolescent growth and development for the age levels of the school. Can relate to student needs and interests. Works with teachers and others to match resources to a variety of learning styles and requirements and to adapt the curriculum and program for students with special needs.

1.5.   has expert knowledge in evaluating learning resources in different formats and media, both on-site and remote, to support the instructional program.

Examples: Works within written school and district policies on the selection of learning resources and their appropriate use. Works within a written school policy on the purchase and management of all school resources and their access. Evaluates print, CD-ROM and online versions of databases. Selects the best books, journals, nonprint and electronic resources for specific curriculum areas and specific learning outcomes using authoritative selection "tools." Organizes teacher involvement in evaluation. Compiles guides to resources both on- and off-site. Develops and manages a collection of quality materials that reflect resource-based units of study.

1.6.   develops and promotes the effective use of informational and imaginative resources in all formats through cooperative professional activities.

Examples: Promotes voluntary reading throughout the school. Develops themes and celebrations that reflect the school's curriculum and unique community. Designs and produces materials for specific instructional purposes, where commercial materials are not available. Assists students and teachers in the effective use of resources and technologies.

1.7.   provides appropriate information, resources or instruction to satisfy the needs of individuals and groups.

Examples: Recommends learning resources for specific learning outcomes. Works with individuals and groups to identify problems, frame questions, check authority, evaluate information and develop critical thinking. Provides guidance on accessing information appropriate to the specific need. Understands the design and structure of bibliographic and other databases. Conducts searches from complex or difficult sources. Answers questions using on-site and remote resources. Assists students and teachers with using authoring tools in print, electronic and multimedia formats. Supports colleagues who are accessing information services from the classroom.

1.8.   uses appropriate information technology to acquire, organize and disseminate information.

Examples: Establishes, maintains and teaches the use of an online catalog of the library collection. Works on information management teams to select appropriate software, hardware and security for desktop access. Contributes to a home page for the World Wide Web for the school. Links the library page to other relevant curriculum sites. Informs school community of copyright issues. Keeps up-to-date with new products and modes of information delivery. Plans and participates in the development and provision of information networks.

1.9.   manages library programs, services and staff to support the stated educational goals of the school.

Examples: Develops an integrated library program linked to the curricular goals of the school. Develops procedures for the cost-effective selection, acquisition, organization, management and use of resources. Manages professional and support staff. Recruits, selects, trains and motivates volunteers. Manages space and equipment. Maintains an inventory of materials and equipment.

Plans and manages a budget which reflects the instructional program. Develops a marketing plan for specific audiences. Plans strategies for securing support for learning resource services in the school and community.

1.10.   evaluates program and services.

Examples: Actively seeks opportunities for improvement and strives for excellent programs and services. Involves school staff in program evaluation. Conducts regular needs assessments using research tools such as questionnaires, focus groups and interviews. Prepares oral and written reports on program development. Reports regularly and confers with the principal and staff on program implementation. Conducts research related to the solution of information management problems. Demonstrates how library and information services add value to the school. Refocuses programs and services on new needs.

Personal Competencies

The teacher-librarian:

2. 1.   is committed to program excellence.

Examples: Seeks feedback and uses it for continuous improvement. Celebrates own success and that of others. Takes pride in a job well done. Shares new knowledge with others at conferences and in the professional literature. Uses the research base of education and teacher-librarianship as a resource for improving services.

2.2.   seeks out challenges and sees new opportunities both inside and outside the library.

Examples: Takes on new roles in the school community that require an information leader. Uses library-based knowledge and skills to solve a variety of information problems. Expands the library collection beyond traditional media such as books and journals. Creates the "library without walls."

2.3.   sees the big picture.

Examples: Recognizes that information seeking and use are part of the creative process for individuals. Sees the library and its information services as part of the bigger process of making informed decisions. Anticipates trends and proactively realigns library and information services to take advantage of them.

2.4.   looks for partnerships and alliances.

Examples: Provides leadership in information management. Forms partnerships with other libraries for resource sharing. Seeks alliances with vendors to improve products and services. Seeks alliances with researchers in education and library and information studies to conduct relevant studies.

2.5.   creates an environment of mutual respect and trust.

Examples: Knows own strengths and the complementary strengths of others. Is dependable. Values and acknowledges the contributions of others in a problem-solving environment.

2.6.   has effective communications skills.

Examples: Runs meetings effectively. Presents ideas clearly and enthusiastically both orally and in writing. Requests feedback on communications skills and uses it for self improvement.

2.7.   works well with others in a team.

Examples: Seeks out opportunities for team participation. Asks for mentoring from others when needed. Looks for ways to enhance personal performance.

2.8.   provides leadership.

Examples: Exercises leadership as a member of teams within the school and community. Seeks opportunities for leadership.

2.9.   plans, prioritizes and focuses on what is critical.

Examples: Recognizes that ongoing planning and time management are required. Reviews goals with administrators and colleagues on a regular basis.

2.10.   is committed to lifelong learning.

Examples: Advocates for a learning environment to encourage the contributions of staff members. Participates in professional associations.

2.11.   is flexible and positive in a time of continuing change.

Examples: Willing to take on different responsibilities and respond to changing needs. Maintains a positive attitude and helps others to do the same. Looks for solutions. Uses technology as an enabler.

Students' Bill of Information Rights

Our students face an information-rich future in which change will be one of the few constants of their life experience. Their ability to adapt and fulfill their individual potentials will require them to be lifelong learners and independent decision-makers.

We believe that all students should have the opportunity to:

- master the skills needed to access information in print, non-print and electronic sources;
- understand and master effective research processes and reporting skills;
- develop the ability to evaluate, extract, synthesize and utilize information from a variety of sources and media;
- utilize data and information to expand their own knowledge base;
- explore the creative use of information;
- develop an understanding of our Canadian cultural heritage and history, as well as cultures and histories of other societies;
- enhance their own self knowledge through developing a love of reading;
- explore the values and beliefs of others by reading world literature;
- think critically, and make decisions based on personal needs and values as well as upon factual evidence, and
- actively participate in decisions about their own learning.

Information is a vital component in the development of critical thought and independent decision-making, and, consequently, access to the ever-increasing body of available information is vital to the development of students' potentials.

We believe that all students should have the right to:

- access a wide range of print, non-print and electronic learning resources at an appropriate level;
- explore materials expressing a variety of opinions and perspectives, and
- freely choose reading, viewing and listening materials for recreational and study purposes.

Glossary of Terms

Teacher-librarian: A professional teacher with a minimum of two years of successful classroom experience and additional qualifications in the selection, management and utilization of learning resources, who manages the school library and works with other teachers to design and implement resource-based instructional programs.

School library: The instructional centre in a school that coordinates and provides on-site and off-site access to information, resources, services and programs that integrate information literacy, the intellectual access to information, with teachers, to develop independent learners who are effective users of information and ideas and committed to informed decision-making.

School library program: The collaboratively planned and taught units of study developed through the shared expertise and equal partnership of classroom teachers and teacher-librarians, based on the principles of resource-based learning and designed to achieve the educational goals of the school.

Support staff: Under the direction of a teacher-librarian, may include graduates of a post-secondary library technician program who organize and maintain the resources and equipment and provide reference and technical support services to teachers and students; clerical staff who provide support services in areas such as acquisition, circulation and processing of resources, and typing or word processing; adult and student volunteers.

Information literacy: The ability to: recognize the need for information to solve problems and develop ideas; pose important questions; use a variety of information gathering strategies; locate relevant and appropriate information; access information for quality, authority, accuracy and authenticity. Includes the abilities to use the practical and conceptual tools of information technology, to understand form, format, location and access methods, how information is situated and produced, research processes, and to format and publish in textual and multimedia formats and to adapt to emerging technologies.

Provincial Guidelines

Newfoundland and Labrador: *Learning to learn: Policies and guidelines for the implementation of resource-based learning in Newfoundland and Labrador schools.* Newfoundland and Labrador Department of Education, 1991.

Prince Edward Island: *School library policy for the province of Prince Edward Island.* Prince Edward Island Department of Education, 1989.

Nova Scotia: *Nova Scotia school libraries: Standards and practices.* Nova Scotia Teachers Union, 1987.

New Brunswick: *Standards and practices for New Brunswick school libraries.* New Brunswick Teachers Association Library Council, 1989.

Quebec: *Library resources in the schools: Pedagogical and organizational aspects.* Québec Ministère de l'Education, 1987.

Ontario: *Partners in action: The library resource centre in the school curriculum.* Ontario Ministry of Education, 1982. Also: *Information literacy and equitable access: A framework for change.* Ontario Ministry of Education, 1995.

Manitoba: *Resource-based learning: An educational model.* Manitoba Education and Training, 1994.

Saskatchewan: *Resource-based learning: Policies, guidelines and responsibilities for Saskatchewan learning resource centres.* Saskatchewan Education, 1988.

Alberta: *Focus on learning: An integrated program model for Alberta school libraries.* Alberta Education, 1985. Also: *Focus on research: A guide to developing student's research skills.* Alberta Education, 1990.

British Columbia: *Developing independent learners: The role of the school library resource centre.* British Columbia Ministry of Education, 1991.

Northwest Territories: *Guidelines for the development of school information centres.* Northwest Territories Education, 1990.

This document is based on prior work by the Association for Teacher-librarianship in Canada and the Canadian School Library Association, as well as the Special Libraries Association (Washington, DC).

Prepared by a joint committee of the Association for Teacher-librarianship in Canada (ATLC) and the Canadian School Library Association (CSLA)—Joan Harper (CSLA); Ken Haycock (ATLC/CSLA, Chair), Judith Kootte (CSLA); Pat Parungao (ATLC); with Liz Austrom—in consultation with provincial and national education groups and associations and a national response panel.

Research evidence has been reported in scholarly and professional journals and monographs in Australia, Canada, the United Kingdom and the United States.

PART FOUR

INFORMATION LITERACY

Teacher-librarians have evolved in their thinking about how students learn to learn and our role in that process based on considerable research and "best practice" in education and library and information studies. We've moved in terminology from "library skills" (whatever they were) to reference skills (using specific subject materials) to research and study skills (focusing on how to organize our work) to information skills and information strategies (to denote a broader conceptualization of teaching students how to access and make effective use of information) to information literacy (with greater attention to identifying the specific need for information, accessing and evaluating it, and deriving and making meaning from it).

These information processes have built on research about student information-seeking behaviors and incorporated subject area standards for problem-solving and decision-making. In order to make these processes more manageable they have occasionally been labeled according to the number of major functions required of the student, from nine steps, to the Big Six, to the essential three.

To a considerable extent these build on the work of Benjamin Bloom and of the British Library's Research and Development Unit twenty years ago.

Christina Doyle begins by defining information literacy in an information society and traces the recent development of the concept, noting that political and business figures alike have endorsed the need for better programs to teach effective information use. Dr. Doyle incorporates the impact of technology, educational reform and curriculum standards in her review, which originally appeared as an *ERIC Digest,* sponsored by the Center for Information and Technology at Syracuse University.

Next to a parent, television may well be a youngster's most persistent and influential teacher. Mary Megee reminds us that information comes to students most commonly through visual media and we ignore it at our peril. Media literacy moves up and down the educational priority list but if we are serious about information literacy we need to incorporate media literacy in our definitions and programs as well. Critical viewing skills are a core competency for citizens and students.

Doug Johnson adds technology to the mix by exploring student access to the Internet and reminds us that we can assure both physical access to information (getting the information on the screen or in hand) and intellectual access (making meaning from it) only by teachers and teacher-librarians working together. He provides a useful skills rubric developed in his school district as a model. Mary Ann Fitzgerald assists teacher-librarians in evaluating online information by pointing out the difficulties with Internet information and how to identify problem areas. There are many causes of Internet misinformation but there are also actions and theories that can be applied to correct them, from censorship (a non-solution) through teaching essential evaluation skills.

Coming to terms with the plethora of skills and strategies necessary for effective and productive users of information can be a daunting task for the teacher and teacher-librarian unless there is a clear process for their articulation and development. Carol-Ann Page provides one such approach through a school-based continuum, designed by teachers to guide their own school's teaching and learning program for information literacy. Sharon Straathof carries this further to a school-based research strategy, providing many examples of a school-wide approach developed with her colleagues. Doug Johnson and Michael Eisenberg bring these important papers into the current technological environment by showing how computer literacy and information literacy work together and support information problem-solving.

"All that glitters may not be gold," however, and David Loertscher points out how programs can operate at a lower level of thinking; he encourages a thoughtful approach to curriculum work with deep reading and deep thinking around significant issues and problems. Teaching information skills and strategies in a planned, purposeful, integrated way can still be insignificant, however, unless the process assists students to learn and to think by engaging their minds and by applying their learning to real problems.

CHAPTER ELEVEN

Information Literacy in an Information Society

Christina Doyle

Information literacy is the ability to access, evaluate and use information from a variety of sources. As students prepare for the twenty-first century, traditional instruction in reading, writing and mathematics needs to be coupled with practice in communication, critical thinking and problem-solving skills (Costa, 1985).

Definition

An information-literate person is one who:
- recognizes that accurate and complete information is the basis for intelligent decision making;
- recognizes the need for information;
- formulates questions based on information needs;
- identifies potential sources of information;
- develops successful search strategies;
- accesses sources of information including computer-based and other technologies;
- evaluates information;
- organizes information for practical application;
- integrates new information into an existing body of knowledge;
- uses information in critical thinking and problem solving (Doyle, 1992).

Concept Evolution

A basic objective of education is for each student to learn how to identify needed information, locate and organize it, and present it in a clear and persuasive manner (Hashim, 1986). In "Educating students to think: The role of the school library media program" (Mancall, Aaron, & Walker, 1986), the role of the school library media program in achieving this basic objective was described: (1) school library media programs need to be involved in helping students develop thinking skills; (2) school library media programs need to take into account current research on how children and adolescents process information and ideas; and (3) school library media programs need to assist with the development of an information skills program in all curricular areas.

In 1987, Kuhlthau advanced the concept of information literacy further when she included library skills and computer literacy in the definition. Kuhlthau's work pointed the way toward the integration of information literacy with curriculum, and presages the current development of the concept of information literacy with the library media center as the starting platform.

In 1988, the American Association of School Librarians (AASL)—a division of the American Library Association (ALA)—published *Information power* (ALA, 1988), national guidelines for school library media programs. The stated mission of *Information power* is "to ensure that students and staff are effective users of ideas and information." This mission is accomplished by:

- providing intellectual and physical access to materials in all formats;
- providing instruction to foster competence and stimulate interest in reading, viewing and using information and ideas; and
- working with other educators to design learning strategies to meet the needs of individual students.

The concept of information literacy was advanced still further when the first meeting of the National Forum on Information Literacy (NFIL) took place on November 9, 1989. NFIL is a coalition of over 60 organizations from business, government and education, all sharing an interest in and a concern for information literacy.

Information Literacy in Context

For an innovation to be successful, it needs to be integrated into the fabric of existing practice. Two major events driving information literacy into the arena of ideas are the Secretary's Commission on Achieving Necessary Skills (SCANS) report, *What work requires of schools* (1991), and *Goals 2000,* the national agenda for education. The SCANS report outlined the economic shift in contemporary American society toward information services. It suggested and recommended skills that all Americans will need for entry-level employment. These recommendations were phrased as outcome measures, and included both foundation skills and practical competencies. SCANS recommended a three-part skills foundation that included (1) basic skills, such as communication and understanding in reading, writing and speaking; (2) thinking skills, such as problem-solving, knowing how to learn, the generation of new ideas, setting goals and choosing best alternatives; and (3) personal qualities, such as responsibility, self-esteem, sociability, self-management, integrity and honesty. There is a very close relationship between the full definition of information literacy and the recommendations of the SCANS report, and this congruency provides a powerful argument for advancing the concept of information literacy.

In 1975, the National Governors' Conference publicized a list of national educational goals, but little was done to implement them. In 1990, the goals were widely publicized by President Bush's administration. In 1994, President Clinton signed legislation authorizing *Goals 2000,* giving the national education goals legal status. The aim of *Goals 2000* was expressed as: "individually, to promote higher levels of individual student achievement, and collectively, to build a globally competitive American workforce" (*America 2000,* 1991, p. 2). Six goals were proposed, covering issues ranging from the education of preschool children to adult literacy. In 1992, a panel of experts from the organizational memberships comprising the National Forum on Information Literacy collaborated in a Delphi study that looked at the national education goals. Success in reaching this objective would result in listing the ways in which these education goals could be attained by applying the process of information literacy. Results of this research showed that the panel members reached consensus on 45 outcome measures for information literacy in the context of selected national education goals.

Both the SCANS report and *Goals 2000* agree on much of what is needed. There should be a greater focus on teaching all students to become independent lifelong learners, to become critical thinkers, to use a variety of technologies proficiently and to work effectively with others.

Impact of Technology

The process of information literacy requires not only the learning of a constellation of skills, but also a new way of thinking in order to derive meaning from learning. Technological storage and sharing of information has increased the availability of data tremendously. Much of this information is available only through telecommunications. Information literacy in telecommunications is achieved when learners know when to use online resources, know how to access information competently, know how to evaluate information as to accuracy and pertinence for each need, and know how to use this information to communicate effectively. Learners who are able to do this will have lifelong skills they will need in the Information Age.

Educational Reform

Much of what occurs in classrooms today was first conceived in the early part of the twentieth century, during the industrial period of American economic history. School curriculum was viewed as a means for passing down to the student all the skills necessary for effective citizenry. As America moves toward a postindustrial or information society, critical thinking skills, problem-solving skills and competence in information literacy in order to process information become increasingly more important for all students. Information literacy needs to develop in the context of school reform, restructuring, assessment and national goals. Currently, the professional curricular organizations of major subject areas are engaged in the process of redefining their national standards.

Curriculum Standards

The National Council of Teachers of Mathematics (NCTM) paved the way for all national standards curriculum reform efforts. Curriculum and Evaluation Standards for School Mathematics views mathematics as "more than a collection of concepts and skills to be mastered; it includes methods of investigating and reasoning, means of communication, and notions of

context. It involves the development of personal self-confidence" (NCTM, p 5) Information literacy, as presented within the mathematics curriculum, involves problem-solving, the use of estimation, thinking strategies for basic facts, formulating and investigating questions from problem situations, use of computers and calculators and other technologies. Assessment of mathematics also fits within the larger picture of information literacy because the focus of evaluation is on using information in meaningful ways to demonstrate understanding.

The National Council for Social Studies (NCSS) has been in the process of revising their standards, with several steps yet to be completed before publication of Curriculum Standards for the Social Studies. To understand and apply the concepts covered in the social studies curriculum, all students will need practice in information literacy skills. The standards state that "it is important that students be able to connect knowledge, skills and values to action as they engage in social inquiry" (NCSS, 1993). Helping students acquire the skills to make good decisions is the basis of the new social studies standards, and information literacy is implicitly and explicitly intertwined.

The National Committee on Science Education Standards and Assessment (NCSESA) is in the process of producing *Science for all* (NRC, 1993), national science standards. The section on "The nature of science" includes "knowledge of the inquiry process, the ability to design and carry out an investigation, perspectives associated with critical thinking or habits of mind, and other positive attitudes usually associated with learning." This is an excellent application of information literacy using a hands-on approach appropriate to a particular subject matter.

Summary

As American society has shifted from an economy based on capital goods (industrial) to an economy based on services (information), there has been a corresponding shift in what is expected from American education. Knowing how to ask the right questions may be the single most important step in learning. The process that is conducted in order to find answers to the right questions leads to the point at which information becomes knowledge. Information literacy—the ability to access, evaluate and use information from a variety of sources—is central to all successful learning and, by extension, to all successful living.

References

American Association of School Librarians & Association for Educational Communications and Technology. (1988). *Information power: Guidelines for school library media programs.* Chicago: American Library Association.

American Library Association Presidential Committee on Information Literacy. (1989). *Final report.* Chicago: American Library Association.

Costa, A. (Ed.). (1985). *Developing minds: A resource book for teaching thinking.* Alexandria, VA: Association for Supervision and Curriculum Development.

Doyle, C. (1992). *Final report to National Forum on Information Literacy.* Syracuse, NY: ERIC Clearinghouse on Information Resources. (ED 351 033).

Hashim, E. (1986). Educating students to think: The role of the school library media program, an introduction. In *Information literacy: Learning how to learn.* A collection of articles from *School Library Media Quarterly, 17.* Chicago: American Library Association, 1991.

Kuhlthau, C. (1987). *Information skills for an information society: A review of research.* Syracuse, NY: ERIC Clearinghouse on Information Resources. (ED 297 740).

Mancall, J., Aaron, S., & Walker, S. (1986). Educating students to think: The role of the library media program. A concept paper written for the National Commission on Libraries and Information Science. *School Library Media Quarterly, 15(1),* 18–27.

National Commission of Excellence in Education. (1983). *A Nation at risk: The imperative for educational reform.* Washington, DC: U.S. Government Printing Office.

National Council for the Social Studies. (1993). *Curriculum standards for the social studies, draft 2.* Washington, DC: National Council for the Social Studies.

National Council of Teachers of Mathematics. Commission on standards for school mathematics. (1989). *Curriculum and evaluation standards for school mathematics.* Reston, VA: National Council of Teachers of Mathematics.

National Research Council. (1993). *National science education standards: An enhanced sampler.* A working paper of the National Council on Science Education Standards and Assessment. Washington, DC: National Research Council.

Secretary's Commission on Achieving Necessary Skills (SCANS). (1991). *What work requires of schools: A SCANS report for America 2000.* Washington, DC: U.S. Government Printing Office.

U.S. Department of Education. (1991). *America 2000: An educational strategy sourcebook.* Washington, DC: U.S. Government Printing Office.

This paper was adapted from the author's *Information literacy in an information society: A concept for the information age* (ERIC Clearinghouse on Information & Technology).

CHAPTER TWELVE

Media Literacy: The New Basic—
Will the Real Curriculum Please Stand Up?

Mary Megee

In the 19th century, the knowledge inside the classroom was higher than the knowledge outside. Today it is reversed. The child knows that, in going to school, he is in a sense interrupting his education.
Marshall McLuhan, 1960

Next to parents, television is a child's "most persistent and most influential teacher," according to the late Ernest Boyer of the Carnegie Foundation for the Advancement of Teaching. David Hamburg, former president of the Carnegie Corporation of New York, calls television "a vast school…whether so intended or not." Through repetition, certain elements of television programming constitute an informal curriculum taught at home to all children, beginning at an early age, with the following themes: consumption, sex, violence and anti-intellectualism. Says National Telecommunications and Information Director Larry Irving, "The discourse is getting coarser and coarser. People aren't paying attention to the needs of our children or what [we] need as a democracy."

Children only spend five or six hours a day, five days a week, maybe 30 weeks a year, in school. In the average home, however, TV is on six or seven hours a day, seven days a week, 52 weeks a year. As the first arm of organized society that children meet, it has the effect of "sanctioning" or socially certifying whatever and whoever appears on the screen. Its compelling complex of sound, pictures and text largely determines which issues, people and actions, we regard as "real" or important.

Even before we have fully comprehended the nature of this force, the scope of its effects, or the economics of its multi-billion-dollar outreach, a tidal wave of new technologies has hit us, delivering even more information and a new set of implications to evaluate. As educators, we know that we must harness the power of emerging technologies like the Internet, but we have a lot of catching up to do. Now that "TV" is more than broadcast and cable, now that it is merging with the telephone and the computer, it is becoming even more pervasive and more powerful.

What Are the Effects of Media Illiteracy?

Historically, the inability to exchange ideas through text has denied non-readers and non-writers full access to the richness of their own culture, has limited educational, social and professional opportunities, and has hampered informed participation in local and national policy decisions. Does the same hold true for those who are "media illiterate"— who cannot decipher the cultural, political and economic implications of the myriad messages they encounter daily? More than 50 years of research says yes.

The problem is not if they see it on TV, they'll do it. The problem is if they see it often enough, they'll see it as part of the norm and it becomes part of their repertoire of possible behavior. Few scholars would deny that TV's influence colors all kinds of transactions, from grocery purchases and fashion trends to language patterns, political choices, religious practices and daily exchanges among family members, friends, co-workers and strangers.

In brief, investigators have found that "heavy users" of TV feel the greatest "need" for advertised products and feel inadequate compared to the seeming perfection shown in TV ads. They adopt a distorted view of sexuality and tend to believe "everyone is doing it except them." They are more fearful and anxious about the "scary world" seen on TV, are "desensitized" to other people's feelings, and exhibit more violent and criminal behavior. And, not surprisingly, they often regard school as a backward, irrelevant, or violent place, as commonly portrayed on TV. Among school-aged children, those who spend the most time watching television generally do least well in the educational system, according to the National Assessment of Educational Performance. More likely to "believe" TV implicitly, a majority of heavy-viewing, underachieving students also live in poverty, have only one parent or guardian and belong to a cultural minority.

For these children in particular, the "real world" is defined increasingly by what they see on television. But what they see only minimally hints at the kind of preparation and skills they need for social development, responsible citizenship, further learning and productive employment. When

people cannot decipher, produce, or exchange information in the language that others use regularly, they tend to suffer psychological effects akin to those stemming from traditional illiteracy— feelings of anxiety, isolation, powerlessness, inadequacy and persecution.

Most commonly, media illiteracy can lead to cynicism. The least understood of these effects, cynicism is the result of a reversal from "total belief" to "total rejection" of media messages. That is, if it's not all true and real, it must be all false and irrelevant. It's useful to distinguish here between cynicism and skepticism. Fatalistic, inflexible and predetermined, cynicism says everything's phony, nothing's important. Students and educators alike would do well to avoid cynicism while promoting skepticism, which is the ability to question, judge, make distinctions and recognize motives and techniques. Skepticism requires more work...and that's where media literacy comes in.

What Is Media Literacy?

In 1992, conferees at the Annenberg School for Communication agreed upon this definition:

> Media literacy is the ability to choose, to understand, to question, to evaluate, to create and/or produce and to respond thoughtfully to the media we consume. It is mindful viewing, reflective judgment...an ongoing process, requiring parents and teachers who are themselves media literate and are nonjudgmental, reflective, yet rigorously valuative in their teaching.

Media literacy is a new, expanded view of traditional literacy, which acknowledges and includes the role and the impact of the mass media. Underlying it is the idea that electronic and other popular media are "texts" that require comprehensive understanding. Reading printed text requires more than simply decoding letters into words or sounds, it involves finding meaning, motive, structure and affect. The same goes for "reading the electronic text."

Media educator Elizabeth Thoman, Executive Director of the Center for Media Literacy in Los Angeles, cautions, "Media literacy is not just being critical of the media; it's learning to appreciate the power of the most powerful medium that the world has ever known."

We may consider the swiftly expanding media environment beyond our control if we continue to teach just the old "basics"—reading, writing, arithmetic—as though they were somehow unrelated to the world of information in which we are immersed. Adults and children must be colearners of a whole new language, made up of sound, image, text, and data bits, with its own grammar and syntax. Rather than standing alone as yet another subject to claim a spot on the school curriculum, media literacy is an extension of traditional literacy, to be integrated into each of the disciplines we teach in the schools: language arts and communications, social studies, civics, mathematics, health, etc. In 1997, media educators largely concur on the following basic tenets of media literacy:

Access: The use of the full range of media and new technologies for receiving and sending information, through broadcast, cable, interactive and other media forms.

Analysis: The ability to decipher the elements of media messages and media systems;—to understand their forms and functions, ownership and management structures, economic and policy implication, message, content, intent and effects; and de-coding and re-contextualizing their meaning.

Evaluation: The ability to make judgments about media, assess and apply journalistic ethics, critique aesthetic elements, and compare and contrast the values of media messages and systems to those of other individual and community value systems.

Production: The ability to create messages, in a variety of media, including text, video and computer, with a view toward sharing the results of this production with the larger community.

Media Education: Teaching Critical Viewing Skills Across the Curriculum

Since children are immersed in the television experience, everyday schooling or parenting that omits an examination of TV's curriculum also ignores the world that children know. The challenge for education is to help young people navigate the sea of messages flooding into their lives daily through TV, movies, radio, music, video games, magazines, newspapers; even billboards, bumper stickers and T-shirt logos. The complexity of the relationship between what we see and hear, what we believe, and how we interact with one another underscores the need for across-the-curriculum teaching of critical thinking and critical viewing skills, that is, media literacy.

In October 1996, the On Television Project at Rutgers University and the New Jersey Network held a video conference on media literacy. Benjamin Barber of Rutgers' Walt Whitman Center said during the conference, "The term 'media education' is redundant; media education is education. The challenge ahead involves nothing short of a revolution for American schooling and, at the same time, a return to the fundamental principles of public education: helping young people learn to ask questions, gain access to information resources, analyze and evaluate media messages, and create their own messages through mastery of the tools of modern communication."

In *Television and America's children: A crisis of neglect,* Edward Palmer asserts that we have failed to use the world's most powerful informational tool to address the nation's educational problems. There is a wealth of programming on public TV, cable and satellite TV, interactive multi-media systems, and commercial TV that we can use selectively at home and in school as a valuable adjunct to instruction in all disciplines. Teaching critical viewing skills bolsters students' skills in traditional disciplines, combats problems of youth apathy, violence, and substance abuse, and improves students', parents' and teachers' attitudes toward school.

Exercises designed to extend understanding of the content, context, impact and social roles of TV foster critical thinking, reading, writing and comprehension. Jerome and Dorothy Singer of the Family Television Research and Consultation Center at Yale University, who have developed curricula for elementary and secondary levels, find that "media literate" students show decided gains in traditional scholarly skills. They learn to analyze material; interpret messages; note details; understand sequencing; integrate aural and visual elements; distinguish fact from opinion; identify emotional appeals, reactions and motives; recognize inferences; make predictions and draw conclusions.

The application of these skills to young people's television experiences helps abate their "need" for advertised products, puts TV images of sexuality into perspective, tempers fears about a violent world and improves students' attitudes about education. Further, the teachers, families and community members involved in critical viewing activities with children increasingly regard school as an important center for communication and connection. Most important, media education orients young people to the role of communicator—as "sender" rather than merely a "receiver" of information, as analyst and maker of media rather than simply a "believer."

Media Literacy in the Classroom

As in any new approach to teaching, there is always a risk. The teacher who points out the disparity between the content, intent and impact of such messages and the ideals on which our society was founded may not achieve instant popularity. Nonetheless, if the teacher opens up discussion for students to evaluate the implications of such messages and the possible motives of the message-makers, a surprising range of viewpoints will emerge as young people begin to connect the world they know well—commercial media—with concepts and principles inherent to traditional educational standards.

From these discussions, assignments involving research, writing and production by students often result in displays of initiative and insight that eclipse students' prior academic achievements. Student work products—in the context of almost any traditional discipline or course—may include written reviews of TV shows, movies, books, music, letters to the editor of local and national publications, self -published magazines, public service announcements on audiotape or videotape, multi-media features or news reports on a full range of investigations. Distribution of these works through school newsletters, local newspapers, libraries, radio and TV broadcasts,

and cable access channels helps students see themselves as part of the community and as viable candidates for the increasing number of professions that require communication skills.

Media Education and Citizenship Education

America is sound asleep. This is not the way to be treating one-sixth to one-seventh of the American economy. This is the bill, and we are taking it up at midnight?! Ladies and gentlemen, this is about more than how many gigabits one company or another might provide. This is about how we transmit ideas in our society—how our children's minds are formed.

> Representative Edward Markey
> (Democrat-Massachusetts), testifying before the
> House of Representatives on the passage of the
> Telecommunications Bill in 1995

Preparing young people for effective participation in their own governance is a primary purpose of education. From the beginning, liberty and literacy have been twin articles of American faith. First Amendment freedoms depend upon an informed, responsible citizenry able to share ideas through reading and writing. Today, the electronic media have to a large degree replaced print—even school, government and the family—as the primary sources of information. Information Age freedoms hinge upon a new basic—our ability to read, write and comprehend the media of our time. Only an individual with access to, and mastery of, the tools of modern communication is adequately prepared for responsible citizenship.

Veteran TV journalist and media literacy activist Hugh Downs says, "If democracy is to survive, people who vote must have access to the facts so they can sort out biases, they can know whose ax is being ground, they can know the political climate, they can know the economic considerations of messages that are hurled at us all the time."

Media educator Renee Hobbs of Babson College explains, "Being able to critically analyze media messages turns us from being spectators into citizens. Of course, we have evolved into a kind of democracy where we watch other people do democracy. And that's very dangerous, turning a democracy into a spectator sport is absolutely the way to lose your democracy."

Kathryn Montgomery, Director of the Center for Media Education in Washington, DC, observes, "Most people don't have a sense of what the institutions are that determine what comes into your house, what the policies are that govern the whole shape of the media system and, generally, the media, with some very few exceptions, don't deal with these issues either. So, it's sort of an invisible part of the picture. And I think that's why one of the key roles of media education is to reveal to people what those structures are; how networks and cable systems are structures. Who owns them? Why do they put the programs on that they do? What relationship does the policy environment have to all of that? And then to really be aware of why it is we see what we see— and what we need to do to change that."

One of the critical issues for a media literate person to understand is the ongoing conflict between commerce and culture, between the public interest and market interests.

What the Educational Community Can Do

Although television has played a major role for almost half a century, and although the United States produces more and consumes more TV than people in any other country, we teach less about who is communicating, for what purpose, with what effect, on behalf of which individuals. Unlike other developed nations, the United States has not yet established media education as a priority for everyday schooling. Great Britain's David Buckingham and Canada's Barry Duncan describe media literacy in their countries as an integral part of all traditional disciplines—language arts, social studies, science. "Even in math, we deal with polls, ratings and the like," says Duncan. "There's got to be a feeling that everybody is making a difference. That's the turning point, when everyone understands the term 'media literacy' and, as it is in Ontario, media literacy is taught on all levels. When that happens, it's part of the school culture and it's part of the educational system." Ontario

requires media education in all schools for grades 7–12. For more than 20 years, Australia and Great Britain have also offered media education as part of schooling on every level.

The United States lags behind the rest of the world both in teaching about TV and using it for education. Whereas the U.S. government spends only one dollar per person a year on public television, Japan spends $17, Canada $32, and Great Britain $38 per person. Even in Asia and Latin America, as well as throughout Europe, some nations devote 12 or 15 percent or more of their broadcast schedule to educational programming for children, while U.S. commercial TV devotes only about one percent. Although the Children's Television Act of 1990 requires that every broadcast licensee "serve the educational and informational needs of children" with quality programming, the fact remains that some stations claim re-runs of *The Flintstones*, *The Jetsons* and *Saved by the Bell* fit the mandate.

There is a growing media literacy movement but there are many obstacles, including our general attitude toward education itself, cuts in school budgets and what one observer calls "rampant technophobia." While teachers have made some laudable efforts, they are unconnected, of varying quality, with limited communication about priorities, goals, effective methods and available materials.

Except in New Mexico and North Carolina, and in selected cities and districts, U.S. schools are not required to provide media education. Most of our academic curricula take into account neither the problems nor the opportunities television presents for the education of students. The vast majority of teachers surveyed by the California-based Strategies for Media Literacy reported that they would like to teach about media more often, but were inhibited by lack of time and teaching materials.

Arguably the most urgent issue of our time is systemic education reform that effectively prepares young people for citizenship in the Information Age. An effort of this scope requires a sea-change in public understanding of the functions and impacts, and educational potential, of the media. It's not a job that can be done easily, or alone; but it can be accomplished as a collaboration by teachers, administrators, family members, business leaders—and media literate children—who are similarly motivated and uniquely positioned to make a difference.

Only public recognition of the importance of understanding media can move education leaders to support the development of comprehensive, accessible materials for teacher training, to ensure broad-based dissemination of learning materials for students on all levels and to make critical viewing an integral part of the school curriculum. The following must happen if the promise for national literacy—that includes and in large degree requires media literacy—is to be realized:

- federal support for model programs and multimedia materials for teacher education and in-class use by students;
- state support for preservice training on college level, or technological enrichment, and staffing for maintenance;
- district and school support for in-service training;
- community collaboration with industry leaders in media production and communications technologies, including challenge grants and matching programs;
- community demand for better media coverage of schools, reports on school aims, successes and achievements;
- selective and creative personal use of media within individual homes.

This last action means that all of us must learn more about the Internet and other new technologies, set an example for members of our families, communities and schools. We must encourage those around us to get the most out of every media moment as well as to produce their own messages in the media of their choice. If the promise of the new technologies for education is to be realized, the voices and messages of students, teachers, principals, families and other members of the education community must be an integral part of the new information environment.

CHAPTER THIRTEEN

Student Access to the Internet: Librarians and Teachers Working Together to Teach Higher Level Survival Skills

Doug Johnson

All students need full access to the Internet's resources in order to learn the skills they need to participate successfully in today's, and especially tomorrow's, society. Success in education, in employment and in civic involvement all increasingly demand the ability to use technology to access, process and communicate online information. All parents and citizens should insist that students at all grade levels have successful experiences with major technologies, including the Internet. Full access to the Internet has two components: physical access and intellectual access. This paper will define both components and explore issues involving each, including how teachers and librarians must work together to ensure access for all students.

Physical Access

Physical access to the Internet for both students and their teachers includes the availability of computer equipment at school and at home,

adequate time online to learn and explore, and adequate skills instruction in using the basic tools of online research. These online tools include e-mail, file transfer, gopher menus and search programs like Archie, Veronica, WWW and WAIS. Physical access also includes the availability of online resources such as personal e-mail addresses and file space, access to listservs and news groups, the capability of telnetting to other computers, the capability to download files into a personal file space and adequate print resources that can serve as skill and resource references. The Mankato Internet Skill Rubrics (see Table 13.1) outlines some beginning skills that Mankato State University (Minnesota) Library Media Education classes have taught. These skills, which are needed for physical access to the Internet, could be adapted to serve as a model for teacher Internet competencies and serve as a discussion starter when designing a beginning scope and sequence of Internet skills for students.

Table 13.1   The Mankato Internet Skill Rubrics

Level 1: Unaware   Level 2: Aware   Level 3: Mastery   Level 4: Advanced

1. Personal and Educational Uses of Networks

☐ Level 1: I do not understand how networks work, nor can I identify any personal or professional uses for networks.

☐ Level 2: I can identify some personal or professional uses for networks, and understand they have a value to my students and myself. I do not have the skills or access to use networks.

☐ Level 3: I can describe what a computer network does and how it can be useful personally and professionally. I can distinguish between a local area network, a wide area network, a value-added network and the Internet. I can describe student and professional uses for each type of network in a school setting.

☐ Level 4: I use multiple types of networks on a daily basis to access and communicate information. I can serve as an active participant in a school or organizational planning group, giving advice and providing information about networks. I can speak knowledgeably about network topologies, protocols, speeds, wiring and administration.

2. History and Structure of the Internet

☐ Level 1: I know nothing about the Internet.

☐ Level 2: I have heard the term used and feel like I should learn more. I've read some articles about the Internet in the popular press.

☐ Level 3: I can describe the history of the Internet and recognize its international character. I know to a large degree the extent of its resources. I can explain the governance of the network and can relate all this information to K–12 education. I can speak to the social and educational issues of equitable access. I know what TCP/IP stands for and why it is important.

☐ Level 4: I recognize current issues surrounding membership and access to the Internet, including the rapid growth of commercial interests. I understand what is meant by the Information Highway and can speculate on its effect on culture and society.

3. Personal Accounts and Access Points

☐ Level 1: I do not have an account on any network nor would I know how to get one.

☐ Level 2: I can use a commercial value-added network like CompuServe or Prodigy. I can directly use dial-in access to a library catalog.

☐ Level 3: I have personal access to the Internet which allows me to receive and send e-mail, telnet and read news groups. I can use a modem or hard wired terminal to log-on to my account. I know that I must protect my password, and should restrict access by others to my account. I can help others obtain Internet access.

☐ Level 4: I can access the Internet using SLIP or PPP, and understand the difference between it and terminal emulation.

4. E-mail and Listservs

☐ Level 1: I do not use e-mail.

☐ Level 2: I understand the concept of e-mail and can explain some administrative and educational uses for it.

☐ Level 3: I can use the e-mail services of the Internet to:
  • read and delete messages;
  • send, forward and reply to messages to accounts in both the same and different domains;
  • interpret domain names;
  • subscribe to, contribute to, and unsubscribe to a listserv, and understand the uses of listservs;
  • I read and contribute to professional listservs such as LM_Net.

☐ Level 4: I can send group mailings and feel confident that I could start a listserv. I use activities which require e-mail in my teaching.

5. News Groups

☐ Level 1: I have no knowledge of news groups.

☐ Level 2: I can locate the news groups available from my account and can read news groups.

☐ Level 3: I understand the organization of news groups and can navigate easily through them. I read several news groups which interest me on a regular basis. I can speak to issues about censorship and online resources.

☐ Level 4: I can contribute to news groups and use a utility like Nuntius or Newswatcher. I use information I have found in news groups as a resource for my students.

6. Gophers and Library Catalogs

☐ Level 1: I do not use the Internet to locate information.

☐ Level 2: I know that there are resources available on the Internet, but cannot confidently access them.

☐ Level 3: I understand the use of Gophers and can locate several which help me. I can use the Gopher to get to other Gophers and to remote catalogs. I can write directions to locating a Gopher so that others can find it as well.

☐ Level 4: I am aware that some Gophers are subject specific. I can use a utility program like TurboGopher to set bookmarks to and download information from Gopher. I use information I have found in Gophers as a resource for my students.

7. Telnet and FTP

☐ Level 1: I cannot access information from remote computers.

☐ Level 2: I know that information and computer programs which are useful to myself and my students are stored on computers throughout the world. I cannot retrieve this information.

☐ Level 3: I can access a remote computer through the telnet command. I can transfer files and programs from remote locations to my host machine by using FTP.

☐ Level 4: I can use a utility such as Fetch to retrieve files and programs. I use information I have retrieved as a resource for and with my students.

8. Search Tools

☐ Level 1: I cannot locate any information on the Internet.

☐ Level 2: I can occasionally locate useful information on the Internet by browsing or through remembered sources.

☐ Level 3: I can conduct a search of Internet resources using at least two tools like Archie, Veronica, WAIS or Mosaic. I can explain why such tools are important to the researcher using Internet. I can state some guidelines for evaluating the information I find on the Internet.

☐ Level 4: I can identify some subject specific search tools, and can speculate on future developments in online information searching.

Table 13.1 The Mankato Internet Skill Rubrics (continued)

Level 1: Unaware   Level 2: Aware   Level 3: Mastery   Level 4: Advanced

9. Netiquette and Online Ethics
- Level 1: I am not aware of any ethics or proprieties regarding the Internet.
- Level 2: I understand a few rules which my students and I should follow when using the Internet.
- Level 3: I have read a guideline for Internet use such as Rinaldi's "The Net: User Guidelines and Netiquette" or other source, and follow the rules outlined. I know and read the FAQ files associated with sources on the Internet.
- Level 4: ??? (Isn't courtesy an absolute?)

10. The Media Specialist's Role in Telecommunications and the Internet
- Level 1: I cannot identify any role for a school media specialist in telecommunications.
- Level 2: I understand the role of media specialist as information specialist and the skills that role requires for many media. I am knowledgeable and support resource-based education in the school. I have not, however, applied these skills to information gathered electronically from remote sites.
- Level 3: I can identify, demonstrate, and teach to other teachers and students basic Internet skills. I can also apply many skills and philosophies to electronic information sources I now apply to print information sources. These include evaluation of information, intellectual freedom, equity of access and integration of media into the learning process.
- Level 4: I am an active proponent of bringing Internet access to all my media center patrons.

The issues surrounding the Internet regarding physical access to the equipment and time and training for students are the same issues that can be raised when allocating any educational resource: how can it be funded; who controls the funds; how is effectiveness evaluated; when can funding be considered equitable; how will staff development be structured; and so on. These are important questions but are not unique to providing Internet access.

There are unique issues regarding the physical access to resources on the Internet that need professional discussion, however. The content of the Internet is unregulated and not moderated in whole. Its genesis was as a resource for adult users. The sheer size and number of users on the Internet have created a huge diversity of opinions, tastes and interests. There are materials that in many school districts may be deemed inappropriate for student use. However, the presence of potentially objectionable materials on the Internet cannot become a justification for denying children their rights to information.

The same selection criteria should apply to online resources as they do to other educational materials. Board-adopted selection policies must cover online resources if they do not do so already. Schools can, to a degree, control the Internet resources that are available to their students. Schools that have their own Internet nodes can select which news groups they will carry, and can structure their gophers and other menus to give easy access to some resources and not to others. (If schools do not have their own nodes, the selection of a commercial provider of Internet service can be made using the board-adopted selection policy.) The selection of Internet resources should be done by professionals at a local level. With all types of resources, there are titles that do not meet the educational standards of some districts, while the same titles are deemed appropriate in other districts. This also applies to Internet resources. Not only are materials judged as educationally suitable or unsuitable, but also whether the resources are essential to individual programs.

A few students will use the Internet to obtain materials that may be viewed as inappropriate to their age or maturity level, as some students now use interlibrary loan to obtain materials that are unavailable in their school or local public libraries. Some materials on the Internet will be judged as obscene. The diversity of political, religious and ethical views expressed on the Internet will be threatening to some teachers, parents and community members. Teachers, librarians and administrators must work together to prepare for challenges to online materials similar to those that have been made in the past regarding library books, textbooks, magazines and audiovisual materials.

Librarians, in their role as intellectual freedom advocates, must inform district decision makers that the same freedoms children now have to read and view must be extended to computing. The format of the information should in no way be a factor in whether a child has access to it. There are many highly regarded documents which already address children's First Amendment rights in regard to access of materials. These include:

- The Library Bill of Rights (American Library Association);
- Access to Resources and Services in the School Library Media Program (American Association of School Librarians);
- Censorship Statement (International Reading Association);
- Freedom to Read Statement (American Association of Publishers and American Library Association);
- Freedom to View (American Film and Video Association);
- Statement on Intellectual Freedom (Association for Educational Communications and Technology);
- Student's Right to Read (National Council of Teachers of English).

Some state intellectual freedom groups and the American Association of School Librarians are currently drafting policies which address censorship and online resources.

Programs that give students physical access to the Internet must also teach them responsible and ethical use of online resources. Guidelines, rules and behavior such as those outlined in Rinaldi's "The Net: User guidelines and netiquette" should be taught and their use encouraged, with self-moderating behavior by students the essential outcome (Rinaldi, 1992). A specific set of student guidelines has been developed by some schools. Those outlined for the CoVis Network are exemplary (Fishman, 1994). Yet as Howard Rheingold writes:

> If a hacker in Helsinki or Los Angeles connects to the Internet and provides access to his digital porno files, anybody anywhere else in the world, with the right kind of Internet connection, can download those steamy bits and bytes. This technological shock to our moral codes means that in the future we are going to have to teach our children well. The locus of control is going to have to be in their heads and hearts, not in the laws or machines that make information so imperviously available. Before we let our kids loose on the

Internet, they better have a solid moral grounding and some common sense. (Rheingold, 1994)

The most effective way to make online ethics meaningful may well be to have students create building or program gophers and moderate their own local discussion groups. Given the availability of the Internet from any computer with a modem and phone or any computer on a network that is linked to the Internet, to enforce student compliance with a set of guidelines will be difficult, if not impossible. And by eliminating a valuable resource from schools that is available in homes, public libraries and colleges, schools run the real risk of being viewed by students as irrelevant to their information and learning needs.

Too many restrictions may also kill the excitement and motivation inherent in active inquiry. In response to a fictitious "boss" who wanted to "restrict access to a few menu items and make sure there's no possible way anyone can get somewhere they're not supposed to be," Richard Fritz (1993) wrote:

> But you'll take all the fun out of exploration and discovery! It's a wilderness out there. The Internet is a new frontier. It's not cut-and-dried. It's living and growing and changing every second of the day. Today's dead-end will be tomorrow's doorway to knowledge…. It's my gut feeling that too many controls and restrictions on access will kill the spirit and adventure needed to kindle progressive learning.

Intellectual Access

Students also need intellectual access to the resources of the Internet. These skills are more critical to the student's education while being far more difficult to teach and far less likely to be taught by traditional education methods. Locating data is not difficult, but using it productively is. In the past, the researcher's major challenge was to locate enough data to make meaningful use of it. The Internet researcher has the opposite challenge: to select useful data from the glut of information on the networks of over 11 million computers. A single search on the Internet can produce literally thousands of references.

Jamison MacKenzie identifies three processes that must occur when converting findings from the Internet into something of value to learners:

- decoding, selecting and evaluating symbols to create data;
- organizing data to reveal patterns and relationships to create information; and
- using information to suggest an action, a solution to a problem, or a supportable opinion to create insight (MacKenzie, 1993).

He also suggests skills that will be imperative for effective Internet use. These include:

- knowing the difference between information and knowledge or insight;
- sorting and evaluating information and information sources;
- understanding the problem;
- identifying what information is needed for a problem;
- knowing the need to be recursive when problem solving;
- creating or cultivating information;
- framing essential questions;
- identifying subsidiary questions;
- planning a search;
- modifying the search when new information suggests it;
- using chance findings;
- using online help tools;
- analyzing data;
- building and testing models;
- synthesizing information to create fresh answers and insights.

The number and complexity of skills required for intellectual access to the Internet demand that students have a wide variety and large number of learning opportunities that make use of the Internet. This makes Internet access as important to primary students as it is to high school and college students. Teachers and teacher-librarians must create a scope and sequence of learning objectives associated with the higher-level thinking skills involved in research—including those that may be specific to the Internet—and integrate these skills into the content areas. It will only be through the cooperative efforts of the teacher-librarian (the research skills specialist) and the classroom teacher (the subject specialist) that this integration will occur.

The biggest stumbling block to intellectual access to the Internet is the lack of progressive teaching methods in schools. The traditional lecture/test teacher does not teach or encourage intellectual inquiry, or use activities in which students use information to solve meaningful questions. Only certain types of teaching methods will make effective use of Internet resources. These include:

- resource-based teaching;
- constructivist teaching (Brooks, 1993);
- authentic teaching and learning;
- project-oriented education using authentic assessment (Sizer, 1992).

The less physically and intellectually accessible Internet resources are even less likely to be used than traditional library resources by teachers who are uncomfortable with ambiguity, open-ended questioning, or authentic assessment. Unfortunately, too few educators have themselves been learners in classrooms that promote open inquiry, and do not have authentic learning skills that they can model. Traditional school structures such as content-specific classes, short, inflexible class periods, norm-referenced testing and textbook-driven curricula also make the use of a wide range of instructional resources for authentic learning difficult. Traditional teachers and institutions, as much as censors, will keep students from having Internet access. Teacher-librarians, as "instructional consultants," must bring their expertise in resource-based teaching to bear in helping to restructure education.

The Relationship of Physical Access to Intellectual Access

Physical and intellectual access to the Internet are interdependent. A student who cannot get time on a computer, does not have an e-mail box, or cannot use FTP, cannot develop the intellectual access skills associated with using the Internet. Likewise, if Internet resources are not going to be used by teachers, teacher-librarians and students in meaningful ways, there is no reason for schools to provide students physical access to the Internet.

The digitization of information will continue at a rapid rate. One estimate is that while only 20 percent of the world's information is currently in a digital format, by the turn of the century, over 90 percent of information will be accessible by computer—much of it accessible *only* by computer. The push for digitization is both global and economic. The U.S. Commerce Department believes that the Internet or its successor will improve the manufacturing base, speed the efficiency of electronic commerce and business communication, improve health care delivery, promote access to the educational system and enable government to dispense services to the public faster, more responsively and more efficiently (NII Report, 1994). We must educate our children to work in an economy that will harness this powerful tool.

Librarians, teacher-librarians, administrators, parents and community members will need both courage and faith if children are to have Internet access. Facing the censor or the traditionalist requires tremendous courage. It is only by having the faith of our convictions that we will be able to summon the courage needed to create an educational environment that will prepare our children for success in an information- and technology-dependent future.

References

Brooks, M. (1993). *In search of understanding: The case for constructivist classrooms.* Alexandria, VA: Association for Supervision and Curriculum Development.

Fishman, B. (1994). The internetworked school: A policy for the future. *Technos, 3 (1),* 22–26.

Fritz, R. (1993, November 28). *Posting.* LM_Net listserv.

MacKenzie, J. (1993). Grazing the Net. *From Now On, 4 (4),* 2–13.

NII Report released. (1994, May 8). Edupage distribution list.

Rheingold, H. (1994, April 6). Why censoring cyberspace is futile. *San Francisco Examiner.*

Rinaldi, A. (1992). *The Net: User guidelines and netiquette.* (Available for downloading from a variety of anonymous FTP and gopher sites.)

Sizer, T. (1992). *Horace's school.* Boston: Houghton Mifflin.

CHAPTER FOURTEEN

Misinformation on the Internet: Applying Evaluation Skills to Online Information

Mary Ann Fitzgerald

A student visits the library in the hope of researching the pros and cons of abortion, a controversy which interests her. She chooses the Internet as her resource because she wants her information to be recent. The first source she finds includes this information: "There is a significant and alarming correlation between abortion and breast cancer...having an abortion raised a woman's risk of contracting breast cancer 50 percent on average" (Plagal, 1994). A second source says this: "A study...on induced abortion and risk for breast cancer discusses whether an association exists, but the findings are not conclusive. Further research is needed to interpret the results" (Advanced Research, 1994). How will the student decide which source to believe?

This example is highly representative of the kinds of contradictory information that can be found on the Internet. Some contradictions are the results of differences of opinion, while others are the result of misinformation. No one knows how much misinformation occurs on the Internet, and this topic has not been adequately explored. Several incidents of Internet hoaxes, rumors and fraud have been reported (Roseman, 1995; Aycock & Buchignani, 1995; Stephens, 1995) that represent deliberate attempts to mislead readers. Hardware and software problems persist that can potentially damage information. The loosely-controlled architecture of the Internet can lead to misinformation also. Other problems have been so common in traditional media that they are likely to transfer to electronic information dissemination, if this has not already occurred. Adherence to the First Amendment prevents librarians or information service providers from separating information from misinformation for the patron. Only the user, who holds a unique concept of the nature of truth, may do this for herself. Therefore, the Internet user must be equipped with critical thinking tools to distinguish good information from bad information, insofar as this is possible.

The purpose of this article is to suggest a specialized set of critical thinking skills designed to enable the user to read critically and evaluate online information. These skills resemble closely the ones needed to evaluate all types of information, with several refinements. In order to accomplish this purpose, the first section of this paper describes the types of Internet misinformation. The second section lists and explains skills that empower online information users to evaluate Internet information critically.

Problems with Internet Information

Electronic formats provide powerful tools for information dissemination and consumption. Highly touted virtues of online formats include speed, space efficiency, instant revisability and pervasive access. Proponents of the Internet enthusiastically promote electronic communication while often remaining mute about problems of misinformation.

In order to describe some of the types of Internet misinformation, the term "misinformation" must be defined. A simplistic definition is "false information." However, individuals possess different ideas of what truth is. While some people see truth as a static reality that can be discovered through science, others feel that truth is unique for each individual. Given this conundrum, "misinformation" cannot be defined to the satisfaction of everyone. It is best to refer to misinformation in a generic sense, talk about its origins and describe certain clues and signs that sometimes point to its existence.

The literature lists many types of misinformation, in fact, more than can be thoroughly discussed in this article. For the sake of convenience these problems are categorized as hardware and software problems, Internet architecture problems and traditional problems that may transfer from print into electronic publishing. Users forewarned with knowledge of these misinformation types may recognize problems more readily.

Hardware and Software Problems

Several hardware and software problems that can potentially damage data persist despite technological progress, and the person at the Internet terminal may not suspect that information has been affected (Eisenberg, 1989). Through the absence of information that should or could be present, the user can encounter information that is incomplete to the point where it becomes misinformation. Incompatibility and inadvertent data loss are just two ways that the information base can become incomplete or fragmented (Hickey, 1995). Another kind of problem is translation errors, which occur when data transfers across different machines, operating systems or storage media. Scanning technology, which inputs data through an optical reader, seldom translates data with 100 percent accuracy. Scanned text and photographs almost always contain subtle differences from the original (Eisenberg, 1989; Hickey, 1995). Computerized photographs can be altered through the translation process so that they no longer reflect reality (Lafollette, 1992).

Internet Architecture Problems

In contrast to technological problems likely to be solved in the near future, there are two characteristics of the Internet that are not likely, nor desirable, to change. When the Internet was originally constructed for military communication, several features were built into it that remain today. Two of these features, lack of central authority and data malleability, are perhaps the Internet's greatest weaknesses as well as its greatest strengths.

Lack of Central Authority

As a safeguard against nuclear attack, the Internet was built without a centralized controlling authority to distribute the information base throughout the country (Stoker & Cooke, 1995). Large segments of the Internet lack "gatekeepers," or people who control the flow of information. Messages to most forums, listservs and discussion groups are processed by software packages that automatically distribute postings to subscribers, regardless of content. Other discussion groups are moderated, but the user may be unable to tell who the gatekeeper is or if there is one at all. Often, no one evaluates or edits information before it is posted onto gophers or web pages. Because of this lack of control "anybody can publish anything" (Neavill, 1984, p. 87). Without editorial control, documents flawed by bias, mistakes, lies, scholarly misconduct or any of a number of other flaws can be circulated instantly. Because the Internet allows anonymity, authors publishing misinformation fear no reprisals.

Data Malleability

Partially because the Internet lacks central authority, online data is highly malleable. Most Internet files are protected from revisions by outside parties. However, authors and system administrators can revise text or delete files at any time. Neavill asks the question, "How can scholarship be based on something so easily altered?" (1984, p. 88). If a researcher wishes to cite an Internet source, nothing guarantees that the source will remain intact. Authors may not realize that their words have been changed by someone else. Internet security is an issue, also, because hackers can access protected data. Hackers often break into government servers, intercepting, interrupting and changing data without discovery (Stephens, 1995). If hackers can access data, they can change it. University servers, the most complete repositories of online information, are particularly vulnerable to hacker attack because of inadequate preventive measures (Coutorie, 1995). Data malleability leads to the entirely separate issue of archival integrity. An electronic information structure is vulnerable to political editing, data loss and environmental disasters to a far greater degree than print archives, a problem that circles back to misinformation through missing information (Graham, 1993).

Old Problems in a New Form

Print publishing, despite editing, source-checking and prepublication review, has never completely eliminated misinformation. The threat exists that through the lack of gatekeeping, print problems can transfer to telecommunicated information. Some Internet misinformation incidents are old schemes dressed in new electronic disguises. For example, chain letters, long a manipulative device propagated through surface mail, now flourish

through e-mail. Other problems are merely potential at this point, but could at any time cross the barrier between print and electronic publication. Transferable problems include human error, misconduct, removal of information from context, lack of currency and bias.

Human Error

Inadvertently created misinformation, although easily forgiven, may still cause harm. Often readers catch an online error quickly and report it to the poster who then retracts the error and apologizes. In this respect, the Internet is a vast improvement over print because errors are easily revised. Other mistakes, however, go unnoticed and instead may be believed for long periods before detection. To illustrate the pervasiveness of errors even among carefully researched data, medical database indexers find as many as 200 substantive errors per month involving clinical treatment and dosages (Kotzin & Schuyler, 1989).

Misconduct

People deliberately transmit flawed information for a variety of reasons. Jokes and pranks are common. The Good Times virus hoax, an e-mail message warning of a nonexistent virus, still circulates and dupes people after several years (Roseman, 1995). Motives for misconduct are sometimes financial. Nonexistent stocks and bonds can be sold for profit through the manipulation of financial records (Stephens, 1995), thus altering the financial information many investors depend upon. More pertinent to the misinformation problem is scholarly misconduct. Gains in knowledge depend heavily upon the research mill, which rewards scholars and scientists for productive research through university promotion and grant awards. Because of this reward structure, motivation for producing research quickly is high, and therefore the likelihood of "sloppy research" and falsification is high (Hernon & Altman, 1995). Several studies suggest that this problem is "far from uncommon" (Hernon & Altman, 1995; Stewart & Feder, 1987). Several have been widely publicized and discussed, most notably Darsee (Swazey, Anderson, & Lewis,

1993; Kochan & Budd, 1992). These cases occurred within the domain of print publishing, despite its verification structure of peer review, editing and replication. With greater freedom and fewer safeguards, scholarly writing published on the Internet may be even less trustworthy. Neavill (1984) is particularly concerned that researchers may electronically self-publish articles after rejection from print journals.

Removal of Information from Context

Another old problem is the intentional or unintentional removal of statements from context and thus subtly or blatantly changing the author's intent. In online discussion groups such as listservs and newsgroups, dramatic misunderstandings occur because of failure to read preceding discussions. Neavill (1993) asserts that electronic discussions are neither linear nor nonlinear but layered or networked, and that readers must recognize this multidimensionality to maximize understanding.

A special form of the context removal problem is caused by hypertext. Within electronic databases, texts and the World Wide Web, browsing tools and search functions make it particularly easy to find relevant bits of information instantly, skipping the visual skimming and sifting process. However, skimming helps to establish context, and thus the hypertext-hopping reader may miss important information and completely misinterpret the author's intent (Tenopir, 1988). Jumping from site to site also encourages readers to suspend critical judgments about authority by allowing them to ignore origin, URL address and bibliographical information (Johnson, 1995). Another phenomenon, that of becoming "lost in hyperspace," is one of disorientation that occurs especially in hyperlinked media (Gygi, 1990, p. 283). Users, following link after link, become disoriented and completely lose track of context. Thus, hypertext presents several new contextual problems for which strategies have yet to be devised.

Lack of Currency

Currency (which refers to whether information is up to date) and bias are misinformation problems that can infest any kind of media. Only broadcast media rivals online information in providing immediacy. Unfortunately, virtually instantaneous information requires a sacrifice of accuracy. Information quickly gathered and disseminated is prone to errors that are potentially immortalized through archival storage. Although it is simple to publish retractions of errors, information searchers often find errors separated from retractions. To maintain currency, information must be updated regularly. The Internet is theoretically the most up-to-date information source, yet updating may be done inconsistently or neglected altogether (Stoker & Cooke, 1995; United States Congress Office of Technology Assessment, 1988). For example, homepage writers often forget to update information when they move or change positions.

Bias

Sometimes the inadvertent result of subjectivity and sometimes deliberately crafted for a specific purpose, bias is arguably present in all communication to at least a minor degree. Political bias towards the Western world is present in computerized texts because there are no ASCII characters for Eastern-language alphabets (Stoker & Cooke, 1995). Stoker and Cooke go so far as to say that because the Internet was established by military, business, academic and government institutions that consist in high proportion of Caucasian, male, middle-class employees, the whole system may be subtly biased toward the typical mindset of that population. Dunmire (1992) asserts that most spoken discourse is opinion and listeners must interpret conversations as naturally biased. Readers must remember that most of the discourse on newsgroups, listservs and chat groups of the Internet is opinion.

Technology glitches, lack of control, data malleability, misconduct, human error, context removal, currency and bias comprise an incomplete list of the problems to be found on the Internet, but they serve to establish the necessity of carefully evaluating all Internet information. As the Internet matures and more people gain access, misinformation may increase and the need for users to critically evaluate this information will likewise increase.

Action: Theories that Apply to Misinformation Problems

What can be done about the problems of misinformation? Some recommend that gatekeepers who will prevent misinformation from being transmitted be more widely employed. Software packages that electronically screen information are available. The censorship approach, however, is probably not the best answer to the misinformation problem.

Censorship: A Non-Solution

Educators and librarians might be tempted to solve the multiple difficulties with Internet misinformation by eliminating, filtering or labeling misinformation. The networked K–12 environment has witnessed a resurgence of censorship owing to the concern for children's exposure to inappropriate materials over the Internet. Censorship is an untenable solution to misinformation for several reasons. The Internet promotes democracy because it encourages the free flow of information and must be protected. Censorship, regardless of beneficial intent, threatens the availability of information (Eisenberg, 1989). Missing information is misinformation and librarians have fought the censorship battle at regular intervals for many years.

Another proposed solution is the attachment of warning labels to questionable information along with corresponding catalog entries and indexed abstracts. Labeling constitutes another type of censorship because it may prejudice the reader's evaluation. The American Library Association firmly supports intellectual freedom and values it more highly than accuracy (American Library Association, 1992). Sachs describes an example of the censorship issue in electronic communication. In the words of one of his respondents, "Any kook who wants to (post) a piece…that's just nuts can do it. Now the facilitator of that conference can delete it. But there's always the question, 'Is this being undemocratic and what about the First Amendment?'" (1995, p. 92).

Whether censorship is exercised, it is unlikely that all misinformation can ever be removed from the Internet, just as it has never been removed from other media. Thus, users must learn to evaluate online information. Educators have been teaching information evaluation strategies for years, but few strategies for electronic formats are available.

Skills for Electronic Information Evaluation

The skills set outlined here constitutes a realistic information evaluation strategy for Internet users ranging from approximately fifth grade through adulthood. The skills are essentially the same as general information literacy skills as described by Stripling and Pitts (1988) and Weisburg and Toor (1994), but have been translated to the Internet context and made more specific.

1. Adopt critical consciousness for all Internet interaction.

The Internet user must learn the types of misinformation, apply skepticism to all Internet material, and constantly scan for triggers that may indicate misinformation. The wise Internet user considers carefully before committing money, time or emotions based solely upon the authority of Internet communication because deception is simple in this new medium. The adoption of critical consciousness is the most important skill in this set because it makes the user aware of vulnerability.

2. Establish prior knowledge through wide browsing, searching and reading.

Wide reading in the content area helps to establish a contextual framework, a necessary component of effective communication. Wide reading translates into wide browsing on the Internet. Surfing, following relevant links and making numerous searches help the user construct contextual frameworks. Readers should track their paths, pay attention to "where" they are and save irrelevant but tempting links for later. The Internet researcher should remember to include print sources in this wide reading.

Figure 14.1   Triggers: Signs That May Indicate Misinformation

☛ Requests or demands for money, especially credit card numbers

☛ Contradictions and internal inconsistencies

☛ Author credentials that do not match subject matter

☛ Error: Spelling, punctuation, grammar, mathematical

☛ Appeals to emotion: flattery, fear messages; language that evokes guilt, sympathy

☛ Opinion markers: words as could, might, would, believe, "I think," assume, etc.

☛ Logical Fallacies

☛ Oversimplification

☛ Unstated Assumptions

☛ "Pass" messages: instructions to pass a communication to other people

☛ Unsupported claims

3. *Distinguish between fact and opinion.*

A large proportion of Internet discourse is opinion, sometimes stated as fact. Opinions unmarked by linguistic tags may be difficult to recognize (Dunmire, 1992). It is probably safest to classify all electronic dialogues (listservs, newsgroups, chat groups) as opinion unless supported by references or logical arguments. Often, however, opinions are marked by subjunctive verbs, opinion verbs, qualifiers, hypothetical situations, predictions of the future and adjective qualifiers. Footnotes, references, bibliographies, active verbs, statistics and specific provable details help to mark facts (Stripling and Pitts, 1988). Internet users must learn these markers and remember to scan for them (see Figure 14.1).

4. *Evaluate arguments.*

It is essential that Internet users be able to differentiate arguments from facts and detect the logical fallacies that many arguments contain because the Internet is growing in popularity as a public platform for debate. There are many types of fallacies. They may be recognized by these markers: proof by select cases, unstated assumptions, false analogies, oversimplification, appeal to tradition or authority and the "everybody's doing it" argument. Stripling and Pitts (1988) describe these logical fallacies in detail (p. 114).

5. *Compare and contrast related pieces of information from different sites, sources and search engines.*

It is seldom safe to accept a solitary piece of information without comparing it with other related pieces, which may confirm or contradict. The online searcher should perform multiple searches with different search engines to cross-check for data agreement. Confirmation supports reliability and often adds new knowledge. Contradiction requires further searching to gather support for one or the other of the conflicting facts. Sometimes an information conflict is unsolvable and the searcher must then tolerate the ambiguity for as long as necessary to find a satisfactory answer, or even indefinitely.

6. *Evaluate the reliability of online sources.*

There are several ways to evaluate reliability, although it is possible to disguise misinformation to the extent that it is undetectable. Four points to consider are format authority, writer authority, internal validity and currency. Different information formats cover issues in varying degrees of depth and credibility and so readers must learn to choose among them. The range of format authority is yet to be established for online sources and there is need for research to rank various Internet features, sites and domains in an order of perceived validity (Hernon & Altman, 1995). Personal authority of individual authors is harder to establish, but credentials may be examined to determine if a person has the background to write authoritatively in the area of publication. Easy methods of investigating authority include consulting an online library catalog for a comprehensive list of the author's output, performing a search on the author's name to examine other references, and e-mailing the author with probing questions. Students must treat any unidentified source with suspicion. Readers may carefully analyze articles and studies for internal validity (Stewart & Feder, 1987). Self-contradictions such as opposing facts and statistical inconsistencies are signs of possible haste or incomplete analysis on the part of the author, as are spelling, typographical and grammatical errors (Schrock, 1996). In current online sources, data may change from day to day and it is imperative to access the latest version of the facts. Most Internet communications bear dates that must be evaluated in light of the information they contain.

7. Identify and detect bias.

All writing is biased in some way because writers naturally express their personal perspective, regardless of attempts toward objectivity. Online readers should know that much of the material published on the Internet is raw personal opinion, highly biased and sometimes abusive. Internet users should remember to consider the sponsor of the site in the light of political agendas and commercialism. Advertisements are ubiquitous and sometimes cleverly disguised as information. As in the abortion example, political agendas of groups sponsoring Web sites may slant information to the best advantage of the group's goals.

8. Learn to interpret the conventions of the Internet.

Any good Internet manual describes Netiquette, emoticons, acronyms and other online conventions. FAQ (frequently asked questions) lists are available for many Internet features, and should be read. These conventions are as essential to

understanding Internet communication as body language is to understanding spoken language. It is important for users to remember that humor plays a large part in much Internet communication, but that often the communicator fails to label jokes.

9. Examine assumptions.

There are three special tendencies representing subconscious assumptions that Internet users must guard against. First, Internet users must combat the natural tendency to believe that all onscreen information is true ("Computerized information found more convincing," 1986). They must realize that print information is generally more reliable than online information due to professional editing, and consult print references as needed. A second assumption to resist is the tendency to believe facts that agree with the reader's bias, which means that it is important for readers to recognize their own biases. Finally, online information users often mistakenly assume that electronic information represents the universe of information, which is not yet true (Lynch, 1994). In addition, users must be alert for other, yet-unidentified assumptions which may be present in their consciousnesses or in the minds of writers.

Conclusion

In this paper, Internet misinformation types have been named, described and classified. From critical thinking and information literacy a set of nine skills has been proposed to evaluate information in a new medium. This set of skills is in a formative stage and further research is needed to validate and expand it.

Information is crucially important to democracy. It is imperative that the electorate be information-wise and tolerant of individual differences and ensuing debates (Callison, 1993). Furthermore, only information literacy can prevent a "two-tiered society" of the informationally rich and poor (Breivik & Senn, 1993, p. 25). The free flow of information unhampered by censorship is one of the most important of the democratic freedoms (Swan & Peattie, 1989). Because of its ability to freely, widely and speedily transmit information, the Internet more than any communication medium promotes democracy. It is likely that information will increasingly flow on the Internet and its successors and users must develop the critical thinking skills necessary to evaluate this information. Perhaps through providing this incentive to adopt critical consciousness the Internet will contribute to educating a populace better equipped for the future.

References

Advanced Research Corporation Community Services. (1994). *Abortion and possible risk for breast cancer: Analysis and inconsistencies.* Available: <http://cancer.med.upenn.edu/pdq/600342.html>.

American Library Association. (1992). *Intellectual freedom manual* (4th ed.). Chicago: American Library Association.

Aycock, A., & Buchignani, N. (1995). The e-mail murders: Reflections on "dead" letters. In S. G. Jones (Ed.), *Cybersociety* (pp. 184–231). Thousand Oaks, CA: Sage.

Breivik, P. & Senn, J. (1993). Information literacy: Partnerships for power. *Emergency Librarian, 21(1),* 25–28.

Callison, D. (1993). Expanding the evaluation role in the critical-thinking curriculum. In C. Kuhlthau (Ed.), *School Library Media Annual* (pp. 43–57). Englewood, CO: Libraries Unlimited.

Computerized information found more convincing. (1986, October 8). *Chronicle of Higher Education, 33,* 16, 18.

Coutorie, L. (1995). The future of high-technology crime: A parallel Delphi study. *Journal of Criminal Justice, 23(1),* 13–27.

Dunmire, P. (1992). *Constraints on critical thinking: An analysis of news narratives.* Paper presented at the annual meeting of the Conference on College Composition and Communication, Cincinnati, Ohio. (ERIC Document Reproduction Service No. ED 345 268).

Eisenberg, D. (1989). Problems of the paperless book. *Scholarly Publishing, 21(1),* 11–26.

Graham, P. (1993). Intellectual preservation and the electronic environment. In R. S. Martin (Ed.), *Scholarly communication in an electronic environment* (pp. 71–101). Chicago: American Library Association.

Gygi, K. (1990). Recognizing the symptoms of hypertext…and what to do about it. In B. Laurel (Ed.), *The art of human-computer interface design* (pp. 279–287). Reading, MA: Addison-Wesley.

Hernon, P. & Altman, E. (1995). Misconduct in academic research: its implications for the service quality provided by university libraries. *Journal of Academic Librarianship, 21(1),* 27–37.

Hickey, T. (1995). Present and future capabilities of the online journal. *Library Trends, 43 (4),* 528–543.

Johnson, P. (1995). Desperately seeking sources: Selecting on-line resources. *Technicalities, 15(8),* 1, 4–5.

Kochan, C. A., & Budd, J. M. (1992). The persistence of fraud in the literature: The Darsee case. *Journal of the American Society for Information Science, 43(7),* 488–493.

Kotzin, S. & Schuyler, P. L. (1989). NLM's practices for handling errata and retractions. *Bulletin of the Medical Library Association, 77(4),* 337–342.

Lafollette, M. (1992). *Stealing into print.* Los Angeles: University of California.

Lynch, C. (1994). Rethinking the integrity of the scholarly record in the networked information age. *Educom Review, 29(2),* 38–40.

Neavill, G. (1984). Electronic publishing, libraries, and the survival of information. *Library Resources and Technical Services, 28(1),* 76–89.

Neavill, G. (1993). Libraries and texts in the electronic environment. In R. S. Martin (Ed.), *Scholarly communication in an electronic environment* (pp. 53–69). Chicago: American Library Association.

Plagal Memoranda. (1994). *Breast cancer update.* Available: <http://copper.ucs.indiana.edu/~ljray/lifelink/plagal/brcan2.html>.

Roseman, M. (1995). *Re: virus alert (hoax).* In LM-NET Archives [Online]. Available: Gopher ericir.syr.edu/Education Listservs Archives/LM_NET/Messages from 1995/Oct_1995/#843.

Sachs, H. (1995). Computer networks and the formation of public opinion: An ethnographic study. *Media Culture and Society, 17(1),* 81–99.

Schrock, K. (1996). *Critical evaluation survey: Elementary school level.* Available: <http://www.capecod.net/Wixon/evalelem.htm>.

Schrock, K. (1996). *Critical evaluation survey: Middle school level.* Available: <http://www.capecod.net/Wixon/evalmidd.htm>.

Schrock, K. (1996). *Critical evaluation survey: Secondary school level.* Available: <http://www.capecod.net/Wixon/evalhigh.htm>.

Stephens, G. (1995, September/October). Crime in cyberspace. *Futurist, 29(5),* 24–28.

Stewart, W., & Feder, N. (1987, January 15). The integrity of the scientific literature. *Nature, 325(6101),* 207–214.

Stoker, D. & Cooke, A. (1995). Evaluation of networked information sources. In A. Helal & J. Weiss (Eds.), *Information superhighway: The role of librarians, information scientists, and intermediaries* (17th International Essen Symposium, pp. 287–312). Essen, Germany: Essen University Press.

Stripling, B., & Pitts, J. (1988). *Brainstorms and blue-prints: Teaching library research as a thinking process.* Englewood, CO: Libraries Unlimited.

Swan, J. & Peattie, N. (1989). *The freedom to lie.* Jefferson, NC: McFarland.

Swazey, J. Anderson, M., & Lewis, K. (1993). Ethical problems in academic research. *American Scientist, 81(6),* 542–553.

Tenopir, C. (1988). Searching full-text databases. *Library Journal, 113(8),* 60–61.

United States Congress, Office of Technology Assessment. (1988). *Informing the nation: Federal information dissemination in an electronic age* (Publication No. OTA-CIT-396). Washington, DC: U.S. Government Printing Office.

Weisburg, H. & Toor, R. (1994). *Learning, linking and critical thinking.* Berkeley Heights, NJ: Library Learning Resources.

CHAPTER FIFTEEN

Information Skills in the Curriculum: Developing a School-Based Curriculum

Carol-Ann Page

A few years ago educational and societal buzz words centered around the "knowledge explosion" and today we are constantly reminded that we live in an "information age." These are not fads…they are here to stay and they require a substantial redefinition of the verb "to know." At one time it was reasonable to learn a body of information by rote memory and to call this knowledge; today there is a distinct need for a shift from passive absorption to interactive processing and use of information in a variety of contexts.

Just as teacher-librarians have moved from the term "library skills" (skills to use the library taught in the library by the librarian) to "research and study skills" (skills to locate and use materials taught either in the classroom or resource center by the teacher and teacher-librarian together) it is time to move to "information skills," denoting more clearly a total school commitment to assisting young people to develop the skills necessary

for purposeful inquiry, informed decision-making and lifelong learning.

While the importance of information skills is receiving increasing acknowledgment, there tends to be decidedly little specificity and clear articulation in their development. Without a school-based continuum of information skills, classroom teachers and teacher-librarians face the difficulty and even professional danger of operating in a vacuum, without a framework or "curriculum," if you will. As a specifically trained professional in working with colleagues to teach young people to access and use information efficiently and effectively, the teacher-librarian should be able to specify and articulate information skills and guide sequential development. Information skills are perhaps more easily understood if organized into smaller discrete parts. These component clusters of information skills suggest the broad categories of skills needed by students.

Definitions

Resource Center Orientation, e.g., location of the resource center, physical layout, basic procedures, etc.

Research Strategies, e.g., defining the problem and its scope and procedures to address it, knowing where/how to start, where to look next, steps to follow, etc.

Locating Information—General and Subject Sources, e.g., use of the catalogue and indexes to encyclopedias, use of magazine indexes, use of specialized reference materials, maps and globes, etc.

Acquiring and Analyzing Information, e.g., using keywords, skimming and scanning, listening, viewing, comparing and contrasting, recognizing bias, etc.

Organizing and Recording Information, e.g., taking notes, outlining, keeping a record of sources, crediting direct quotes.

Communicating and Presenting Information, e.g., written and oral reports, slide-tape presentations, debating, etc.

While it is certainly not difficult to locate such a list of skills, and indeed many teacher-librarians have and use such a list, if it is not *integrated* with classroom instruction its short term value for the student, and the possibility of long term retention, are severely limited. Skills taught at each grade level are arbitrary and should differ from school to school, precisely the reason for a school-based continuum. The exact level at which skills are introduced is not important; what is important is that a school have a plan for the *sequential development* of information skills and that the plan reflect the goals and priorities of the school. This definitely leads to an improved basis for discussing objectives in planning with classroom teachers.

The National Council for the Social Studies (33rd yearbook, 1963) offers a well-accepted and often quoted list of criteria or principles for effective skill development:

1. The skill should be taught functionally, in the context of a topic of study, rather than as a separate exercise.

2. The learner must understand the meaning and purpose of the skill, and have motivation for developing it.

3. The learner should be carefully supervised in his (or her) first attempts to apply the skill, so that he will form correct habits from the beginning.

4. The learner needs repeated opportunities to practise the skill, with immediate evaluation so that he (or she) knows where he (or she) has succeeded or failed in his (or her) performance.

5. The learner needs individual help, through diagnostic measures and follow up exercises, since not all members of any group learn at exactly the same rate or retain equal amounts of what they have learned.

6. Skill instruction should be presented at increasing levels of difficulty, moving from the simple to the more complex; the resulting growth in skills should be cumulative as the learner moves through school, with each level of instruction building on and reinforcing what has been taught previously.

7. Students should be helped, at each stage, to generalize the skills, by applying them in many and varied situations; in this way, maximum transfer of learning can be achieved.

8. The program of instruction should be sufficiently flexible to allow skills to be taught as they are needed by the learner; many skills should be developed concurrently.

If we accept these basic principles—the need to provide for different learning styles, the need to provide for alternative means of reporting and presenting information, and a critical need to evaluate the processes of information use, as well as the final product of student research—then the planned sequential development of information skills and their integration with all aspects of the program become essential—to ensure that students are moving along a continuum towards independence and to ensure that some skills are not taught repeatedly to some students while not at all to others.

The Process

The question which arises is how to develop such a skills continuum for a school. The process outlined here is not sophisticated but it is systematic. The process does not require an extensive skills background but it does require initiative on the part of the teacher-librarian. The process does not intimidate or alienate teachers…it does work and has been implemented in a large number of schools through in-service programs.

The teacher-librarian, as stated, must take the initiative and be prepared to provide leadership and expertise in the articulation and specification of information skills. It is essential to involve the entire staff, starting with the principal, who must understand the purpose for the process and the concrete benefits for the school. It is difficult to implement any change, particularly one involving staff participation, without the understanding and support of the school administration.

The process can take place over a series of short sessions, before and after school or at lunch hour.

Step 1—Locate a list of information skills for the staff to react to. This can be derived from district guidelines for information skills development, from state or provincial curriculum guides, or from other school examples. For ease of implementation, sample lists used for this process at a number of schools are included here. (See Tables 15.1 and 15.2.)

Step 2—Provide only the appropriate section(s) to groups of staff for reaction. Do not expect a second grade teacher or a seventh grade teacher to respond to a K–7 list. Work with specific grade levels or primary/intermediate groups depending on the size of school. This is most effective if done sequentially. Meet with each group to come to some consensus. Have each grade level provide input/feedback both a grade level below and a grade level above the level they are presently teaching. The role of the teacher-librarian as both a team partner at each grade level and as a liaison between grade levels is key to development of the continuum.

Step 3—Seek ratification of the initial draft sections of the continuum from the primary and intermediate staff.

Step 4—Take the complete draft to the total staff for reaction. Pay particular attention to the transition years, Grades 4 and 7. Is too much expected at year four? Will students be sufficiently prepared for secondary school by the final year (in this case, Grade 7)?

Step 5—Seek final ratification and perhaps adoption as school policy…the emphasis must be on teachers accepting shared responsibility for information skills development.

The timeline for this process will vary according to the size of the school and the approach taken. If, for example, meetings are scheduled sequentially by grade level at Step 2 of the process, the timeline may be two to four weeks.

Meeting by primary and intermediate groups may be appropriate in small schools, but not as effective in large schools, though this approach takes less time. It is important to recognize that this stage of involvement in the process is where teachers develop a sense of ownership and commitment to the continuum of information skills which will serve as the future framework on which to build cooperatively planned and taught programs.

An information skills continuum for the intermediate grades is provided as an example of the developmental approach from year to year. Standardized formats for paragraphs, outlines, oral and written reports and bibliographies also ensure that teachers, teacher-librarians, and students share expectations and a common approach to both processes and products of student research. Most importantly, standard formats contribute to success-oriented inquiry and learning. As students gain confidence in what to do and how to do it, they are freed to absorb information, process it and use it in a meaningful way.

Table 15.1 Information Skills: Primary (K-3)

Indicate the grade level at which you *introduce* each skill. (Introduction means (a) students at that level *need* the skills and (b) the majority of students could master the skill appropriate to the grade level.) The student...

	Grade Level
1. demonstrates enjoyment in the resource center without supervision	_____
2. learns borrowing procedures of the resource center	_____
3. learns to recognize favorite authors, illustrators, characters	_____
4. learns the parts of a book's cover...title, author, illustrator	_____
5. learns to recall information based on print or non-print materials	_____
6. alphabetizes to the first letter and locates words in a picture dictionary	_____
7. learns the location of easy books	_____
8. learns the location of nonfiction books	_____
9. locates story books and nonfiction books	_____
10. alphabetizes to the second letter and locates words in a picture dictionary	_____
11. alphabetizes to the third letter and locates words in a picture dictionary	_____
12. recognizes main idea and sequence in stories	_____
13. learns the location of nonprint materials	_____
14. is aware of the newspaper as a source of information	_____
15. learns a beginning knowledge of the catalog	_____
16. demonstrates careful use of equipment (e.g., viewer and tape recorder)	_____
17. knows how to take care of books	_____
18. learns how fiction books are arranged	_____
19. recognizes the difference between a dictionary and an encyclopedia and what each is used for	_____
20. learns to pick out the key words in a question	_____
21. learns to use the table of contents and index as guides to the contents of a book	_____
22. learns how nonfiction books are arranged	_____
23. is aware of magazines for recreational reading	_____
24. recognizes main idea, sequence and characters in stories	_____
25. understands and selects root words	_____
26. is able to convey information orally using complete sentences	_____
27. is aware of magazines for information purposes	_____
28. is selective in choosing a book for enjoyment or appropriate for a purpose	_____
29. conveys information orally, with confidence, using complete sentences	_____
30. uses books to locate specific information	_____
31. learns to use an encyclopedia of the appropriate reading level	_____
32. uses filmstrips to locate specific information	_____
33. recognizes main idea, sequence, characters, mood and setting in stories	_____
34. learns to take notes using key words and phrases	_____
35. is able to convey information in written sentences	_____
36. learns to present information in a variety of ways and can select from 2 or 3 given choices	_____
37. uses pictures to gain information and to present information	_____

From *Foundations for Effective School Library Media Programs.* © 1999 Ken Haycock. Libraries Unlimited (800) 237-6124.

Table 15.2   Information Skills: Intermediate (4–7)

Indicate the grade level at which you *introduce* each skill. (Introduction means (a) students at that level *need* the skills and (b) the majority of students could master the skill appropriate to the grade level.) The student...

	Grade Level
1. learns to use guide words as aids in locating specific words	_____
2. learns to use entry words	_____
3. learns to use context clues in selecting the appropriate meaning of new words	_____
4. learns to use a junior thesaurus as a source of synonyms	_____
5. learns that the catalog is divided into subject, author, title	_____
6. learns to use an atlas for information purposes	_____
7. understands (can state) a purpose for reading for information	_____
8. learns to paraphrase information or take point form notes on a given subtopic(s), using one source	_____
9. learns to understand and use an atlas, index and map guide	_____
10. learns to use point form notes to write a paragraph in his/her own words	_____
11. learns to use dictionary aids such as pronunciation, symbols, syllabication and accent marks	_____
12. learns the arrangement of nonfiction materials on the shelf (i.e., a basic understanding of the Dewey Decimal System)	_____
13. learns to use the catalog to locate a specific book, either by author or title	_____
14. learns to use the pamphlet file as a source of information	_____
15. is aware of and learns to make use of resources available outside the school (public library, community resource people, government agencies)	_____
16. learns to use "see" and "see also" references in the catalog	_____
17. learns to write a simple bibliography	_____
18. learns to use a variety of reference books as sources of information	_____
19. learns to use a variety of indexes to locate information (i.e., Children's Magazine Guide)	_____
20. learns that the copyright date is a way of evaluating currency in a given resource	_____
21. learns to take notes on a given subtopic(s) using more than one source	_____
22. learns to present an oral report using point form notes as a guide	_____
23. learns to develop a report outline to organize information	_____
24. learns to interpret information in graphs/charts/diagrams	_____
25. learns to present information in graph/chart/diagram form	_____
26. learns a search strategy for locating resources on a specific topic	_____
27. learns to use dictionary aids (e.g., tenses, parts of speech, word origins)	_____
28. learns to use an outline to write a short report using his/her own words	_____
29. learns to use titles, chapter headings, subheadings as a guide to contents and to establishing a purpose for reading	_____
30. learns to compare information from different sources and identify agreement or contradiction	_____
31. understands (can state) a purpose for viewing for information	_____
32. demonstrates careful use of equipment (projectors, cameras)	_____
33. learns basic interview techniques for gathering information	_____
34. learns to use different types of maps (e.g., physical, political, population, contour)	_____
35. understands (can state) a purpose for listening for information	_____
36. learns to participate in group discussions for various purposes (e.g., sharing of information, ideas, opinions, and/or reaching consensus)	_____

From *Foundations for Effective School Library Media Programs.* © 1999 Ken Haycock. Libraries Unlimited (800) 237-6124.

The teacher-librarian and school resource center provide three levels of services:

Curriculum Implementation
    Curriculum Planning and Development
    Cooperative Program Planning and Team Teaching
    Professional Development Services for Teachers

Curriculum Enrichment
    Promotion of Materials and Services
    Guidance for Readers, Listeners, Viewers
    Information Services
    Design and Production of Materials
    Cooperation with Outside Agencies

Curriculum Support
    Administration of the Resource Center
    Selection of Materials
    Acquisition of Materials
    Organization of Materials
    Circulation of Materials

If the teacher-librarian endeavors to operate at the level of curriculum implementation, then he or she must have some knowledge and understanding of curriculum at all grade levels and in all subject areas. In other words, the teacher-librarian must know and appreciate the curriculum as interpreted through school-based programs. The teacher-librarian must also be able to analyze curriculum for entry points for the development of information skills through cooperative program planning and team teaching.

Most scope and sequence charts and much curricula have a materials orientation, stressing the location and selection of materials and content mastery. These skills are perhaps the most taught and least transferable. As with higher order thinking skills, more attention needs to be paid to comprehension, communication and production skills, to ensure that students have the ability to analyze and synthesize information.

With a strong commitment to a well-defined role emphasizing cooperative program planning and teaching, and a school-based continuum of information skills, the teacher-librarian has a basis at each grade level on which to focus the planning and implementation of resource-based programs which build on prior process learning and lead to further independence for the student. It is only at this level that the resource center program has educational validity and a political chance at survival!

Sample Information Skills Program: Intermediate Level

This Information Skills Program is organized into six categories or skills clusters:

1. *Orientation:* Finding the way to the library, feeling comfortable in the library, learning the proper handling and care of books, learning borrowing procedures, etc.

2. *Research Strategies:* Techniques for searching for information (knowing where/how to start, where to look next, steps to follow, how to narrow a topic, etc.)

3. *Locating Information:* Using the catalogue and other indexes to locate specific, general or subject-related information.

4. *Acquiring and Analyzing Information:* Using key words and the techniques of skimming and scanning to locate specific information, comparing and contrasting, classifying, recognizing bias and prejudice.

5. *Organizing and Recording Information:* Note-taking, outlining, interviewing, bibliography.

6. *Communicating and Presenting Information:* Written and oral reports, audio-visual and dramatic presentations, etc.

Grade 4

Locating Information:

1. uses guide words as aids in locating specific words in dictionaries and encyclopedias.

2. uses context clues in selecting the appropriate meaning of new words.

3. can use a junior thesaurus as a source of synonyms.

4. can use a variety of dictionaries appropriate for the fourth grade level.

5. can use a variety of encyclopedias appropriate for the fourth grade level (e.g., *Childcraft, Young People's Illustrated*).

6. has a beginning knowledge of the catalogue (e.g., searching by author or title or subject).

7. can use the catalogue to locate a specific book, either by title or by author.

8. locates title, author and illustrator (a) on the book cover and (b) on the title page.

9. locates the call number on the book spine.

10. is aware of the atlas for information purposes (i.e., as a source of maps).

11. is able to make use of resources available outside the school (public library, community resources, and resource people).

Acquiring and Analyzing Information:

1. uses context clues in selecting the appropriate meaning of new words.

2. uses titles, chapter headings, subheadings as a guide to contents.

3. uses pictures for a specific purpose (i.e., to gain information on specific topics).

4. identifies key words (phrases) in a question.

5. uses key words (phrases) to locate information needed to answer questions.

6. understands that different questions ask for different kinds of facts/information (e.g., Who? asks for facts/information about people).

Organizing and Recording Information:

1. is able to paraphrase information or take point form notes on a given sub-topic(s) using one source.

2. can state the source and authorship of information.

3. uses a given report outline to organize information.

4. makes point-form notes on a given sub-topic(s).

5. takes notes from (a) filmstrips and (b) a tape.

Communicating and Presenting Information:

1. can state a purpose for reading information.

2. understands (can state) a purpose for viewing information (videos and filmstrips).

3. understands (can state) a purpose for listening for information.

4. paraphrases information to answer questions (i.e., uses own words).

5. can participate in group discussions for various purposes (e.g., sharing of information, ideas, opinions, and reaching consensus).

6. can write an expository paragraph of five sentences (including indentation, topic sentence and appropriate punctuation).

Grade 5

Research Strategies:

1. is able to use a simple search strategy for locating resources on a specific topic.

Locating Information:

1. uses dictionary entry words.

2. uses dictionary syllabication as a guide to pronunciation.

3. can select the correct meaning from the dictionary.

4. uses the index to an atlas to locate maps.

5. can use the *Children's Magazine Index* to locate information in magazines.

6. uses the catalogue to locate a source on a given subject or topic.

7. uses the pamphlet file as a source of information.

Acquiring and Analyzing Information:

1. can interpret information presented in graph/chart/diagram form.

2. can develop a simple report outline to organize information.

3. can use a simple outline to write a short two or three paragraph report using his or her own words.

4. is able to compile a simple list of resources available on a topic.

Communicating and Presenting Information:

1. presents an oral report using point-form notes as a guide and using concrete or visual aids.

2. can present information in simple chart/ diagram form.

Grade 6

Locating Information:

1. uses dictionary aids such as accent marks and symbols for parts of speech (n., v., adj., adv.).
2. knows the organization of the newspaper and the use of its index.
3. can make use of "see" and "see also" references in the catalogue.
4. uses latitude and longitude to locate specific places on a map.

Acquiring and Analyzing Information:

1. is aware of the newspaper as a source of information.
2. recognizes different types of maps (e.g., physical, political, population, contour).
3. understands that the copyright date is a way of evaluating the currency of information in a given resource.

Organizing and Recording Information:

1. takes notes on a given (sub) topic(s) using more than one source.
2. lists resources used including author, title, date.
3. can use basic interview techniques for gathering information.

Communicating and Presenting Information:

1. demonstrates careful use of equipment (overhead projectors, opaque projectors, cameras).

2. writes a narrative paragraph of five sentences (including indentation, topic sentence, developing sentences, concluding sentence, proper punctuation).

Grade 7

Locating Information:

1. can use indexes to encyclopedias to locate information.
2. uses the newspaper as a source of information.

Acquiring and Analyzing Information:

1. can compare information from different sources and identify agreement or contradiction (e.g., encyclopedia articles, newspaper articles, etc.)
2. can use a given map scale to measure distance on a map.
3. is able to proofread, using simple standard symbols, and identify omissions, insertions, spelling, punctuation, paragraph indentation, tense.

Organizing and Recording Information:

1. can write a simple bibliography, in proper format, for resources used.

Communicating and Presenting Information:

1. writes an explanatory paragraph of five sentences (including indentation, topic sentence, developing sentences, concluding sentence, proper punctuation).

CHAPTER SIXTEEN

Developing a School-Based Research Strategy K–7

Sharon Straathof

The teacher-librarian whose goal is to develop a school-wide, developmental, cooperatively planned and taught program is constantly in search of ways to involve staff and students in well-organized, systematic approaches to the development and application of information skills. The task of working with teachers to implement skills programs in the context of the curriculum is facilitated by an agreed upon approach to, and expectations for, skills development. A school-based research strategy, particularly when coupled with a continuum of information skills, provides a logical reference point on which to base unit and yearly planning and permits both teachers and the teacher-librarian to assess progress towards goals in the classroom and the resource center.

The developmental nature of a research strategy ensures consistency in student approaches to information gathering, recording and reporting, while tailoring activities and expectations to individual needs and abilities. The strategy suggested here is divided into three developmental stages involving nine sequential steps (see Table 16.1).

Three Stages

At Stage I the nine steps in the process are introduced in their simplest forms. Much skills instruction and practice are necessary outside the context of a complete research project, but students also should be given frequent opportunities to work through the whole process. Stage I involves much instruction and direction as it is critical that students experience success in all aspects of the strategy.

At Stage II skills are developed and refined to greater levels of sophistication and greater independence. Frequent opportunities are again provided for the student to use the strategy in a variety of situations. Less direction is required at this stage as the process is monitored through a series of checkpoints as defined in the glossary (see Table 16.2). Individual needs-based instruction is offered as problems are identified. Relatively sophisticated standard formats for outlining, presentation, and bibliographies are used.

Table 16.1   Elementary Research Strategy: The Three Stages

The Nine Steps	Stage I Introduction	Stage II Development	Stage III Application
1. Identification of Topic (Brainstorming, Clustering)	Assigned by teacher and teacher-librarian; topic could be the same for all students or differ for groups or individuals. Brainstorming: "What do we want to find out about our topic?"	Student choice of a specific topic from a given list. Brainstorming: "What do we want to find out?" Clustering: "Can we group our ideas into clusters (subtopics)?"	Student choice of specific topic from a range of topic areas, with the option to develop own topic. Assistance, as necessary, in narrowing topic, deciding suitability. Independent or small group brainstorming, clustering.
2. Webbing (Organization of Research)	Provided by format; group discussion to clarify specific areas of investigation	Teacher-led discussions to develop webs of increasing complexity; moving towards student independence in completing webs.	Student develops web independently or with other student(s). Checked by teacher, teacher-librarian.
3. Selection of Suitable Materials	Selection by teacher and teacher-librarian.	Selection by student from a set of given materials (print, non-print). Student makes decisions re suitability of content, reading level, according to learned criteria.	Independent selection using knowledge of types of materials available, locational skills, learned criteria for deciding suitability.
4. Selection of Needed Information	Resource format (Web) dictates information required; preselected materials permit easy identification. Students move from finding information in pictures using captions, reading simple text, using simple indexes.	Student applies skills within the context of the web. Scope limited. More sophisticated skills introduced (headings, subheadings, skimming, etc.). Skills for using non-print materials developed. Process monitored frequently by teacher, teacher-librarian.	Student applies skills within the context of the web. Scope is broader. Teacher and teacher-librarian monitor at checkpoints.
5. Recording Sources of Information	Simple recording of author, title, on a given format. Introduce publisher, copyright date as appropriate.	Recording of bibliographic information given "Fill-in-the-blanks" forms for various media. Information compiled according to simplified standard format.	Student records and presents bibliographic information independently, following standard format.
6. Notetaking	A picture or key word is recorded on a given format	Key words or phrases are recorded on a given form. Information recorded by subtopics.	Notetaking cards used; students record information by subtopics as dictated by the web.
7. Outlining (Organization and Evaluation of Information)	Research format is both web and outline	Teacher-led discussions to develop outlines which correspond to webs. Increasing complexity and student independence in completing webs.	Student develops outline independently from web and notes, following standard format.
8. Preparation for Presentation (written, oral, visual)	Dictated by format, age, skill level. Drafting and editing introduced in written work. Planning for oral and visual presentations via group discussions.	Partially dictated by format; much direction via group discussion, instruction. Drafting, editing of written work. Guidelines established for oral, visual presentations. Frequent monitoring by teacher; moving towards independence.	Guidelines provided; progress monitored at checkpoints. Independent editing of written work. Speaking cards prepared for oral presentations. Visual presentations planned on paper. Frequent opportunities for practice.
9. Presentation	Will vary according to choice of presentation medium. Criteria are established for presentations; frequent opportunities for feedback from teacher(s) and students; audience expectations are set. Guidelines become more sophisticated, with increasing complexity and independence expected.		
LEVELS	Early Primary ⟷ Middle Primary ⟷ Late Primary	⟷ Early Intermediate ⟷ Middle Intermediate	⟷ Late Intermediate

Table 16.2   Research Strategy—Glossary

Brainstorming is a pre-research activity to help the student establish the scope of research and to develop some areas of inquiry which will be appropriate. In brainstorming, the student is asked or asks "What kinds of things should I find out about this topic?" All possibilities are recorded.

Checkpoints are points built into an assignment at which the student working independently through the research strategy, must check in with the teacher or teacher-librarian to ensure satisfactory completion of a step in the strategy. This permits the teacher to provide direction, encouragement, and individual review and/or instruction. Checkpoints also help to clarify the steps in the strategy, as checkpoints are at the end of each step.

Clustering is the intermediate step between brainstorming and webbing, in which the student groups the ideas from the brainstorming session in logical clusters in order to provide a focus for research. Clusters become subtopics on the web.

5-Finger Rule is a means by which students can quickly evaluate the suitability of reading level. The student chooses a "typical page" and reads, recording the number of unknown words on fingers of the hand. If three "problem words" are found, the student should question the usefulness of the material. If more than three words are found, the material is probably too difficult.

Notetaking is the recording of key words or key phrases in the student's own words to the greatest extent possible.

Outlining is based on a web, or a combination of a web and notes. An outline provides a guide for drafting, paragraphing and editing a report, essay or oral presentation. At Stage I, the outline is provided by the research format. At Stage II outlines are developed through the teacher-directed discussions. At Stage III the student develops an outline independently, following a given standard format.

Scanning is perusing materials to decide on suitability by looking at such things as tables of contents, headings, subheadings, indexes, and reading level.

Skimming is quick reading of appropriate sections of material, looking for key words related to the web topics and subtopics. More detailed reading of significant sections following skimming.

Webbing is a technique for establishing clear goals for research by defining and limiting the direction the research takes. The web becomes the student's guide to locating significant information. It is also helpful in writing outlines, as the web is, in effect, a research outline.

While the three stages may be viewed as roughly corresponding to: early to primary (K–3), late primary to middle intermediate (Grades 3–5), and mid to late intermediate (Grades 5–7), it is important to reiterate that the process is developmental. In addition, since this type of strategy should be modified to suit the unique needs of the school, specifics at each stage would vary. In the early years of implementing the strategy, elements of skills instruction may need to be compressed in situations where school-wide skills instruction has not been consistent. For example, intermediate students may need early webbing-related skills compressed and taught if they do not possess these skills.

The overall goal of a research strategy in the elementary school is to enable students to select and narrow a topic, plan the scope and direction of research, locate sources, identify and record significant information and prepare to make a presentation based on standard formats appropriate to the level. However, total independence is not expected and the process is monitored with guidance and instruction provided.

The implications of such a research strategy for secondary schools are several: students entering secondary school cannot be expected to be totally independent in research; clear outlines of expectations are still needed; more sophisticated versions of each step in the research strategy require instruction; some skills will need to be introduced, such as footnoting and the use of direct and indirect quotations. This K–7 research strategy lends itself, though, to an extension at the secondary level, with the addition of Stage IV and perhaps V leading to independence and a high level of sophistication in research. Secondary stages would involve increased expectations in terms of complexity of sources, quality and quantity of research and sophistication of standard formats and presentation techniques. Skills needed for doing research from primary sources would also be introduced.

Related Skills

The nine steps in the strategy are skills clusters rather than separate, discrete skills (see Table 16.3).

1. *Identification of a topic* is a sophisticated process involving the broadening or narrowing of a topic within a range of possibilities. Brainstorming and clustering (see Table 16.2) are introduced at the earliest stages, usually as large group activities to give students experience in expanding and narrowing topics and organizing information searches.

Table 16.3   K-7 Research Strategy—Related Skills

1. Identification of Topic
- brainstorming
- clustering (ability to group ideas, concepts)
- narrowing or broadening a topic

2. Webbing
- recognizing subtopics as parts of the whole
- recognizing most significant concepts, ideas
- structuring a web

3. Selection of Suitable Materials
- scanning
- use of tables of contents, indexes, headings, subheadings
- recognition that copyright date can indicate usefulness of information
- analysis of reading levels to judge suitability of materials
- knowledge of a variety of media (i.e., books, encyclopedias, magazines, audio-visual material)
- locational skills (use of catalogs, knowledge of Dewey Decimal System, etc.)

4. Selection of Needed Information
- use of indexes
- skimming
- distinguishing fact from fiction
- selecting significant information (information appropriate to web)
- reading captions
- interpretation of charts, tables, diagrams

5. Recording Sources of Information
- knowledge of reasons for recording sources
- identifying author, title and subtitles, titles of articles, chapters, publishers, city of publication, copyright date
- knowledge of standard formats (from simplest to most complex) for citing various media
- alphabetization

6. Notetaking
- identification of key words, phrases
- recording key words, phrases
- organizing information gathered
- notetaking from both print and non-print sources

7. Outlining
- knowledge of outline format
- recognition of subtopics as parts of a whole
- recognition of logical sequence of information
- editing out of inappropriate or less significant information
- organizing information in logical groupings. (This will have been covered at the webbing and notetaking steps as well.)

8. Preparation for Presentation
- (A very wide range of skills needed, depending on medium chosen)
- writing sentences form key words
- paragraphing
- writing introductory and closing statements
- knowledge of essay and paragraph formats
- editing
- proofreading
- preparation of notes for oral presentations
- preparing illustrations, diagrams, charts, graphs
- planning presentation (i.e., sketch of visual presentation, plan for oral presentation)
- layout, lettering and other "artistic" skills

9. Presentation
- Many presentations will be a combination of the following:

Written
- paragraphing
- essay format
- ability to present information in an attractive manner

Oral
- ability to speak from prepared notes
- voice control
- use of illustrative material or objects
- ability to respond to questioning

Visual
- technical skills, depending on medium chosen

---

2. *Webbing* (see Table 16.2) is a means of organizing and focusing research. Clusters of ideas developed during brainstorming are organized in a visual format which the student refers to, and modifies as necessary, during the research process. Webbing allows students to make decisions about the scope and direction of research and helps to classify information. Webbing also limits the student's impulse to copy. With a clear idea of the kind of information required, the student is less likely to resort to the "quantity vs. quality" approach to research. The web also serves as a guide for developing an outline and for preparing the final presentation (see Table 16.4).

3. *Selection of suitable materials* is essential for success. At Stages I and II resources are pre-selected by the teacher and teacher-librarian and student choice takes place within this set of materials. Independent selection at Stage III should involve monitoring and guidance. The selection of materials involves much

Table 16.4   Webbing and Outlining Web Development

Web Development
Stage I
The web is provided by the research format.

Cover (topic)	(Illustration) Key word
(Illustration) Key word	(Illustration) Key word
(Illustration) Key word	Bibliography

Grades K-1

Cover (Topic)	Table of Contents
Key word or phrase and Illustration	Key word or phrase and Illustration
Repeat	Repeat
Index	Bibliography

Grades 2-3

Students work on a large sheet of paper divided into 6 or 8 sections. Sections are set aside for cover, bibliography, table of contents, etc. Information to be recorded in the remaining sections is defined in the brainstorming session. Notes are recorded either on the research paper (K-1) or on a separate note-taking sheet (Grades 2-3). When research and illustrations are completed, the sections are cut apart and stapled to form a booklet.

Stage II
The web is developed in a large group, teacher-directed discussion. Individuals use the web generated by the group.

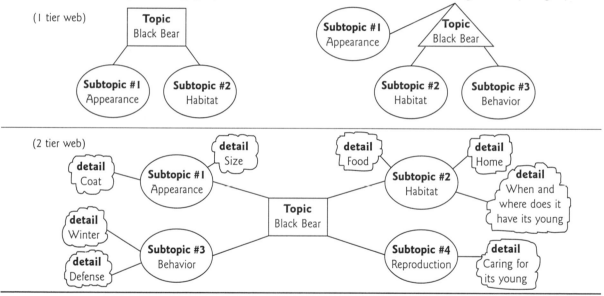

(1 tier web)

Stage III
Independent (individual or small group) development with guidance and /or checkpoints.

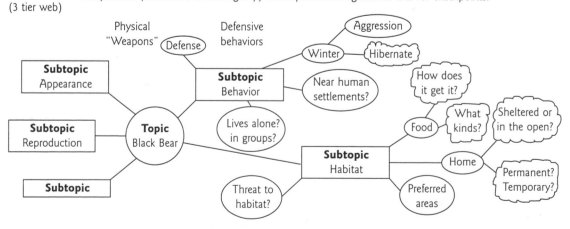

(3 tier web)

Table 16.4   Webbing and Outlining Web Development (continued)

Outlining
Stage I
Format provided.

Stage II
A simple outline is developed as a group activity, based on a web. The next stage is to develop an outline format to the subtopic level as a group, then allow students to work independently to add details to the outline in logical order.

Topic — Black Bear	I. Topic — Black Bear
A. Subtopic — Appearance	A. Subtopic — Appearance
B. Subtopic — Habitat	1. (detail) — Size
C. Subtopic — Reproduction	2. (detail) — Coat
	B. Subtopic — Habitat
	1. (detail) — Home
	2. (detail) — Food
	C. Subtopic — Reproduction
	1. (detail) — When it has its young
	2. (detail) — Where it has its young
	3. (detail) — How it cares for them

Stage III
Students develop an outline independently, following a given standard format and basing the outline on a combination of the revised web and notes.

I. Topic	II. Topic
A. Subtopic	A.
1. Detail	1.
a) Additional detail	a)
b) Additional detail	b)
B. Subtopic	B.
1. Detail	1.
2. Detail	2.
a) Additional detail	
b) Additional detail	

instruction regarding varieties of sources, selection of materials with an appropriate reading level and suitable, relevant content, as well as the many locational skills involved in use of the resource center (see Table 16.3). The "5-finger rule" facilitates selection at Stage I and II, while the technique of scanning is stressed at Stages II and III (see Tables 16.2 and 16.4).

4. *Selection of needed information* involves a wide variety of skills (see Table 16.3) which require instruction and frequent practice in many varied contexts. At Stage I, required information is clearly specified and dictated by the brainstorming session and web development, but more scope is involved and the student must read more carefully to identify appropriate information. At Stage III the process is much more open-ended as it is expected that the student will have developed the skills and confidence necessary to select information independently.

5. *Recording sources of information* is included at all stages but a simplified standard bibliographic format is expected only at Stage III.

6. *Note-taking* from both print and non-print resources follows the web format. Notes are organized by sub-topics as they are recorded. In kindergarten and early first grade, pictures are drawn to record information. Later, keyword note-taking is introduced, followed by a combination of key words and phrases.

7. *Outlining* facilitates the organizing of information gathered and the preparation of the presentation. At Stage I, the research form

(see Tables 16.2 and 16.4) provides the outline, and, in fact, becomes the presentation in booklet form. At Stages II and III formal outlines are prepared using both the web and notes, moving from a simple outline to a more sophisticated standard format (see Table 16.4). While the web may appear to be a good organizer in itself, the process of developing an outline involves the editing and reorganization of information gathered. The student has been encouraged to modify the web as research proceeds and it is at the outline stage that the final decisions made regarding content of the presentation and sequencing of information are made. The outline is less necessary for visual presentations (see Table 16.4).

8. *Preparation for presentation* varies according to the medium of presentation (see Tables 16.1 and 16.5). Where the presentation is written, emphasis is placed on the writing process, including drafting, editing and proofreading skills.

9. *Presentation* may be written, oral or visual and some combination of these. Options should be varied to include posters, dioramas, slide-tape or dramatizations, as well as written reports.

Process writing (see Table 16.6) is a logical extension to this approach. The research strategy is the writing process applied to the gathering, recording and processing of information rather than creative writing. A school-wide commitment to the writing process is not essential to the development of a research strategy but the benefits to the student of using the parallel processes are significant.

A School-Wide Approach

The school-based K–7 research strategy is based on the three stages and breaks the developmental process into specific elements for each grade level, providing for a logical progression of skills and expectations. Like the continuum of information skills, it is essential that there be a total staff involvement in and commitment to the development of the school-based strategy to ensure common goals, logical progression and suitability to the needs of students. Staff involvement also clarifies the teacher's goals and responsibilities and re-emphasizes the cooperative nature of program and the desirability of teacher/teacher-librarian partnerships in program development. The research strategy can be implemented in schools that have not developed a school-based continuum of information skills; however, the strategy works best where it is seen as being a step beyond the information skills already designated appropriate at each grade level. In addition, teachers are more likely to see the inherent logic of developing a school-wide strategy where the information-skills continuum has already been developed and implemented.

The teacher-librarian interested in developing a school-based strategy may choose several different paths towards this goal. It is possible to begin using the strategy with certain interested teachers or at certain grade levels, with the aim of demonstrating its effectiveness and drawing in other staff members. Where staff is receptive, where a continuum of information skills has already been developed or where the writing process is in place, an in-service presentation to staff may be appropriate, followed by grade-level meetings to develop specific expectations and goals. Using the Three Stages outline, and if possible, the information skills continuum, staff decides which aspects of the strategy will be emphasized at each grade level. In the sample school-based strategy, movement from one stage to another is not lockstep; some developmental stages require more emphasis than others (see Table 16.5).

In addition, an interim version of the strategy, providing for "catch-up" in later grades where a formal process has not been previously used school-wide, may be necessary before the final K–7 research strategy can be put in place.

Yearly review of the strategy is essential to ensure its continuing effectiveness. Teachers may find that students can move more rapidly through the stages to an even more sophisticated level by seventh grade. Alternatively, the developmental process may be slower and expectations may need to be adjusted accordingly.

Table 16.5 Sample School-Based K–7 Research Strategy

	K	1	2	3	4	5	6	7
1. Identification of Topic (Brainstorming Clustering)	Teacher decision Brainstorming to establish criteria: "what do we want to find out?"	Teacher decision Brainstorming established purpose, guidelines for choosing key words	→	Teacher decision Group brainstorming, clustering led by teacher. Number of sub-topics determined by teacher	Students select from a range of well-defined topics. Teacher-led brainstorming, clustering.	→	Students select from a range of topic areas; narrow topic with assistance. Small group brainstorming, clustering.	Students choose and narrow topic given guidelines and assistance where needed. Option to choose own topics. Individual brainstorming, clustering.
2. Webbing (Organization of Research)	Provided in the form of booklet or research page.	→		Teacher directed with web outline provided for students to complete. (Two subtopics). Second tier of web added.	Teacher-directed with web outline provided (3-4 subtopics). Second tier of web added.	Sample web developed as large group; students develop own webs from model.	Review of webbing techniques. Students develop own webs to second or third tier.	→
3. Selection of Suitable Materials	Selection by teacher, teacher-librarian. Students have limited choice.	→	Selection by teacher and teacher-librarian, provision for range of reading levels. Students choose appropriate materials using 5-Finger Rule & simple scanning techniques.	Some selected by teacher and teacher-librarian; some independent selection, using established criteria and techniques. Non-point materials introduced. Two sources required.	Guided independent selection where appropriate for skill level of students. Two-three sources required.	Guided independent selection. Variety of sources required (i.e., book, encyclopedia, filmstrip).	Independent selection, monitored by teacher, teacher-librarian. Variety of media.	→
4. Selection of Needed Information	Webbing format dictates information required. Pictures as information sources.	Webbing format dictates information required. Pictures and simple texts as information sources.	Web provides strict focus for identifying needed information. Simple indexes introduced.	Web limits scope but student must make more decisions in selecting significant information. Skimming introduced. Teacher monitors closely.	→	Independent selection monitored by teacher at checkpoints.	→	Independent selection
5. Recording Sources of Information	Record title of book.	Record author, title.	→	Record author, title of print or non-print materials alphabetically.	Recorded on "fill-in-the-blank" forms. Compiled according to simplified standard format.		Student records and presents bibliographic information independently, according to standard formats.	→
6. Notetaking	Pictures to illustrate concepts in web.	Pictures or key words, recorded on "web."	Key words recorded on notetaking form.	Key words recorded on notetaking form by subtopic.	Key words, phrases recorded on notetaking form by subtopic.	Key words, phrases recorded on notetaking cards by subtopic.	→	
7. Outlining (Organization and evaluation of information)	Provided by format.	→		Boxed on web: main point outline developed in teacher-led group discussion.	Based on combination of web and notes: main point outline in standard format developed as a group. Increased independence in completing.	Based on web and notes. Simplified standard format, developed independently with assistance as needed.	Standard outline format developed independently. Monitored at checkpoint.	→

Table continues

Table 16.5 Sample School-Based K–7 Research Strategy (continued)

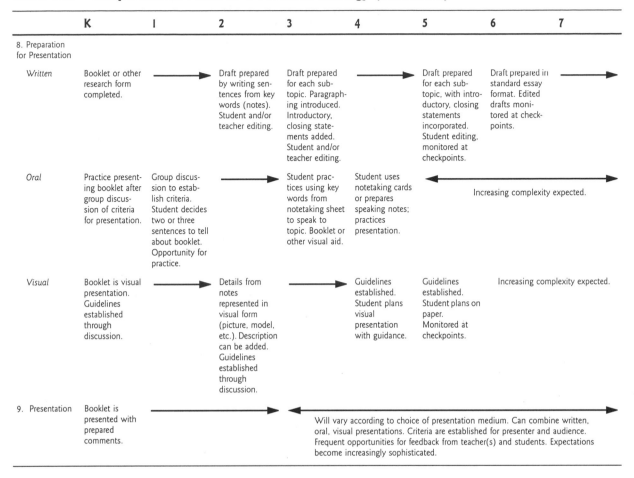

	K	1	2	3	4	5	6	7
8. Preparation for Presentation								
Written	Booklet or other research form completed.	→	Draft prepared by writing sentences from key words (notes). Student and/or teacher editing.	Draft prepared for each subtopic. Paragraphing introduced. Introductory, closing statements added. Student and/or teacher editing.	→	Draft prepared for each subtopic, with introductory, closing statements incorporated. Student editing, monitored at checkpoints.	Draft prepared in standard essay format. Edited drafts monitored at checkpoints.	→
Oral	Practice presenting booklet after group discussion of criteria for presentation.	Group discussion to establish criteria. Student decides two or three sentences to tell about booklet. Opportunity for practice.	→	Student practices using key words from notetaking sheet to speak to topic. Booklet or other visual aid.	Student uses notetaking cards or prepares speaking notes; practices presentation.	← Increasing complexity expected. →		
Visual	Booklet is visual presentation. Guidelines established through discussion.	→	Details from notes represented in visual form (picture, model, etc.). Description can be added. Guidelines established through discussion.	→	Guidelines established. Student plans visual presentation with guidance.	Guidelines established. Student plans on paper. Monitored at checkpoints.	Increasing complexity expected.	
9. Presentation	Booklet is presented with prepared comments.	→		← Will vary according to choice of presentation medium. Can combine written, oral, visual presentations. Criteria are established for presenter and audience. Frequent opportunities for feedback from teacher(s) and students. Expectations become increasingly sophisticated. →				

Table 16.6 Process Writing and the Research Strategy

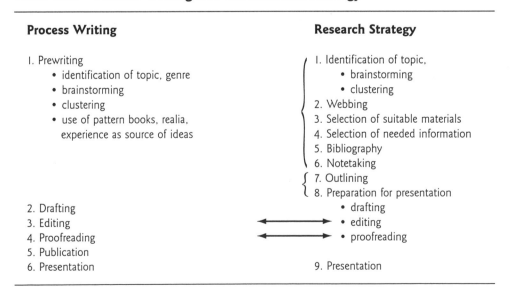

Process Writing	Research Strategy

1. Prewriting
  • identification of topic, genre
  • brainstorming
  • clustering
  • use of pattern books, realia, experience as source of ideas
	1. Identification of topic,
	  • brainstorming
	  • clustering
	2. Webbing
	3. Selection of suitable materials
	4. Selection of needed information
	5. Bibliography
	6. Notetaking
	7. Outlining
	8. Preparation for presentation
	  • drafting
	  • editing
	  • proofreading

2. Drafting 3. Editing 4. Proofreading 5. Publication 6. Presentation	9. Presentation

Consideration must also be given to the evaluation of the process. Evaluation is based on the student's ability to apply the overall strategy in a variety of situations as well as to use the many component skills. It is important to stress that evaluation must be of the process and not of the final product alone. Evaluation must be ongoing and based on frequent contact with the students at all steps. Once again, cooperatively planned and team taught programs facilitate such evaluation as both teacher and teacher-librarian are available to guide students. The step-by-step progression of the strategy also makes evaluation of the process easier, as do the checkpoints which are built into Stage III assignments. The student should be aware of expectations and evaluation criteria before beginning research so that the aims and responsibilities are clearly understood.

A school-wide program has many advantages:

- guided sequential development ensures that students grasp the strategy and can internalize the process for application to research in many subject areas;
- success is built in at all steps and stages. Expectations are clearly defined, the process is familiar no matter what the subject area or grade level or the teacher assigning the project, and instruction and monitoring of progress are an integral part of the strategy;
- the strategy provides for the introduction of skills and processes in the early grades and therefore permits relative sophistication and independence by sixth and seventh grades;
- numerous opportunities are provided for students to apply skills and attain mastery and transference;
- a school-wide program developed in cooperation with the staff ensures that teachers remain aware of skills required at each stage and that they incorporate skills instruction into their program;
- a school-wide strategy limits assumptions teachers may make about the scope of an assignment and the abilities of the students. Teachers will be more inclined to tailor the assignments to the developmental level and stage of the students. On the other hand, a school-wide commitment to a research strategy permits teachers to make assumptions about the skills background of students and to proceed to expand expectations and instruction. Consistency of approach and working cooperatively towards goals mean clearer objectives for the teacher and for the students;
- a K–7 research strategy developed by the total staff in cooperation with the teacher-librarian ensures this consistency and, equally important, ensures commitment and participation at all levels. Students can then become secure in their approach, as expectations and processes are consistent.

Teacher-librarians are effective when they plan and develop units of study with classroom teachers to integrate information skills, and then teach these units together. The school-based research strategy builds on the information skills continuum to assure well-planned, well-integrated team taught programs for young people.

CHAPTER SEVENTEEN

Computer Literacy and Information Literacy: A Natural Combination

Doug Johnson and Mike Eisenberg

The pressure is on. Government officials, school boards and the general public all seem to have finally seen the light and acknowledged the message that technology can play an important role in the education of our young people. Nationwide, funds are becoming available for computers, Internet connections and other information technologies for school labs, for classrooms, and yes, even for school library resource centers.

This is obviously good news. However, this increased funding is accompanied by increased accountability. Educators are being asked to show something for the investment. Although there is increasing support for computers in schools, there doesn't seem to be a correlated increase in understanding (among the public and even among educators) of how technology can and should be used, nor an understanding of the differences that technology can make in education. The public intuitively senses that children today need to know about computers and how to use them. They hope that technology can improve teaching and learning, but few individuals have a

deeper understanding of the role and application of computers in schools. Yet that lack of understanding doesn't stop them from asking difficult and important questions:

- What evidence is there that the money spent on technology is being spent wisely?
- What are the best uses for a finite number of computers and limited amount of related technologies in the schools?
- How much difference is technology making in student achievement?

Ensuring technology is used in effective ways requires knowledge, vision and leadership. Teacher-librarians are in an excellent position to provide this leadership. Over the past 10 years, the profession has made significant progress in accepting an important role in the educational technology arena. In many schools and districts, the school library resource center has been the first place technology has been successfully used. As a result of automation projects, electronic research resources and computer labs located in or adjacent to resource centers, teacher-librarians have played central roles in technology planning and implementation.

This active role in technology has clearly benefited many students. Teacher-librarians are committed to equal and open physical access to technology for all students and staff through establishing non-departmental computer facilities and networks in their libraries and throughout the school. Library media professionals understand that meaningful school-wide implementation of technology requires regular and unrestricted access for all students and staff. Technology cannot be isolated in "special" classrooms or only a few departments.

But now teacher-librarians must also begin providing the knowledge, vision and leadership to the critical area of computer instruction. We must be able to provide not only physical access to the technology but also intellectual access. Again, the public and educators agree that students need to be proficient computer users— students need to be computer literate. Yet there seems to be only a vague notion of what computer literacy really means.

Can the student who operates a computer well enough to play "Doom" be considered computer literate? Will a student who has used computers in school only for running tutorials or an integrated learning system have the skills necessary to survive in our society? Will the ability to do basic word processing be sufficient for students entering the workplace or post-secondary education? Clearly not.

In too many schools, most teachers and students still use computers only as the equivalent of expensive flash cards or electronic worksheets. The productivity side of computer use in the general content area curriculum is neglected or grossly underdeveloped. Productivity tools (Moursund, 1995–96) (such as word processors, databases, spreadsheets, graphic tools, chart makers) are often taught only in special computer classes and most students have very limited access to the technology outside those actual class sessions. Computer productivity skills may be a significant part of special courses like business education or technology education, but unfortunately these courses are only taken by a minority of students, despite the fact that these skills would benefit all students.

Teacher-Librarian Leadership

There are, however, some encouraging signs concerning computers and technology in education. For example, it is becoming popular for educational technologists to advocate integrating computers into the content areas. Teachers and administrators are recognizing that computer skills should not be taught in isolation and that separate computer classes do not really help students learn to apply computer skills in meaningful ways. This is an important shift in approach and emphasis. It is a shift with which teacher-librarians are very familiar.

Teacher-librarians know that moving from isolated skills instruction to an integrated approach is an important step that takes a great deal of planning and effort. Over the past 20 years, teacher-librarians have worked hard to move from teaching isolated library skills to teaching integrated information skills. Effective integration of information skills has two requirements:

1. the skills must directly relate to the content area curriculum and to classroom assignments, and

2. the skills themselves need to be tied together in a logical and systematic information process model.

Schools seeking to move from isolated computer skills instruction will also need to focus on both of these requirements. Teacher-librarians can play a significant role in this transition. From experience, teacher-librarians know that successful integrated information skills programs are designed around collaborative projects jointly planned and taught by teachers and themselves. Computer skills instruction can follow the same approach. Teacher-librarians, computer teachers and classroom teachers need to work together to develop units and lessons that will include computer skills, general information skills and content-area curriculum outcomes.

Teacher-librarians must also provide leadership in developing a meaningful, unified computer literacy curriculum. Most computer literacy curricula are little more than "laundry lists" of isolated skills, such as:

- knowing the parts of the computer,
- writing drafts and final products with a word processor, or
- searching for information using a CD-ROM database.

While these specific skills are certainly important for students to learn, the "laundry list" approach does not provide an adequate model for students to transfer and apply skills from situation to situation. These curricula address the "how" of computer use, but rarely the "when" or "why." Students may learn isolated skills and tools, but they will still lack an understanding of how those various skills fit together to solve problems and complete tasks. Students need to be able to use computers flexibly, creatively and purposefully. All learners should be able to recognize what they need to accomplish, determine whether a computer will help them to do so, and then be able to use the computer as part of the process of accomplishing their task. Individual computer skills take on a new meaning when they are integrated within this type of information problem-solving process, and students develop true computer literacy because they have genuinely applied various computer skills as part of the learning process.

Teacher-librarians can do a tremendous service to their students by combining their district's computer literacy and information literacy curricula. Separate computer and information skills programs result in confusion on the part of students, teachers and parents.

The curriculum outlined below, "Computer Skills for Information Problem-Solving," demonstrates how computer literacy skills can fit within an information literacy skills context. The various computer skills are adapted from curricula developed by the state of Minnesota (Minnesota Department of Education, 1986) and the Mankato Area Public Schools (Mankato Schools Information Literacy Curriculum Guideline).

These basic computer skills are those which all students might reasonably be expected to demonstrate before graduation. Since Internet-related skills are increasingly important for information problem-solving, they are included in this curriculum and are noted by an asterisk.

A comprehensive set of computer skills fits easily and logically within the various steps of the Big Six process (Eisenberg & Berkowitz, 1988, 1992) (see Table 17.1). The computer skills support and enhance the student's information problem-solving abilities, but they do not supplant the more general information skill. One day, it may well be assumed that information skills automatically include technology skills, but currently specific computer skills need to be defined and clearly stated because:

- Many districts already have some form of computer skills curriculum which is seen by some teachers or parents as valuable, and this approach shows how its skills can be easily included into an information problem-solving framework.
- It is not realistic to expect most teachers and many teacher-librarians to understand that information literacy automatically assumes computer literacy.
- The business world, academic community and public seem to readily accept that students must have computer skills, but the need for the broader information skills is less "hyped." Focusing on readily understood computer skills may help to raise the visibility and importance of the information problem-solving curriculum.
- Clearly stated computer skills help determine the resources needed to effectively teach a skill. For example, if it is the expectation that information be communicated through a computer-generated graph, then the need for a certain number of computers, types of software and level of teacher proficiency is more easily established.

Table 17.1   The Big Six Model

The framework for the entire curriculum is the Big Six skills information literacy model developed by Mike Eisenberg and Bob Berkowitz. The Big Six skills approach is one of the most widely-used models of information literacy. The Big Six represents a systematic approach to information problem-solving. It is a set of skills that is transferable to school, personal, or work applications, as well as all subject areas across a full range of grade levels. According to the Big Six approach, whenever a student has an information-oriented problem, it is appropriate and useful to initiate the following six steps and substeps:

1. Task Definition
   1.1 Define the problem.
   1.2 Identify the information requirements of the problem.
2. Information Seeking Strategies
   2.1 Determine the range of possible sources.
   2.2 Evaluate the different possible sources to determine priorities.
3. Location and Access
   3.1 Locate sources (*intellectually and physically*).
   3.2 Find information within sources.
4. Use of Information
   4.1 Engage (e.g., read, hear, view) the information in a source.
   4.2 Extract information from a source.
5. Synthesis
   5.1 Organize information from multiple sources.
   5.2 Present information.
6. Evaluation
   6.1 Judge the product (*effectiveness*).
   6.2 Judge the information problem-solving process (*efficiency*).

Although presented in a logical order, the Big Six approach does not assume that information problem-solving is always a sequential process. In completing tasks and solving problems, students may locate and use a source (steps 3 and 4) and later loop back to figure out exactly how they will handle the situation (step 1). In other situations, students may decide to use one source at a time, going through steps 2–5 a number of times. However, to solve information problems successfully, students must successfully complete all the various steps at some point.

Computer Skills for Information Problem-Solving: A Curriculum Based on the Big Six Skills Approach

1. Task Definition

The first step in the information problem-solving process is to recognize that an information need exists, to define the problem and to identify the types and amount of information needed. In terms of technology, students will be able to:

A. Use e-mail and online discussion groups (e.g., listservs, newsgroups) on the Internet to communicate with teachers regarding assignments, tasks and information problems.

B. Use e-mail and online discussion groups (e.g., listservs, newsgroups) on the Internet to generate topics and problems and to facilitate cooperative activities among groups of students locally and globally.

C. Use desktop conferencing, e-mail and groupware software on local area networks to communicate with teachers regarding assignments, tasks and information problems.

D. Use desktop conferencing, e-mail and groupware software on local area networks to generate topics and problems and to facilitate cooperative activities among groups of students.

E. Use computer brainstorming or idea-generating software to define or refine the information problem. This includes developing a research question or perspective on a topic.

2. Information-Seeking Strategies

Once the information problem has been formulated, the student must consider all possible information sources and develop a plan for searching. Students will be able to:

A. Assess the value of various types of electronic resources for data gathering, including databases, CD-ROM resources, commercial and Internet online resources, electronic reference works, community and government information electronic resources.

B. Identify and apply specific criteria for evaluating computerized electronic resources.

C. Use Internet electronic interest groups (e.g., newsgroups), e-mail and online forums (e.g., listservs) to query such groups as part of a search of the current literature.

D. Use a computer to generate modifiable flow charts, Gantt charts, time lines, organizational charts, project plans and calendars which will help the student plan and organize complex or group information problem-solving tasks.

3. Location and Access

After students determine their priorities for information seeking, they must locate information from a variety of resources and access specific information found within individual resources. Students will be able to:

A. Locate and use appropriate computer resources and technologies available within the school library resource center, including those on the center's local area network, (e.g., online catalogs, periodical indexes, full-text sources, multimedia computer stations, CD-ROM stations, online terminals, scanners, digital cameras).

B. Locate and use appropriate computer resources and technologies available throughout the school including those available through local area networks (e.g., full-text resources, CD-ROMs, productivity software, scanners, digital cameras).

C. Locate and use appropriate computer resources and technologies available beyond the school through the Internet (e.g., newsgroups, listservs, WWW sites via Netscape, Lynx or another browser, gopher, ftp sites, online public access library catalogs, commercial databases and online services, other community, academic and government resources).

D. Know the roles and computer expertise of the people working in the school library resource center and elsewhere who might provide information or assistance.

E. Use electronic reference materials (e.g., electronic encyclopedias, dictionaries, biographical reference sources, atlases, geographic databanks, thesauri, almanacs, fact books) available through local area networks, stand-alone workstations, commercial online vendors or the Internet.

F. Use the Internet or commercial computer networks to contact experts for help and referral services.

G. Conduct self-initiated electronic surveys through e-mail, listservs or newsgroups.

H. Use organizational systems and tools specific to electronic information sources that assist in finding specific and general information (e.g., indexes, tables of contents, user's instructions and manuals, legends, boldface and italics, graphic clues and icons, cross-references, Boolean logic strategies, time lines, hypertext links, knowledge trees, URLs, etc.) including the use of:

i) Search tools and commands for stand-alone, CD-ROM, and online databases and services (e.g., DIALOG commands, America Online, UMI, Mead), and

ii) Search tools and commands for searching the Internet (e.g., Yahoo, Lycos, WebCrawler, Veronica, Archie).

4. Use of Information

After finding potentially useful resources, students must engage (read, view, listen) the information to determine its relevance and then extract the relevant information. Students will be able to:

A. Connect and operate the computer technology needed to access information and read the guides and manuals associated with such tasks.

B. View, download, decompress and open documents and programs from Internet sites and archives.

C. Cut and paste information from an electronic source into a personal document.

D. Take notes and outline with a word processor or similar productivity program.

E. Record electronic sources of information and locations of those sources in order to properly cite and credit in footnotes, end notes and bibliographies.

F. Use electronic spreadsheets, databases and statistical software to process and analyze statistical data.

5. Synthesis

Students must organize and communicate the results of the information problem-solving effort. Students will be able to:

A. Classify and group information using a word processor, database or spreadsheet.

B. Use word processing and desktop publishing software to create printed documents, applying keyboarding skills equivalent to at least twice the rate of handwriting speed.

C. Create and use computer-generated graphics and art in various print and electronic presentations.

D. Use electronic spreadsheet software to create original spreadsheets.

E. Generate charts, tables and graphs using electronic spreadsheets and other graphing programs.

F. use database/file management software to create original databases.

G. Use presentation software to create electronic slide shows and to generate overheads and slides.

H. Create hypermedia and multimedia productions with digital video and audio.

I. Create World Wide Web pages and sites using hypertext markup language (HTML).

J. Use e-mail, ftp and other telecommunications capabilities to share.

K. Use specialized computer applications as appropriate for specific tasks (e.g., music composition software, computer-assisted drawing and drafting programs, mathematics modeling software).

L. Properly cite and credit electronic sources of information in footnotes, endnotes and bibliographies.

6. Evaluation

Evaluation focuses on how well the final product meets the original task (*effectiveness*) and the process of how well students carried out the information problem-solving process (*efficiency*). Students may evaluate their own work and process or be evaluated by others (i.e., classmates, teachers, teacher-librarians, parents). Students will be able to:

A. Use spell and grammar checking capabilities of word processing and other software to edit and revise their work.

B. Apply legal principles and ethical conduct related to information technology concerning copyright and plagiarism.

C. Understand and abide by telecomputing etiquette when using e-mail, newsgroups, listservs and other Internet functions.

D. Understand and abide by acceptable-use policies in relation to use of the Internet and other electronic technologies.

E. Use e-mail, and online discussion groups (e.g., listservs, newsgroups) on local area networks and the Internet to communicate with teachers and others regarding their performance on assignments, tasks and information problems.

F. Use desktop conferencing, e-mail and groupware software on local area networks to communicate with teachers and others regarding student performance on assignments, tasks and information problems.
(Eisenberg, Johnson, Berkowitz, © 1996)

Other Considerations

Included here are skills and knowledge related to technology that are not part of the computer and information technology curriculum. These items should be learned in context (as students are working through various assignments and information problems using technology). Students will be able to:

A. Know and use basic computer terminology.

B. Operate various pieces of hardware and software—particularly operating systems—and be able to handle basic maintenance.

C. Understand the basics of computer programming. Specific courses in computer programming should be part of the school's curricular offerings.

D. Understand and articulate the relationship and impact of information technology on careers, society, culture and their own lives.

Identifying and placing computer skills within the Big Six model are only the first steps in assuring all our children become proficient information and technology users. The remaining tasks for cooperating teacher-librarians and teachers include:

- continuously improving their own technology skills in order to be effective information skills teachers;

- developing a school-wide expectation that every child develops a working understanding of how information and technology can be used to solve problems;

- systematically analyzing the curriculum to ensure that students receive instruction in the full range of Big Six and computer skills and sub-skills;

- designing a variety of units which integrate the technology-enhanced Big Six curriculum with classroom curriculum; as students move up in grade level, the depth and specificity of skills instruction should increase;

- designing authentic assessments which help students evaluate the effectiveness of their information and technology skill use and

methods of communicating with parents and the public student acquisition of those skills;

- identifying how emerging technologies fit into the information problem-solving context, and then providing opportunities for students to learn and use them.

(Eisenberg, Johnson, Berkowitz, 1996)

Incorporating computer skills into the Big Six model is a flexible, dynamic approach to computer education. It provides a meaningful framework for students and a practical one for educators, and for teacher-librarians; it places them center stage as vital, indispensable teachers who can help assure that all their students master the skills needed to thrive in a information-rich world.

References

American Association of School Librarians. (1995). Information literacy: A position paper on information problems solving. *Emergency Librarian, 23(2),* 20–23.

Eisenberg, M. & Berkowitz, B. (1988). *Curriculum initiative: An agenda and strategy for library media programs.* Norwood, NJ: Ablex.

Eisenberg, M. & Berkowitz, B. (1990). *Information Problem-Solving: The big six skills approach to library & information skills instruction.* Norwood, NJ: Ablex.

Eisenberg, M. (with B. Berkowitz). (1992, January). Information problem-solving: The big six skills approach. *School Library Media Activities Monthly.*

Mankato Schools Information Literacy Curriculum Guideline. (Available at <http://www.isd77.k12.mn.us/resources/infolit.html>)

Minnesota Department of Education. (1986). *Model learner outcomes for educational media and technology.* St. Paul, MN.

Moursund, D. (1995–96, December/January). Effective practices (Part 2): Productivity tools. *Learning and Leading with Technology,* 5–6.

CHAPTER EIGHTEEN

All That Glitters May Not Be Gold

David Loertscher

In my home town of Park City, Utah, there was a creek that ran down the center of this high mountain mining town. It contained the runoff of the many silver and lead mines above the city and was labeled "Poison Creek." No one was to go near it (except for all us naughty children who could not resist the temptation). What attracted us to Poison Creek? It was all the flecks of glittering fool's gold that were liberally sprinkled throughout the thick "soup" ambling slowly down the sandy creek bottom. I still have my hair and haven't died of cancer, but who knows what was in that irresistible goop!

A very respected colleague and I were talking not too long ago about the progress she was making in her district. She had done a lot of work with the local teacher-librarians concerning collaboration, and reports of many projects were coming in from the various schools. What she heard disturbed her to no end. Let me explain. Consider the following scenario:

Suppose you are the teacher who has sent students to the resource center to do a report. When the deadline arrives, you get the projects back and they seem to divide themselves into three different types. Which do you think would get the highest grade?

1. Student uses one encyclopedia article; paraphrases the article; and turns in a neat report with one citation.

2. Student uses one encyclopedia article, two periodical articles, and one map; paraphrases the three articles; and turns in a word processed report complete with map and four citations.

3. Student uses ten periodical articles, four books, three videos, four Internet sites, two CD-ROM databases, and one videodisc; cuts and clips various relevant pieces and devises clever transitions; and presents a multimedia demonstration as a collage with 24 citations.

The obvious question hits us all: Is more better? More variety of information sources? More flashiness in report format? Are we carried away by the glittering specks in the soup of presentation? The answer, of course, is that all the reports can be junk and all can be marvelous examples of learning, but there may be no correlation between the amount learned, the presentation format, or the number of sources used.

Figure 18.1   The Research Process

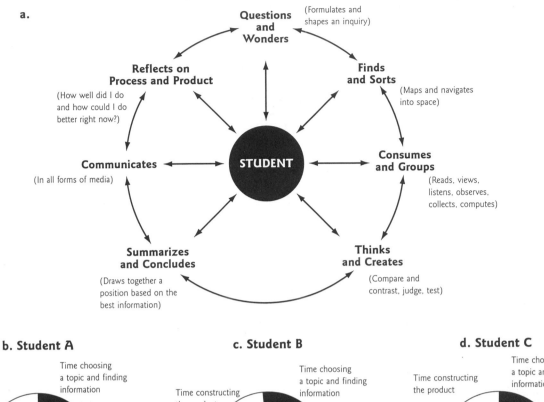

a.

Questions and Wonders
(Formulates and shapes an inquiry)

Reflects on Process and Product
(How well did I do and how could I do better right now?)

Finds and Sorts
(Maps and navigates into space)

Communicates
(In all forms of media)

STUDENT

Consumes and Groups
(Reads, views, listens, observes, collects, computes)

Summarizes and Concludes
(Draws together a position based on the best information)

Thinks and Creates
(Compare and contrast, judge, test)

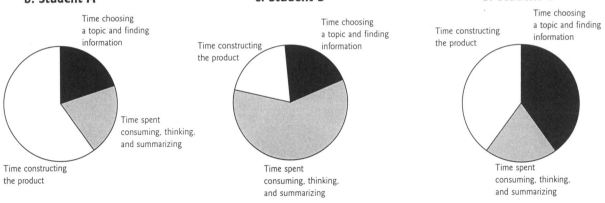

b. Student A

Time choosing a topic and finding information

Time spent consuming, thinking, and summarizing

Time constructing the product

c. Student B

Time choosing a topic and finding information

Time constructing the product

Time spent consuming, thinking, and summarizing

d. Student C

Time choosing a topic and finding information

Time constructing the product

Time spent consuming, thinking, and summarizing

In the information world and the world of multimedia, we often advocate that more is better. While we have been preaching, the information pool has increased exponentially; suddenly, the information age has come upon many schools. Thus, a few years ago where students were able to wrest only a few tidbits of information from our collections, now they are flooded. Students accustomed to mud-puddle libraries now have Olympic-size pool libraries. Lots of young people are being thrown into the deep end of these new pools without any swimming lessons.

The Research Process

Consider the model illustrated in Figure 18.1a. When we divide the research process into a number of steps and teach students the process, do we also help them understand some sort of time distribution across the model? In other words, if you were a student facing an assigned project, where would most of your time be spent? Finding? Product production? Think back to several projects just completed in your school using the library as a resource. Students using the library resource center might be observed doing the following:

1. Student selects topic rapidly—chooses something "easy"—grabs a couple of resources, and immediately starts creating the assigned product.

2. Student only seems concerned that she has the required "three" sources of information to include in the bibliography—she doesn't care which three sources, just as long as she gets the project in on time. She spends very little time reading or thinking, but a lot of time coloring, constructing, gluing and assembling.

Has the student gained any more learning from the entire project? Perhaps. At least the student might be more engaged and interested. But I suspect that actual learning has increased very little. In graphic form, this scenario might look like Figure 18.1b.

There could be a reason, however, why this scenario might be viewed positively rather than negatively. For example, if students were learning to do computer graphing as part of creating the product, or designing a web page to communicate their results, we might say that time was well spent helping students develop their technology tool skills. While there are literally hundreds of projects a student might do, their contribution to learning ought to be assessed before being assigned.

Suppose the scenario was that illustrated in Figure 18.1c.

Here, students are doing the hard work of actually reading the material they photocopy or print off the CD-ROMs. They are spending time thinking about what they have read, comparing ideas across information sources, pondering, solving problems, and taking time to just let things "sink in" as they work toward the "Ah-hah" experience. More common, however, I suspect the scenario looks something like Figure 18.1d in the new Olympic-size libraries.

Consider the student who exits the resource center with an armload of printouts, several books, some periodical articles, and a bibliography of sources to check at the public library. If it is Wednesday and the product is due Friday, there is little chance that productive thinking will go on; and without that critical component, the amount of learning will be affected.

This is why just throwing money at technology, deepening the information pool, and connecting to networks doesn't automatically make a difference in that holy grail—academic achievement. I believe that it is the desire to capitalize on the thoughtful use of the resources and technology that justifies the hiring of an information professional.

It is very easy to make major errors as teachers and teacher-librarians collaborate to use technology and information resources. Let us suppose we allocate two weeks to a topical unit. We can make elaborate plans to help the students find and locate their materials and produce their products. But have we made equally elaborate plans to see that students have the time needed, the encouragement, and the assistance they need as they consume, think, and synthesize what we can provide? Time spent planning with the teacher for this critical phase is essential.

This area of the research process is often unpopular with learners because it requires work and time. By the time a student has found some relevant information, the project deadline looms so large, there is little choice but to skip the reading and reflecting time. Procrastinators are memorable resource center users. Many of them enjoy the thrill of the deadline; some seem overwhelmed and frightened. In either case, they sweet talk us into finding the "nugget" they need to quickly complete their assignment. It is satisfying to help the "damsel in distress," and we should, but we should also remind them that there are other more appropriate ways to tackle learning assignments.

Enhancing Motivation to Learn

The work ethic of actually spending time reading, viewing and listening, then thinking and summarizing comes from two sources, as Eshpeter and Gray (1989) remind us: intrinsic motivation and extrinsic motivation. If the task or the material is interesting to the student, the amount of engagement time increases. Likewise, if the heavy hand of the teacher "requires" engagement either through direct assignment or as a part of the assessment, then time on this critical task will generally increase. It seems that human nature takes over quickly in schooling—even with graduate students—who constantly question the teacher on how little they have to do to get by. It is a pleasant surprise when learners get so motivated that they want you to suggest more and more and more for them to devour.

In most of the professional literature I read these days, authors are suggesting that school must be more relevant; that is, we should use various tactics to maximize intrinsic motivation. As teacher-librarians work to construct beneficial learning activities with teachers that exploit the information pool, there are mechanisms that can be set in place to encourage the student naturally to engage in more thoughtful activities (see, for example, Association for Supervision and Curriculum Development, 1996, an excellent and very practical source created by teachers for teachers, and Newmann, Secada & Wehlage, 1995, also useful). Consider a few:

1. Turn assignments into more engaging problems. The higher the students' interest is at the outset, the more likely they are to spend more time on the task. Here are a few suggestions:

    - Connect assignments to the real world. (Have students tackle a real community problem, an actual political dilemma, an ethical dilemma in science.)
    - Connect assignments to topics you know students are already interested in.
    - Connect abstract learning to a required performance. (Show what you know through what you can do.)
    - Design a task that will end with exhibition to an authentic audience (parents, experts, peers across the world).
    - Design exhibitions in ways that will connect with careers, entrepreneurial ventures, successful businesses, contributions to quality of life. (Students use their web design skills to put up an actual business on the web.)
    - Have students track the process of learning as part of the learning project itself, assessing both the product and the process at the conclusion of the unit.

2. Plan for time for students to consume, think and synthesize. You might even conduct mini-lessons that focus the students' attention on this valuable activity. Some of the study skills literature might help here—although the mini-lessons suggested in various books and manuals suffer from the same problems as our old library skills models—busy work unconnected with any project the students are doing in the classroom. Examples of mini-lesson topics might be:

    - techniques to extract ideas from text, lectures, visuals and electronic sources;
    - self questioning or reflecting techniques;
    - techniques of comparison, contrast, rejection of misinformation;
    - ways to increase time on task;
    - ways to increase persistence and enhance work habits;
    - ways to judge when enough is enough;
    - ways to increase memory and concentration.

3. Construct product assignments that require the students to think rather than cut, clip and copy. In other words, students won't be able to find "the answer" in any source.

    - compare and contrast various information sources, consider alternative ideas, create several perspectives or points of view;
    - verification of data in several sources before use;
    - analysis of trends or big picture looks;
    - take a position other than X source does;
    - change the genre (transform one medium into another).

4. Create assessments or rubrics so that students know that they are being measured on the thoughtful way they approach the work, interact with the resources and transform substance into the product. Sample statements in the rubric might be:

    - Each main point is supported by relevant, accurate and specific pieces of information.
    - Main points and supporting details come from numerous sources.

Figure 18.2   An Example of a Challenging, Engaging Problem

A Remnant of the Donner Party

Engaging problem:

One night about the last day of January 1847, Reasin P. Tucker was out and about the Johnson Ranch northeast of Sutter's Fort in California when he saw a man coming down the Bear River. As he came closer, Reasin could see that the man was very haggard and in great distress. This living skeleton told Reasin that he was of the Donner Party and told briefly how their wagon train had been caught in the snow east of the mountains by Donner Lake and was unable to go backward or forward. Everyone was starving. He did not know if any of the Party were still alive but begged Reasin to find help. Thus began four expeditions to save the infamous Donner Party.

Quest:

Using every piece of information available and several retellings of the rescue of the Donner Party, construct two timetables of the first rescue party—one timeline above the other. On the top horizontal timeline present a day-by-day account beginning January 31, 1847 of what is happening at Donner Lake. On the second, lower timeline, present a parallel day-by-day account of the first rescue party.

Some things you will have to consider:

What happens to the human body when it is deprived of food for a long period of time? How long can a person survive? What extreme measures will prolong life? When food finally becomes available, how can the body begin to accept food again without harm? (Science)

What kind of person will risk life and limb on a rescue of others when the odds for success are near zero? What preparations are needed and what strategies are needed to launch and survive a rescue attempt? (Social Studies and Science)

When people reconstruct an event through various retellings, why do details and descriptions of major events conflict? How does the historian construct what actually happened from conflicting stories and very little actual evidence? (Social Studies)

Exhibition:

Construct the parallel timelines (in small groups) and then present a collaborative retelling of the entire event from two perspectives. A culminating activity might be a reader's theater of the dramatic story using the real characters. (Language Arts)

Notes to the Teacher and Teacher-Librarian:

Any kind of unit requiring reconstruction of an event will require original resources and copies of various retellings by numerous authors. This type of unit requires time to weigh evidence and think through a reconstruction of the events since no one source will provide the opportunity to simply cut and clip. Background knowledge of the Donner Party, the terrain they encounter, and weather patterns of the Sierra Nevada Mountains will be critical to the understanding and recreation of the events.

- Information from personal experience or data from personal experimentation or observation provide additional support to the argument.
- It is obvious to the reader or viewer of the project that a great deal of thought has gone into the presentation (Association for Supervision and Curriculum Development, 1996).

When concern for all the steps of the research process is reflected in collaborative planning, particularly those which require the student to actually spend time consuming, thinking and summarizing, then amazing things happen in resource-based teaching and learning. You know you are achieving success when someone asks: "Tell me about some great learning experiences that happened in the library resource center this past year." Numerous examples will come to mind rather than a stupor of thought.

And the results will be laced with more than flecks of fool's gold.

References

Association for Supervision and Curriculum Development. (1996). *Performance-based learning and assessment.* Prepared by educators in Connecticut's Pomperaug Regional School District 15. Alexandria, VA: Association for Supervision and Curriculum Development.

Eshpeter, B. & Gray, J. (1989). *Preparing students for information literacy: School library programs and the cooperative planning process.* Calgary, AB: Calgary Board of Education.

Newmann, F., Secada, W. & Wehlage, G.. (1995). *A guide to authentic instruction and assessment: Vision, standards and scoring.* Madison, WI: Wisconsin Center for Education Research.

PART FIVE

Collaborative Planning and Teaching

Almost twenty years ago I labeled the process of teacher and teacher-librarian collaboration as "cooperative program planning and teaching." This term entered the professional literature and became commonly used to describe the foundation of the teaching role of the teacher-librarian. As with most things, however, language changes and develops, and some commentators now distinguish between "cooperation" and "collaboration," a reasonable position and one that I certainly accept. However, the term "cooperative program planning and teaching" was always used to denote an equal teaching partnership between teacher and teacher-librarian, a collaborative relationship if you will.

Regrettably, we have yet to reach that rarified state of joint curriculum planning and team teaching with colleagues in every school to integrate information skills and strategies. The school library media program rests on collaboration with classroom teachers, yet the process for achieving active involvement in the curriculum planning process is not easy. While teacher-librarians advocate a joint approach to instructional programs,

teachers have traditionally been educated and rewarded for a more isolated approach to curriculum planning; happily, this situation is changing as principals and other school leaders, including teacher-librarians, work to achieve more collaborative work environments.

Ray Doiron explores the historical development of curriculum encounters between teachers and teacher-librarians and identifies at least three phases of development. We have moved from simple "assistance" to "integration" with a perhaps too great reliance on behaviorism and the teacher-librarian as sole advocate for change, without recognizing the more organic nature of planning and the importance of "deliberation" around the basic components of learners, content, milieu and teachers. Antoinette Oberg expands on the notion of curriculum planning as deliberation and provides insights into how individual teachers plan and the implications for teacher-librarians as co-planners.

Through this overview and explication of how teachers plan, it becomes more apparent that the world of the teacher-librarian, with its mainly school focus, and the world of the teacher, with its mainly classroom focus, can easily clash. Jean Brown notes that newer curriculum guides for teachers encourage collaboration and resource-based teaching and learning but current classroom practices do not reflect these mandates, making the challenge that much greater. Teacher-librarians will need to work with and through others to effect change.

Patti Hurren focuses on the needs of English-as-a-Second-Language students and identifies the advantages of adding other non-classroom teachers to the planning team. Her paper is particularly useful in adding to our understanding of the collaborative process from another field's perspective and providing examples of serving student needs through a different teaching and learning framework.

While it is important to acknowledge the different platforms from which planning models emerge, it is also important to know and use a model which can then be adapted for specific individuals. Some years ago, a group of teacher-librarians identified the need for a formal planning guide to provide structure and a common basis for staff development and training. Carol-Ann Page outlines the results of that planning. The model is also designed as a means for recording units of study for future adaptation and use with others and thus appears very linear; however, it is designed to be flexible and holistic in use. The planning checklist and process provides a basis for understanding "collaborative planning" and how it works in practice.

CHAPTER NINETEEN

Curriculum Encounters of the Third Kind: Teachers and Teacher-Librarians Exploring Curriculum Potential

Ray Doiron

A tremendous growth in the understanding and acceptance of the role of the school library in curriculum has taken place over the past 10 years. Most states and provinces have in place clearly defined policies and guidelines for the school library within the overall goal of developing students as independent, lifelong learners. These policies affirm the importance of school libraries in education and establish the right of students to have access to quality resources and services. They articulate a vision of the school library resource center as an integrated and integral part of the overall school curriculum, with resource based learning as the principal strategy for students using the school library, and cooperative program planning and teaching as the chief method teachers and teacher-librarians use to bring about resource based learning.

Most of the policies have included guidelines for realizing this vision, with particular focus on the roles of administrators, teachers and teacher-librarians as partners working to achieve these goals. Each of them emphasizes the importance of cooperative program planning as the process to build curriculum and implement a plan for instruction. This curriculum planning process depends heavily on the working relationship between the school's administrator and the teacher-librarian, and between the classroom teacher and the teacher-librarian. This places the teacher-librarian in a position of instructional leadership in the school, with a heavy responsibility to advocate, coordinate and implement a resource based curriculum philosophy.

Several of these policy documents clarify the concept of cooperative program planning with a definition, a rationale, or a model of the relationship among the partners. However, most of the information available on cooperative program planning comes in the form of testaments to its usefulness, or written examples of the success of learning activities developed with this process. Few attempts have been made to address the dynamics and the nature of the relationship between the classroom teacher and the teacher-librarian, a relationship that is consistently referred to as a cornerstone of the school library program.

The purpose of this paper is to probe the complexity of this curriculum planning process and identify key concepts that classroom teachers and teacher-librarians need to recognize as forming the essence of their curriculum encounters. An exploration of historical developments in school libraries will highlight the original curriculum encounter between classroom teachers and teacher-librarians. This lays the groundwork for the second type of encounter commonly used by the partners today, which sees planning as a linear process utilizing the predominant behavioristic model. A rationale will then be advanced for a third kind of curriculum encounter that reorients this linear approach toward a more dynamic process based on a mutual respect for teachers' "personal practical knowledge" (Connelly & Clandinin, 1988) used in the active exploration of curriculum potential. Reinforced with this understanding, both partners become empowered to develop their own personal strategies that stimulate the potential inherent in the concept of the school library resource center.

Encounters of the First Kind:
The Historical Perspective

Going back to the mid-nineteenth century, libraries were conceived by Melvil Dewey as part of a large plan for education in general. Long considered the "father of modern libraries," Dewey (1888) envisioned the key educational role of libraries as institutions that nurtured and prepared students for lifelong learning. In his view, education was divided into two parts: the formal education from kindergarten through college, and home education that continued throughout life. He even referred to these libraries as "universities for the people," where the general public could continue their learning after work and on weekends. Dewey was a founding member of the American Library Association, founded the first journal dedicated to libraries, developed his classification system and established

the first university school dedicated to training librarians. Dewey's early writings on the role of libraries addressed many issues in education and helped motivate municipalities to start small public libraries and staff them with professional librarians. His career centered on advocating the need for professionally educated librarians, working in well-equipped public facilities, filled with an abundance of good quality books. He envisioned these public librarians as teachers who taught visitors to the library all they needed to know to find books and information.

Prior to the middle of this century, few efforts were made to give the school library any real role in the curriculum of the school (Carroll, 1981). Instead of going to the public library for books, some schools started building their own collections of material and housing them in the school (Davies, 1979). School libraries basically became warehouses for books and reference materials and usually operated outside the school program, more in the model of a typical public library of the time. Their collections consisted of essential reading for young scholars serious about purely academic endeavors. The librarian was a keeper of the collection, knowledgeable in the management of materials and recognized as a literary expert. Most school libraries were located in urban centers and in senior high schools, with one or two bookcases of "old favorites" forming the basis of a library in the rural or small urban elementary school.

It was during the 1950s and then into the '60s that school libraries took on their first real curricular role (Davies, 1979). With advances in technology and America's perception of having to "catch up" in the space race, increased pressure came to add resources to schools to better equip them for teaching. School library collections grew, and with them the belief that librarians should continue to act as experts in literature. As well, they should now teach sets of skills designed to educate students in accessing the school library collection and using its reference materials. In addition, a new responsibility for acquiring and using audiovisual materials became an integral part of the school library's mandate (Carroll, 1981).

Just as most aspects of curriculum were influenced by Ralph Tyler's rationale (1949) for curriculum development, a library curriculum emerged that had listed appropriate skills, organized them, arranged them into manageable units, suggested learning activities and identified measurable objectives. This standardization of a library curriculum helped legitimize and extend the role of the school librarian. During this time and into the early '70s, school librarians continued to manage and promote their collections, as well as operate a distinctive program that took students through a detailed set of "library skills."

In most situations, school librarians helped students with classroom-generated projects, assigned by their teacher with little or no communication beforehand with the school librarian. Students often arrived unannounced proclaiming, "We're doin' a project!" In some cases, the two teachers (classroom and library) did meet to plan activities that would be done during regularly scheduled library periods, but these usually happened in isolation from the classroom program. So the school library curriculum was an entity unto itself, a separate subject- or content-area that existed apart from the classroom curriculum, with the possible addition of a few opportunities to work together. Any curriculum encounter between classroom teachers and teacher-librarians was incidental or even accidental, not part of any overall school plan. In actuality, the school library could be removed from the school altogether with little or no effect on the basic curriculum. In some cases, this is what happened, as staffing allocations to the school library were eaten away by demands to meet higher priorities in other areas.

The late 1960s and the early 1970s saw several pressures begin to build, influencing the operation of the school library and giving rise to a new vision of the school library as the center of a school's literacy program. More funding was available, and society placed more emphasis on education and innovative new programs. The classroom curriculum was becoming more learner-centered, with less attention paid to covering content and more consideration placed on the processes needed to deal with the content (Carroll, 1981). Teachers were realizing that information on any subject was increasing so rapidly that no one textbook could contain it all (Davies, 1979). We began to hear about the "information explosion" and that we had entered the "information age." Computers were gaining momentum in their ability to store and process vast amounts of information. Curriculum programs relied less on a core book and became more resource-based. Whole language empowered classroom teachers to create learning environments where literacy was nurtured in naturalistic ways. Planning curriculum was no longer focused on implementing a set of curriculum materials, but on deciding what experiences would best facilitate literacy development. Learning also became more contextualized, making purpose and meaning key factors in designing curriculum. Programs like the school library program were in danger of being left by the wayside if they didn't actively search for ways to become more integrated into these new classroom directions. Classroom teachers also searched for broader contexts in which their students could pursue their independent interests and experiences. These evolving experiences set the stage for a new vision of the school library as a learning resource center where students and teachers actively searched for information, processed that information and used it in all sorts of meaning centered experiences.

Ironically, we can look to the words of Melvil Dewey and hear haunting glimpses of this vision in one of his first statements on the role of libraries in education:

> The time *was* when a library was very like a museum, and a librarian was a mouser in musty books, and visitors looked with curious eyes at ancient tomes and manuscripts. The time is when a library is a school, and the librarian is in the highest sense a teacher, and the visitor is a reader among the books as a workman among his tools. (Dewey, 1886; Dewey's emphasis)

A New Partnership Emerges

Through the swirling dust of the dynamic changes occurring in classroom and school library programs, several elements consistently settled out and formed the basis of a curriculum partnership between the school librarian and the classroom teacher. Educators began to see there were many similarities in the nature of each role and that much could be gained by integrating the school library resource center into the school's overall curriculum plan. First of all, the teaching of "skills in isolation" was seen as counterproductive to learning (Carpenter, 1963). Classroom teachers no longer wanted to teach skills that were not part of the immediate learning needs of students. The school librarian was realizing that teaching the use of an encyclopedia in November was of little use to students who didn't need to know it until the spring.

Second, the demand for resources to support classroom programs became a pervasive cry, placing increased emphasis on literature (that traditional area of expertise for the school librarian), good quality nonfiction and up-to-date and user-friendly texts. Teachers began building extensive classroom libraries and school librarians scrambled to select quality materials to support the burgeoning school curriculum.

Third, both classroom teachers and school librarians began to recognize that each of their traditional programs taught many of the same skills. For instance, both programs taught how to use the parts of a book, like the table of contents, glossary and index. Both taught students how to use dictionaries and encyclopedias. All these skills and dozens more began to be referred to as research and study skills, and later, information skills—those skills needed to access, process, critically evaluate and apply information.

A fourth factor was the growing attention paid to learning processes and less of a fixation on learning outcomes. This forced teachers to examine their traditional curriculum plans, which used learning objectives written with attention to only one expected student product; and to consider what learning processes they hoped to develop, what experiences would activate these processes and what the potential outcomes might be. Students operated at their own ability level, with their personal learning style and with lots of input into the products they produced.

A fifth element in this educational change was the shift in the role of the teacher from an imparter of knowledge or discloser of information

to a facilitator, coach, model and guide. It was empowering of teachers, giving them more control over the development of their programs. School librarians felt this sense of empowerment so strongly that they lobbied to be known as teacher-librarians, a term emphasizing their role as a teacher with special skills in using a wide variety of learning resources. The direction for classroom teachers and teacher-librarians was away from their traditional role as "sage on the stage" to become a "guide on the side."

Classroom teachers were developing an understanding that learning is an active process that happens in social situations. They recognized that fundamental changes were taking place in how classrooms looked and operated, and that students should have more control of their learning. The teacher-librarian saw the same things, and embraced resource-based learning as a concept that embodies this new philosophy and frames it within the context of the school library resource center. With this rationale, a natural link was established between the classroom and the school library as both colleagues looked for ways to develop their partnership and make full use of this potentially powerful curriculum endeavor. Cooperative program planning and teaching became the term applied to the curriculum planning process activated by classroom teachers and teacher-librarians. It was defined as "a concept...a strategy or approach to teaching and learning"(Haycock, 1988, p. 29). It is not a "program of instruction, but rather a philosophical framework for the development and implementation of resource-based programs that reflect what we know about how students learn" (Ibid.).

Encounters of the Second Kind: Applying the Tyler Rationale

For teacher-librarians, cooperative program planning became their principal modus operandi, as they embraced the new vision for the school library and stepped up efforts to move their schools in this direction. They advocated change by entering into partnerships with their administrators to work together to make the vision of an integrated school library resource center a reality.

They became curriculum leaders on the staff, perfectly positioned to bring teachers together and improve the school's overall program. Once the school was committed to the new mission of the school library, it was often up to the teacher-librarian to initiate cooperative program planning and, in partnership with classroom teachers, set up resource-based learning experiences.

While considerable effort was spent articulating and advocating the vision, little attention was given to the nature of the renewed relationship between classroom teachers and teacher-librarians. The main concern soon moved from "What is cooperative program planning and teaching?" to "How do we do cooperative program planning and teaching?" The focus was on implementation, on getting the process into action so that working examples could be used as models for others just starting the process. Quick definitions and detailed examples of the "process in action" could be given, but without attention to the curricular dynamics of the relationship of teacher and teacher-librarian, our traditional understanding of what curriculum is and how it develops was applied.

For most teachers, that understanding of curriculum is rooted in the behavioristic principles of identifying learners' needs, setting learning objectives, designing activities and evaluating outcomes. These principles, which were first described by Ralph Tyler in 1949 and have since permeated most teacher education programs and published curriculum materials, were so instilled in teachers' minds that they became the main way used to bring about cooperative program planning. Mary Kay Urbanik (1989) outlines several curriculum planning models, all rooted in the Tyler Rationale, in her book, *Curriculum planning and teaching using the library media center*. While some adapted the model to give more attention to the diagnosis of needs (Taba, 1962, as cited in Urbanik, 1989), or to a continuous feedback loop for evaluation (Saylor, Alexander, & Lewis, 1974, as cited in Urbanik, 1989), or to sharing the unit of study with others (Doll, 1982, as cited in Urbanik, 1989), they are still basically focused on developing a well organized, structured and easily measured set of learning objectives.

For classroom teachers and teacher-librarians, this approach means determining the needs of the students, setting objectives, designing activities to teach these goals and evaluating students to check if they have reached the intended outcomes. Figure 19.1 represents the relationship among various curriculum concepts using this traditional framework (adapted from Urbanik, 1989). The sources of curriculum and the planning structure form the basis of the curriculum planning process, which leads to a definition of curriculum as the set of intended learning outcomes, implemented through the instructional plan, producing measurable outcomes.

Since this framework is so familiar to teachers, it provides a common language to assist them as they meet to build resource-based units of study. In practice, classroom teachers bring knowledge of their students and of the expected classroom curriculum to any planning session, while teacher-librarians bring expertise in resources and information skills to the discussion; together they can work through the steps in any one of the behavioristic models and develop activities for students that seem to combine the objectives of the classroom and the library. The strength in these models lies in their establishment of goals or ends to be reached. Teachers get an overall view of the intent of the unit of study, the work their students will do and how they will evaluate their work. These models also establish the important relationship between the provision of meaningful student experiences and the meeting of educational aims. While working in this type of planning session, the partners examine their programs and attempt to match common skills that could be developed through the resources available on the desired topic. This provides a certain amount of professional satisfaction and comfort to have examined learning goals and matched them with resources that help enhance the learning experiences of students. There is a sense of order, development and organization resulting from this process that can be traced throughout the implementation, and is useful to demonstrate what actually happened once the unit of study is completed.

Figure 19.1   The Traditional Curriculum Framework

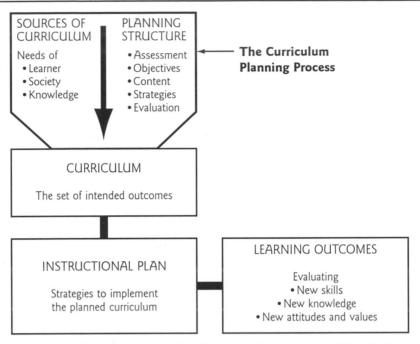

Adapted from *Curriculum planning and teaching using the library media center* (Urbanik 1989).

In summary, the nature of cooperative planning implied by an application of the behavioristic curriculum planning process is one in which learning activities are designed, divided up and delivered to students through a linear planning process controlled by the explicit detailing of behavioral objectives. It can best be described as two programs coming together and aligned by the classroom teacher and the teacher-librarian. During this brief alignment, the partners place their programs on the table, as it were, and search through them for common objectives that can be taught using the rich resources of the school library and the teaching assistance of the teacher-librarian. The focus is on their programs, or the knowledge, skills and strategies they hope to develop in their students. Careful attention is made to match learning objectives to a variety of interesting and heterogeneous learning experiences. These experiences are described as resource-based and designed to guide students in the independent use of the resources. When completed, evaluation of learning outcomes can easily be accomplished, and the planning partners can look at the completed unit of study and make suggestions for ways to improve it next time.

In essence, the curriculum encounter is a transaction between teachers and content, characterized by the feeling "if you do this for me, I'll do that for you." The classroom teacher remembers the experience as positive and wants to repeat it again next year, while the teacher-librarian feels he or she has involved one more staff member in the school library program. The partners have basically entered into an agreement to provide a service for each other, keeping the relationship in the transactional state, rather than moving it to a transformational level where real change in beliefs, values and attitudes toward the school library can be affected. What is needed for this change to take place is a process that empowers each partner to activate their personal strengths and experiences in a more transformational relationship.

The Need for a Different Starting Point

Having worked in these curriculum planning sessions for six years as a teacher-librarian and with colleagues in university courses and professional development sessions, several observations have led me to believe that this behavioristic model can only approach, but never fully reach, our goal of integrating the concept of the school library resource center into our school curriculum. First of all, while classroom teachers usually come into the planning model at the activity level (what they would like to do with their students), the teacher-librarian's tendency is to begin at the goal setting point, which is seen as the necessary first step, so that a common ground can be established for the planning work to proceed. So, what the teacher feels comfortable doing in the school library, what their past experiences have been in the library and what they have identified as lacking in their program are all part of what they bring to partnerships with the teacher-librarian. Efforts to move the planning process away from activities in order to set goals meet with varying levels of success. Some classroom teachers recognize the need to set goals and then design learning experiences to meet these goals, but many resist and focus on the experiences they want to provide and from these determine the expected outcomes. This indicates a fundamental difference in the starting point for the curriculum planning process, one that moves the process in a different direction and bases it on teacher-to-teacher interaction, rather than the teachers-to-content relationship working in the traditional planning process.

A second observation centers on the tendency for this activity-oriented model to make curriculum planning a purely objective process. Units of study developed through this process tend to establish a neat and tidy curriculum package simply to be carried out by the teachers. They are often written up (and even published) as if they could easily be "copied" by someone else and applied to whole new situations. We often operate with the belief that if we plan this particular unit of study once, it will be available for every other time we want to use it. Of course, we expect to have to "tinker" with it for future applications, but the bulk of the work is done and we can simply repeat it. However, experience tells us that these units can never really be applied to another group of students at a later time. Teachers always want to change something, or feel the new group of students is more or less capable of handling the

work. This indicates a second problem with these models, they fail to take into consideration emerging factors in the classroom environment, student idiosyncrasies, or developments in teaching styles that are constantly affecting the dynamics of curriculum development.

A third observation focuses on efforts of teacher-librarians to implement cooperative planning in their schools. These efforts often begin by building a vision of the school library resource center and advocating certain changes to the existing management structures to allow a greater role for the teacher-librarian in curriculum development and implementation. Most teacher-librarians report that these early efforts are often quite successful, and that they are settling into the real work of developing planning and teaching partnerships with teachers. Most begin these efforts with the behavioristic model applied to the cooperative planning process. What often emerges is an awareness that there is resistance among some teachers to the change in the relationship between them and their teacher-librarian. This resistance is common among classroom teachers who use a more informal or organic process when designing their classroom programs, as they resent being put into a planning session that expects them to walk through a very programmed planning model. While there are those who would suggest teachers should be more concerned with setting objectives and following a structured plan for implementation, this ignores the reality of different teaching styles and different planning styles.

Many teacher-librarians complain that their efforts are going nowhere fast, that some teachers just don't want to sit down and plan with them. For support, their colleagues encourage them to be patient and keep working at it. Perhaps, as teaching professionals, we need to look at the nature of the planning process we presently use to see if it really is the best way to involve all teachers in the benefits of the school library/classroom partnership. Does it respect the variety of teaching styles that exists in any one school? Does it place learning objectives at the center of the planning process rather than the teacher-to-teacher partnership that we claim is so essential? Do teachers have a variety of planning styles that need to be identified and respected before any meaningful partnership can occur? Can the behavioristic model ever meet the needs of these divergent planning styles? Perhaps we need to place these two teachers at the center of the planning process, or, at the very least, accept teachers as the "starting point" of any curriculum deliberations (Ben-Peretz, 1989). In this way, we envision our partnership not simply as an alignment of objectives or activities, but as two teachers working to transform their relationship into a mutually supportive opportunity for each to grow professionally and be as effective as possible.

Encounters of the Third Kind:
Exploring Curriculum Potential

Several curriculum educators (Ben-Peretz, 1989, 1990; Connelly & Clandinin, 1988; Oberg, 1986) have attempted to describe the nature of the curriculum planning process in terms that reflect a more dynamic and transformational role for teachers. While all these educators wrote in the context of professionally developed curriculum materials (published programs) being implemented into a school's program, many of the concepts they articulate have direct application to the cooperative planning process. For one, they describe teachers as "active participants" in the curriculum planning process, and dismiss the concept of teacher as "a mere transmitter of curriculum" (Connelly & Clandinin, 1988). Ben-Peretz (1990) encourages teachers "to see their major role in the partnership of curriculum development as that of informed and creative interpreters who are prepared to reflect on their curriculum and to reconstruct it" (p. xv). Teachers come together to explore the curriculum potential of materials and how they could be used in specific classroom situations. Connelly and Clandinin (1988) believe that "curriculum development and curriculum planning are fundamentally questions of teacher thinking and teacher doing" (p. 4). Applying these premises to the teacher/teacher-librarian curriculum encounter offers an exciting alternative view embodying a more flexible and responsive notion of cooperative program planning.

Classroom teachers and teacher-librarians come to planning sessions with a wide variety of classroom experiences, personal experiences, background knowledge, personal interests, abilities and personalities. Connelly and Clandinin (1988) empower teachers in the curriculum planning process by recognizing their "personal practical knowledge" as the vital and respected essence of their "lived experience" in the classroom. This knowledge is where they begin the planning process, and it is that knowledge that guides their deliberations and most greatly affects how they will carry out the planned curriculum. Teacher-librarians also come to the encounter with a vibrant, personal practical knowledge that serves them capably throughout the planning process. What is necessary for success is the mutual acceptance and respect of each other's personal practical knowledge, so that this becomes the true starting point of the partnership inherent in cooperative planning.

Most of these concepts are rooted in the work of Joseph Schwab, who dismissed many traditional curriculum theories as being out of touch with and inappropriate to the "practical" nature of curriculum endeavors. Until recently, curriculum educators saw theory and practice as separate fields, with theory taking precedence over practice, as exemplified in the breakdown of the discipline into curriculum and instruction. Schwab (1969) feels it is inappropriate for theory to dominate, since most theories fail to "clear disparities between knowledge yielded by the enquiries and behaviors of the subject matter which the knowledge purports to represent" (p. 3). He takes exception to the "inadequacies of principles," and calls for a redirection of our "curriculum energies" toward making the practical the dominant component, since it is concerned "with choice and action, in contrast with the theoretic, which is concerned with knowledge" (p. 2). He referred to the "arts of the practical" (1969), which are applied to "curriculum in action," and include such activities as identification of curricular weaknesses, implementing change in small doses and exploring alternative solutions to problems.

He called the method for developing the practical, "deliberation," whose main goal is making "a decision about action in a concrete situation" (1969, p. 20). Deliberation is a complex process that can be difficult and time consuming but one that more clearly describes the natural way teachers work together. "It treats both ends and means and must treat them as mutually determining one another" (Schwab, 1969; p. 20). It weighs alternatives and searches "not for the right alternative...but the best one" (p. 21). It allows planners to discuss, debate and reflect on situations where they worked successfully in the past and in which they hope to provide new learning experiences for students.

Schwab (1973) details four "commonplaces" that must be central to all curriculum deliberations—learners, teachers, content and milieu. Any curriculum building process must consider each of these factors equally, and must also be approached with a personal knowledge of the curriculum making process itself, so that all five "bodies of experience" interact during curriculum deliberations. Some details about these commonplaces should help clarify the role of each.

1. Learners. Planners obviously have to know their students well and not be limited by general knowledge about the age group with which they work. They need to ask what these students already know; what they are able to learn at this time; what their strengths and weaknesses are academically, socially, etc.; what affective components need to be considered; what choices students will have in the learning; what special attributes these students might have that should be considered; what interests and attitudes characterize these students? All these considerations will form part of the deliberation.

2. Content. The planners have likely come together because they wish to develop students' knowledge, skills and/or strategies, usually within the context of a defined topic. This subject could come from teacher interests, student interests, or a textbook or curriculum program. Within the context of the teacher/teacher-librarian curriculum encounter, deliberations will center on what information, concepts, or principles are to be developed; what resources will best achieve this; what the relationships of the concepts are to the everyday life of the students; important historical perspectives to be considered; the content presenting a balance of social and cultural issues; and how the subject will be integrated with other subject areas.

3. Milieu. One area of consideration often overlooked but especially important in teacher/teacher-librarian curriculum endeavors is the milieu or situation in which teaching and learning takes place. The prevailing influence of the larger society's needs and the local community's interests should be represented. Other major milieus to be considered are the classroom and the school library resource center, where independence and self-sufficiency are encouraged. Planners need to decide where the learning will take place. Will students work in groups or as whole classes? Will they work cooperatively or individually? How will their families be involved? How will the community be involved? Will students from other classes or other schools be involved? How will teachers work together? Will students have flexibility in the completion of their learning?

4. Teachers. Teachers know students, content and milieu very well, and they use that knowledge to design their programs. Teachers have preferred methods and favorite activities that they know work for them as effective teaching strategies. They have a wealth of teaching experience, plus planning experiences that they rely on to develop new learning activities. Planning sessions need to recognize each teacher's strengths and build on these strengths to design mutually supportive activities that empower each partner to grow and develop professionally.

Usually in the cooperative planning process, we consider that the classroom teacher brings expertise in students' needs and in the classroom curriculum to any planning session, while the teacher-librarian brings knowledge of information skills and expertise in resources. While this is certainly true, it can limit any real change in

Figure 19.2   Teacher/Teacher-Librarian Curriculum Encounters

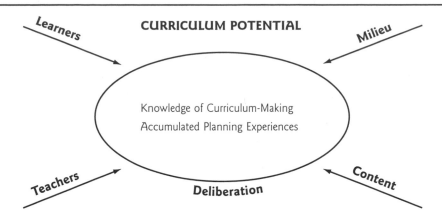

teachers' understanding of the role of the school library resource program. It relies on a transactional partnership, a give and take, rather than a partnership rooted in the coordination and balance among the four commonplaces, a growing knowledge and experience with curriculum making, a process of evaluation operating concurrently during the deliberations and an acceptance of curriculum materials as "resources" considered "in the service of the student" and not as ends in themselves (Schwab, 1973).

With the four commonplaces forming the basic components around which we build our deliberations, and with our working knowledge of curriculum contributing the fifth ingredient, successful planning sessions then become "those in which all five commonplaces…are thoroughly considered, alternatives have been considered before choices were made, and planners can justify their decisions…"(Oberg, 1986). Cooperative program planning and teaching is a teacher-to-teacher relationship where the practical implications of several factors are thoroughly considered, rather than assuming that the nature of the partnership is to simply apply prescriptive behavioristic methods to an identified content.

Figure 19.2 represents one way of visualizing the teacher/teacher-librarian curriculum encounter using some of the concepts described here. The use of terms like encounter, potential and milieu all reflect a more naturalistic or organic view of the curriculum planning process and suggest a holistic, dynamic mode of operation. The

four commonplaces are brought together through deliberations grounded in a knowledge of curriculum making. Rising from these deliberations are sets of learning experiences that realize a curriculum potential. In this way, curriculum potential becomes a concept including all parts of the curriculum making process, and not one based solely on a rigid linear model.

If this diagram (Figure 19.2) represents one encounter, then we can conceive of several of these models stacked on top of each other as the "accumulated planning experience" of several encounters. The curriculum potential reached in one set of experiences adds to our curriculum knowledge and becomes the basis of the next encounter, with the four other commonplaces constantly growing and changing as well. This kind of curriculum encounter recognizes the growth and development taking place over several of these planning experiences, and builds into the teacher/teacher-librarian partnership a mutual respect for the personal practical knowledge of each teacher, plus the accumulated planning experiences shared together.

Across a school, the partnership will be at different stages of development with different teachers, depending on the length of time the partners have worked together, the frequency of their deliberations and the successes of the learning experiences developed. Perhaps by approaching the planning process with a common understanding of each partner's personal involvement in curriculum development and an appreciation for a more holistic view of the cooperative planning process, teachers and teacher librarians will be able to build on their past experiences and present conditions in order to develop resource-based learning units that truly exemplify a shared vision of the school library resource center.

We must be careful that our school library programs do not become defined by a set of planned units that are accumulated and repeated over time. That limits the concept of "program" to a set of identifiable materials or activities, much as we think of a mathematics or reading program. By basing our school library program on a series of curriculum deliberations that recognize teachers' personal practical knowledge and the dynamic concept of curriculum potential, we interact with teachers about beliefs, values and attitudes, and together change previously held ideas about the school library and develop a shared vision that will ensure the program is truly an essential and integrated component of our schools.

Leadership for Change

Many teacher-librarians will recognize this third level of curriculum encounter as one that reflects more accurately their position as an instructional leader in the school. With the more traditional behavioristic model, there is a real danger of being perceived as an instructional leader who leads from the front, waving a flag, setting the route, showing the way and calling for all others to follow. In this context, the vision for the school library program could be described as one person's vision, not one developed by all the educational partners. When we stop and think, we know this is not the attitude we want to give. Brown (1993) describes our instructional role as "a collegial, collaborative one, and although we have our visions, we must realize that we work in a particular school culture; that others have their visions as well; that other teachers' visions may be as valid as our own; that vision-building takes time as it is a learning process; and that we can all learn from one another" (p. 18).

Each curriculum encounter, then, is not meant to be an application of a fixed planning model, but rather an exploration of possibilities based on an emerging collective vision that generates mutually agreed learning activities. It does not limit the leadership role of the teacher-librarian to designing learning contracts between two teachers. Instead, the third level of curriculum encounter advocated here demands a more transformational type of leadership, one that "facilitates the redefinition of a people's vision, a renewal of their commitment, and the restructuring of their systems for goal accomplishment" (Brown, 1993; p. 18). Instead of trying to change teachers' more informal methods for curriculum planning and becoming frustrated with their seeming unwillingness to take part, we need to reexamine how we are approaching fellow teachers to assure ourselves that we respect their personal practical knowledge, and are willing to empower them to share in the constant refining of the role of the school library resource center. Without this flexibility in our cooperative planning process, we leave classroom teachers with little choice but to accept our vision of the school library and how it develops or to resist efforts to activate their partnership with the school library.

Teacher-librarians working at the school level, and curriculum consultants attempting to implement school library policies at the district level, need to recognize the limitations of founding the planning partnership on a teacher-content relationship, and begin to explore the powerful curriculum potential inherent in using the teacher-teacher relationship as the starting point for process. All teachers are at differing stages in their curriculum literacy skill, and their personal practical knowledge will work against the growth of the cooperative planning partnership if it is not recognized as a valuable and essential element that can assure the success of the entire process. In-service and professional development activities should focus on the nature of the curriculum planning process, and link theory and practice more closely.

Curriculum encounters and curriculum potential represent concepts about possibilities—the practical, the attainable—not sets of open and shut experiences beginning and ending with objectives. Those educators committed to the concept of the school library as a vital, active and energetic learning center within a school will see curriculum encounters of the third kind as opportunities for close contact, for real communication to take place, and for all learners to feel empowered to explore and experience new and exciting worlds.

References

Ben-Peretz, M. (1975). The concept of curriculum potential. *Curriculum Theory Network, 5(2),* 151–159.

Ben-Peretz, M. (1989). Teachers' role in curriculum development: An alternative approach. *Canadian Journal of Education, 5(2),* 52–62.

Ben-Peretz, M. (1990). *The teacher-curriculum encounter: Freeing teachers from the tyranny of texts.* Albany, New York: State University of New York Press.

Brown, J. (1993). Leadership for school improvement. *Emergency Librarian, 20(3),* 8–20.

Carpenter, H. M. (Ed.). (1963). *Skill development in the social studies.* Thirty-third Yearbook. Washington, DC: National Council for the Social Studies.

Carroll, F. L. (1981). *Recent advances in school librarianship.* New York: Pergamon Press Inc.

Connelly, E. M., & Clandinin, D. J. (1988). *Teachers as curriculum planners: Narratives of experience.* Columbia University, New York: Teachers College Press.

Davies, R. A. (1979). *The school library media program: Instructional force for excellence.* 3rd edition. New York: R. R. Bowker.

Dewey, M. (1886, June). The library quartet and its work. *Library Notes, Boston Library Bureau, 1(1),* 5–7.

Dewey, M. (1888, June). Libraries as related to the educational work of the state. *Library Notes, Boston Library Bureau, 3(1),* 333–348.

Haycock, C. A. (1988). Cooperative program planning: A model that works. *Emergency Librarian, 16(2),* 29–38.

Oberg, A. (1986). The school librarian and the classroom teacher: Partners in curriculum planning. *Emergency Librarian, 14(1),* 9–14.

Schwab, J. (1969). The practical: A language for curriculum. *School Review, 78(1),* 1–23.

Schwab, J. (1973). The practical 3: Translation into curriculum. *School Review, 81(4),* 501–522.

Tyler, R. (1949). *Basic principles of curriculum and instruction.* Chicago: University of Chicago Press.

Urbanik, M. (1989). *Curriculum planning and teaching using the library media center.* Metuchen, NJ: Scarecrow Press.

CHAPTER TWENTY

The School Librarian and the Classroom Teacher: Partners in Curriculum Planning

Antoinette Oberg

The role of the teacher-librarian has expanded to include cooperation with classroom teachers in planning the instructional program. This cooperation takes many forms, depending on the skills and inclinations of both teacher-librarians and teachers. When a full planning partnership develops, the teacher-librarian can provide not only a welcome support to the classroom teacher, who usually faces the complex and demanding task of curriculum planning alone, but also an occasion for expanding and improving the curriculum planning process. The extent to which this occurs depends largely on the teacher-librarian's knowledge of curriculum planning.

Curriculum planning is something every teacher does daily. Regardless of how detailed the provincial or state curriculum guides may be, teachers have a great deal of planning to do to tailor guide suggestions or prescriptions to their own and their students' knowledge and interests. Although most teachers plan their programs with apparent ease and efficiency, curriculum planning is actually a very complex process. Proper planning requires not only a thorough grasp of the subject matter of a lesson or unit, but also a sensitive understanding of the learners for whom it is intended, and awareness of the many contextual factors which define and influence the situation, as well as knowledge of the planning process itself.

Ideally, in order to marshal the knowledge and resources necessary, curriculum planning is carried out in groups rather than individually, by people who all have first-hand knowledge of the situation for which they are planning. School department or grade level groups are best suited for this task. However, regardless of how well experienced and proficient their members may be in individual curriculum planning, such groups typically lack knowledge of the subtleties and complexities of joint curriculum planning.

It is in this area that the teacher-librarian can make an important contribution. When department and grade level groups are not active in joint planning projects, the teacher-librarian's role becomes even more important. It is the teacher-librarian who can change the teacher's solitary curriculum planning into a more broadly based and cooperative venture.

The teacher-librarian is ideally positioned for this role as a member of a large or small curriculum planning team. First, as a regular member of the school staff, the teacher-librarian has first-hand, intimate knowledge of the school setting—school curriculum policies; principal expectations; teacher predilections, interests and non-interests; parent sentiments; available facilities and materials. Second, the teacher-librarian has expert knowledge of prescribed curriculum and of available print and non-print resource materials. When knowledge of the curriculum planning process is added to this already substantial body of expertise, the teacher-librarian is in a position not only to respond to teacher requests but also to go beyond teacher requests and make suggestions that can improve the curriculum planning process.

A Traditional View of the Curriculum Planning Process

For the better part of this century, teachers and curriculum developers have been taught that the ideal curriculum planning process is a rational series of steps beginning with the definition of goals and objectives (sometimes preceded by identification of student or societal "needs") and ending up with a check on the accomplishment of those objectives and subsequent revision of instructional plans.

A typical version of this Tyler planning model, named after the man who first laid out its rationale (Tyler, 1949) can be summarized in eight steps:

1. Specify goals and objectives.
2. Assess student status.
3. Determine needs.
4. Rank needs.
5. Plan a program.
6. Implement program.
7. Evaluate program.
8. Continue, modify or abort program based on the evaluation.

(Tankard, 1970)

This view of curriculum planning has a number of things to commend it as a prescription for the planning process. For one thing, curriculum planners should certainly consider what educational ends they are aiming for, although these need not and often should not be stated in terms of precise student behaviors, as later interpreters of the Tyler rationale (Mager, 1962; Popham, 1970) have insisted.

Another commendable feature of the Tyler model is its emphasis on what happens with students as an important ingredient in subsequent planning. The teacher's sensitive judgment of the nature of the students' experiences in relation to educational aims should be the primary determinant of what is subsequently planned.

Unfortunately, these emphases have tended to be overshadowed by a view of curriculum planning as a technical process initiated and controlled by the precise specification of behavioral objectives. Not only does this view mistake important features of education, as Stenhouse (1975) argues, but it fails to capture what little is known about how teachers go about the planning process either individually or in groups.

Curriculum Planning and Deliberation

A better representation of the curriculum planning process as it actually occurs in groups of experts is the model developed by Walker (1971). The three key elements in this model are the curriculum's platform, its design, and the deliberation associated with it. (See Figure 20.1.) The platform consists of the curriculum planner's assumptions and it is the source of educational aims and goals. The platform includes conceptions or beliefs about what exists and what is possible. For example, "We believe there is a learnable strategy for interpreting historical events," states a conception about what is learnable. The platform also includes theories, or beliefs, about what relations hold between existing entities. An example given by Walker, "The teacher imparts attitudes toward a subject, and, indeed, attitudes towards learning itself," states a theory about how attitudes toward learning develop.

Figure 20.1   Walker's Naturalistic Curriculum Planning Model

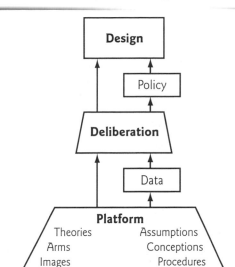

From *Foundations for Effective School Library Media Programs.* © 1999 Ken Haycock. Libraries Unlimited (800) 237-6124.

Beliefs about what is educationally desirable are also part of the platform. Another of Walker's examples, "We teach a subject not to produce little living libraries on that subject, but rather to get a student to think mathematically, to consider matters as a historian does, to take part in the process of knowledge getting," states a general aim of education. Two other less explicit but nevertheless important platform components are images and procedures. Images are another form in which some educationally desirable condition or state of affairs is thought of, without specifying why or in what way it is desirable. Heroes are cultural images. So are outstanding works of art or admired scientific theories. The image of home may be a very important source of aims and goals for an elementary teacher (Clandinin, 1983).

Images are realized through procedures, which specify courses of action or decisions that are desirable without specifying who or in what way they are desirable. Some people would also call these principles (Elbaz, 1983; Oberg, 1987; Peters, 1959).

Examples include "Be honest," and "Minimize the time necessary to learn," and "Create situations in which learners can share with each other."

The significance of the platform is two-fold. First, every curriculum planner has a platform whether it is made explicit or not. When teacher-librarians plan with a teacher, they work from a platform. When curriculum planners appear to speak at cross purposes or do not see eye to eye, it is often because they are working from different curriculum platforms. Making platforms explicit is a useful way to get beyond misunderstandings and even disagreements about curriculum and curriculum planning. Secondly, the curriculum planning platform is the source of justification of all the decisions made during planning. A teacher decides to have students generate their own questions about air pollution rather than answer the ones on the worksheet because he or she believes the development of inquiring citizens is an important educational aim. In order to defend a curriculum or a curriculum decision, one refers to the platform on which it is built.

The key element in Walker's model with which teacher-librarians are likely to be most concerned is the process of deliberation. This is a way of describing the planning process teacher-librarians and their teacher colleagues undertake. According to Walker (1971),

> The main operations in curriculum deliberations are (1) formulating decision points, (2) devising alternative choices at these decision points, (3) considering arguments for and against suggested decision points and decision alternatives, and finally, choosing the most defensible alternatives subject to acknowledged constraints. (p. 54)

The process is actually more circular than it sounds in this description, with each decision influencing every other one, so that early decisions must always be considered in light of later ones. There are five important bodies of experience which must be considered during deliberation. These are (1) the subject matter, (2) the learners for whom the plan is intended, their abilities, aspirations, anxieties, (3) the milieu in which the learning is to take place, that is, the classroom, the school community, biases, expectations, beliefs and values, power relationships, social norms, and so on, (4) the teacher, his or her approach to learners, to the subject matter, to planning, to teaching, and to colleagues, and (5) curriculum planning. All of these must be considered equally, without overdue emphasis on any one, especially subject matter and the materials which embody it.

As Walker points out, deliberation is a horribly complicated process.

> We should not be surprised to find out that curriculum deliberations are chaotic and confused. But we must not be misled into believing either that such confusion is worthless or that it is the inevitable consequence of deliberation. Deliberation is defined by biological, not sociological, criteria, and it may take many forms. The most common form in current practice is argumentation and debate by a group of people. But it could be done by one person, and no logical barrier stands in the way of its being performed by a computer. (p. 55)

Schwab (1978) makes the same point and adds another. He argues that "the process of deliberation is not only difficult and time-consuming; it is also often unsatisfying because there is no point at which it is clear that the course has been completed and completed well" (p. 292).

The final component of Walker's model is the design of the curriculum. His conception of design is different from the traditional definition of design as the arrangement of the parts of the curriculum, that is, the relationship among objectives, activities, content, materials, and evaluation. Instead, Walker sees design as the set of

relationships embodied in the materials-in-use which can affect students. He explains:

> We are accustomed to speaking of curricula as if they were objects produced by curriculum projects. The trouble with this view is that the curriculum's effects must be ascribed to events, not materials. The materials are important because their features condition the events that affect those using the materials. The curriculum design—the set of relationships embodied in the materials-in-use which are capable of affecting students—rather than the materials themselves are the important concerns of the curriculum specialist. The trouble with the concept of design is that the curriculum's design is difficult to specify explicitly and precisely—one way to specify a curriculum's design is by the series of decisions that produce it. A curriculum's design would then be represented by the choices that enter into its creation. (p. 53)

This concept of design reminds us that students may demonstrate accomplishment of objectives in ways not anticipated, depending on how the lesson proceeds. When teachers are oriented to learners and what they are experiencing rather than to subject matter or prescribed outcomes or discipline or the clock, what happens in the classroom is and ought to be unpredictable except in very general terms. The teacher works with the potential inherent in the curriculum materials, in students, and introspectively to create the best possible opportunities for learning.

Let us return to the core of the curriculum planning model, deliberation. This conception of curriculum planning as deliberation is quite different from the objectives-first, subject matter dominated model on which we have all been brought up. It portrays curriculum planning as circular, indeed circuitous, uncertain, complex, and time consuming rather than as a unidirectional, ends-driven deductive process. Perhaps the most important difference between the deliberative and the Tylerian models is that while the Tylerian model was developed to guide curriculum developers through a tidy planning procedure, the deliberative model was developed to describe what groups of teacher-experts actually did in planning a curriculum. Understanding that it is the inherent nature of the curriculum planning process-in-action to be unstraightforward might alleviate some of the frustration of finding it so.

The aim of this planning process is to clarify what kinds of learning (not behaviors) are desired and why, and what materials, arrangements, and activities are likely to contribute to them. If realizing that planning is as complex as teaching is little comfort for the teacher-librarian attempting to facilitate it, perhaps some general knowledge of how teachers tend to approach curriculum planning may help. Interestingly, this description of deliberative curriculum planning as it occurs in groups is compatible with an entirely different body of literature which describes what we know about individual teachers' planning predilections. Although teacher planning may not always exhibit the ideal characteristics of deliberation as described by Walker and Schwab, it is closer to the deliberative model than to the objectives-first model, into which curricularists so often try to force teachers.

How Individual Teachers Plan

One group of teacher planning studies divides teachers into two sorts of planners: comprehensive and incremental. Comprehensive planners build detailed plans of how the lesson content and activities will be worked out, based on expectations of how students will react. Incremental planners, on the other hand, plan only an initial activity and then try it out on the students before planning further (Clark & Yinger, 1979). Most teachers do not begin their planning with statements of objectives (Zahorik, 1975). Some consider objectives later in the planning process, and some do not consider them at all, although they are implicit in every planning decision, buried subconsciously in the teacher's platform.

There are also some differences depending on subject matter and grade level. Teachers of English and social studies tend to consider broad goals more, and more often, than do teachers of math, science and geography, who tend to focus instead on content (Taylor, 1970). It seems that many teachers rely on the teacher's manual or the curriculum guide statement of objectives and see planning

as the generation of a set of reminders about how they intend to go about accomplishing what is prescribed in the guide (McCutcheon, 1979). The emphasis on plans of secondary teachers is typically on content, while the emphasis in plans of elementary teachers is typically on activities.

The biggest influences on the selection of content and activities are the teacher's perception of student interests and anticipated student responses. Teachers plan what they think will grab student interest and keep the lesson flowing smoothly. The second strongest influence on planning decisions is the teacher's own preference, knowledge and skills. Teachers will select activities and content which they themselves like and feel comfortable handling. The third most important influence on teacher planning decisions is curriculum materials (Leithwood, Ross, & Montgomery, 1978). Here is a particularly potent point of influence for the teacher-librarian. Teachers tend to plan around materials they have at hand. They avoid topics for which they lack materials.

Some teachers do not write down many plans at all. For them, planning is a mental activity during which they rehearse the lesson privately (McCutcheon, 1979). The actual plan comes alive only in interaction with students. Most teachers plan, as they teach, in isolation. They typically do not refer to the professional publications, colleagues, consultants or the principal (Oberg, 1975). Given all these things that teachers tend to consider during planning, one might ask in what order teachers typically make these considerations. The answer is that there is no typical order of consideration. Moreover, there is no correlation between order of consideration and quality of the plan which results. Planning procedures are variable among expert planners as well as regular classroom teachers (Oberg, 1978). The circularity and circuitousness characteristic of deliberation seem to be the order of the day.

Implications for Teacher-Librarians as Co-Planners

If we adopt deliberation as our view of the planning process, then successful planning sessions are those in which all five commonplaces (subject matter, learners, milieu, teachers, planning) are thoroughly considered, alternatives have been considered before choices were made, and planners can justify their decisions in terms of their curriculum platform. Achieving success in these terms is a tall order even for expert planners. A group of experienced teacher-librarians with whom these ideas were shared listed some key points for those who undertake curriculum deliberation to keep in mind:

1. Objectives need not be considered first.

2. The platforms of both teacher-librarian and teacher should be clarified.

3. Planning involves risk-taking.

4. Some platforms may not mesh.

5. Knowing student interests helps teachers plan.

6. Find out what student responses the teacher expects.

7. Make teachers aware of resources appropriate for their particular students.

8. Be aware of the content of curriculum guides.

9. Focus on process as well as content learning.

10. Build good relationships with teachers and supervisors.

11. Teacher-librarians need many different approaches to curriculum planning.

12. Flexibility in planning approach is essential.

13. Planning is different in each situation.

Some Concepts in Curriculum Planning

Other points useful in curriculum planning can be gleaned from some distinctions among key curriculum concepts, curriculum materials, curriculum content, and learning activities.

Curriculum materials. Materials are an embodiment of subject matter and although they loom large as an influence on the teacher's planning, Schwab (1973) advises that they should not overshadow the importance of the other commonplaces, namely learners, milieu, the teacher, and the curriculum planning process itself. Schwab's admonition is easily taken into account if curriculum materials are used not, as teachers typically use them, to define de facto the curriculum, but

in the way teacher-librarians are more likely to see them, as resources which can be used in a variety of ways. Decisions about how to use any given set of curriculum materials are made in light of students' needs, community and school expectations, and teacher preferences. For example, students who are knowledgeable about a particular historical event may be given (by a teacher who values critical thinking) two sets of source materials from that era, not to learn more about the historical event, which they could do with those materials, but to compare the opposing points of view presented in the materials. Schwab says that any given materials may be used by students in three different ways: (1) to learn what the materials convey, for example, a story, a scientific explanation, an historical event; or (2) to learn how a story, scientific event or historical account is constructed; or (3) to learn how to interpret the story, scientific explanation, or historical account. Helping teachers see the potential in curriculum materials in varied ways is a valuable function of the teacher-librarian. It is easier to see the varied potential uses of curriculum materials if one is clear on the distinctions between curriculum content and curriculum goals.

Curriculum content. Conceptions of curriculum content are often fuzzy. Teacher-librarians who can clarify what is meant by curriculum content in their own minds will be of greater help to teachers than those who cannot. Content is the facts, ideas, concepts, skills, attitudes and so on which make up the curriculum. Sometimes the content is defined entirely by the goal or objective statement. "Students should know the causes of the revolution" is a goal statement which also defines the curriculum content. The content is the concepts and generalizations which define the causes of the revolution. Sometimes the content is only instrumental to the goal. If the goal is that students should learn skills of critical thinking, any of a wide variety of content areas, likely one from the social sciences or humanities, may be used for this purpose. Typically, content plays an instrumental role when the goal is a cognitive skill. Clarifying the kind of learning intended puts curriculum content and materials in perspective.

In order to determine the appropriate relationship between content and materials then, it is important to know which type of goal is intended. Curriculum goals are of four types: cognitive knowledge, cognitive skills, affect, and psychomotor skills. Teacher-librarians are most often working with teachers concerned with one or more of the first three types. If teachers are not explicit about the goals they intend, then teacher-librarians must uncover these goals in their conversations with them. Note that goals are statements of intentions about what students will learn, that is, what they will know about (cognitive concept knowledge), what they will know how to do (cognitive skill knowledge), what they will be able to do (cognitive skills), what traits they will exhibit (affect). Note also that goals or objectives need not be stated behaviorally, except for psychomotor skills goals. There is usually a variety of observable indicators of what a student has learned, and to restrict the demonstration to one behavior is unnecessarily and harmfully limiting. So, for example, "to build a cedar box" is not a goal because it does not reveal what students are intended to learn. As soon as the teacher explains that she wants the students to understand about West Coast native culture through the activity of building the box, the teacher-librarian as well as the teacher will be in a much better position to suggest appropriate learning materials.

Activities. Knowing what kind of goal is intended is also important for determining appropriate activities. The crucial feature of learning activities (presuming we are intending some kind of cognitive or affective learning) is what kind of mental activity they occasion. Building a cedar box is an appropriate activity if students are to calculate and measure, to attend to the physical or aesthetic qualities of the wood, to demonstrate artistic prowess in the decoration of the box, to show care, diligence, and attention to detail in their work, to reflect on the lifestyle and values of the native people who produced such boxes, or any of a number of other worthwhile goals. Notice that the goals, along with other elements of the planner's platform, provide the justification for the learning activities.

This paper has touched only briefly on a number of complicated curriculum matters. The aim here has been not to present recipes and formulae, but to share some theoretical and practical distinctions and some empirical findings which might be helpful to teacher-librarians in thinking about their role as a help to teachers in their curriculum planning. Because the planning process is inherently complex, unpredictable, and contingent, it cannot be accomplished well with straightforward technical procedures. What is required for successful curriculum planning is broad and deep knowledge of subject matter, learners, teachers, and milieu; sensitivity to the way these elements combine in any given case; and a capacity to revel in the many intricacies and multiple possibilities in any given instance of planning.

References

Clandinin, J. (1983). *Conceptualization of image as a component of teacher personal practical knowledge in primary school teachers' reading and language program.* Unpublished doctoral dissertation, University of Toronto.

Clark, C. & Peterson, P. (1984). *Teachers' thought processes* (Occasional Paper No. 72). Institute for Research on Teaching, Michigan State University.

Clark, C. & Yinger, R. (1979). *Three studies of teacher planning* (Research Series No. 55). Institute for Research on Teaching, Michigan State University.

Elbaz, F. (1983). *Teacher thinking: A study of practical knowledge.* Croom Helm.

Leithwood, K., Ross, S. & Montgomery, D. (1978). *An empirical investigation of teachers' curriculum decision making processes.* Paper presented at the 1978 annual meeting of Canadian Society for the Study of Education, Fredericton, New Brunswick.

Mager, R. (1962). *Preparing instructional objectives.* Fearon.

McCutcheon, G. (1979). *How elementary school teachers plan their curriculum: Findings and research issues.* Paper presented to the 1979 annual meeting of the American Educational Research Association, San Francisco, CA.

Oberg, A. (1975). *Information referents and patterns in curriculum planning of classroom teachers.* Unpublished doctoral dissertation, University of Alberta.

Oberg, A. (1978). *Characteristics of classroom teachers' curriculum planning decisions.* Paper presented at the 1978 annual meeting of the Canadian Society for the Study of Education, Fredericton, New Brunswick.

Oberg, A. (1987). Using construct theory as a basis for research into teacher professional development. *Journal of Curriculum Studies 19(1)*, 55–65.

Popham, W. & Baker, E. (1970). *Systematic instruction.* Prentice Hall.

Schwab, J. (1969). The practical: A language for curriculum. *School Review, 78(1)*, 1–23.

Schwab, J. (1973). The practical 3: Translation into curriculum. *School Review, 81(4)*, 501–22.

Schwab, J. (1978). The practical: Arts of eclectic. In I. Westbury & J. Wilkoff (Eds.), *Science, curriculum, and liberal education: Selected essays of Joseph J. Schwab.* University of Chicago Press.

Schwab, J. (1983). The practical 4: Something for curriculum professors to do. *Curriculum Inquiry, 13(3)*, 239–365.

Shavelson, R. & Stern, P. (1983). Research on teachers' pedagogical thoughts, judgments, decisions and behavior. *Review of Educational Research, 51*, 455–498.

Stenhouse, L. (1975). *An introduction to curriculum research and development.* Heinemann.

Tankard, G. (1974). *Curriculum improvement: An administrator's guide.* Parker.

Taylor, P. (1970). *How teachers plan their courses.* National (UK) Foundation for Educational Research.

Tyler, R. (1949). *Principles of curriculum and instruction.* University of Chicago Press.

Walker, D. (1971). A naturalistic model for curriculum development. *School Review, 80(1)*, 54–65.

Zahorik, J. (1975). Teachers' planning models. *Educational Leadership, 33*, 134–139.

CHAPTER TWENTY ONE

Changing Teaching Practice to Meet Current Expectations: Implications for Teacher-Librarians

Jean Brown

School library resource centers are an integral and essential part of the school's instructional program, at least in theory, with teacher-librarians involved as teaching partners with classroom teachers. However, in actual practice many school libraries are viewed as frills, or as merely a storehouse of recreational reading materials, existing on the periphery of the school's instructional program. Rather than seen as essential, the teacher-librarian is often seen as dispensable, a rather expensive clerk or technician, the first to be laid off in times of staff reductions. Why does the gap between theory and practice exist, and what, if anything, can be done about it?

Since it is generally accepted (again in theory) that a school library resource center ought to be an integral part of the school, an obvious place to begin in attempting to understand the problem is with the school itself. Since the school is part of a school district, and also part of the larger society, it is also necessary to examine conditions in the

school district and to consider national concerns that affect the school. Since the major concern here is with the implementation of school library media programs, conditions and factors which affect this program are focused on.

The World of the School

Interestingly, the gap between theory and practice does not exist in school library media programs alone. There is a considerable gap between theory and practice in all areas of the curriculum. Schools today, in spite of the literature which would make you believe otherwise, are very similar to what they were years ago. The many reforms which curriculum planners envision for the schools are, in actual fact, found in very few classrooms. Studies show that rather than a change in teaching practice, there has been a change in expectations for that practice. It is a situation which has caused many concerned educators to lament, "The more things change, the more they stay the same."

The 1980s was not a particularly good time for schools or teachers. It was a time of major social and economic crisis. Unemployment rates were high; inflation figures soared. Although government measures reduced the rate of inflation, the effects of the recession are still being felt. Many government workers, including teachers, have had to accept wage freezes. The threat of budget cuts and teacher layoffs has increased the insecurity of teachers. All these conditions have led to low teacher morale. On the national scene, teachers have been bombarded with negative reports on education. *A nation at risk*, the report of the National Commission on Excellence in Education, and approximately a dozen others published in 1982–83, expressed concern that standards seem to be falling, and placed most of the blame on the school system. The reactions to these reports are reminders that the schools are indeed part of the larger society. Block, a superintendent of education in Minnesota, angrily reacted to *A nation at risk*, which he called "a foul shot at American education."

> Mediocrity? Maybe—but we know the roots of it. We are a nation that has become so materialistic that we refuse to give up the second snowmobile or the second car or the bigger house or the speedboat so that we can pay for excellence in education (Block, 1983, p. 183).

School districts have had to contend with declining enrollments and declining dollars. Elementary and secondary enrollments in Canada, for example, declined by 17 percent, from 1970-71 to 1983-84. This decline occurred at the same time that governments experienced the effects of the recession. The result was that money allocated to elementary and secondary education declined dramatically between 1970 and 1981, "from 22 percent to 16 percent, and the downward trend is continuing" (Brown, 1985, p. 7). Faced with such restraints, many boards are unable to maintain the quality of education; Burke and Bolf, after surveying 3,724 educators, concluded that the school environment had deteriorated, especially "when it came to the availability of funds for repairing or replacing supplies,

equipment and buildings, for increased class size, or for professional development and supply [substitute] teachers (Burke & Bolf, 1985, p. 9).

At the same time as they are experiencing financial cutbacks, school boards have been faced with demands for new programs. Legislation has been passed requiring school boards to make special arrangements for the mentally and physically handicapped. Parents have demanded and obtained classes in second languages. In some areas, the needs of gifted students have been recognized through special programs, and special program teachers are being recruited while others are being laid off. Other classroom teachers are declared redundant due to declining enrollments. Boards wishing to hire new teachers with special expertise are often prevented from doing so by collective agreements requiring that teachers declared redundant be given priority.

Scarcity of funds and the reality of teacher layoffs have forced district offices to look at what is essential to schooling and what is not. Few districts have attempted to broaden their programs in such a climate. Many principals and superintendents feel that they are winning the battle if they can simply maintain their present staff and programs. Only positions and programs which are seen as essential have survived. How essential are school library media programs and teacher-librarians to education? To answer that question, it is necessary to examine classroom teaching.

Classroom Teaching Practices

What goes on in most classrooms? There is an abundance of studies to provide glimpses behind the classroom door (see, for example, Crocker, 1983; Eisner, 1979; Eisner, 1983; Goodlad, 1984; Jackson, 1968; Lortie, 1975; Sarason, 1982) and show that, in general, "a school is a school is a school," regardless of location.

The classrooms observed generally looked much alike. The teacher was usually explaining or lecturing to the whole class or to a single student, often asking questions which required recall answers.

Teachers, when not lecturing, were usually supervising students who worked individually at their desks. Students were usually engaged in passive activities, involved with writing answers to questions asked by the teacher, listening to the teacher, or waiting and preparing for the next class. Despite curriculum guidelines which suggest that teachers provide for student individuality in learning rates and styles, there was little indication that individual differences were considered.

There was ample evidence that the many changes advocated by curriculum developers and recommended in curriculum guidelines are not being integrated into classroom practice. Goodlad (1984) concluded "Over the years, these ways of schooling have proved to be extraordinarily resistant to change, encouraging the view that nothing changes; there is only the appearance of change (p. 267).

In order to summarize the findings on teaching practice, it is useful to categorize them under the following generalizations:

Teaching is an isolated activity. Most teaching occurs behind closed doors in a self-contained classroom, and that is the way most teachers want it. In fact, some teachers said they could not work with another adult in the room and refused to use a teacher's aide (Sarason, 1982). Most teachers have never observed a colleague teaching, they do not really know their fellow teachers' educational beliefs, teaching competency, or treatment of students. Teaching, it was revealed, is not discussed by many staffs, and most teachers work in total isolation.

Teachers perceive themselves to be autonomous in their classrooms. Most teachers guard the autonomy of their classrooms, and feel threatened if their superiors make demands that reach into the classroom. Teachers recognize that they have to teach certain subjects but how and when they do it is seen by them as their decision. Requiring teachers to plan in advance was perceived as a threat to the teacher's autonomy (Jackson, 1968). Visitors are not welcome in most classrooms, mainly because most teachers fear them as being critical or evaluative.

Teaching goals are vague rather than specific. Teachers, working in isolation in their own classrooms, are often vague as to their goals, and are uncertain as to whether or not they have certain objectives. What happens in the classroom may

be radically different from the rational model: instead of a linear progression from objectives, to change, to evaluation of how objectives were met, teachers tend to allow action to precede goals. "We saw teachers begin to team teach, change their reporting procedures, create a totally new classroom atmosphere, and years later begin to talk about the goals of the school" (Lieberman & Shiman, 1973, p. 53).

Teachers work with groups, not with individuals. A reality of most classrooms is that goals must be met in a group context. Teachers are generally responsible for a class of thirty to forty students. The physical limitations imposed by such sizes force teachers to adopt certain instructional practices as a means of crowd control. Goodlad (1984) saw the classroom as "a crowded box" (p. 175) within which teachers have little opportunity to work with individual students. He observed (p. 126), "In the secondary schools no teacher could get to know many students well. Many students were not well known by any teacher."

Teachers rely on textbooks and are concerned with coverage of all the content in it. Given the demands placed on today's teachers, Eisner asked, "Is it any wonder that many teachers—perhaps most—would welcome textbooks and other kinds of workbooks that in effect decide for them what children shall study, in what order, for what ends?" (Eisner, 1979 p. 27). The textbook provides security for both teacher and student, for it outlines the course, suggests activities, provides practice exercises and discussion questions, and even helps in the evaluation process. The trend in many schools seems to be that "The textbook and its partner, the workbook, provide the curricular hub around which much of what is taught revolves" (Eisner, 1979, p. 27). Reliance on textbooks has been shown to lead to concern with coverage of all the content in the textbook. Part of the reason for this is the way textbooks are organized. Packaged as complete, sequential programs, textbooks convey the idea that if children do not cover all the material, and use all the parts of the program (workbooks, practice sheets, etc.), then they are missing out on important learning activities.

Teachers have to control the class in order to teach. The important matter of classroom management, discipline, and control has been shown to exert influence on the delivery of curriculum content and of the activities introduced in the classroom. Studies show that teachers are aware of better teaching methods than they employ, but the necessity for them to maintain control discourages the adoption of teaching strategies such as use of small groups and discovery learning. Certain realities facing classroom teachers are identified as factors contributing to discipline problems: Compulsory education means that some students are in school against their will, and in addition, there is the ever-present distraction of the crowd. The classroom puts friends together in a small, crowded room, and then requires them to pay attention to the teacher and ignore each other. Maintaining discipline and control under such conditions is a time-consuming, and nerve-wracking, part of the teacher's job. As much as 40 percent of the teacher's time is directed toward this end (Lortie, 1975).

Teachers see themselves as the essential catalysts in the learning process. Teachers may limit their teaching strategies partly due to the need for classroom control but they also base their actions on the belief that most students must be subjected to direct teacher instruction in order to learn. This may also help to explain why teachers make limited use of small groups, self-instructional non-print materials and other types of learning experiences outside the teacher-dominated, whole class teaching method. It may also help to explain why teachers do most of the talking in the classroom. Goodlad (1984) observed that teachers outtalked students by a ratio of three to one. He concluded (p. 229), "If teachers in the talking mode and students in the listening mode is what we want then we have it." Even when teachers ask students questions they will seldom give them time to respond. Eisner (1983) noted that the response time for students to answer was an average of three seconds! This point of view may also help to explain why teachers pay so little attention to independent study during school hours. The teachers observed in these studies wanted to teach, and anything which distracted students or

teachers from classroom instruction was viewed as counterproductive.

Teachers prefer to teach in self-contained classrooms. Uninterrupted teaching can best occur when the classroom is self-contained and teachers can shut their doors. Teachers wanted clearly defined boundaries, a self-contained classroom, and no interference from other adults. This desire for what Lorties (1975) refers to as "boundedness," is undoubtedly linked to the teacher's notion of how learning occurs (the teacher as the essential catalyst), the autonomy of the classroom, and the teacher's need for maintaining control. It influences the relationship teachers have with others. With parents, teachers want to determine the time and the conditions. Their relationship with the principal is more delicate. On the one hand, they recognize their need for support from the principal, and yet they want to protect their own boundaries. In many schools the practice seems to be allowing the principal hegemony over all areas of the school other than the classroom. As far as colleagues are concerned, teachers respect each other's boundaries, and tend to stay out of each others affairs unless invited to participate.

Teaching, Change and the School Library Media Program

The concept of the school library media program has developed as a response to what schools are expected to do. Documents such as *Partners in action* (Ontario Ministry of Education, 1982) and *Resource services for Canadian schools* (Branscombe & Newsom, 1977), developed as a response to the needs of the curriculum. According to curriculum guides, instruction is individualized, geared to meet the learning needs and learning styles of individual students. Teachers select from many resources, in different formats, as they develop learning experiences which will help students master clearly defined objectives. Students are actively involved in the learning process. They read, write, discuss, and listen; and also view, record, photograph or videotape. One aim is to produce graduates who can cope with the information needs of the modern world, independent learners equipped with the skills required for lifelong learning.

Table 21.1   The Nature of Teaching and Expectations for Teaching as Exemplified in School Library Media Programs

Nature of Teaching	Expectations for Teaching
Isolated activity	Cooperative planning
Teacher autonomy	Team teaching
Vague goals	Precisely defined goals and objectives
Group instruction	Individual instruction
Reliance on textbook	Variety of resources, different formats
Teacher control	Maximum freedom for the learner
Teacher as essential in the learning process	Teacher as creator of learning experiences leading to students becoming independent learners
Self-contained classrooms	Different locations

However, most schools are not meeting these expectations. There has been a change in expectations rather than a change in actual practice. Whether or not a school library resource center is seen as important and essential will depend upon what is actually happening in the classrooms. Teachers who rely on textbook teaching, workbooks and worksheets will have little need for a resource center. Students will not use it because it will be perceived (correctly) as not important in their overall evaluation. Another important factor to consider is teachers' sense of autonomy in their own classrooms. Teachers who jealously guard the classrooms will resist any attempt that appears to threaten that autonomy. Only in schools where teachers are seriously attempting to implement current expectations as expressed in curriculum guides will the school library resource center be seen as essential.

The perceived need for a school library media program, then, depends upon how serious we are about implementing current curriculum. Are classroom teachers really expected to follow current curriculum guidelines? If so, they will need considerable support. Teacher-librarians are familiar with the support needed for resource-based learning (as most of the curriculum is currently), and know that classroom teachers using that approach will require a centralized, organized collection of carefully selected resources and the specialized services provided by a fully qualified teacher-librarian. However, there is

another area in which classroom teachers will need support that is perhaps not as familiar to teacher-librarians, and that is support in making a major change in teaching practice.

Major differences exist between what classroom teachers are actually *doing*, and what they are *expected* to be doing, as reflected in guidelines such as *Partners in Action* (Ontario Ministry of Education, 1982).

For teachers accustomed to textbook teaching with its accompanying workbooks and practice sheets, this recommended approach will require learning how to use many resources effectively, in different formats, as part of the instructional process. If teachers are to feel comfortable with resources in different formats, and if they are to learn how and when to use them effectively, then they will need assistance.

However, to meet current expectations will also mean that teaching will no longer be an isolated activity (see Table 21.1). If the classroom teacher is to participate as a partner with the teacher-librarian, then the whole notion of a self-contained classroom in which the teacher has full autonomy is challenged. For many teachers, it will be a major change to accept another teacher as a partner in the instructional process. And for some it will be a major change to carefully plan learning experiences based on precisely stated objectives formulated to meet the learning needs and learning styles of individual students. If teachers are expected to work cooperatively and incorporate resource-based teaching and learning strategies into classroom instruction, then they will need support.

To ask teachers to change the materials they use for teaching, and the teaching approaches they use, is to require a change in their basic beliefs about how students learn. Teachers who believe that students must receive direct instruction in order to learn will find it very difficult to give students the freedom to learn independently, within carefully planned learning experiences. Many teachers will have to be shown that students can learn in situations where the teacher is more of a guide and a creator of learning experiences than a transmitter of information.

In recent years there has been a considerable body of knowledge accumulated on how best to achieve change in the school system (see, for example, Berman & McLaughlin, 1978; Fullan, 1982; Sarason, 1982). This research has important implications for all those wishing to implement school library media programs, for it recognizes how complex such a change is, and how best to go about successful implementation. Goodlad (1984) has been forceful in presenting the view that "the individual school is the key on which to focus for affecting improvement within the formal education system (p. 36). He, and others, recognize the classroom teacher as the central figure in implementing the curriculum, and point out that school staffs must work together for school improvement.

The consensus in the literature is that change will not occur through isolated and occasional in-service sessions. Teachers need time for guided reflection and integration, they need personal support and challenges and they need to try out new ways of teaching in a nonthreatening environment. The best place to provide this is in the school itself, with in-service involving the whole staff, including the principal, working together to improve instruction within the school.

Certain strategies were more effective than others in implementing change in the school system. Generally, the best practices are "essentially learning-by-doing" (Berman & McLaughlin, 1978, p. 28). Although "these strategies were not a panacea," (Berman & McLaughlin, 1978, p. 28) and they may not work at all if applied separately,

the following strategies did work together in an overall implementation strategy:

- concrete, teacher-specific, and ongoing training;
- classroom assistance when needed;
- opportunities for teachers to observe in classrooms where the change had already been successfully implemented;
- regular staff meetings which focus on practical problems arising from the change;
- involvement of the teachers in the development of any materials required for the change; and,
- the active involvement of the school principal (this last strategy is seen as vital for "it signaled the staff that their efforts were supported and valued" (p. 30).

The teacher-librarian has an important role to play in providing the school level support that classroom teachers need if they are to live up to current expectations. The qualified teacher-librarian is in a unique position to work as a partner with the classroom teacher, so that the expert in the content to be taught (the classroom teacher) can be assisted by the expert in learning resources (the teacher-librarian). It is an impossible task, based on a naive notion of change, for the teacher-librarian within a particular school to attempt to single-handedly change teaching practice in the school. This is a complex change, and will require the active support of the principal and the involvement of the school staff. The literature on change in education reveals that change will only occur if administrators and teachers feel a definite need for it and if there is a broad base of support.

The impetus for improvement at the school level will not come from the teacher-librarian. The position has neither the authority nor the prestige to create such a demand. The impetus must arise from the recognition that good teaching requires such an approach. At the school level, the drive for change and improvement must be spearheaded by the principal. But in the long term, it is the classroom teachers who will either accept or reject the notion of teaching exemplified by the school library media program.

This does not mean that teacher-librarians have no role to play in the change process.

Indeed, they have very important roles to play. Their first, and probably most important role, is that they interpret and communicate to teachers, students, administrators, and parents what a quality school library media program should be. This demands that they fully understand it themselves. They must be mindful that they will be judged by the tasks they perform. Teachers who only see the teacher-librarian performing clerical or technical duties will perceive the role as only clerical or technical. If teacher-librarians want to be taken seriously as professional "partners in action," then the literature on change is clear that they must act like professionals.

Those who presently work as teacher-librarians must be enthusiastic optimists, willing to prove to colleagues that different teaching approaches can work. They need to understand the curriculum and the teacher's world, so that they can work with the classroom teacher to help implement the school's program. They need to understand the nature of educational change, so that they can function as change agents at the school level. School people need extroverted personalities, allowing them to work well with others and to have the confidence to try out innovations. Being on the forefront of expectations in the curriculum, teacher-librarians have a responsibility to understand what is expected, to communicate this to their colleagues, and to show how a school library media program is necessary to provide the essential resources and services that teachers need to teach and students to learn.

References

Berman, P. & McLaughlin, M. (1978). *Federal programs supporting educational change*. Volume VIII: Implementing and sustaining innovations. The Rand Corporation, 1978. (ED 159289).

Block R. (1983). We already know our problems out here in the field. *Phi Delta Kappan, 65(3),* 183.

Branscombe, F. & Newsom, H. (Eds.). (1977). *Resource services for Canadian schools*. McGraw-Hill Ryerson.

Brown, W. (1985). Education spending cuts: Pulling up the ladder on young Canadians. *ATA Magazine, 65(2),* 4-7,

Burke, R. & Bolf, C. (1985). Economic recession and the quality of education. *ATA Magazine, 65(2),* 7–11.

Crocker, R. (1983). *The use of classroom time: A descriptive analysis*. St. John's, NF: Memorial University of Newfoundland.

Crocker, R. (1983). Determinants of implementation of an elementary science program. *Journal of Research in Science Teaching, 21(2),* 211–220.

Eisner, E. (1979). *The educable imagination*. New York: Macmillan,

Eisner, E. (1983). The kind of schools we need. *Educational Leadership, 41(2),* 48-55.

Fullan, M. (1982). *The meaning of educational change*. Toronto: OISE Press.

Goodlad, J. (1984). *A place called school*. New York: McGraw-Hill.

Jackson, R. (1968). *Life in classrooms*. New York: Holt, Rinehart & Winston.

Lieberman, A. & Shiman, D. (1973). The stages of change in elementary school settings. In C. Culver & G. Hoban (Eds.), *The power to change: Issues for the innovative educator*. New York: McGraw-Hill.

Lortie, D. (1975). *Schoolteacher: A sociological study*. Chicago: University of Chicago Press.

Ontario Ministry of Education. (1982). *Partners in action: The library resource centre in the school curriculum*. Toronto: Ontario Ministry of Education.

Sarason, S. (1982). *The culture of the school and the problem of change* (2nd ed.). Boston: Allyn & Bacon.

CHAPTER TWENTY TWO

Expanding the Collaborative Planning Model

Patti Hurren

This paper examines the collaboration process between a classroom teacher, a teacher-librarian and a language specialist. A cooperative planning and teaching model between classroom teachers and teacher-librarians has been widely used in many schools (Driscoll, Shields, & Austrom, 1986). Recent changes in the population of many schools have seen the English as a second language (ESL) population grow dramatically. There are rarely enough trained language specialists to meet the needs of ESL learners, nor is there typically adequate funding to hire additional specialists. Therefore, the task of meeting the needs of mainstreamed ESL students falls primarily to the classroom teacher.

The inclusion of a language specialist into the planning team is one way of addressing the needs of ESL learners. In this case, the goal of the collaboration session was to plan an integrated language and content novel study unit for fifth grade students. The teachers were working at an elementary school with a population of approximately 800 students. Close to 80 percent of the students in the school speak English as a second language, and of those almost all speak Punjabi.

The novel selected for the study was *The hostage* by Theodore Taylor.

The findings are discussed in three sections. The first section defines the process by answering the following questions: (1) What is meant by collaboration?; and (2) What constitutes language and content instruction? Evidence of the concepts as defined is presented. In the second section, the principles that guide the collaboration and language and content instruction are presented, followed by teacher interactions. Finally, in the third section, the process is evaluated in order to make choices and statements in regard to the success of the collaboration between a classroom teacher, teacher-librarian and language specialist.

Defining the Process

Before describing the collaborative planning among the three teachers, it is important to define the terms of reference. In order to do this, it is possible to pose two questions.

First, "What is meant by collaborative planning?" Lieberman (1986) states that "the forms of collaborative activity are as varied as the numbers and kinds of people involved" (p. 6). The process of teachers working together to plan and/or teach has been defined in many ways and called many things, such as: collaborative consultation, collegiality, teamwork and cooperative planning (Idol, Paolucci-Whitcomb, & Nevin, 1986; Little, 1982; Little & Bird, 1984; Rosenholtz, 1987). It is likely that a specific definition of the form of collaboration used by teachers in this study may emerge from the data collected. However, it is possible to identify a definition from the literature. The type of collaboration evident in this study is best described by Idol, Paolucci-Whitcomb and Nevin (1986) in the following way:

> Collaborative consultation is an interactive process that enables people with diverse expertise to generate creative solutions to mutually defined problems. The outcome is enhanced, altered, and produces solutions that are different from those the individual team members would produce independently. (p. 1)

Individuals who work together often take different types of roles (Bravi, 1986). In a true "collaboration" model, the teachers enjoy an interactive form of communication that emphasizes shared responsibility for the planning and teaching process. There is a great deal of evidence in the data to support this type of role identification.

The second question that can be posed is "What constitutes integrated language and content instruction?" Since this is the goal of the collaborative planning, it is important to determine what this will look like within the collaboration session. There is much support for integrated language and content instruction among language and classroom teachers (Langer & Applebee, 1987; Penfield, 1987; Swaim, 1988). The process is best described by Mohan (1990), when he recommends that:

> ...cooperating language teachers and content teachers should:
> 1. agree on target tasks which can be both language and content goals. These will often be tasks essential to content classrooms;

> 2. develop language-sensitive ways to support LEP (limited English proficiency) students' work on content tasks. (p. 59)

Inherent in integrated language and content instruction are the various skills that the teachers introduce or reinforce from previous units of study. These may include information skills, thinking skills and skills that are specific to the particular content area. Having defined the terms of reference, it is now possible to begin describing the actual collaboration sessions.

Each of the teachers in this collaboration brings an area of expertise to the process. The following comments are typical of the type of information the classroom teacher (CT) shares with the planning group:

> CT: We've already been to the aquarium. We went this year and we did do marine biology way back in the fall—so they've had a fair bit of looking, but mostly at invertebrates, not mammals.
>
> I have had limited success with that. I tried a learning log with the kids and about half of them finally caught on, after I flogged it for I don't know how many months with none of them ever responding to anything I wrote back. The logs are sitting on my desk right now in dejection because I just got so frustrated with it.

The classroom teacher not only brings an extensive experience with fifth grade curriculum, but also an understanding of the background knowledge the students are likely to have. In addition, the CT is able to comment on the strengths and weaknesses of the students in light of previous classroom experiences.

The teacher-librarian (TL) is experienced in cooperative planning and teaching at all levels. She made these statements:

> TL: I was really impressed with the way sort and predict worked with J's class when we did religions. It worked really well. I was very skeptical because I thought the language there was too difficult. But it wasn't. A lot of good thinking, and a lot of relationships.
>
> Magazine articles are just great and there is a lot on that topic. We have some local newspapers written at an appropriate reading level too.

The TL not only brings an expertise in information skills. She also has an extensive knowledge of available resources and can explain how specific teaching strategies worked with similar groups.

Finally, the language specialist (LS) can guide the planning as indicated below:

> LS: The students should learn the language that goes with that, for expressing those ideas. I would ideally like to put up a chart with the language on it and they could have that chart in their books. We could refer to it as we go through, because it seems to me that if we're going to focus on any kind of language, this would be the language we want to focus on in this particular book…one of the things we are going to do, if we do that, is bring in the language of sequence, and we're going to give them a way of expressing what's in it.

Clearly, each of these specialists contributes to the improved quality of the planned instruction. It would be expected that the final instruction would be enhanced by inclusion of all these components. It is probable that none of these individuals would have planned as comprehensively on their own.

In this case, the teachers are working together for the first time. Consequently, some time is taken during the collaboration process to actually clarify the roles that each teacher will take during the teaching. The following comments refer to this clarification.

> CT: Are we looking at doing group work or how we are going to incorporate all of us? Are we all going to take turns doing it, or am I doing it and you guys are watching, or what?

> LS: That's what we thought—that we would both just watch you and I'll tape-record you.

> TL: And I'll video. [laughter]

> LS: The idea is that all of us will take part in the teaching. That's what collaboration is all about. You shouldn't have to feel as though you're doing the whole thing and there are a lot of different ways that we can do that. There will be times when we are doing group work and each of us will have a group. There will be times when each

of us will be teaching the whole class. That's what I had foreseen doing, as long as you're comfortable doing that.

In addition to the collaboration shown above, there is evidence that the teachers are working toward integrated language and content instruction.

> TL: What about presenting the idea before they start, the idea of evaluation…What I'm trying to do is get them thinking about the whole idea of captivity verses freedom.

> CT: …before we start.

> LS: It would be interesting to do something like a matched thinking activity where we pick vocabulary out of the book, and we could purposely pick vocab which is evaluative.

This interaction gives evidence that the teachers are identifying tasks that will combine content knowledge and language development as well as specific thinking skills. It is interesting to note that the emphasis on language development is not directed solely at ESL students but is seen to be valuable for all students.

Underlying Principles

There are two areas in particular that are governed by a set of principles. These areas are directly related to the topics of focus for section one. They are: (1) collaboration between teachers; and (2) integrated language and content instruction.

There are particular rules or assumptions that contribute to a successful collaboration process. Babcock and Pryzwansky (1983) describe a typical process by which collaboration occurs. This process includes: (1) "problem identification," where the collaborators jointly identify the problem to be solved; (2) "intervention recommendations," where possible strategies for dealing with the problem are discussed; (3) "implementation of recommendations," where the collaborators each implement some of the proposed solutions; and (4) "nature and extent of follow-up," which includes continuous communication and modification of the problem solving process (p. 360).

Figure 22.1   A Framework for Teaching and Learning

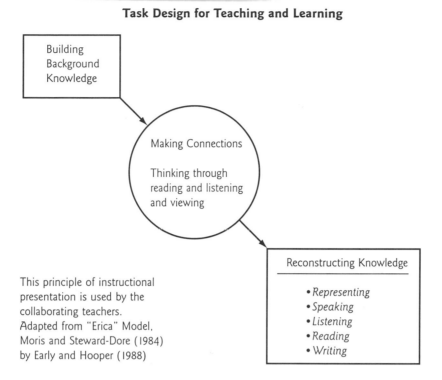

Task Design for Teaching and Learning

Building Background Knowledge

Making Connections

Thinking through reading and listening and viewing

Reconstructing Knowledge

- *Representing*
- *Speaking*
- *Listening*
- *Reading*
- *Writing*

This principle of instructional presentation is used by the collaborating teachers. Adapted from "Erica" Model, Moris and Steward-Dore (1984) by Early and Hooper (1988)

Steps one and two of this model are directly applicable to the data collected.

There are also principles that underlie teaching. The scope and sequence of these principles is too vast to be fully described here. However, it is possible to identify a particular principle of teaching in effect in this situation. The "Task Design for Teaching and Learning" is a three step model for instruction developed by Early and Hooper (1988). This model, which originates in content area reading research, looks at (1) Building Background Knowledge; (2) Thinking Through Reading, Viewing and Listening; and (3) Reconstructing Knowledge. It can be represented graphically in the following manner:

This principle of instructional presentation is used by the collaborating teachers.

It is possible to identify discourse that follows the process of collaboration as described by Babcock and Pryzwansky (1983). However, it is clear that although the teachers work at "problem identification" and "intervention recommendations," they do not follow a strict sequential model. Discussion of different parts of the problem, or more

appropriately the planned instruction, is more cyclical, with continuous revision and restatement as indicated below:

CT: We're starting from scratch...We do know that it deals with evaluation of keeping a whale captive or letting it free. So we're looking at how long, [LS]?

LS: Well, when we first talked about this, you said two weeks.

Is that still what you have in mind?

CT: So we need to do a little bit on the whale.

Comments by the teachers move fluidly back and forth between exploration of the topic and concerns about length of time and organization.

Throughout the planning process, the teachers discuss possibilities for teaching strategies or "intervention recommendations."

LS: Now, [TL] mentioned using some of the strategies that we learned during the professional development last year. There's building from clues, but I'm not entirely sure that building from clues would be a good one with this. It's hard to get artifacts to introduce a story about captivity for whales.

CT: It seems to me…that an activity which would be really good to do with this would be some kind of debate.

LS: It would be interesting to do something like a matched thinking activity where we pick vocabulary out of the book, and we could purposely pick vocab which is evaluative and then put it on a sheet, and they have to cut it up and come up with their own groups.

TL: Like a sort and predict.

The principles for the progression of the teaching are stated early in the collaboration process in the following way:

LS: OK, if you look at the planning sheet I gave you—what it looks like is: building background knowledge, thinking while reading, sharing the information and putting it into another form—which is a pretty basic progression for any study you're going to do in any subject area. It's very generic.

Through the use of the planning sheet the LS guides the collaborative session. The teachers discuss and agree on the importance of the different components contained in the planning model, and set about planning tasks to fit each of the steps.

TL: I want to tie in their background knowledge. What do you think is the best way to go—to talk about dealing with the kind of issues at hand, or their understanding of evaluation in general?

The teachers finally decided on a sort and predict activity to look at the students' background knowledge and to build a common understanding of the key vocabulary of the novel. The words were not selected for difficulty, but rather because they were pertinent to one of the themes of the story. To deal with the second step of the model, the teachers planned a thinking log.

LS: …a reading journal and have them after each chapter…write two or three lines as a response to literature—about what they thought—about what they heard.

CT: Not what they heard but what they think.

LS: Um-hmm, or it could be what they heard but that's a different thing. A thinking log sort of idea. You can ask a thinking question like: "Today when you write in your thinking log, I want you to think about this particular stance or this particular person and how they feel or whatever."

TL: It would be a good way to find out how much they are understanding and whether or not they can express what they know.

Finally, the teachers discussed the third step of the model.

LS: An activity which would be really good to do with this would be some kind of debate.

CT: Um-hmm.

LS: …and force them to have an opinion, even if it's not their own, about what should happen in the book.

CT: Um-hmm, I would guess that would be near the end where he makes his decision, if that's sort of what the whole book is about.

LS: The debate would give the students a chance to sum up everything they have learned about captivity verses freedom for killer whales, and present it to the class.

Throughout the planning process, the teachers discuss various possibilities, but in the end, they choose activities that are directly supportive of the three stages of the task design model.

Evaluation and Choices

There are costs and benefits to this type of collaborative planning model. Evidence has been presented through the data to indicate that these teachers were collaborating to produce integrated language and content instruction. It is important to evaluate the process itself, as well as determine whether it is an effective model.

The benefits to the teachers involved are numerous. Zahorik (1987) states: "Collegiality among teachers and between teachers and administrators is recognized by many as an important source of professional growth" (p. 386). He goes on to list eleven different types of help that teachers often exchange in a collaborative situation, including: (1) Materials; (2) Discipline (including ideas for motivating students); (3) Activities; (4) Individualization; (5) Evaluation; (6) Methods (including models for teaching and "how to" information); (7) Objectives; (8) Reinforcing; (9) Lecturing (how to model various processes); (10) Questioning; and (11) Room Organization (including ways to group students). Lieberman (1986) adds that "collaboration…can serve as…another meeting ground for ideas and support and a context for understanding and sharing different worlds" (p. 8).

On the other hand, reality reinforces the costs inherent in this model. Research tells us of many obstacles that can interfere with collaboration, such as teacher isolation, space restrictions, lack of funding and traditional school cultures of individualism (Lortie, 1975; Hargreaves, 1989; Minnes, 1991). However, it is evident that the teachers involved in this particular collaboration have overcome these initial obstacles. But they do have to contend with a serious cost related to the process, which is the extensive amount of time needed to plan together. Teachers are dealing with increasing demands on their time and it is difficult to "find" time for collaboration.

In the end, when judging the effectiveness of the collaborative planning sessions, it is necessary to weigh the benefits described above against the cost in terms of time spent by the teachers involved. Obviously, the cost and benefits in regard to collaboration will vary depending on the players and the school culture in which they operate. In this case, it is possible to make some conclusions about the particular collaboration sessions examined.

After the collaboration sessions, the teachers made the following comments:

TL: She's so articulate. That's exactly what I meant. That's also what I was thinking of.

CT: The part I liked best was planning the thinking log. I didn't have success with that before, but I really want to do something like it. Now that we've talked about how it works, I think it will be much better.

TL: Great, that's a new strategy I've learned. Thanks, guys.

LS: This was so much fun. I can hardly wait until we meet again. When can we get together again?

It is apparent that all three participants in the collaborative planning sessions felt it was a positive experience. As shown above, the participants had an opportunity to learn about new strategies, discuss how to improve practice and enjoy positive interaction with colleagues. This last point is perhaps the strongest point in favor of collaboration, and it is one that seems largely neglected in the literature. In addition to building respect among professional colleagues, collaborative planning is "fun." If teachers view collaborative planning as both effective and enjoyable, it is likely that the time spent will be considered worth the cost.

Generally, one can recommend collaborative planning for integrated language and content instruction based on the overwhelming benefits to the teachers and students involved. Specifically, it appears that by adding a language specialist to the already effective partnership between classroom teachers and teacher-librarians, the planning process is strengthened.

References

Babcock, N. & Pryzwansky, W. (1983). Models of consultation: Preferences of educational professionals at five stages of service. *Journal of School Psychology, 21,* 359–366.

Bravi, G. (1986). *Support personnel as consultants.* Paper presented at University of Manitoba, Department of Educational Psychology, Winnipeg, MB.

Driscoll, D., Shields, P. & Austrom, L. (Eds.). (1986). *Fuel for change: Cooperative program planning & teaching.* Vancouver, BC: British Columbia Teacher-Librarians' Association.

Early, M. & Hooper, H. (1988). *Task design for teaching and learning.* Unpublished. Vancouver, BC: Vancouver School Board.

Hargreaves, A. (1989). Curriculum policy and the culture of teaching. In G. Milburn, I. Goodson, & R. Clark (Eds.), *Re-interpreting curriculum research: Images and arguments* (pp. 26–40). London, ON: Althouse Press.

Idol, L., Paolucci-Whitcomb, P. & Nevin, A. (1986). *Collaborative consultation.* Rockville, MD: Aspen Systems.

Langer, J., & Applebee, A. (1987). *How writing shapes thinking.* Urbana, IL: National Council of Teachers of English.

Lieberman, A. (1986). Collaborative work. *Education Leadership, 43(5),* 4–8.

Little, J. (1982). Norms of collegiality and experimentation: Workplace conditions of school success. *American Educational Research Journal,* 19 (3), 325–340.

Little, J. & Bird, T. (1984). *Report on a pilot study of school-level collegial teaming.* (ED 266540).

Lortie, D. (1975). *Schoolteacher: A sociological study.* Chicago: University of Chicago Press.

Minnes, W. (1991). *Teacher collaboration around computer use: CT with English as a second language students.* Unpublished master's thesis, University of British Columbia.

Mohan, B. (1990). *LEP students and the integration of language and content: Knowledge structures and tasks.* Paper presented at National Symposium on Limited English Proficient Students Research Issues. United States Department of Education, Office of the Director for Bilingual Education and Minority Languages Affairs.

Penfield, J. (1987). ESL: The regular classroom teacher's perspective. *TESOL Quarterly, 21(1),* 21–29.

Rosenholtz, S. (1987). Education reform strategies: Will they increase teachers' commitment? *American Journal of Education, 95(4),* 534–562.

Swaim, M. (1988). Manipulating and complementing content teaching to maximize second language learning. *TESL Canada Journal/Revue TESL du Canada, 6(1),* 68–84.

Zahorik, J. (1987). Teachers' collegial interaction: An exploratory study. *The Elementary School Journal, 87(4),* 385–396.

CHAPTER TWENTY THREE

Collaborative Planning:
A Model That Works

Carol-Ann Page

"Separating learning experience into blocks of time or into subjects taught in isolation is contrary to what is known about how children learn. . ."

Cooperative program planning and teaching is a concept...a strategy or approach to teaching and learning. The term does not constitute a "set" program of instruction, but rather a philosophical framework for the development and implementation of resource-based programs which reflect what we know about how students learn. For the classroom teacher it is one more strategy or approach to be added to their teaching repertoire.

We know that people learn best when they can relate present learning to past knowledge and experience or create connections to the knowledge and experience of other areas of their lives. We know that it is only through such connections or meaning that the transfer of learning is facilitated. The purpose of cooperative program planning, then, is to develop learning experiences or units of study that effectively *integrate* the student's resource center activities (whether literature or research) with other learning experiences.

There are some cornerstones that lay the foundation for effective cooperative planning. First, the role of the teacher-librarian as a professional colleague and equal teaching partner must be clearly defined and understood in order to develop the partnership necessary for cooperative planning. Such a partnership does not place the teacher-librarian in a subservient, service role, nor in a superior, consultant role. Rather, each partner brings specific expertise to the planning process. Second, a school-based information skills continuum, developed by the staff, and for which each staff member acknowledges some ownership and accepts some responsibility, provides a necessary framework for the planning process. Finally, a planning model, or checklist, facilitates the efficiency and effectiveness of the planning process.

There are also some conditions that are conducive to effective planning sessions. First, teacher-librarians must be prepared to initiate planning with teachers, rather than waiting for teachers to come to them. If teachers don't know about, or understand, the service they can't be expected to seek it out. Second, the teacher-librarian must be prepared to present suggestions in such a way that the teacher can respond. Responses to "May I help you?" or "How may I help you?" may vary from silence, to "No thanks," to "I'm not sure." Determining a teacher's needs and preferred teaching strategies, and offering specific suggestions about the options that might be pursued, affords the teacher a greater, more positive opportunity to respond as a full partner in the planning process.

There are many paradigms of the planning process. If one holds the view that the teacher is a professional decision-maker, there are several decisions teachers make before, during and following instructions. Such decision-making is an ongoing, cyclical process, and may be represented as follows:

Program Planning Process

Objectives. Teachers determine what the students they are responsible for are going to learn. Direction, in many subject areas, is provided by curriculum guides and similar documents. But the teacher, based on a knowledge of student backgrounds, abilities, interests, and needs, makes the final decision about specific learning objectives.

Content. Teachers decide the content of student learning, including what the content will be and how much, or how little, will be taught.

Organization. Teachers make decisions about how the content will be organized to best facilitate student learning. Topical, thematic, chronological, and a variety of other organizational approaches are possible.

Methodology. Teachers make decisions about the instructional methods to be employed to best facilitate student learning. A variety of approaches such as direct teacher instruction, audio-visual presentation, discovery learning, resource-based learning (to name but a few) are possible.

Activities. Teachers make decisions about the learning activities to be developed to best facilitate student learning. Again, a variety of learning activities are possible and both instructional strategies and learning activities should be varied enough to appeal to each of the learning modalities.

Evaluation. Teachers make decisions about how student growth and learning will be evaluated, as well as how the effectiveness of a unit of study will be judged.

Traditionally, resource center use and teacher-librarian involvement have "plugged in" to the teacher's program at the learning activities stage. At this stage, the emphasis is on what students are to do and on what adjunct services, if any, are required. Typically, a teacher may contact the teacher-librarian with requests for resources to support a unit of study, "starting tomorrow," or to schedule a class in to undertake a research activity. In many instances, it may be only after the third or fourth student request for information that the teacher-librarian is able to determine that an assignment has been given somewhere, by someone. Frustrating? Certainly. It is professionally difficult, if not impossible, to be placed in a service role that purports to help teachers meet their teaching/learning objectives, if in fact these objectives are not known but, instead, must be deduced…either from written research assignments carried by students, or from the oral interpretation of students.

The cooperative planning process moves the involvement of the teacher-librarian back to the objectives stage, where the focus is on what students are to learn. Graphically the cooperative partnership looks like this:

Objectives…what students are to learn
Content
Organization
Methodology
Activities…what students are to do
Evaluation

Teacher-librarians in successful programs move from the activities phase to the objective setting phase, cooperatively established by the teacher and teacher-librarian.

When teachers and teacher-librarians are planning for resource-based learning programs, the learning objectives established involve both content or knowledge objectives as well as information skills objectives. This is an important point to emphasize, since both teacher-librarians (who are not, and can't be expected to be, subject specialists in every area) and teachers (who are classroom generalists or subject specialists) often express some confusion with, and even lack of confidence in, the planning partnership until this is understood. What each partner contributes to the cooperative planning process can best be represented as follows:

What the Teacher Brings to the Planning Process

- knowledge of the student
- knowledge of the content area

What the Teacher-Librarian Brings to the Planning Process

- knowledge of resources
- knowledge of information skills

The teacher librarian's contribution is considerably more complex than a superficial glance at this graphic representation might suggest. Rather than a "simple" knowledge of the availability of resources to support a given topic of study (and that, in itself, is not a "simple" task), more importantly, and at a much more sophisticated level, the teacher-librarian requires the skills necessary to determine the suitability of those resources to support the learning objectives and to meet student ability levels and learning styles. And, rather than a "simple" knowledge of information skills, and again at a much more sophisticated level, the teacher-librarian requires a knowledge of suitable strategies for integrating information skills instruction and application into units of study.

Cooperative program planning is a process of communicating...of creating something. In planning sessions, communication will not proceed in a rigid way, nor will it necessarily proceed in the order outlined in the planning checklist. Often, many of the points in the checklist will be addressed simultaneously and almost always there will be a back and forth flow between the points or stages in the process.

All of the information suggested by the checklist is crucial for successful and effective teaching/learning experiences and programs. The teacher-librarian needs to be skilled at employing effective questioning techniques to get at this information as expeditiously as possible.

- Initiate contact and schedule planning time
- Establish subject/topic/grade and ability level(s)
- Review previous skills and activities
- Establish general goal
- Establish specific objectives
    - knowledge/concept objectives
    - information skills objectives
- Select and locate resources
- Determine teaching strategies and learning activities
    - minimum expectations for students
    - responsibility for preparation and teaching of each component
    - scheduling of learning activities
- Evaluation
- Record and retain unit (note strengths/weaknesses on completion).

The Planning Checklist and Planning Process

Initiate Contact and Schedule Planning Time. Planning operationalizes the cooperative partnership. Planning must therefore be seen as a priority, and time must be set aside for it. Scheduling planning time to follow an initial contact allows each partner valuable "think time" in preparation for a planning session. The teacher might be asked to think about proposed learning objectives, preferred instructional strategies, and a timeline for a unit of study. The teacher-librarian might be thinking about the availability and suitability of resources to support a proposed topic of study and proposed techniques for grouping students and integrating information skills, given the number and nature of the resources available.

Establish Subject/Topic/Grade/ Ability Levels. The discussion of student ability levels will most often include the following areas of consideration:

- conceptual level...what concepts are involved in the area of study? how can this be determined?

- knowledge base…how much information or knowledge do students already have about the area of study? how can this be determined?
- skill level…what skills will students need to access and/or process the information required? what skills do students possess?
- reading ability…what is the range of reading ability among a given group of students?
- learning styles…what is the range of learning styles among a given group of students?

Review Previous Skills and Activities. An information skills continuum greatly facilitates this stage. Reference to a school- or subject department-based continuum assists the planning process in determining what has been mastered and, developmentally, what the next steps in skill development should be.

Establish General Goal. A goal may be defined as a statement of the purpose of a unit of study in terms of the individual learner. A goal statement should answer the question "Why are we studying this? (i.e., what are students to learn?)." It is most effective to approach establishing the purpose (general goal) for a unit of study by talking in terms of the learner(s) rather than in terms of the teacher(s).

Establish Specific Objectives. An objective may be defined as a statement of the behavior a student will be able to demonstrate at the end of a lesson or unit of study. Objectives break the goal into specific components. This stage of the planning process is one of refining and more specifically structuring a topic of study, since objectives provide the basis for selecting instructional strategies, learning activities, and evaluation procedures. Both knowledge and skill objectives need to be addressed.

Selection of Resources. The selection of suitable resources involves matching available resources to each of those considerations identified under "Student Ability Levels"…concepts to be included, the knowledge base of students, their skill levels, reading abilities and learning styles. Once this has been done, the next stage is to determine what information resources still need to be sought out or prepared (i.e., rewritten, taped, presented in picture or graph form).

Determine Teaching Strategies and Learning Activities. As stated, the learning objectives will provide the basis for selecting both teaching strategies and learning activities. At this stage in the planning process it is perhaps most effective for the teacher-librarian to be prepared to present things in such a way that the teacher can respond…to specific questions, suggestions or examples of specific approaches.

Minimum expectations. Minimum expectations should be designed to assure success for all students but should not act as a "ceiling" for more capable students. Minimum expectations should be established for the processes of gathering, recording and presenting information. This may involve structuring assignments to guarantee success, through such techniques as built-in checkpoints, or it may involve differentiating assignments to allow for varying ability levels.

Responsibility for preparation and teaching. Specific responsibility for the preparation and teaching of various components of a unit of study should be determined during the planning process. Teachers who are new to the cooperative planning process sometimes presume their responsibility ends with planning, and sometimes teacher-librarians who are new to the process corroborate this by assuming sole responsibility for the preparation and teaching of resource center learning experiences. This approach reduces cooperative program planning and teaching to "parallel" planning and teaching, which differs considerably from effecting the full integration of information skills and resource center experiences into the curriculum. The important point to emphasize here is that while responsibility may not be shared 50–50, it needs to be shared.

Scheduling of learning activities. The scheduling of learning activities depends on the overall time frame for a unit of study and on student grouping. These factors will determine the time and sequence of scheduled activities, as well as the location of students and resources.

Evaluation. Discussion of evaluation procedures should include some focus on each of the following aspects:

Evaluation of process (i.e., information skills): This type of evaluation, obviously, is on-going throughout a unit of study, and involves both teacher and teacher-librarian in the observation of students and in record-keeping to track individual student progress. These evaluation procedures are largely tied to minimum expectations set for students.

Evaluation of product: Criteria for evaluation of student products should be determined and made clear to students at the outset of a unit of study.

Student involvement: Students may be involved in evaluating their progress in process skills and the quality of their final product.

Evaluation of unit: Criteria for evaluating the effectiveness of a unit of study should be discussed during the planning process and time for this procedure established at the end of a unit of study.

Record and Retain Unit. Strengths and weaknesses and suggested revisions should be recorded at the end of a unit of study. This facilitates revision and adaptation for future use—the unit can be used again the following year, again stressing with appropriate revision and adaptation, and introduced and used by other teachers working at the same grade level, or serve as an example for teachers one is just beginning to plan with, or can be shared with other teacher-librarians and teachers in the district. A copy can also be taken by the teacher or teacher-librarian leaving the school. Retaining units of study is important for total program strength and growth over time.

Conclusion

The results of the cooperative program planning process are resource-based learning programs and experiences for students which (a) maximize the use of all school resources to the best possible effect for the student population, (b) ensure the integration of information skills instruction and application, developmentally, across the curriculum and (c) guarantee successful learning

experiences for all students. The impact of this approach on the rate and degree of student learning can and should be measured.

The successful implementation of this approach has been documented in the Vancouver (British Columbia) school district, as well as in many school systems across Canada. Both Australia and New Zealand launched a concerted national training program to assist teacher-librarians in the implementation of the approach. The philosophy is reflected in the U.S. national guidelines for school library media programs and is being successfully implemented in school districts across the United States.

Collaborative Planning Guide and Record of Unit of Study

The term "cooperative program planning and teaching" was coined in 1978 by Ken Haycock based on research and professional experience in teacher-librarianship. It refers to the essential role of the teacher-librarian in planning units of study with classroom teachers to integrate those skills and processes necessary to develop students committed to informed decision-making, cultural and literary appreciation and lifelong learning. Cooperative program planning and teaching provides the philosophical framework for the work of the teacher-librarian; it is not just another service function. The approach differs from team teaching, which in many instances became "turn teaching." It also differs from parallel planning and teaching where, following a brief "planning session," the teacher plans and executes classroom instruction and learning experiences and the teacher-librarian plans and executes library instruction to parallel those of the classroom. This approach to the effective use of non-classroom collaborative personnel in the school is now being used with similar success in learning assistance programs and gifted and talented programs.

Almost two decades ago, when planning a half day workshop for all teacher-librarians in the Vancouver (British Columbia) school district on cooperative program planning, a group of teacher-librarians identified the need for a formal planning guide to provide structure for the in-service program and support for follow-up work in schools. Working with Ken Haycock, then coordinator of library services, Ruth Lindgaard provided original impetus for a district approach, and Carol-Ann Page brought a structure and process for cooperative planning which she had developed and used successfully in her school for individual, grade-wide and school-wide cooperative planning.

The committee consolidated this structure and process with other planning guides and developed a draft guide for district use. The resulting "model" was field-tested in a number of schools prior to district workshops and revised accordingly.

Following the six half-day in-service programs, led for groups of 25 teacher-librarians, additional field testing took place in more than 75 schools. The original guide of four pages was expanded to six; objectives and evaluation were placed side by side to ensure that it was in fact the learning objectives that were being evaluated and not simply completion of the activities; the format was revised to allow inclusion in three-ring binders; and a number of smaller changes were made as well.

The resulting planning guide and record unit of study is used extensively throughout the Vancouver school district. In most schools, it is used to refer to the planning checklist and record units so they can be revised and adapted rather than begun again each year; many schools, however, use the form for collaborative planning with teachers. It is perhaps interesting to note that the initial response was more favorable from classroom teachers and curriculum and program consultants than from teacher-librarians themselves but this changed with use. Everyone is looking for more efficient and effective ways to plan and this guide has provided considerable direction and support to that end. It also facilitates the development of the district's index to cooperatively planned and taught units of study throughout the system, arranged by subject, topic, skill area and grade level.

Editor's addendum: In light of changing terminology in schools and in teacher-librarianship the process of "cooperative program planning and teaching" has been renamed "collaborative planning and teaching" here. Similarly, the design of the planning model has been revised to reflect newer initiatives and concerns in schools. The process of joint curriculum planning and team teaching, however, and the commitment to collaboration as two equal teaching partners, committed to student learning and success, remains unchanged.

Figure 23.1   Collaborative Planning and Teaching—Record of Study

Subject: _____

Topic: _____

Grade and Ability Levels: _____

PLANNING CHECKLIST	SUMMARY IN BRIEF DEVELOPERS' NOTES
❑ Inititiate contact and schedule planning	_____
❑ Establish subject, topic, grade, and ability level(s)	_____
❑ Review prerequisite knowledge, skills/strategies and activities	_____
❑ Establish general goal [the "big idea"]	_____
❑ Establish specific objectives	_____
❑ Select and locate resources	_____
❑ Determine teaching stategies and learning activities	_____
❑ Specify criteria for student assessment	_____
❑ Record and retain unit	_____

Figure continues

From *Foundations for Effective School Library Media Programs.* © 1999 Ken Haycock. Libraries Unlimited (800) 237-6124.

Figure 23.1   Collaborative Planning and Teaching—Record of Study (continued)

GENERAL GOAL
"The Big Idea"—Why are we doing this?

_____

_____

_____

_____

ENABLING PREREQUISITES
• knowledge • skills • attitudes • activities

_____

_____

_____

_____

CHECKPOINTS FOR DISCUSSION
❑ School's continuum of information skills [see clusters below]
❑ Time allotment/scheduling [classroom/library]   ❑ Special needs students
❑ Introductory lesson/motivation   ❑ Concluding lesson/culminating activities
❑ Student preparation for research
[key vocabulary; connections with prior knowledge; strategies]

_____

_____

_____

_____

> **Information Processing and Use General Clusters**
> Resource center orientation
> Information problem solving strategies
> Locating information—general sources
> Locating information—subject sources
> Acquiring and analyzing information
> Organizing and recording information

❑ Be very clear —Specify and articulate skills and strategies
　　　　　　　　　—Specific examples will be in the school's continuum

Figure 23.1   Collaborative Planning and Teaching—Record of Study (continued)

NOTES AND WEBS

Brainstorm to establish web of **Content Objectives:**

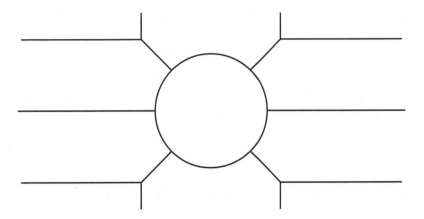

Brainstorm to establish web of **Skill Objectives:**

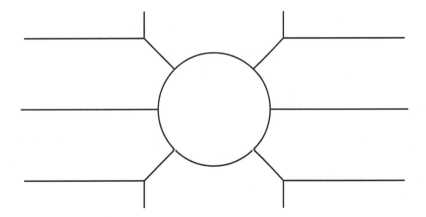

Sequencing of Content:

_____

_____

_____

_____

Figure continues

Figure 23.1   Collaborative Planning and Teaching—Record of Study (continued)

OBJECTIVES

What is the student to learn?

Things to consider:

• knowledge   • attitudes   • skills and strategies to access and use the information

Content/concept	
Skill/strategy	

ASSESSMENT

How will learning be measured?

Match to objectives:

observation; checkpoints; monitoring; formative assessment; summative evaluation

Figure 23.1   Collaborative Planning and Teaching—Record of Study (continued)

TEACHING STRATEGIES

What is the student to do in order to accomplish the objectives?

How will the unit be differentiated for ability levels and learning styles?

Match to stated objectives and assessment.

Activity: _____   Number of students: _____

_____

_____

Resources and location: _____

_____

_____

Minimum expectations: _____

_____

_____

Remediation? _____

_____

_____

Who will prepare? Other responsibilities? _____

_____

Activity: _____   Number of students: _____

_____

_____

Resources and location: _____

_____

_____

Minimum expectations: _____

_____

_____

Remediation? _____

_____

_____

Who will prepare? Other responsibilities? _____

_____

Figure continues

Figure 23.!   Collaborative Planning and Teaching—Record of Study (continued)

TEACHING STRATEGIES

What is the student to do in order to accomplish the objectives?
How will the unit be differentiated for ability levels and learning styles?
Match to stated objectives and assessment.

Activity: Number of students:

_____

_____

Resources and location:

_____

_____

Minimum expectations:

_____

_____

Remediation?

_____

_____

Who will prepare? Other responsibilities?

_____

_____

Activity: Number of students:

_____

_____

Resources and location:

_____

_____

Minimum expectations:

_____

_____

Remediation?

_____

_____

Who will prepare? Other responsibilities?

_____

Figure 23.1   Collaborative Planning and Teaching—Record of Study (continued)

NOTES AND WORKSHEETS
Materials to be added to this plan:

❑ Unit plan   ❑ Detailed lesson plans
❑ Assignment sheets   ❑ Bibliography of resources
❑ Student worksheets   ❑ Resource lists
❑ Evaluation forms   ❑ Other

_____

_____

_____

_____

_____

_____

_____

_____

_____

_____

_____

_____

_____

_____

_____

_____

_____

_____

_____

_____

_____

Figure continues

Figure 23.1   Collaborative Planning and Teaching—Record of Study (continued)

SUGGESTIONS FOR INCLUSION AND EXCEPTIONAL STUDENTS

_____

_____

_____

_____

_____

_____

_____

_____

_____

_____

_____

_____

_____

_____

_____

_____

_____

_____

_____

_____

_____

Figure 23.1   Collaborative Planning and Teaching—Record of Study (continued)

PARTICULARLY GOOD RESOURCES

Easier

_____

_____

_____

_____

_____

More difficult

_____

_____

_____

_____

_____

Highly recommended

_____

_____

_____

_____

_____

CHECKPOINTS FOR DISCUSSION

Checked: ❑ District's collections specialization inventory
❑ District collections
❑ Union list of periodicals
❑ Electronic resources
❑ Other libraries, agencies, museums, etc.
❑ Are adequate resources available?

Figure continues

Figure 23.1   Collaborative Planning and Teaching—Record of Study (continued)

EVALUATION OF THE UNIT
Strengths

_____

_____

_____

_____

_____

_____

_____

Weaknesses

_____

_____

_____

_____

_____

_____

Recommendations for improvement and revision

_____

_____

_____

_____

_____

_____

_____

PART SIX

PROGRAM DEVELOPMENT: A SYSTEMATIC APPROACH

With the foundations for effective school library media programs at least understood it becomes important to plan for implementation in the school. Carol-Ann Page provides a systematic approach through three phases: establishing school-based systems and structures; establishing a profile and team planning; and establishing school-wide programs. Mary Tarasoff and Sonya Emperingham provide a specific example of moving the "library program" to a "learning resources program" in their school through collaborative planning and teaching.

One of the most challenging stumbling blocks to a strong elementary school program is the issue of scheduling. Jean Donham van Deusen explains the necessary pre-requisites to flexible scheduling and points to the importance of developing an information skills continuum, of addressing issues of access, of engaging in team planning through principal expectations and of maintaining a commitment to resource-based learning.

At the secondary level, scheduling is less an issue than developing true collaborative units that emphasize process as well as content. Liz Austrom and her colleagues have planned units of study in large secondary schools that give meaning to a systematic approach and to the close monitoring of student learning. Several examples are provided in different subject areas and at different grade levels. While these units were developed before the pervasiveness of information technologies in schools the underpinning principles are clear and easily adapted to other situations. Similarly, Debra Simmons takes a common elementary school approach, learning stations, and uses this strategy with success at the secondary school level. Connecting writing and research is also possible through the "I-Search" paper, which Julie Tallman explains through the partnership of teacher and teacher-librarian.

Three other issues facing teacher-librarians are explored in this section. Jean Donham van

Deusen and Paul Brandt explain why thematic units are helpful to student learning, how to construct a thematic unit, the importance of sequencing and key questions and offer suggestions for culminating the unit and resources to use. Rita Dunn, well-known for her work in learning styles, writes with Mark Beasley and Karen Buchanan on the characteristics of culturally-diverse students and their learning styles. Their Personal Belief/Bias Scale may prove illuminating to you.

The partnership of the principal and teacher-librarian as a foundation for leadership and change has been clarified earlier, but Patricia Wilson, Martha Blake and Josette Lyders articulate what principals need to know and why through the results of their national survey.

Of course, no program will be developed without positive and effective communication skills and strategies. Barbara Howlett offers practical suggestions for improved interpersonal skills and for "selling the service."

With a clear understanding of the foundations for effective programs, with partnerships with teachers and principals and a systematic approach to improvement, teacher-librarians will better ensure that their students are effective users of information and ideas.

CHAPTER TWENTY FOUR

Developing the School Resource Center Program: A Developmental Approach

Carol-Ann Page

The need for clearly defined approaches to developing a resource-based program is expressed frequently, but university classes and articles are too often of the "glad tidings" or "how I run my library good" nature. The three- to five-year plan outlined here refers to a resource center program based on cooperative program planning with colleagues to develop, teach, and evaluate units of study in a flexibly scheduled resource center.

This approach necessitates that the teacher-librarian clearly understand and be able to articulate this role, and have a strong commitment to it. The major function of the role is to plan, develop, and teach programs cooperatively with classroom teachers as equal teaching partners. To suggest that this is but one facet of the role, or one that takes place after the resource center is made technically perfect, or one that takes place at a different level—once teachers have been "won over"—is to move it from a central focus to a peripheral position.

Two common attitudes tend to characterize teacher-librarians who do not have a clearly defined role that is internalized. First, there are those who, because they presume rejection, continue to function as reactors rather than initiators. Second, there are those who hold the view that they must start "where the teachers are at."

Each of these types operate from positions of servitude or relative powerlessness because they lack not only a clear understanding of this specialized role, but also of the process of change itself.

The very nature of the role of the teacher-librarian is that of initiator and change agent. This includes not only encouraging teacher and student use of the resource center, but also involvement as an equal partner in planning for research and study skill development and language improvement. A jointly planned and taught program such as this often involves a change in the teaching strategies and learning activities commonly used in the school. The collaborative input and involvement of teachers becomes essential for a successful resource center program.

It is important for teacher-librarians to be aware of both the formal and informal structure of the school and to be prepared to work at both levels, particularly since the fate of most programs is decided at the informal level. The "informal covenant" or agreement that exists between administrators and teachers regarding the day-to-day operations of the school supports the administrator as spokesperson for the school and grants some decision-making power regarding school policies and programs; the teacher, however, maintains final authority in the classroom and expects (and gets) administrative support for instructional decisions. Any school program then needs a two-level implementation plan—administrators are critical in the adoption phase of a program while teachers are critical in the implementation phase.

Three Phases of Development

The developmental approach is described in three phases. Throughout these phases, strategies for change and a multi-level plan for implementation are interwoven.

Phase I—Establishing Systems and Structures

1.   Assess the Current Situation

Knowledge of the present status, behavior, and expectations for people and programs in the school is important. Analyze the strengths and weaknesses of the facility, collection and budget. Also analyze the administration, teaching staff, support staff, student population, and community. Identify key people on staff. On any given staff, ten percent "set the tone" and "run the school." They have a lot of power, whether they recognize it or not. Support from people in these positions is essential for successful change. Identify key programs or subject areas in the school and look for entry points into them. The focus might be on the effective use of existing materials for a new social studies program or an emphasis on inquiry skills in the science program, or the need for a sustained silent reading program. Based on this assessment, identify the discrepancies between the current and the desired resource center program.

2.   Define the Role

One of the major tasks in the development and implementation of any new program is to define the program itself and the roles and responsibilities of those to be involved. This is also an important step when the teacher-librarian is new to the school. Never presume that the role of the resource center and the teacher-librarian is understood. Similarly, never confuse support for the teacher-librarian as an individual with understanding of, and commitment to, the *role* of the teacher-librarian.

Roles and responsibilities need to be defined formally, through discussion with the principal, through in-service sessions, and through staff meeting presentations. In all cases, the purpose is to provide information and seek support. (Seeking permission is a dangerous approach! What if the answer is "no"?) Adopting a collaborative approach, assuming a partnership and a trial period, asking for a chance to try out a role or an approach with teacher and administrator support is a much more successful way to gain acceptance and bring about program adoption. For example, you might conclude an orientation for teachers by saying, "My major goal for this term is to plan just one unit with each of you. I hope you will support me in this. I'll get in touch with each of you tomorrow to schedule some planning time."

Definition of the role of the resource center and the teacher-librarian should also take place informally, through the school's daily bulletin, a corner in the monthly newsletter, displays of new materials, and over coffee or lunch in the staff room.

3.   Establish Guidelines

Two sets of guidelines can serve the teacher-librarian well: guidelines for flexible scheduling and guidelines for cooperative planning and resource sharing.

Guidelines for flexible scheduling should specify that:

1.   Cooperatively developed programs take precedence for teacher-librarian time and available space.

2.   Classes are not booked on a regular (every Tuesday at 9:30) basis.

Figure 24.1 Topics for the Month

Topics	For the month of _____	Teacher _____
		Please return by _____

Language arts	
Social studies	
Science	
Math	
Other	
Support materials needed	Library
	School
Planning time	Do you wish to arrange *Planning Time* for cooperative teaching? ☐ *Yes* ☐ *No*

From *Foundations for Effective School Library Media Programs*. © 1999 Ken Haycock. Libraries Unlimited (800) 237-6124.

3. Total class bookings presume cooperative planning between the teacher-librarian and teacher and that the two are functioning as partners in the teaching and supervision of the class.

4. Small group bookings may involve cooperative planning followed by either the teacher-librarian and students working together, or independent work on the part of the students for which space and materials have been made available.

5. Individual students are welcome at any time with a library tag; in this instance, the classroom teacher assumes responsibility and is reasonably confident that the student understands

and can carry out the specific task, whether it is to select a book for recreational reading or to find information. The teacher also establishes a specific time limit with the student.

Guidelines for cooperative program planning and resource sharing can be provided through the use of a monthly topics sheet. The topics sheet should be a "two minute item" for teachers—filling in the topics to be covered in each subject area for the upcoming month and checking off whether resources are required and planning time needed (see Figure 24.1). Resources are pulled or secured and shared among teachers on the basis of the topics sheets submitted each month Through this approach, one teacher doesn't end up with all the dinosaur books or all the resources on insects while other teachers go without. The topics sheets are compiled into a monthly program chart which is distributed to the entire staff. The administrator's copy is asterisked to indicate the teacher-librarian's involvement in programs for each grade level. The monthly program chart indicates the curriculum that is being taught throughout the school at a glance. It facilitates the communication and sharing of ideas among staff as well as the sharing of resources.

The rationale for, and benefits of, the topics sheet should be discussed first with the administrator and then outlined, with examples, in a presentation to the staff. Most teachers are very receptive to this approach, and even a partial return of forms means that the teacher-librarian has more information than would have otherwise been the case.

The topics sheet facilitates cooperative planning in both a formal and informal sense. There is a place provided on the sheet for teachers to indicate whether or not they would like planning time. Entry points into other programs can often be identified and informal approaches to teachers made on this basis. One of the advantages of this system is that it provides specific information for the teacher-librarian and points of discussion with teachers, thus eliminating the "how can I help you?" shopkeeper approach to teacher-librarianship.

4. Communicate Often and Well

Regular communication with the administrator, as well as with staff members, is of paramount importance. Effective communication can create an awareness of, and support for, the adoption of the program. Possible strategies for implementing changes, based on assessment of the current situation, should also be discussed. Through such discussion, priorities can be established and both teacher-librarian and administrator can concentrate efforts in specific areas.

Focus on program strengths and weaknesses, not individuals and personalities. Keep in mind that the most successful approach is to emphasize the positive aspects of the program and the progress being made *before* introducing the

problem or issue to be discussed. Remember—all of the problems in the school end up at the principal's door! Seek advice, but don't presume the administrator is going to take action. Be prepared to act on suggested approaches or solutions if they will indeed enhance the program.

5. Start with One Teacher (Start Small... Think Big)

Based on the initial assessment, identify the teachers who appear to be most receptive to new ideas and programs or with whom you succeed in establishing rapport quickly. Start with them to ensure that you and they meet with success! Never underestimate the "ripple effect"—accept small increments of change and avoid large-scale disappointment. Keep the developmental approach clearly in focus!

Be sure to write up units of study which are developed with teachers and keep these on file as a basis for sharing with others and to ensure availability for use in subsequent years. This is well worth the extra time and effort in the long run; it provides a foundation for continued development and saves time when redesigning and revising units and programs to use again. The importance of this component cannot be over-emphasized.

6. Establish a School-Based Skills Continuum

It is essential that a continuum of information skills be developed and agreed to by staff to ensure that some skills are not being omitted, that a developmental approach is being taken to skills coverage, and that skills instruction is being integrated with, and embedded in, the curriculum. This provides a framework for cooperative planning and a needed structure for resource-based programs.

Teacher involvement in this process is crucial. If teachers work as partners in developing a continuum that is relevant to the teaching and learning situation in a specific school, they will assume some responsibility for skills development. (The terms "research and study skills" or "information skills" help to overcome this problem.) Appropriate aspects of cultural and literary appreciation might also be included in this type of continuum.

The following five-step process has been initiated and successfully worked through with several staffs in order to develop a school-based, research and study skills continuum.

Step 1: Select or devise a research and study skills list as a starting point for staff to react to. Provincial or state curriculum guides, school district guidelines, or any one of a variety of standard sources of information skills lists might be used. The simpler the list, the easier the task.

Step 2: Don't ask each staff member to react to a long skills list initially. Provide the appropriate sections to groups of staff. For example, ask primary teachers to react to a list of primary skills and intermediate teachers to react to a list of intermediate skills. Work with grade levels or primary/intermediate groups, or subject groups, depending on the size or nature of the staff. Meet with each group, in sequential grade level order, to come to a group/grade consensus.

Have each grade level provide input/feedback both a grade level below and above the level at which they are presently teaching.

Step 3: Seek ratification from the primary and intermediate/junior sections of staff. Meet with each group and look at the continuum for each grade level within the group.

Step 4: Submit the rough draft to the total staff for reaction. Discuss the "transition" years, such as grades 3–4, 6–7, and 9–10 in particular.

Step 5: Seek final staff ratification of the document as a statement of expectations for which they accept responsibility.

The teacher-librarian has several important roles to play in this process—initiator, partner, and liaison, among them. Regardless of the particular expertise which the teacher-librarian may bring to this task, it is important to keep these roles in mind, or teachers may be inclined to view the final product as the teacher-librarian's list and, therefore, not a shared responsibility.

7. *Be Accountable*

Establish credibility and support through regular reporting procedures. A monthly written report to the administrator might consist of a listing of planning meetings, cooperative programs, and other professional undertakings such as committee involvement and in-service presented or attended. Technical or support services which have involved a considerable amount of teacher-librarian time or energy might also be listed in this category; examples might include the preparation of major book and media orders, or reorganization of the audio-visual collection. Written reporting can also provide the basis for oral reporting to both staff and administration.

An annual report is mandatory for teacher-librarians who are operating a flexibly scheduled resource center based on cooperative program planning, whether or not it is required by the district or administrator. The annual report serves several purposes. It provides an overview of the year, highlights the progress made in program development, and assists the teacher-librarian in feeling some sense of closure at year end. The annual report also serves as the basis for establishing program priorities for the following year.

If cooperative program planning and teaching is the framework for the resource center program, then the emphasis in the annual report should be placed here. A chart of cooperatively developed programs can be drawn as a major part of the annual reporting procedure. The chart provides an overview of the year and highlights the strengths and weaknesses of the program. It serves as a useful discussion paper with the administrator. It can also be used to facilitate sharing of program ideas among staff.

The various strategies described for Phase I can be accomplished over a period of one year to eighteen months, provided that there is effective, continuing communication with the administrator and no "waffling" on the part of the teacher-librarian. Strategies for Phase II extend and build on those outlined in Phase I.

Phase II—Establishing a Profile and Team Planning

1. *Be High Profile*

The teacher-librarian must be as visible, accessible and involved as possible in order to be viewed as a professional *teaching* colleague. Continue to initiate or provide in-service for staff. Provide an in-service session for new teachers at the beginning of the year and invite all teachers—and be sure that the administration attends. Provide in-service for student teachers. There are double dividends here. Student teachers provide one or more avenues to working with staff. And who knows—one of those student teachers may be a colleague one day!

Where teacher-librarians are part-time, work in two different schools, or in a situation where there are multiple buildings onsite, post and distribute a timetable, indicating locations for morning coffee and lunch breaks. Times and locations for planning with teachers should also be established.

Become a member of the professional development committee, or other key committees in the school. Is there a school budget committee? How are budget decisions made? Is there a school interviewing committee? There is sound rationale for the teacher-librarian being a member of this committee. If in fact the teacher-librarian is expected to plan and work with all other teachers on staff, then it seems only reasonable to have some involvement in the decisions made regarding the hiring of new staff members. This involvement may be in a variety of forms. If a staff interviewing committee exists, the teacher-librarian should be a member. If it is a committee of one—the administrator—then the process of interviewing for new staff members and the criteria by which decisions are made are still worth discussing. Perhaps the administrator would include a question about resource center use in his or her interview format! Examples: "Can you tell me how you have made use of the resource center in your teaching?" "How have you worked with the teacher-librarian?" "How have you ensured coverage of the necessary information skills?" Through questions such as these, the administrator will have an idea of the candidate's experience with, and attitude towards, resource center use. The administrator is essentially saying, " I feel the resource center is important in this school."

Establish a profile with the community. Set an objective to attend all parent meetings, or every second one, or select those which you feel are important and be there. Arrange to make at least one presentation to the parent group each year. Make every effort to find out what their questions, concerns or perceived needs are. Communicate through interpreters if necessary in a multi-ethnic community and provide pamphlets and written messages in translation. One of the most effective means of addressing parent groups is through a brief slide presentation. Let parents see their children at work in the resource center.

Seek out adult volunteers in the community. Be sure to talk to them about the role of the teacher-librarian and resource-based programs in the school. Adults who give their time are often the community members who have a wide sphere of influence.

Establish liaison with the local public library branch. Invite the children's librarian to tell stories, give booktalks, collaborate on a puppet show, and explain the services of the public library. Encourage student and class visits to the public library.

Maintain visibility through report card inserts—a bookmark will do! Send notes home with student library monitors. When assessing student work in cooperatively planned and taught programs, always comment on the work and sign your name. That always gets home!

2.   *Change the Approach/Not the Tune*

Continue to meet with the administrator on a *regular* basis. Be careful not to stop at the "awareness level" and silent support! Place the emphasis in Phase II on the administrator's role regarding expectations of and for teachers. It is unreasonable to expect that the teacher-librarian will succeed in working well with all teachers on a staff without administrative support. If the resource center program is viewed as a partnership, there will be some expectation that classroom teachers will work with the teacher-librarian to ensure adequate development of research and study skills, and effective resource center use, on the part of the students for whom they are primarily responsible. The only place this expectation is going to come from is the administration.

Active, positive, administrative support can increase teacher commitment to a successful resource center program. Suggest subtle ways that the administrator might commend a staff member for a program that has been planned. Visiting the resource center while the program is in operation, a note in the teacher's mailbox, a word in passing in the hallway, or, better still, in the staff room where other staff members will overhear, are all effective ways of intrinsically rewarding teachers and reinforcing desired approaches.

3. Take Bigger Steps: Grade Level Planning

Once you have succeeded in planning at least one unit with the majority of teachers, there is another approach to be taken in Phase II. Approach teachers at one grade level and attempt to plan a program together as a team. Base the approach and planning on the information skills continuum developed in Phase I. Emphasize the importance of those skills outlined in the continuum that require resource center use. Again, start at the grade level where there is the greater likelihood of success, and persuade other grade levels by effective example.

Highlight the benefits of grade level planning. Sharing ideas, materials, and the preparation workload can be stimulating, challenging and time-saving. When a group plans, develops, and implements a program together, everyone tends to put forth his or her best effort. The benefits for students lie in what are often better programs. The prerequisite should be that at least one cooperative program exists for each grade level.

Hold grade level meetings to discuss the progress being made with research and study skills commitments. Are all areas being taught? If some are being missed, or need greater emphasis, how can this be done? Is revision of the continuum necessary? At the same time, review the cooperatively developed programs which are on file for that grade level and attempt to agree on a program, or choice of programs, that will provide for development of a specific skill and a common experience for all students at that grade level. This helps strengthen the developmental aspect of the resource center program by providing a link from year-to-year, yet it remains a strong, curriculum-integrated approach.

There are other benefits to this type of approach as well. Most importantly, it allows some teachers to become involved at the cooperative teaching or implementation stage, rather than at the planning stage. If it is a positive, successful experience in which educational benefits and student enjoyment are demonstrated, those more reluctant or hard-to-convince teachers may be inclined to get involved at the cooperative planning stage in future programs.

Phase III—Establishing School-Wide Programs

By the beginning of Phase III, there is a solid foundation and a strong framework for the resource center program, firmly establishing it as an integral part of the school curriculum.

The teacher-librarian's initiative and leadership to this point create a position to take the development of the resource center program to its logical conclusion.

Take a Giant Step: Total School Programming

In its simplest form, total school programming is often undertaken in preparation for a theme day, week or month. The type of total school program referred to here, however, is one which, regardless of the curriculum area(s) included, involves extensive cooperative planning and teaching with all staff members and working with all students in the school. It is one in which the resource center is truly the central focus, or such an integral part that the total school program could not function without it. It is developmental and it is one which staff have a long-term commitment to.

The key to total school programming is often a staff member with expertise and interest in an area, whether it be environmental education or computer literacy. The "seed" for a total school program can be most successfully planted by first working through a program with that teacher and subsequently developing a proposal to take to the entire staff.

Planning for a school-wide program includes:

- the identification of a subject-related scope and sequence continuum of content and skills, to ensure a developmental approach across the grades;

- the integration of research and study skills from the school-based continuum at each grade level;
- a specific approach to program planning, development, and implementation to determine and facilitate the process staff will work through;
- a realistic timeline;
- opportunity for evaluation and revision of the program by all teachers; and finally,
- provision for the maintenance of grade-wide units developed in Phase II.

Essentially, throughout Phase II, this means that there will be a minimum of two grade-wide programs in existence, providing a strong basis for further program development of this nature.

Conclusion

The introduction of any change involves a number of steps. For teacher-librarians, one might identify five stages in the change process:

Awareness—

An understanding of the roles and responsibilities of teachers, teacher-librarians, and administrators in developing an effective resource center program is not going to happen by osmosis. While district leadership is important, effective program implementation requires someone at the school level to take responsibility for explaining the program. If not the teacher-librarian, then who?

Understanding—

A well-articulated rationale and full information can assist administrators and teachers to understand the conceptual framework of a resource center program. Understanding can streamline communication and planning.

Acceptance—

Demonstration and practice lead to acceptance. Interaction among the teacher-librarian, administrator, and teachers promotes cooperation.

Commitment—

Professionalism is determined not only by level of academic achievement, but also by degree of commitment. The professional teacher-librarian will have a strong commitment to a clearly defined role in resource-based learning. Administrative support is critical and is also the most effective means of gaining and solidifying teacher commitment to the implementation of a program.

Renewal—

Review and revision should be an ongoing part of the change process. If teachers remain active partners in implementation, the continuation of a program is much more assured. And the measure of successful implementation is in program continuation.

New areas of expertise take time to develop. Implementation should be viewed as a process. As a process, it should involve a well thought-out plan covering a three- to five-year period. If this three phase approach cannot be accomplished in a period of five years, it is probably time to decide that it is just not going to happen in this school, or that someone new might be better able to do it in this particular situation…and in either case, transfer!

The key criteria to success with this approach are a strong commitment to a well-defined role, administrative support, a high profile, and accountability.

The result should be a resource center program that is embedded in, and essential to, the school curriculum and, as a consequence, is both educationally viable and politically justifiable.

CHAPTER TWENTY FIVE

From Library Program to Learning Resources Program: Cooperative Program Planning and Teaching

Mary Tarasoff and Sonya Emperingham

Over the past five years, we have expanded our school library program beyond the walls of the library to include other school-based and community resources. The resulting learning resources program enables our students and teachers to access a wider variety of learning materials and experiences that support classroom programs and to provide instruction and resources that more closely match student needs, interests, and abilities.

Our learning resources program views the library resource center as one source of information along with classroom, district and community resources. The teacher-librarian's role is to facilitate and maximize student and staff access to this broad range of resources; in our school the teacher-librarian's title has been changed to "learning resources teacher" to reflect this change. The teacher-librarian and teachers work collaboratively to plan and teach programs that help students learn how to access and process information and

ideas as well as to understand and appreciate literature and nonprint resources.

This paper describes the process over the past five years which has resulted in the redefinition of the library program and the implementation of a learning resources program in our school (see Figure 25.1).

This year, we have established a stronger link with our school-based team (SBT) that already exists to meet needs of specific students (see Figure 25.2). For example, a student in the third grade was referred to the school-based team because of his outstanding ability in mathematics. The teacher-librarian met with the SBT (see Figure 25.2) to identify the student's specific needs and to plan cooperatively. The district mathematics consultant was approached for assessment and resource support. In the end the team decided that a multi-aged group of students (grades 1 to 5) who were highly capable and interested in math would meet regularly with the

Figure 25.1   Changes from Library Program to Learning Resources Program

Library Program	Learning Resources Program
Resources	
■ print, audiovisual (mainly books)	■ print, audiovisual, human, new technologies
Resources Acquisition	
■ teachers suggest themes, librarian chooses book	■ together teachers and teacher-librarian choose specific books, and teacher-librarian chooses books for themes
Scheduling	
■ fixed, regular, yearly	■ flexible, varying length of session, blocks of time (3–12 weeks), maybe not all year
■ 30–40 minute sessions	■ 2–3 times a week
Book Exchange	
■ librarian and library aide present	■ teacher and library aide present
	■ teacher-librarian may be present
■ few book in classrooms	■ teacher-librarian ensures extra books are loaned to classroom libraries
	■ many books in classroom libraries
Instruction	
■ library research skills	■ information accessing and processing skills, research skills
	■ problem-solving, creative and critical thinking
	■ speaking, writing, representing
	■ listening, reading, viewing
■ appreciation and enjoyment	■ appreciation and enjoyment of literature and nonprint resources
Instructional Setting	
■ taught in library	■ taught in library or classroom
Teaching Personnel	
■ teacher-librarian	■ teacher-librarian and teachers
■ individual teaching	■ co-teaching
Support Staff	
■ clerical, library aide	■ clerical, library technician
Program Planning	
■ librarian plans own program not connected to classroom programs	■ collaborative planning to support classroom goals and programs (library program skills are integrated)
Facility	
■ fixed furniture and shelves	■ movable dividers/book displays
■ separate entity	■ connections to other areas

teacher-librarian over a period of two months to pursue cooperative problem-solving projects focused on math. The classroom teacher would provide challenging math activities in the regular classroom setting.

Process of Change

Year 1: The implementation of a new primary program which is centered on active learning, inclusion of all students, acceptance of diverse student needs and abilities, continuous progress,

Figure 25.2   Linking Our SBT with the Learning Resources Program: Service Delivery Model

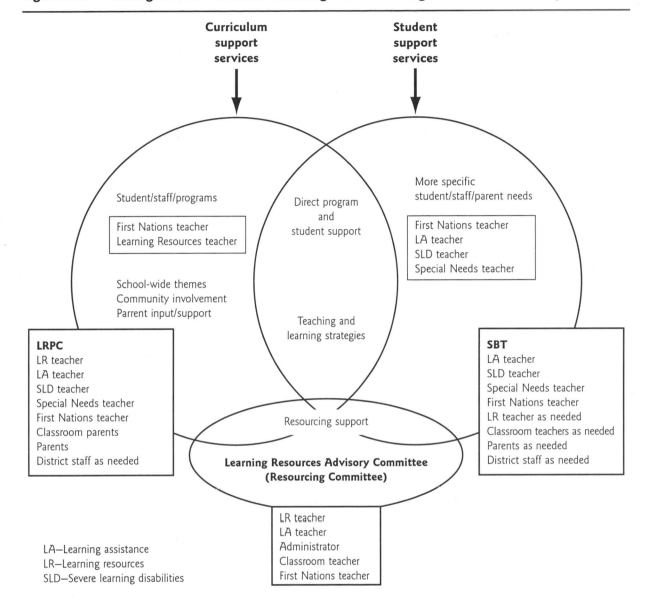

Curriculum support services

Student support services

Student/staff/programs

First Nations teacher
Learning Resources teacher

School-wide themes
Community involvement
Parent input/support

Direct program
and
student support

Teaching and
learning strategies

More specific
student/staff/parent needs

First Nations teacher
LA teacher
SLD teacher
Special Needs teacher

LRPC
LR teacher
LA teacher
SLD teacher
Special Needs teacher
First Nations teacher
Classroom parents
Parents
District staff as needed

Resourcing support

SBT
LA teacher
SLD teacher
Special Needs teacher
First Nations teacher
LR teacher as needed
Classroom teachers as needed
Parents as needed
District staff as needed

**Learning Resources Advisory Committee
(Resourcing Committee)**

LR teacher
LA teacher
Administrator
Classroom teacher
First Nations teacher

LA—Learning assistance
LR—Learning resources
SLD—Severe learning disabilities

and more learner-focused goals, encouraged our staff to emphasize a wider variety of teaching/learning strategies with more open-ended activities. At this time, it became important to us to examine how our library resource center program could best support staff and students within the context of the primary program. In the latter part of the year, a presentation was made to our staff by the teacher-librarian and administrator focusing on the current literature about resource-based learning and the role of teacher-librarian and teachers in cooperative program planning and teaching (CPPT). The

teacher-librarian gave specific examples of cooperatively planned programs that she had already initiated and carried out during the year. By first "doing" and then explaining what she had done in place of the "traditional book exchange and library program," the staff had concrete examples within the school to help them envision the cooperative planning and teaching process.

Year 2: Based on the teacher-librarian's presentation, other classroom teachers became actively involved in CPPT. Some classes continued with regularly scheduled library sessions. During the year a subcommittee of interested teachers, the TL and administrators met to develop the library resource center program model. Plans emerged to connect student support services (special needs and learning assistance areas) more closely with the library resource center. Ordering of resources became more collaborative as teachers, along with the TL, chose specific books and media to be acquired for the resource collection. (Previously, teachers suggested only themes or content areas and the TL chose the specific titles.)

The administrator and TL organized school-based in-service on reading strategies to provide common understanding of some teaching/learning activities. The initial in-service session was followed by the presenter modeling the strategies in several classrooms with our own students. Over the course of two months, the same person presented four more two-hour sessions focusing on different reading/writing strategies. The TL then continued to model these and other strategies when cooperatively teaching. She also incorporated them in cooperative planning with the teachers, which resulted in teachers using these reading/writing strategies in their classroom programs as well.

Year 3: During this year, our school was accredited and established school-wide goals for the next five years. The transition of the library program to learning resources program was identified as one of the major goals and the staff agreed to focus on continuing to develop this program.

Year 4: Implementation of the changes (see Figures 25.1 and 25.3) was facilitated not only by redefining the program and by modeling strategies through CPPT but also by making changes in the physical layout of the library resource center. Although these alterations were not extensive, they were a visible sign of change and were designed to facilitate collaboration and flexibility. For example, an opening created between the library resource center and the computer and learning assistance areas enhanced the cooperative relationship between student support programs and the learning resources program. Purchasing book-display and storage units which doubled as movable dividers allowed the resource center space to be used

more flexibly and efficiently. As a result of collaborative planning, the TL was more familiar with the programs offered throughout the school and, therefore, could schedule more than one class at a time into the learning resource center (LRC). A centralized display area was created to display student projects and ongoing activities resulting from classroom or school-wide themes. For example, the Salmonoid Project (raising salmon from eggs) occurred in this area. A fourth grade class buddied up with a kindergarten class to look after the aquarium and to study salmon using a unit cooperatively planned by the teachers and TL. Students represented their learning in charts, art and poetry. Because of the centralized display, all students (and parents) were able to watch the fish develop and learn from this resource.

Another change in the use of the library came about because the TL often cooperatively taught in the classroom, freeing the library resource center for use by more classes without the TL being present—something that seldom happened before.

During this year, the staff focused on coordinating the science curriculum throughout the school. The TL played a pivotal role in program planning and in accessing science resources by:

1. collaboratively planning with teachers and coordinating parents to develop science kits (now available in the LRC). The teachers chose themes and identified activities and experiments; parent volunteers were given lists of resources and materials to collate into kits;

2. organizing a "Book Week," when families could choose to buy a new science book to donate to the LRC; the books were pre-selected by the TL based on input from teachers and on her expertise of available resources and knowledge of classroom programs;

3. arranging for in-service that focused on science, using a wide variety of literature and hands-on materials. The focus was on developing skills in reading nonfiction, interpreting diagrams, experimenting, researching and reporting information.

Year 5: Our staff agreed to be a pilot school to develop for the district our version of a learning resources program (see Figures 25.2 and 25.3). A

Figure 25.3   Learning Resources Program

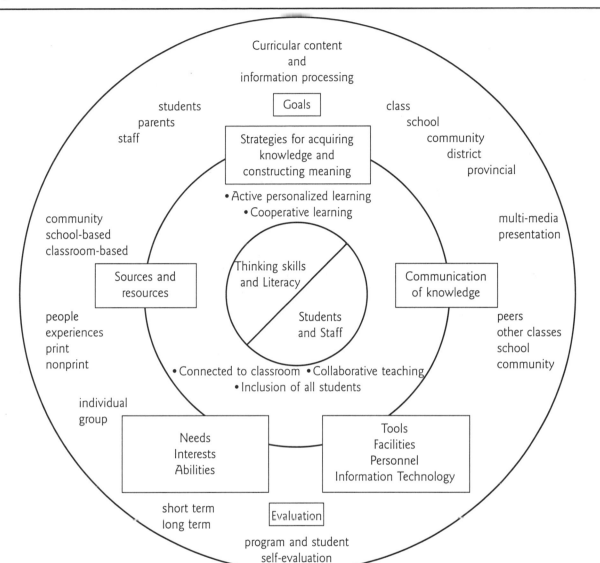

daily journal of the teaching and learning activities that the TL coordinated, cooperatively planned and taught, and otherwise facilitated, was kept and analyzed to elucidate just "what really was working well." A list of a few examples of the learning resource teacher "in action" is given in Figure 25.4.

The Learning Resources Program: A Snapshot

Components:

- Cooperative program planning

- Cooperative teaching
- Accessing and managing material and human resources

Cooperative Program Planning

To the cooperative planning sessions, classroom teachers bring their expertise in curricular areas as well as their knowledge of their own students' needs, interests and abilities. The TL contributes expertise in evaluating and acquiring a wide selection of resources and in teaching ways to access, process and respond to learning resources and experiences. This partnership results in access

Figure 25.4   Examples of Learning Resources Teacher "In Action"

Organizing and Cooperatively Planning Learning Experiences
- book field trips ("Beach Walk")
- organize and conduct interest group for math
- chair Learning Resources Program Committee meeting for school-wide event
- facilitate school-wide theme (art project, story dramatizations, exposure to literature)
- meet with teachers to plan

Teaching in Classrooms and in Library
- develop and facilitate writing project for class
- cooperatively plan and teach "Circle Story Writing"
- teach "comparative story" theme in Grades 1, 3 and 5 classes
- guide students through self-directed research projects
- video-tape students' role-playing as part of novel study
- teach information processing strategies while teacher is teaching a unit on Africa

Resourcing
- based on specific requests from staff on a daily basis
- inform teachers about community resources, field trips, outside learning opportunities
- locate/present wide variety of resources for students to self-select for projects
- cooperatively select and purchase resources with teachers
- coordinate parent volunteers to make/collect resources
- contact and arrange speakers
- support professional and staff development

to a wide variety of resources, processes and learning activities that support the goals of classroom programs and help meet specific student needs, interests and abilities.

Cooperative planning identifies the skills and processes students need to learn for accessing information and resources, thinking about ideas and information and communicating them (see Figure 25.5). During the planning sessions the following need to be discussed:

- Curriculum (Content/Theme/Strategies/Skills/Attitudes)
- Teaching Strategies/Resources
- Learning Activities/Resources
- Representing Knowledge, Skills, Strategies and Attitudes
- Evaluating Student Learning and the CPPT process

Questions to guide the planning of resource-based learning opportunities help focus the planning and ensure a variety of teaching and learning styles are accommodated through this process (see Figure 25.5).

During these sessions, the TL and classroom teacher(s) decide on the curricular content, skills,

strategies and attitudes to be focused on. Using this as a starting point, resources are identified, teaching strategies, learning activities and co-teaching roles are planned. Part of the planning also involves deciding how students will represent what they have learned and how their learning will be assessed. Besides benefiting from sharing instructional strategies and planning time, both teachers gain from sharing their ongoing observations and assessments of student progress. At the end of the program, it is also helpful to reflect on what worked well and what could be modified for next time both for the teachers and students.

The following is an example of the CPPT process in our school's learning resources program that took place this year. During a planning session, a fifth grade teacher mentioned that the students would like to use the televised *Safari '94* program as a resource. This was a program in which scientists explored Barkley Sound underwater and viewers could phone in to have experts answer their questions. The following plan was developed and cooperatively taught around the theme of Ocean Exploration. The *Safari '94* program was the stimulus to generate student interest. Along with this, videos, books, and people were accessed on various

Figure 25.5   Cooperative Planning Framework

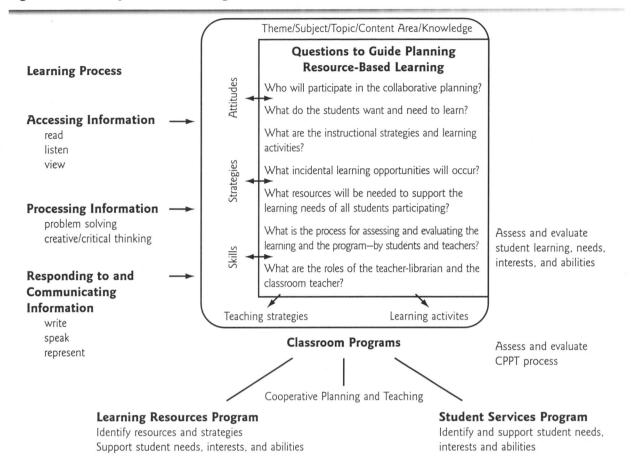

topics that the students expressed interest in. Later, students formed interest groups to research their own topics. The goal was to develop research skills and knowledge of the ocean. The end product was the creation of a multi-media display which the students used to teach other students in the school what they had learned.

As an introduction, the TL scheduled time to "revisit" resources with the whole class to help them decide on their topic. Then she met with the interest groups and assisted them in locating appropriate resources (print, non-print and/or human resources). Over a period of several weeks, regular meetings with the students were conducted to determine if additional resources were required. Both the TL and classroom teacher guided the students through the project, teaching the research skills as needed.

Cooperative Teaching

The time devoted to cooperatively planning a unit will vary in length depending on the purpose of the unit and/or student interest in the topic. As the teacher and TL develop the strategies and activities for each session, they may employ a variety of teaching arrangements. For example:

Initiating and Modeling

The TL may teach the initial lesson(s) modeling the particular teaching and learning strategies for classroom teacher and students. The teacher repeats the strategies using resources and techniques that were decided on in collaborative planning. In this way both teachers and students learn new strategies for gathering, processing and communicating information and ideas.

Another way to initiate and model is for the TL to arrange and accompany the class and teacher on a field trip. To extend the learning after the trip, the TL teaches a follow-up lesson in the classroom modeling how to complete the assigned activity by using resources from the LRC. The classroom teacher then, as planned, expands and completes the activities in subsequent sessions. The teacher later reviews the strategy necessary to complete the task to ensure student success.

Side-by-Side Teaching

During planning, a wide variety of resources and strategies are chosen with the students' needs, interests and abilities in mind. More personalized instruction can be provided because the pupil/teacher ratio is decreased when both teachers are working at the same time with students. For some students, the activities may be their first exposure to the particular skills, strategies and knowledge and they will need more guidance and instruction. Other students who are more experienced can be encouraged to refine and extend their skills and knowledge. Independent and/or cooperative group activities can be set up for students. An added benefit to side-by-side teaching is the opportunity for sharing the evaluation of and reflection about the students' learning as well as evaluation of the teaching methods used.

Parallel Teaching

A third way to cooperatively teach involves the TL emphasizing the same skills, strategies and/or knowledge that the classroom teacher is teaching as part of a classroom theme or unit. The TL may teach the whole class or small groups, but uses different materials and/or methods of presentation which accommodate different learning styles. Parallel teaching is also used to review skills, strategies and knowledge.

Incidental Teaching

During planning sessions, the teacher and TL discuss ways to capitalize on incidental learning—learning that occurs but is not necessarily a focus of the planning and teaching. Some of the ways this is accomplished is by planning open-ended activities, using cooperative learning groups, having a wide variety of resources available, enabling students to have choice, and planning activities that foster self-directed learning.

Accessing and Managing Resources

CPPT allows the TL more knowledge into the types of resources that are needed to support students' learning in the classrooms. The TL coordinates the acquisition of resources, ensures adequate access to them, and keeps staff and students informed about new resources that are housed in the school. In addition, the TL accesses outside sources and resources from the community or district, and coordinates staff and student access to them when needed.

Our learning resources program model has emerged from an expanded view of the library program. It has resulted from an approach that provides support for learner-focused instruction and resource-based learning and maintains a close connection to classroom programs and student needs, interests and abilities. This model includes at its core cooperative program planning and teaching (CPPT) between the classroom teacher who has knowledge of the curriculum and students and the TL who has familiarity with a variety of resources, with curriculum at many levels, and with diverse strategies for actively accessing and processing information and ideas.

The process of change in our school has been gradual and ongoing, involving teachers and administrators working together over the past five years. Success has come from being able to demonstrate the model in practice beginning with a few teachers and then working with others who, after observing the positive effects, asked to be involved in CPPT. Success has been based on the collaboration of all those involved—staff, students, and parents. Success has resulted from leadership by the TL, administrators and interested teachers and from ongoing reflection and refinements to the model to meet our own needs. Through cooperative program planning and teaching, the TL and teachers are enabling students to access a wider range of resources and acquire learning strategies for successful, self-directed learning.

CHAPTER TWENTY SIX

Prerequisites to Flexible Scheduling

Jean Donham van Deusen

The idea of flexible scheduling has been in the culture of the school library media profession for at least 30 years. It is the idea that classes are scheduled for instruction in the library resource center based on instructional need, rather than based on a fixed calendar which dictates that classes will meet in the resource center. Fixed or regularly scheduled library resource center classes compare to the "special" classes taught by art, music and physical education specialists. However, there is a substantive difference; in those specialties, there is the content of the discipline to teach. In the library resource center, the instruction has to do with providing students with the intellectual tools to accomplish work in content areas.

What is flexible scheduling? Simply put, it is a plan wherein classes meet for instruction in the library resource center when they have a specific need driven by activity in their classroom. And they do not have library resource center instruction when no need is generated in their classroom. So, it is possible that a class will come to the library resource center every day for five days in a row for instruction and work on an assignment or project, or every day for two weeks, and then they may not have any instruction in the library resource center for three weeks until an activity in their class calls for it again. Each week is different for the teacher-librarian; each week different groups are coming. Flexible scheduling and flexible access are related terms, but they are not the same thing. Flexible access refers to children having the opportunity to go to the resource center whenever they (usually as individuals or small groups) have a need.

Flexible scheduling has intuitive appeal. It makes sense that we bring classes to the library resource center when there is a specific instructional need. It makes sense that what is taught in the library resource center be integrated with what is taught in the classroom. It makes sense that what is taught in the resource center is taught when students need to know. After all, library resource center instruction is the teaching of information processes. Just as there is no point in teaching keyboarding unless there will be application of those skills in word processing, so there is no point in teaching search strategies or note-taking or evaluation of sources or locational skills if there is no information need.

Likewise, flexible scheduling offers an advantage to the teacher-librarian in freeing time for consultation with teachers. With fixed scheduling, often the teacher-librarian is meeting with students while teachers are planning for instruction. Being unavailable when teachers might most need our help is counter-productive to our accomplishing the consulting role.

Flexible scheduling has varied in the success of its implementation. It seems that research and observation may provide us with some indications of what is needed for flexible scheduling to meet its expectations. What are those expectations?

1. Flexible scheduling should improve the likelihood that instruction in the library resource center is integrated with classroom instruction. When the learner's experiences in school are overtly related to one another, they take on meaning. Cognitive theory tells us that to make learning meaningful, we need to associate learning in one setting with another, contextualize our learning, relate new learning to existing schemata and construct meaning for ourselves. When we give children isolated instruction unrelated to other intellectual events, we leave the application of that instruction and the integration of it into other learning up to the child. Yet, what we know of transfer is that we must explicitly teach for transfer. Flexible scheduling can be an avenue to teaching for transfer, because with it we schedule library resource center instruction purposefully to relate it to classroom instructional events.

2. Flexible scheduling should facilitate consulting between teacher-librarians and teachers. Time is the quintessential resource in a service profession. Working as a teacher-librarian is a service profession; our product is service. By gaining flexibility in our schedules, we can increase the likelihood of being available to work with teachers when they are in need of our services. Attendance to the consulting role demands that we see teachers as important, primary customers; we need to recognize that children will benefit from our work with their teachers.

So, what does it take to make flexible scheduling work? While there may be no one right answer appropriate for all settings, there are some features which seem to make flexible scheduling more likely to succeed. Five key elements seem to be:

- information skills curriculum matched with content area curriculum;
- flexible access;
- team planning;
- principal expectations;
- commitment to resource-based learning.

Information Skills Curriculum

Before advancing flexible scheduling, the teacher-librarian must have a clear plan for what he or she intends to teach. In recent years, several models for information-process curricula have been published; widely known models include those by Eisenberg, Kuhlthau, Stripling and Pappas. These can be the basis for design of a curriculum. The teacher-librarian must have a carefully conceived plan for developmentally appropriate instruction in mind first. Likewise, classroom teachers must have a clear curriculum plan for the disciplines he or she teaches. Next must come the collaboration and negotiation between classroom teachers and teacher-librarians. They must sit down together, roll up their sleeves and work at matching the information skills agenda to the expectations in the disciplines to see how these can be integrated so that information skills reside within the context of the content area curriculum. This planning involves determining the fit, conceiving of appropriate instructional activities which will provide for integration and laying out the timeline for the school year. Such planning can occur between individual teachers and the teacher-librarian, or between teams (grade level or discipline-based). The crucial issue is that such meeting must occur to map the integration. If this process is not comprehensive—every teacher, every grade or team—the information process curriculum is hit-or-miss. Would we allow math to be hit-or-miss? Probably not. Then, how can we, in good conscience, settle for the information curriculum to be hit-or-miss?

This preliminary planning and mapping needs to occur in sustained sessions; one possibility is for some professional development time to be set aside for it. Another possibility is for substitute teachers to be provided so that teachers and the teacher-librarian can map the integration. It is crucial to the success of an integrated information skills curriculum, and therefore, dedicated time is appropriate and necessary. This is a situation in which the principal's shared ownership of the vision for a truly integrated information skills curriculum can facilitate the important planning phase.

Access

Flexible scheduling means that children no longer have a guaranteed weekly visit to the library resource center for book checkout and reading guidance. While we see an increasing emphasis on processing and technology, the goals of the elementary library resource center program continue to call for children to become readers, have guidance in selecting appropriate reading materials and have access to reading materials. When the weekly class period is eliminated, it must be replaced with some kind of opportunity for these reading goals to be met. Flexible access is perhaps the best replacement. Flexible access is complex; its implementation must be systematic. It is not enough to simply say to everyone, "The library resource center is open all day. Children may come whenever they want to." In addition, we must work with classroom teachers to ensure that access is enabled from the classroom as well as into the library resource center. Some teachers have no difficulty establishing with their students internal systems for allowing free-flow between the classroom and the library resource center. For others, concerns about accountability for children and their use of time create the need for more formalized systems. Such systems can be designed so that children have opportunities to go to the library resource center whenever they have the need. Systems as simple as creating laminated passes for use in each classroom (similar to "washroom passes" used in many schools) can create a governance over how many children descend upon the center at one time and how

many children leave a given classroom at one time. Two, three or four passes per classroom, depending on school and center size, may meet the needs. One would hope that a belief system in a school would include the notion that whenever a child encounters an information need, there is a way for that child to try to fulfill the need in a timely fashion.

It may be important to design a system so that access is not hit-or-miss. A concern in some settings with flexible scheduling is ensuring that all children do get into the library resource center frequently to browse and select materials for their personal needs. One possibility is to identify for each classroom a fifteen minute period each week when a class comes to the center with the teacher to ensure that each child has had the opportunity for book checkout. This differs from weekly scheduled classes in two important ways: the intent is not instruction, but rather materials selection, and the teacher accompanies the children to assist. If possible, the teacher-librarian may want to try to schedule these browse-and-checkout times during times when it is unlikely that other teachers would be requesting flexibly scheduled instruction, e.g., during times when other classes are having mathematics, physical education, or other activities less dependent on the use of the library resource center. Another possibility is to suggest that teachers design a record-keeping system to see that all children go to the library resource center. Whatever system is designed, the concern for access for all must be addressed.

Team Planning

In research we have found that schools where teachers plan as teams (by grade-level or content-area), flexible scheduling particularly correlates positively with the consultation role of the teacher-librarian (van Deusen & Tallman, 1994). Perhaps this suggests that the teacher-librarian ought to provide some leadership to help teachers work together as teams if this structure is not in place. If the movement toward teamwork in industry is an indicator of improved performance in team-based settings, we can surely suspect that collaborative schools hold promise of greater success. If teamwork helps us to participate as consultants, then it makes sense for us to be advocates and catalysts toward such collaboration.

Principal Expectations

Our research also indicated that when principals had expectations for the teacher-librarian to participate in instructional planning with teachers, such participation occurred. The importance of principals sharing the vision of the library resource center program as a collaborative partner in classroom instruction cannot be overlooked. The responsibility for communicating that vision to principals and demonstrating how that vision translates into practice lies with the teacher-librarian.

Commitment to Resource-Based Learning

One of the advantages of flexible scheduling is to facilitate the teacher-librarian's role as an instructional consultant working collaboratively with teachers to plan for instruction. An important task which teacher-librarians perform in that role is the task of identifying appropriate electronic and print resources and recommending ways in which those resources can be used in teaching and learning. Resource-based learning facilitates a constructivist approach to learning; it facilitates student engagement and active learning. Resource-based learning also provides the appropriate classroom structures to facilitate free-flow to and from the library resource center; children are engaged in active work and the classroom tends not to be teacher-centered. In such settings, movement to and from the library resource center, as needs arise, is natural. By working collaboratively with teachers to integrate a variety of resources into their teaching, the teacher-librarian acts as a catalyst for these approaches. If there is no commitment to resource-based learning, it is difficult to envision flexible scheduling serving much of a purpose; the teacher-librarian has less to offer in a textbook-bound approach to teaching.

If these five conditions are not in place, it may be premature to advance the notion of flexible scheduling. A concern which must remain in the mind of the teacher-librarian is the possibility that a move away from fixed scheduling could become a move toward no scheduling; that is, children having little or no access to the library resource center and little or no library resource center instruction. Before or during the process of implementation, the teacher-librarian would do well to consider these five conditions.

Other Factors

There are two other factors which have potential to enhance a program with flexible scheduling. The first is support staff. In a follow-up survey to the participants in our flexible scheduling research, we found that when teacher-librarians have support staff, tasks associated with the consulting role are performed significantly more often. In that follow-up survey, three groups were analyzed: those with no paid support staff; those with up to 20 hours per week; and those with 20 hours or more per week. Those teacher-librarians who had more than 20 hours of paid support staff in their library resource centers reported over 150 percent as many occurrences of four of the five consulting tasks than those who had no support staff. Having support staff available in the library resource center means that the teacher-librarian can spend time meeting with a teacher or a team of teachers, and children can still access the center and locate and use resources there. While flexible scheduling can be implemented without support staff, a concern for children having flexible access arises if there is no one available to assist them when the teacher-librarian is working with classes or teachers. No significant differences were found between those with no support staff and those with fewer than 20 hours. Perhaps there is a threshold level to be attained before the availability of support staff can significantly increase the consultation activity. It must be noted that building size must be considered in determining an appropriate amount of support staff.

Another factor which can improve the success of flexible scheduling is a design for student assessment of information-process skills. Having an assessment plan provides a means for the teacher-librarian and teachers to monitor the information skills curriculum. Such monitoring is particularly important for an infused curriculum, that is, a curriculum taught as an integral component of a content area. The assessment plan should identify the characteristics of successful performance of the information processes and should include a system for assessing student progress toward success, as well as a system for record-keeping. Without such a system, it will be difficult at best to know whether the implementation of flexible scheduling has indeed met one of its goals—successful integration of the information process curriculum.

Flexible scheduling makes intuitive sense; it says let's use our instructional time to its best advantage. It is consistent with what we know about retention: that is, when we teach a complex skill, it is more likely that today we can build on yesterday's lesson than on last week's! It is consistent with what we know about teaching for transfer: it is more likely that instruction will have meaning if it meets a need and can be applied to a current problem than if we teach in isolation and hope that students can transfer what they learn at some time when the problem arises. However, for flexible scheduling to meet its promise, there must be a system in place to ensure that the learning opportunities arise, that children have appropriate access to the library resource center and we can articulate what it is we want them to learn. Creating such a system requires the involvement of not just the teacher-librarian, but the entire instructional team of a school—principal, teachers and teacher-librarian.

References

van Deusen, J. & Tallman, J. (1994). The impact of scheduling on curriculum consultation and information skills instruction. *School Library Media Quarterly, 23,* 17–26.

CHAPTER TWENTY SEVEN

Secondary School Assignments: Cooperatively Planned and Taught

Liz Austrom and Colleagues

It is not usually possible to transfer a unit of study or assignment from one situation to another without at least some adaptation, modification or revision, based on the needs of the specific program and the group of students to be taught; nevertheless, it is useful to examine what has been developed by others in order to ascertain the relative value of the approach used, the elements of the particular design and the structure of the assignment for one's own situation. The units and assignments outlined here have proven successful in more than one setting and may provide inspiration or insight to develop something just that much better. We trust that readers will make a similar commitment to sharing the results of their efforts in cooperative program planning and teaching in professional journals and elsewhere.

Social Studies
Industrial Revolution Project, Grade 9

The Industrial Revolution Project was planned to develop and reinforce basic skills in report writing (specifically taking notes and organizing information) in ninth grade. These skills were taught and assessed in the previous grade by teachers and teacher-librarians in a developmental reading program.

This unit was initiated by the teacher-librarians after group discussion about the lack of report writing skills exhibited by students. A one hour in-service with the social studies department was held, focusing our presentation first on the teacher-librarian's role in materials supply and then on team planning and teaching. We ended by sharing our observations about student report writing abilities. The teachers shared concerns and commented on student tendencies to copy directly from text. As a result of this discussion, most of the ninth grade social studies teachers decided to work with us on a unit designed to improve report writing skills. Together we selected the Industrial Revolution as the content area, basing our decision on the availability of materials at many reading levels, since the students in our population exhibited a wide range of prior achievement (see Figures 27.1 and 27.2).

Figure 27.1   Plan for Research Project

		Industrial Revolution, Grade 9: Plan for the Project—Time and Content	
A. Classroom	1 period	Introduction to Industrial Revolution Unit. Preview of assignment	Subject teacher
		Quick review of skills learned in developmental reading e.g., skimming, scanning, previewing techniques. Students look at list of topics—make choices	Reading center teacher or Teacher-Librarian
B. Resource Center	6 periods	*Lesson 1.* Introduction	Teacher-Librarian
		Purpose & process of assignment Skimming: SQ3R technique	Reading center teacher
		Lesson 2. Class in two groups	Teacher-Librarian Reading center teacher
		Group A. Paraphrasing; Bibliographies Group B. Bibliographies; Paraphrasing	
		Lessons 3,4,5. Collection of information Organization of notes and bibliographies	All assist
		Lesson 6. Instruction on report outline	Teacher-Librarian
		Organization of notes Writing of outline	All assist
C. Classroom	1 or 2 periods	Writing report Review of unit	Subject teacher

We established the following unit plan:

Period One—The introduction of the unit in the classroom. The teacher may already have spent several periods on the topic, but this period focuses on the requirements of the assignment and on the selection of individual topics, as well as reviewing the use of key words and indexes, and particularly the use of encyclopedias.

Period Two—Whole class instruction in the resource center. In the first half of the period the teacher-librarian explains the purpose, offers encouragement and reassurance, and demonstrates the process of using the sheets that each student is given in a folder, using overhead transparencies of the sheet.

The *Research Record* is worth 30 percent. Students are told to include every source they look at so as to get credit for the search as well as the notes. This sheet was included so that all students would have a chance to succeed. It is usually done significantly better than the bibliography and pulls up the average mark. In a school where students are less varied or where they have had a lot of prior experience with reports, it might not be necessary. It does have the advantage of telling the teachers whether or not students are using the indexes. All of the possible bibliographic citations are noted on cards on a ring, and each includes a notation about whether there is a good index or table of contents. This is available for teachers and teacher-librarians; it makes marking the sheets much easier. (The same result could be achieved using part of the online catalog record.)

The *Outline* is worth 20 percent. Students are advised that the final period of instruction will show them how to do the outline. The teacher-librarian in this period merely emphasizes the need to have all the notes done by the final period, shows how the note slips will be cut apart, sorted by topic, organized in order, and stapled in order in clumps which correspond to the paragraphs in the final outline. A reminder sheet on the process is stapled to the inside back cover of the folder so that students can check there if they forget which step comes first.

Figure 27.2   Industrial Revolution, Grade 9: Assignment Sheet

I.   **Introduction.** Briefly, the Industrial Revolution means the shifting from hand tools to power machinery and the application of power driven machinery to manufacturing. The Industrial Revolution began about 1750 and is still in progress.

II.   **Purpose.** To gain an understanding of inventors or scientists who made significant contributions to the Industrial or Scientific Revolution and to develop skills in researching and organizing information.

III.   **Materials.** Materials in the school library resource center will be on overnight loan for your use in this assignment.

IV.   **Organization and What To Do.** Following is a list of inventors or scientists who made significant contributions to the Industrial Revolution in the fields of transportation, communication, manufacturing, medicine and engineering.

17th and 18th Century	*19th Century*	*20th Century*
Eli Whitney	George Eastman	Wright Brothers
James Watt	Carl Benz	Henry Ford
Robert Fulton	Isambard Brunel	Vlasimir Zworykin
George Stephenson	Nicholas Otto	Ferdinand de Lesseps
Sir Humphrey Davy	Rudolf Diesel	John Deere
Elias Howe	Heinrich Hertz	Justus von Liebig
John Kay	Samuel Morse	John Dalton
Richard Arkwright	Alexander G. Bell	Werner von Braun
Johna Gutenberg	Thomas Edison	John Rockefeller
Benjamin Franklin	Guglielmo Marconi	Frederick Banting
Edward Jenner	Charles Goodyear	Alexander Fleming
William Harvey	Louis Pasteur	Ernest Rutherford
Isaac Newton	Alfred Nobel	
	Robert Koch	
	Sandford Fleming	
	Joseph Lister	
	Thomas Telford	
	James Simpson	
	Gregor Mendel	

Choose *one* of the assignments listed below.

1.   **Inventor.** Choose one inventor from the list above. Identify the person's invention, explain its importance to the Industrial Revolution and its effect on the way people lived. If your chosen inventor produced a number of inventions, choose only the one that you consider to be most important.

2.   **Invention.** The most significant impact on changing technology has come about as a result of inventions that have been developed and refined by a number of inventors over the years, e.g., the automobile. Choose an invention and explain how it has evolved and improved to its present state. Discuss in more detail the work of two inventors involved in the invention's refinement and explain their contributions. Be sure to mention the machine's impact or significance.

3.   **Field of advancement.** Select a field in which technology has improved rapidly over the last 200 years, e.g., manufacturing, transportation, communication, medicine or engineering. Summarize the improvements made in the field of your choice and explain its impact or significance on people's lives today. Include details of work of two or three inventors/scientists who contributed to this area.

During the six periods you are in the resource center, you will be expected to complete your notes, a bibliography, a report outline and a research record form. You will be given instructions for each and you will be given marks for each.

When you return to the social studies classroom you will be expected to write an in-class report using your notes and outline to assist you. The report will also be marked.

Remember:
It is *your* responsibility to have the assignment completed on time.

Figure 27.3   Samples

Research Record   Name _____

                                                            Topic _____

I used the source materials listed below	complete call number	I used the:		I found this source:		not on my topic
		index	table of contents	useful	not useful	

Notetaking Sheets—worth 30%. Students were told to use one side only, to use one main idea only in each section, to record the necessary information at the top of each section, and to paraphrase only. Although the slips have a section to check "direct quote," students are advised not to use it. The same forms are used by senior students and they are allowed to use quotations. Each sheet contains six notetaking sections with the following layout:

Reference #_____ Page # _____ Paraphrase _____ Direct Quote _____

Resources Used and Preparation of Essays and Bibliographies—worth 20%. Students are told that they will be taught in detail the next period how to do a bibliographic citation or description. In this period the teacher-librarian simply emphasizes through demonstration that if the column headed "Useful" was checked on the *Research Record,* then a bibliographic description should be written before the notes are taken. The reference number on the notetaking sheet is also related to the reference number on the *Resources Used* sheet. Students are advised that they may have many notes from one reference, or they may have only one—depending upon the number of relevant ideas they find in the book. Reference numbers are assigned arbitrarily, 1 for the first book used, 2 for the second, etc. A *Resources Used* sheet sample normally contains space for six references but has been abbreviated for inclusion below.

Topic _____ Student Name _____

Resources Used:

Write down in Correct Form. Use the *Preparation of Essays and Bibliographies* as a guide.

REFERENCE #		CALL #

Terms:

Corollary Information to be checked:

Definitions:

In the second half of period two, the social studies teacher, or the reading teacher if you have one in the school, reviews the Preview/Questions steps in the SQ3R (Survey, Question, Read, Recite, Review) study method, using class sets of a chapter from *Carl Benz and the Motor Car* by Doug Nye, and a page from *Merit Student Encyclopedia* on the history of the automobile (see Figures 27.3 and 27.4).

The focus is to have the students develop questions which will direct their reading. The same handouts are then used, in conjunction with a one page summary of skimming techniques, to practice key word skimming and topic sentence skimming.

Some classes do not require the full hour to complete these activities. When this happens, students are encouraged to begin the search on their topic by looking in encyclopedia indexes and identifying sections that they can use in subsequent periods.

Period Three—The class is split into two groups which are designated on each folder beside the student's name. Instruction is for thirty minutes and then the groups switch and receive the second half of the instruction. In one group the social studies or the reading teacher uses the chapter from *Carl Benz and the Motor Car* for a directed reading exercise where students take practice notes on note-taking sheets. The emphasis is

Figure 27.4   The Outlining Process

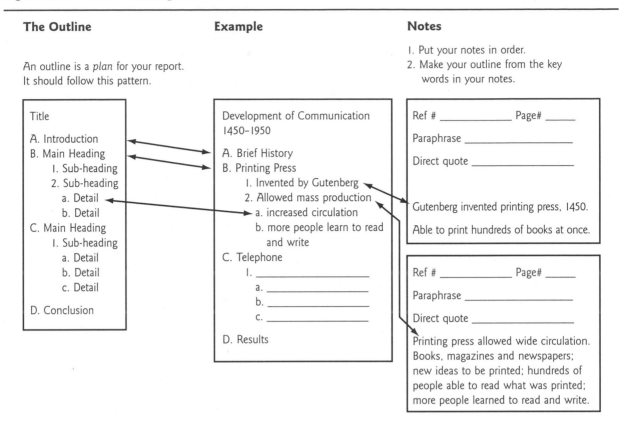

The Outline	Example	Notes

An outline is a *plan* for your report. It should follow this pattern.

1. Put your notes in order.
2. Make your outline from the key words in your notes.

The Outline

Title

A. Introduction
B. Main Heading
   1. Sub-heading
   2. Sub-heading
     a. Detail
     b. Detail
C. Main Heading
   1. Sub-heading
     a. Detail
     b. Detail
     c. Detail

D. Conclusion

Example

Development of Communication 1450–1950

A. Brief History
B. Printing Press
   1. Invented by Gutenberg
   2. Allowed mass production
     a. increased circulation
     b. more people learn to read and write
C. Telephone
   1. _____
     a. _____
     b. _____
     c. _____

D. Results

Notes

Ref # _____ Page# _____

Paraphrase _____

Direct quote _____

Gutenberg invented printing press, 1450.

Able to print hundreds of books at once.

Ref # _____ Page# _____

Paraphrase _____

Direct quote _____

Printing press allowed wide circulation. Books, magazines and newspapers; new ideas to be printed; hundreds of people able to read what was printed; more people learned to read and write.

- skim to locate the answer,
- read the specific section carefully, and
- paraphrase the information using key words.

Recording the reference number and page number at the top of the strips is stressed, as is writing only one idea per strip, and using abbreviations and note codes where possible.

In the other group, the teacher-librarian teaches students how to use the style guide for bibliographic citations, which is stapled to the inside front cover of the folder. It is based on the idea that there is a basic pattern and several variations that cover most book materials. Students each complete one practice bibliographic citation for a preselected book, then modify it for a series. All preselected books are from the Wayland/Priory Press series *Pioneers of Science and Discovery.* Next, the format of an encyclopedia article is taught and practiced. Everyone must be right on task if this is all to be accomplished in 25–30 minutes.

Periods Four, Five and Six—A quick reminder of the process and then everyone gets to work,

using the books that have been pulled and are located on a trolley, plus the encyclopedias which are not pulled into a separate collection. Students who need help are given it by whichever teacher is nearest and not helping someone else. The idea is to supervise closely enough so that students are not practicing errors, but are shown the correct method as quickly as possible. Some never need much help, while others need constant assistance at first. The social studies teacher can often identify the most needy and spend most of the first working period with those few students while the teacher-librarian handles the rest of the class. Students are advised that they must do homework, and all materials are available to be checked out overnight but must be returned before school the following day. We usually put a limit of two regular books or one book and one encyclopedia per student per night. Even so, circulation figures often reach 100-plus per night for this assignment, and the returning task each morning is a heavy one.

Period Seven—Students must have their notes complete for this period. Whole class instruction takes approximately 20 minutes, and emphasizes the process of cutting the strips, sorting them into categories, sorting each category clump into logical order, stapling in clumps which correspond to paragraphs, and making an outline from the notes. Overheads and prepared outlines on chart paper are used to demonstrate, and students are given the one page sample outline format. The bulk of the period is spent with teachers assisting students to organize their notes and get started. None of the students finish their outline within the period. In the last five minutes the teacher-librarian summarizes what must be handed in, what it is worth in marks, and the expectation that the bibliography will be rewritten in alphabetical order on another sheet before it is handed in.

Period Eight—Most teachers give their students some time back in the classroom to finish their outlines. Others do not. However, all teachers allow one or two periods before the student must write their in-class essay using only their notes and study outlines. This allows students to perfect their organization and also to take a few more notes if they feel they do not have enough or if they have a weak area.

Evaluation

Evaluation is shared by all teachers participating. The social studies teacher marks the reports. When we have had a reading teacher participate, she has marked the notes and outline, while the teacher-librarian has marked all of the process sheets. The process sheets are worth twice what the "end product" is worth and all marks become part of the social studies mark. We use marking code sheets so that a standard level of expectation is maintained no matter who marks. When marking is completed, a library volunteer records the marks on a class list and the folders are returned to the students. Excerpts of the marking code are provided here to indicate the range and value of the various concepts evaluated (see Figure 27.5).

In general, students do quite well on this assignment. It must be noted as well that the most difficult part of the assignment is the outline. Composing an outline is a high-level thinking task and is one which needs repeated practice. One danger of doing the unit year after year is that the personnel involved somehow begin to feel that student performance should drastically improve. We have done it so many times that we forget that the students are doing it for the first time. And we forget that it is a sophisticated task that requires repetition to be mastered.

We provided for that repetition by establishing a second unit which is done with all grade nine science students each year, and which includes the use of the periodical index. Further follow-up is provided by an English research essay in grade 10 which adds the use of footnotes via the Harvard system of referencing. These two repetitions of the same process in different subject areas ensure both mastery and transfer of learning. Since we know all students have had the previous instruction we do not have to commit the ultimate sin in students' eyes of reteaching what they have already "had." We simply remind them of what they have already learned and then we add something new to the process. Students then perceive a reason for doing another research project and they are not turned off! The subsequent units do not need to be as lengthy as the original unit, since we are building on the prior instruction. New students in the school are easily identified and given the necessary extra help.

These assignments might be seen to add to the workload of the teacher-librarian but they are worth the work. Students are so much more capable of handling assignments and they do appreciate the help given them. They also view the teacher-librarian as a source of future assistance and become "regulars." Some have come back to the school and said that the one facet of their university experience that they felt totally prepared for was writing essays. When we recall our own experiences in that area, we feel that the work involved in these units is the best, most valuable work that we have ever done. Other teachers and teacher-librarians who have been involved all feel the same way.

Figure 27.5   Grade 9 Research Project Marking Code: Industrial Revolution

Paraphrased Notes	Possible Mark
1. Completed reference details	2
2. Information complete and relevant to the topic	8
3. Paraphrasing skills:	
uses key words, omits unnecessary words	3
uses own words	3
information makes sense	3
one idea per strip	3
4. Organization of information	6
5. Legibility of notes	2
Total	30

The Outline

1. Topic complete (Title, headings for introduction, conclusion, etc.)	10
2. Organization of ideas	6
3. Correct format (numeration, indentation, etc.)	3
4. Neatness	1
Total	20

Research Record

1. Correlation with bibliography and notetaking (including quantity)	10
2. Variety of resources attempted	5
3. Complete call number	4
4. Complete title	4
5. Used index and/or table of contents where appropriate	5
6. Legibility and neatness	2
Total	30

Bibliography

1. Correct form completeness	3
order	2
spelling	3
punctuation	3
capitalization	1
indentation	1
2. Variety of resources	3
3. Complete call number	2
4. Legibility and neatness	2
5. Reference number	2
Total	20

Art
People Perspective, Grade 8

All too often library-based assignments in art rely on the old standards of writing a biography on a famous artist or a report on a period of art history. This particular assignment maintains the integrity of art objectives while integrating specific information skills.

This segment of the grade 8 art program is designed to change students' attitudes toward drawing and image making. Many students come to a class feeling that they cannot draw because they always compare their work to other people's work and find their own inadequate. If students' abilities are to develop, then a primary goal must be to assist them to gain more assurance and to feel more comfortable with drawing as self-expression. Students must be willing to take risks in their drawings. Risk-taking is where all the exciting things happen.

When students say they cannot draw, they are really saying that they are not satisfied with their drawings. To help them become more satisfied, we can do two things. First we can teach them a technique which will give them a method of approaching the task. The contour line drawing is one such method. It becomes a "seeing" tool for students to use. Secondly we must emphasize the individual nature of any art experience: we are all different; we are all important, unique and special; our unique experiences and perceptions affect the way we see and feel about things, therefore our drawings should reflect that uniqueness. Students' drawings must be accepted as a personal individual expression.

Goals

- to give students a method of approach and a skill which will enable them to draw a portrait;
- to build students' confidence and an acceptance of their own work as valuable;
- to broaden students' view of portraits by establishing a context for the variety and uniqueness of expression found in portraits.

Learning Objectives

- the student will make several contour line drawings;
- the student will complete a contour line drawn portrait from life;
- the student will examine and react to six portraits drawn from a representative list of portraits;
- the student will utilize the catalog, tables of contents, indexes and list of illustrations to find the selected portraits;
- the student will evaluate his or her own portrait.

Unit Plan

Periods One and Two: Art Classroom

1. teacher introduces drawing, with an emphasis on contour line drawing.
2. students complete a minimum of four blind contour line drawings per period.

Periods Three and Four: Art Classroom

1. students complete several contour line drawings, looking at the drawing for reference points not more than half the time.

Period Five: Art Classroom

1. students complete a figure drawing from a live model, and using contour line drawing.
2. drawing must fill a paper 24 by 18 inches, lines running off at least three sides of the paper.

Period Six: Art Classroom

1. students complete the drawing, including background, and transfer to black paper.

Periods Seven to Ten: Art Classroom

1. students complete pastel of the portrait on black paper; color choice to be determined solely by the students.

Period Eleven: Art Classroom

1. teacher critique of the work, emphasizing the individuality of expression and uniqueness of

interpretation of each portrait; all portraits to be hung on the wall for display.

Period Twelve: Art Classroom

1. teacher discusses work of Maxwell Bates, using slides; teacher emphasizes the communicative skill of the artist in spite of a technique which students might perceive to be crude.

2. teacher introduces sheet for library assignment *People Hunt*; emphasis is on looking and interpreting.

Periods Thirteen and Fourteen: Library Resource Center

1. teacher reminds students of discussion of assignment previously done in class, stressing the individual, thoughtful response required.

2. teacher-librarian introduces the Resource List, emphasizing:

   - use of subject catalog;
   - difficulty of last names with "Van" or "De" and suggesting that if a two part name is not found under one of the parts the student should try the other part;
   - process of not looking for the title of the painting until they find the source, then they use the index and list of illustrations.

3. students complete the worksheets, with assistance as necessary from both the art teacher and the teacher-librarian.

Evaluation

1. students evaluate their own pastel, assigning letter grades according to established criteria,

e.g., anyone who has made a genuine effort should not get below a C.

2. teacher marks the original drawing on which the pastel was based, assigning letter grades. Both teacher and student letter grades are recorded.

3. library assignment is marked either "acceptable" or "not acceptable," depending upon the thoughtfulness of the work done (see Figures 27.6, 27.7, 27.8, and 27.9).

Social Studies
Simulating International Relations— Population Control, Grade 11

While the topic of this assignment may not suit every situation, the approach is an interesting one and the design elements well worth replicating in this and different subject areas. This assignment builds in a research strategy, one of the most important of information skills but one of the least common. Students do not actually begin "research" until a number of preliminary steps are completed.

The *Resource List* provides for students the general subject headings and specific subject headings which will be helpful for the assignment. It reminds students of general and specific reference materials and particularly useful specialized encyclopedias. Also included is a brief guide to the use of periodical indexes, pamphlet files and audiovisual items, with specific related subject headings (see Figures 27.10, 27.11, 27.12, and 27.13).

Figure 27.6 Instructions for the People Hunt: Art 8

1. Select six portraits from the list you will find in this package of materials.

2. Using the Resource List and the subject catalogue, locate books or pamphlets which have pictures of your selected portraits.

3. Use the *index* or *list of illustrations* in the book to help you in your search.

Note: a. You should find a color picture, not a black and white one.
  b. Make sure that what you have is not a "detail" study of only a part of the whole portrait.

4. Fill in one section of the attached worksheet for each portrait you have selected. Base your answers on what you observe and feel about the person shown in the portrait.

The student assignment sheet (above) is accompanied by a three page worksheet with the following form repeated six times, the only differences being the painting number, which goes from one to six.

Painting #1: _____
Artist/Title of Painting

1. What kind of person is this? _____

2. What does this person do for a living?_____

3. What did the artist think of this person?_____

4. Would you like to meet this person?_____

Why?_____

_____

_____

_____

Note: The portrait list which follows is the one used by students to make their selections of six portraits to find and comment upon. The Teachers' Reference Sheet, which students do not have access to, gives the name of the painting, the name of the artist, the complete call number of the book, and the title of the book. If we run into difficulties during a class we can always consult the list. Also if there has been heavy circulation of art books just prior to the assignment the list can be used for a quick check to ensure that needed titles are indeed on the shelves.

Of course, all portraits were originally checked to make certain that they did appear in books, and that there was relatively easy access to them via the subject catalogue. Many additional subject cards for the painters had to be added to our subject file the first time we did the assignment.

From *Foundations for Effective School Library Media Programs.* © 1999 Ken Haycock. Libraries Unlimited (800) 237-6124.

Figure 27.7   List of Portraits for People Hunt

Name of Painting	Name of Artist	Name of Painting	Name of Artist
A. Durer's Self Portrait	A. Durer	The Old King	Rouault
Absinthe	Degas	Old Peasant	Van Gogh
Anna Christina	Wyeth	Ortukaryooak the Inlander	Winifred Marsh
Bacchus	Caravaggio	Oscar Wilde	Toulouse-Lautrec
Battista Sforza	Piero Della Francesca	Page Boy at Maxins	Soutine
Cafe Singer	Degas	Pere Tanguy	Van Gogh
Cardinal Leger	Lemieux	Portrait of a Man	Antonello Da Messina
Clown	Rouault	Portrait of a Man 1512	Titian
Comtesse D'Haussonville	Ingres	Portrait of a Man with a Medal of Cosino	Botticelli
Don Fernando Nino De Guevara	El Greco	Portrait of a Nurse	Soutine
Dr. Gachet	Van Gogh	Portrait of a Woman (c1900)	Bonnard
Farm Girl	Soutine	Portrait of a Woman (La Schiavone)	Titian
Federigo Da Montefetro	Piero Della Francesca	Portrait of Cardinal Nicholas Albergati	Van Eyck
Genivra Di Benci	Leonardo Da Vinci	Portrait ot Jean Cocteau	Modigliani
Gertrude Stein	Picasso	Portrait of Jules De Jouy	Monet
Girl with Braids	Modigliani	Portrait of Sculpture Miestchaninoff	Soutine
Girl with Veil	Vermeer	Portrait of Vava	Chagall
Half Past Three (or "The Poet")	Chagall	Queen of Hearts	De Kooning
In a Private Room at the Rat Mort	Toulouse-Lautrec	St. Jerome as a Cardinal	El Greco
Jew in Green	Chagall	Self Portrait	Degas
La Goulue Entering the Moulin Rouge	Toulous-Lautrec	Self Portrait	Durer
La Muta	Raphael	Self Portrait	Gauguin
Lacemaker	Vermeer	Self Portrait 1895	Munch
Le Beau Major (Dr. Devariagne)	Modigliani	Self Portrait in Blue Jacket	Backman
The Loge	Renoir	Self Portrait 1901	Picasso
Madam Matisse	Matisse	Self Portrait 1656	Rembrandt
The Madwoman	Soutine	Self Portrait 1629	Rembrandt
Malle Babbe	Frans Hals	Self Portrait with Palette	Cezanne
Man in Armour	Rembrandt	Self Portrait with Palette	Gauguin
The Man with a Pink	Van Eyck	The Tipsy Woman	Manet
Margaretha Van Eyck	Van Eyck	Weeping Woman	Picasso
Marilyn Monroe	De Kooning	Woman Iring 1904	Picasso
Marilyn Monroe	Warhol	Woman I	De Kooning
Mme. Ines Moitessier	Ingres	Woman with Fish Hat	Picasso
Mme. Rene De Gas	Degas	Young Canadian	Charles Comfort
Miss Olson and a Kitten	Wyeth		

Figure 27.8   Teacher's Reference Sheet for People Hunt Portrait List

Name of Painting	Name of Artist	Call #	Title
Absinthe	Degas	759.4 DEG	Degas
Anna Christina	Wyeth	759.13 WHE	Two Worlds of Andrew Wyeth
Bacchus	Caravaggio	759.5 CA	The Complete Painting of Carvaggio
Battista Sforza	Piero Della Francesca	709 HAR VOL II	Art, A History of Painting, Sculpture, Architecture
Cafe Singer	Degas	759.4 DEG	Degas
Cardinal Leger	Lemieux	759.11 DU	Four Decades
Clown	Rouault	759.4 ROU	Rouault
Comtesse D'Haussonville	Ingres	709 HAR	Art, A History of Painting, Sculpture, Architecture
Don Fernando Nino de Guervara	De Guevara	759.6 THE	El Greco
Dr. Gachet	Van Gogh	759.05 PIg	Post Impressionists pg. 53
Ella	Thomas Cook	759.11 HAR	A Peoples Art pg. 91
Farm Girl	Soutine	759.4 SOU	Soutine
Federigo Da Montefetro	Piero Della Francesca	709 HAR Vol II	Art, A History of Painting, Sculpture, Architecture
Genevea Di Benci	Leonardo Da Vinci	750.5 LEO	Leonardo Da Vinci
Gertrude Stein	Picasso	759.6 PIC	Picasso
Girl with Braids	Modigliani	759.5 MOD	Modigliani
Girl with Veil	Vermeer	759.94 VE	The Complete Painting of Vermeer

Figure 27.9 People Hunt—Art 8

Look up headings in the

Subject File—

1. The name of the artist
   e.g., Van Gogh, Vincent
2. Painters, followed by the nationality of the artist
   e.g., Painters, Dutch
3. Other headings:
   Artists
   Painters
   Painting—History
   Portraits

Write the *complete call numbers* of useful books in the spaces above. Then take your list to the shelves and look for the books.

*Remember:

1. R above the call number means the book is in the Reference section.
2. The Card Catalogue will tell you if there are pamphlets on your topic.

Special Reference Source:
McGraw-Hill Encyclopedia of World Art.
- includes information on a wide variety of artists throughout history. As well, it has many color plates of famous works of art.

Important:
Use the *Index*, Volume XV

McGraw-Hill Encyclopedia of World Art
Gogh, Vincent van (Dutch ptr., 1853–90) 14 694–700',
plate 286 292
Les Alyscamps 14 697
and Anquetin 14 696
Apples 14 696
L'Arlesienne 14 697
Back Side of Old Houses 14 696
Basket with Crocuses 14 696
La Berceuse 14 697, 699, plate 292
and Bernard 14 696
Cezanne's comment on 9, 33, 34
Les Chaumieres 14 698

Art 8

People Hunt

From *Foundations for Effective School Library Media Programs.* © 1999 Ken Haycock. Libraries Unlimited (800) 237-6124.

Figure 27.10   Population Control: The Research Process

Staff scientists of the National Research Council are reported to have perfected a new form of contraceptive drug. The drug is effective for one year with only one dose and may be taken by either a man or a woman. There are no harmful side effects and it is soluble and so can be added to water systems. The drug is one hundred percent effective, but an antidote is available.

Unfortunately the drug is expensive to manufacture and, until a commercial plant can be built, only a limited supply will be available. The government has decided to offer this contraceptive to the world. However, because of the small amount produced so far, only one country will be able to receive the drug.

Your country has been called together by the Prime Minister and the Minister for Foreign Affairs. Briefly, your task is to decide which country should receive the drug. You should look at possible countries from these points of view.

1. Which country has the most need? Some factors to consider are:
   - Population per arable acre or hectare
   - Food availability
   - Growth rate
   - Density
   - Degree of urbanization
   - Degree of industrialization
   - Gross National Product or Gross Domestic Product
   - Health facilities
   - Distribution of income
   - Potential for future development

2. What factors will work against widespread acceptance of the drug? These are mainly cultural and religious beliefs, e.g., local customs, need for large families, etc.

Procedure

You will work in groups of three to four people. Use the Country Choice Process Sheet and note-taking form to help you choose your country.

When you have chosen your country you must let your teacher know. Each country may only be done by one group per class. As a group, you will be required to make a three to ten minute report explaining your reasons for choosing a particular country. This report must also contain visual materials. Each group member must participate in the oral presentation.

The teacher and the rest of the class will listen critically as members of the Cabinet. Be prepared to defend your choice during the question period after your presentation.

From *Foundations for Effective School Library Media Programs.* © 1999 Ken Haycock. Libraries Unlimited (800) 237-6124.

Figure 27.11   Country Choice Process Sheet

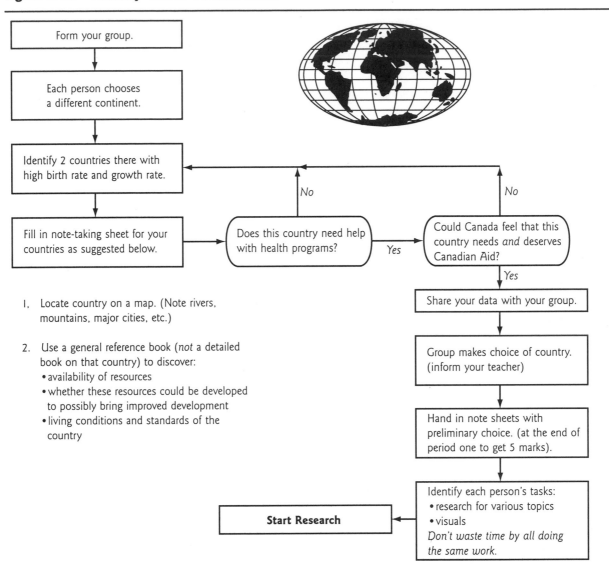

1. Locate country on a map. (Note rivers, mountains, major cities, etc.)

2. Use a general reference book (*not* a detailed book on that country) to discover:
    • availability of resources
    • whether these resources could be developed to possibly bring improved development
    • living conditions and standards of the country

From *Foundations for Effective School Library Media Programs.* © 1999 Ken Haycock. Libraries Unlimited (800) 237-6124.

Figure 27.12   Note-Taking Form—Population Control

Student Name _____

Country _____	Country _____
BR_____ GR_____ GNP_____	BR_____ GR_____ GNP_____
Map	Map
Rivers _____	Rivers _____
Landforms _____	Landforms _____
Resources	Resources

_____	_____
_____	_____
_____	_____
_____	_____

Potential for development	Potential for development

_____	_____
_____	_____
_____	_____
_____	_____

Living standard	Living standard

_____	_____
_____	_____
_____	_____
_____	_____

Group members:	Possible choices:

_____	_____
_____	_____
_____	_____
_____	_____

Group choice:

_____

_____

Figure 27.13   Evaluation Form

	Possible marks

1.   Note sheet
     (if completed during period)

2.   *Teacher evaluation as follows:*
     Factual information
     Concluding argument
     Visual (or audio) materials
     (classroom size charts, graphs, maps, etc.)

3.   *Student evaluation:*
     Argument
     (What did they say, how convincing were they?)

     Presentation
     (Manner, clarity of voice, use of visuals)

These marks will be averaged from each student's evaluation

Total _____

(Late Deduction) 25%

Bonus: 5 marks for most convincing presentation

Time: • Resource Center—3 periods only

         • Books will be available during class time as well as for overnight loan.

         • Presentations will begin _____

CHAPTER TWENTY EIGHT

A Stations Approach to Learning:
The Conversion of a Secondary School Skeptic

Debra Simmons

A "stations approach" to learning can be defined in the most sophisticated educational terms or can be described simply as a series of activities, and supporting resources, designed to develop student knowledge and skills; each of these activities, or stations, is physically separated from one another. Each student moves through these stations following the instructions at each location in order to complete a task or solve a problem.

The first introduction I had to units based on stations convinced me that this approach was like a workbook that walked. In working through the stations, students were asked to examine a number of books on a given subject and to perform tasks using the books. The intent was to expose students to a variety of materials and through using them to learn how information is arranged within the books. But it seemed to me that the questions were not related to anything immediate or useful since reference books come and go, arrangements in books differ and idiosyncrasies abound. Filling in the blank became the primary objective for the students much as filling in the blank in workbooks becomes the end for students. I felt there must be a better, more meaningful and quicker way to teach kids a procedure for locating information than making them go through a three hour exercise of locating how many ships used the St. Lawrence Seaway in a given year or comparing population density for two countries. I acknowledged that some students made reference at a later date to a book they discovered during the exercise, but I was not convinced that stations could be useful for anything other than finding answers to questions for which the overlying objective of the unit was lost to most students.

Then I worked with another teacher-librarian who bullied and cajoled me into creating a series of stations for an eighth grade class studying the Renaissance in Europe. We had a great time locating materials, thinking of questions related to these resources, digging out inviting, interesting and "awesome" facts about the period.

My colleague taught me how to administer such a lesson. She passed on those seemingly insignificant details that separate success from failure. For instance: having students use only pencils so that marks in materials can be erased; having answer booklets instead of sheets to reduce the possibilities of copying; physically separating stations as much as possible to ensure individual work. But like previous stations-based units, there was no purpose other than general exposure. The kids liked it because the situation was different from the usual classroom. They worked in isolation yet could move about. And they, like most people, were intrigued by the pictures, facts and fun of handling a variety of materials. What I felt was lacking was a focus—a purpose. This focus came eventually from classroom teachers. We should have employed cooperative program planning and teaching techniques from the beginning. But we learned. Subsequent stations were planned cooperatively with subject teachers.

What began as a walking workbook has evolved into a sophisticated approach to learning that caters to the content needs of the classroom teacher while integrating information skills and employing every level of Bloom's taxonomy of the cognitive domain. This has come about because of the cooperative and demanding nature of unit development within the social studies department at our school. The stations approach began in social studies but is about to spread to science, now that we know how to make it work and how to ensure the combination of content and development of skills.

Social Studies
The Middle Ages, Grade 8

The transformation began with the restructuring of the eighth grade social studies curriculum. A unit on the Middle Ages in China, India, and Japan was dropped into the middle of the course. There were a number of problems with this unit: teachers were unfamiliar with the material; students lacked a background; the desired concepts were lost in the mass of dates and names in the text.

Because our teachers had used the Renaissance stations, they were receptive to developing a series of stations on the Middle Ages in these areas.

They provided us with specific content goals and learning objectives. To these we added a variety of information skills that needed to be reinforced. The end product was a unit of 43 stations using books, audio and video materials that had a focus and could be used in a variety of ways. The unit allowed for a number of follow-up activities, and was more adaptable because it focused on course content. It could be used to replace, to supplement or clarify the text. It has been used to review note-taking skills, it has led to further research, it became a foundation for discussion, and it has been used later as a basis in comparing this period with the Renaissance in Europe.

In preparing the questions and activities for this unit, we created a matrix of content and skills to ensure that the students were exposed to all the content concepts and used a variety of information skills (see Figure 28.1). The matrix shows content goals and skills used. Most of the questions were of the lower cognitive levels—comprehension and application, with some analysis. Examples of the kinds of activities the students were asked to perform include:

- Using a physical map, imagine a land trip from China to Europe. Would the trip be easy or difficult? Give two reasons for your answer.

- Using specific photographs of castles of the Middle Ages in Scotland and India, identify the country, climate, decoration, construction; give your preference and reasons.

We viewed these stations as a means for teaching complex concepts using basic locational skills. Talking among the students was not allowed; the intent was individual discovery.

Social Studies
Physical and Economic Geography, Grade 10

Last year, the second teacher-librarian and I worked with a teacher to develop a stations approach to the physical regions of Canada. The teacher provided us with very specific concepts related to these regions. We decided that a visual approach would be best so that students would leave the exercise with a visual image of these regions. As a result, these tenth grade

Figure 28.1 Grade 8 Social Studies—Patterns of Civilization

Content: Aspects of life in India, China, and Japan during 500–1600 A.D.		Skim/ Scan	Dictionary Vocabulary Enrichment	Table of Contents	Index	Interpretation of Illustrations, Maps, etc.	Listening	Viewing	Comparing	Recognizing
Research Skills										

India
■ blending of cultures
■ influence of invasion
	1. Customs of daily life, food, clothing, shelter, etc.
	
	2. Arts:
	  painting
	  poetry
	  theatre
	  puppetry
	
	3. Cultural accomplishments:
	  ■ gunpowder
	  ■ printing
	  ■ medical advances
	  ■ magnetic compass
	  ■ etc.									

China
■ cultural accomplishments
■ rise and fall of empire
■ isolation
	4. Warfare
	  ■ weapons
	  ■ leaders
	
	5. Education
	  ■ subjects
	  ■ rigors
	
	6. "Riches of the East"
	  ■ spices
	  ■ silks
	  ■ jewels									

Japan
■ adopt and adapt
■ feudalism
■ isolation
	7. Architecture
	  ■ Taj Mahal
	  ■ mosques/temples
	  ■ other
	
	8. Religions
	  ■ character of
	
	9. Personalities
	  ■ Genghis Khan
	  ■ etc.									

students do very little textual reading. There is also less emphasis on interpretation and analysis.

The 25 stations consist of pictures, slides, maps, pamphlets, graphs and a few books. There is more than one item at every station. Students are led to speculate, compare, and apply knowledge. The unit has been used as an introduction to the subject of physical regions. It has also been used as a closing activity. It has been used with equal success with regular tenth grade classes,

modified classes and with classes of English as a second language students.

There are important differences between this unit and previous ones. A major change is its size. Because we had time to develop and evaluate only 25 stations, we do not have one station per student as is usual. As a result, students frequently doubled up at some stations. The serendipitous benefit that came of this was the discussions which arose between students when the answer

Figure 28.2   British Columbia—Economic and Physical Geography

	Raw materials	Secondary support	Products	Conservation	Techniques Methods	Markets	Employment	Physical	Climate	Pollution
Fishing										
Mining										
Tourism										
Forestry										
Agriculture										
Misc.										

was analytical, speculative or unknown. Questions such as these stimulate discussion:

- Look at the physical map of British Columbia. What problems might there be in developing a transportation system?

- Look at a specific photograph. Make two statements about the climate of the area and speculate about what geographic region is most likely represented. Why?

When students were asked to evaluate the unit they wrote that they enjoyed it, liked not having a lot to read, and acknowledged their inexperience in "seeing" information. Because of the nature of the questions, the stations provide an excellent opportunity for one-on-one teaching and the "teacher" is frequently another student.

Lessons Learned

This year we have pushed the limits even further. In the past we have been able to develop stations that are content relevant, flexible in organization, and adaptable to a variety of materials and students. This year, we were asked to work with a teacher to incorporate the ability to see the relationship between evidence and conclusion into a stations approach to the Industrial Revolution. Instead of giving us specific content, the teacher wanted the stations to provoke the students to generalizing. The basic generalization that was sought was that "The Industrial Revolution continues today and affects your life beneficially and detrimentally." Stations were set up around eight

areas: medicine; transportation; science; war; commerce; communications; personal life; technology. Each area had five stations and each student had to complete two subject areas. The materials were neither predominantly textual nor visual, but a combination of both. Since this was intended to be used with ninth grade students, once again, basic locational skills were reinforced. Each station was formed in such a way that a conclusion could be reached based on the data located. Students were asked to link a station with a given conclusion. The factual information and the conclusions reached led to an in-class essay about the impact of the Industrial Revolution on medicine or war or technology. From these essays came a discussion of the advantages and disadvantages of continued technology in our lives.

This unit has not been as popular with teachers. The absence of specific content makes follow-up activities difficult. The abstract nature of the material requires careful guidance by the teacher. Also, making time in a crowded curriculum to discuss evidence and conclusion as well as the ethical, moral, political and economic aspects of technology requires a skill at juggling time as well as students. It is our intent to alter the unit somewhat and introduce it into the eleventh grade science and technology course. The prime objective of this new course is to help students to evaluate and solve problems. The abstract reasoning abilities of eleventh grade students is more developed than in ninth grade students and older students will be better able to deal with this material. We will of course first involve the teachers and incorporate the principles of cooperative program planning and teaching. We have learned the hard way that which is blatantly evident to many: working in isolation just doesn't work.

Now we are working on a tenth grade unit to supplement the study of physical geography. These stations will be similar in that they will be primarily visual. They deal specifically with the relationship between the physical and economic geography of British Columbia (see Figure 28.2). Content matter has been provided by the teacher. Once again we have added information skills. Greater emphasis is being placed on incorporating the higher levels of cognition—evaluation and synthesis. Once again, a matrix has been created into which we place information about which station covers the content and

which cognitive level is employed. This unit is in preparation and will not be used until next September. We don't yet know how the students will respond to questions that require greater abstract thinking skills as well as locating skills (see Figure 28.3).

I have become very enthusiastic about the possibilities of the stations approach. I have seen it work with students on modified programs, large and small classes, and classes of students with English language difficulties. It need not always use set questions, but can be used to lead students into formulating their own questions. It teaches information skills in conjunction with a content area; it can be used to stimulate imagination as well as to identify factual data. It is an adaptable and viable way to introduce, to enhance, to sum up. I'm convinced. I've been converted.

Figure 28.3   Cognitive Skills Development in a Stations' Approach

	A	B	C	D	E	F
Topic	**Knowledge** tell, label, list, locate, cite, offer, choose , name, find, say, group, show	**Comprehension** translate, propose, define, expand, explain, alter, outline, annotate, restate, infer, offer, contemplate	**Application** relate, operate, utilize, try, solve, exert, use, put to use, adopt, take up, employ, handle	**Analysis** break down, check, examine, reason, look into, divide, uncover, deduce, dissect, include, sift, screen	**Synthesis** create, yield, combine, reorder, make, structure, build, cause, compile, effect, blend, form	**Evaluation** judge, accept, decide, reject, rate, crticicize, prioritize, award, rank, umpire, weigh, settle

Connecting Writing and Research Through the I-Search Paper: A Teaching Partnership Between the Library Program and Classroom

Julie Tallman

"Research is no big deal. It's not very tough to do. All you have to do is look up your subject in an encyclopedia and then write your information in your own words." In essence, here's the question and here's the answer! Do you hear this refrain from your students? Is this how your students feel about research? Do they know how to research effectively for themselves? Do they reflect on what they read and apply the ideas to their problem focus or do they cut and paste?

When one of her freshmen gave this version as his definition of research at the beginning of a school year, Marilyn Joyce, a northern Maine teacher-librarian and process advocate, knew she wanted to see more critical thinking skill development in applying information to research problems and greater use of library resources. She started by rallying her freshman English teacher, Bettie Martin, to use a modified version of Ken Macrorie's I-search writing process (Macrorie, 1988), in place of the traditional freshman biographical essay. Martin had read about the I-search and was willing to experiment.

Macrorie originally developed the I-search process as a writing process for his college composition classes. Its popularity spread through the K–12 community because of its easy adaptability as an effective writing process for middle and secondary students. Students seemed to write more successfully about questions, problems or interest areas that drew their attention and hooked them. Their internalized need to explore these topics served as intrinsic motivation for carrying them through the information search stage. Owning the topic and being able to write their papers in the first-person style gave students a vested interest and confidence in their written expression. The student's personal interest in a topic sustained a need to seek and synthesize information about the topic. For Joyce and Martin, it also provided a natural place to infuse information skills as the students were ready to learn them.

Wanting to see first-hand how the I-search connected with information skills through a collaborative partnership between a teacher-librarian and classroom teacher, I ventured to Maine to study Joyce and Martin's approach at Stearns High School in Millinocket. Interviews with students and faculty and analysis of student papers, journals and worksheets convinced me that teaching research and information skills through a writing process such as the I-search promoted stronger student awareness of research strategies transferable to subsequent assignments and personal information searches. This paper is a report on a unit both teachers and students considered successful.

Planning

Following Macrorie's approach, students chose a topic about something they needed to know for their own lives. Their product was the story of their adventure. In personal logs and in their final three- to five-page papers, students wrote about the search process they took, how they felt about the information they found, and how they used it to answer their questions. The log or journal became a powerful tool for developing their metacognitive abilities and creating material for the I-search paper itself.

Joyce reported that it took them a month to go through the process with their students. Both Martin and Joyce wanted students to have adequate hands-on time in class for research and writing. To help students find and use the information they needed, Joyce and Martin taught the research strategies that matched their information needs. Those needs changed as the searches evolved. Because the I-search paper was the students' first major research assignment, Joyce and Martin knew the students did not have strong, developed research strategies. They discovered they needed to conference with students frequently to follow student progress and identify when information skills instruction and extra guidance was needed individually or for the class. As a result, Joyce developed a written set of questions to guide students in solving their problems and drawing their conclusions (see Figure 29.1).

Steps

Over the last three years, Joyce and Martin have developed a set of steps and strategies that gave students research skills adaptable to their needs during this assignment. In particular, they stressed the pre-search stage when "students formulated a central research question, related the question to prior knowledge, identified key words and names associated with their question, integrated concepts and developed questions to organize their search." Of particular usefulness to the students for relating their topics to prior knowledge was a pre-notetaking sheet that asked them to identify what they knew about a topic, what they didn't know and what they wanted to know.

Choosing the Topic

Choosing a topic that demanded the student's attention seemed to prevent frustration and decreasing interest as the assignment was nearing completion. The topic choice made a difference in how much students enjoyed their research experience and how much they involved themselves in the topic. According to Martin, student topic choice also increased writing quality and the ease with which the students wrote.

Joyce and Martin gave the students three strategies to find an interesting topic. First, they made a personal experience webbing diagram that pictured their interest areas. Joyce reported that topics coming out of the webs included hobbies, family, career choices, education and travel. Students received instruction for using the Social Issues Resources Series (SIRS) CD-ROM database and the Infotrac magazine index in the library resource center. These electronic resources promoted a teacher-student dialogue about topics of interest to the students. Reading in traditionally high-interest materials, such as tales of the weird and supernatural, and looking up possible

Figure 29.1   Sample Conferencing Questions Developed by Joyce

Pre-Notetaking Stage

I. After selection of a potential topic

Goal: to help student find a focus

A. Content questions

1. Why did you select this topic?

2. What do you already know about the subject?

3. Can you tell me more about ... ?

B. Process questions

1. Do you think you have a broad or narrow topic? Why?

2. What will be your next step?

II. After drafting questions on Pre-Notetaking Sheet

Goal: to help students formulate 'what they don't know' questions

A. Content questions

1. What other questions might you ask?

2. Have you created at least one question from each one of your key words?

B. Process questions

1. What strategy can you use to generate more research questions?

2. What is the secret to writing a good research question?

3. What indexes and tables of contents have been the most helpful when creating questions?

4. What obstacles have you encountered? How do you plan to overcome them?

5. What is your next step?

III. While revising question on Pre-Notetaking Sheet

Goal: to determine questions for students "Questions I will answer through my research" column and to formulate the central research question

A. Content

1. Are you satisfied with your central research question? Is it an accurate picture of what you will show through your research? Justify your answer.

2. Do all of the questions to guide your research support your central research question?

3. Have you formulated questions to cover all aspects of your central research question?

B. Process

1. Has your focus changed as a result of your reading? If "yes," how?

2. What have you learned about the pre-search stage of the research process?

The Interpretation Stage

Content

1. Find articles that present opposing points of views. Compare and contrast these articles. Which viewpoint is most "in line" with your opinion on the subject? Why?

2. Can you relate this information to personal experience?

3. Make a prediction. Based on your information, what will happen in the future?

4. Can you find examples of faulty logic in your sources? Cite examples and explain the faulty logic.

5. Evaluate your source for currency, bias and/or point of view.

6. Take a difficult passage to read and "translate" it into language we can all understand.

7. Is this information relevant? Justify your answer.

8. What information can you use to support this generalization? *or* From these specific details, draw a conclusion.

9. Based on your information, propose a plan of action.

10. Establish a criteria for making a judgment (e.g., a criterion for judging scientific research on determining child custody).

11. Suggest some solutions for a problem posed in your research. Evaluate the solutions. Prioritize the solutions. In other words, which potential solutions should be initiated first? Why?

12. Conduct an experiment to determine the validity of your hypothesis or to disprove a theory proposed in one of your sources.

13. Evaluate the quantity and quality of your sources. Do you have enough sources? Do your sources represent different points of view? Are they reliable? Explain your responses.

14. How will you communicate your findings to your audience? Who is your audience? What methods of presentation will they respond to?

Process

1. What is your next step?

2. What obstacles have you encountered? How will you overcome them?

3. Explain your timeline for this project. Are you on schedule? Does your timeline need revision?

4. What is your next step?

5. What strategy or technique has been most successful? Why?

6. What strategy or technique has been least successful? Why?

7. How do you feel at this stage of the process? If you feel frustrated or confused, what can you do?

8. Identify a problem you encountered and explain how you overcame it.

9. Up to this point in the research process, what have you learned about the process itself? about strategies and techniques for accomplishing steps in the process?

10. Develop a criteria for judging your progress. Then do a self-evaluation.

11. What can be done to improve teacher-student/librarian-student conferences? to improve peer conferences?

12. Have you made effective use of the following: class time, library time, peer-conferencing time? Explain. What can you do to improve your use of time? What is the first thing you will do to implement these changes?

13. Have you successfully answered your research questions? Explain.

14. Will your search continue after you finish this project? If "yes," what do you plan to do?

CONNECTING WRITING AND RESEARCH THROUGH THE I-SEARCH PAPER   253

topic choices in print indexes and tables of contents also helped some students.

Still, some students chose something in which they had only passing interest. In the study, it was obvious in comparing topic choices to reactions and value of this project that these students gained less from the experience. Students who did not have a stakeholder position in the topic had trouble focusing on good research questions and found the research process less exciting and less involving. They also did not have the same pride and satisfaction in answering the search questions.

Pre-Notetaking

After choosing the topic, the students wrote about what they knew, did not know and wanted to know about the topic. On a worksheet split into three columns, they answered each of these questions. Students who chose a topic without much personal interest commented on how difficult this exercise was. Returning to this sheet after they had some understanding of their topic improved their ability to decide on what they wanted to know. For many of the students, this was a helpful tool.

The teaching team did not allow the students to write down quotes or take detailed notes when they read for general knowledge on the topic before deciding on research questions. Instead, the students reflected about what they read in journals. This exercise forced them to use their own words and relate the material through their own perspective. Although finding it difficult to do, students appreciated how much it made them think about what they were reading.

Martin used this part of the process to stress student interaction with the topic. She promoted such phrases as, "I think...." Joyce contended that students "do little interpretation and analysis of the information" without a personal perspective.

Choosing Resources

Joyce and Martin worked with each student on their resource choices. Where appropriate, they helped the students find alternative sources of information in addition to library resources. For example, students who chose career topics sought out the resources in the guidance office. Students with topics of known interest to other members of the faculty made arrangements to interview them. Some found community members, such as their doctors, who could help them with their topics. One of the best experiences from this assignment was the realization that a valid resource could be anything or anyone with authority and credibility on the topic.

Martin and Joyce encouraged students to think about additional sources as their focus became clearer. One Native American student chose to write about his tribe. He had books from the University of New Brunswick library and other source material that allowed him to write his paper. But he realized he was not happy with his paper as it progressed and discarded it. A late interview with his father gave the student a new perspective, new questions and eventually, a new version of his paper.

Martin and Joyce encouraged students to photocopy useful material on the library's copy machine. Joyce, the teacher-librarian, taught the students margin note reflection and highlighting skills. She said, "We encouraged them, especially starting out with an encyclopedia, if possible, to see a broad view of their topic, and they highlighted that on their photocopy. Then, after the highlighting, and when they knew something about their topic, they did either a webbing diagram or a formal outline to try to make some sense out of the concepts related to their topics and get some kind of organizational pattern. I found kids who couldn't do a webbing diagram, or could not do an outline and hadn't done enough initial reading. They'd say, 'I can't do my outline,' and I'd say, 'What do you know about your topic? Where are your materials? What have you highlighted?' And they didn't have enough material."

Reflecting in Their Journals

Joyce emphasized that students discuss in their journals the obstacles and problems they encountered as well as the information they collected. The students critiqued their own research process. If students wrote about a problem, they also wrote about how they planned to fix it. If they did not know how to fix it, they interviewed other students for recommendations.

Recognizing Bias and Opinions in Sources

While students gathered resource ideas, Joyce and Martin spent class time discussing types of information from resource materials. Joyce reported that students did not automatically know what to write in their journals when they started to write about what they were reading. She wanted them to be critical readers. "[For] the first couple of years, the kids were writing 'well here's one of my research questions, here's the answer.'" But there was no interpretation or interaction with it. "We were missing out on the whole interpretation process with all the detecting bias and understanding."

Another activity was to have students read news articles on the same topic. Each student split a paper into two columns and jotted down a comparison/contrast of two of the articles; one column contained a quote or passage from the article, the other the student's reaction or reflection. Then students shared their comments with the class, giving the class an opportunity to see the range of possibilities in the different comments they each made. Martin and Joyce extended this exercise to the students' journals.

Student Interaction with Source Material

Martin continually asked students to interact with their new information by evaluating it, comparing it with other information they had learned and reflecting on its meaning to their questions. Martin and Joyce gave students starter phrases to help in the process. For example, "I reacted very strongly when I discovered...; I still want to know...; When I compared this article to that article, I found..." These phrases reduced a common problem in the research exercises. Students will say, "OK, I've read this, what do I write about?" They also helped students do their journal writing in first-person perspective.

Transition to Final Products

The transition from journal notes to the final report completed the steps. Students created their papers by going into their journals and editing them. They decided what ideas were really important in the final copy and what items were integral to their questions. Martin and Joyce did not stress producing as formal a product as a term paper.

Assessment

Martin had the responsibility for checking the strength of the students' reflection about their topics. She gave students an opportunity to redo the paper if they reverted to the question-and-answer format without involvement. She also corrected grammatical and structural errors, content, resources, paragraph flow and transitions. Finally, Martin looked for creativity and personal involvement with their topics.

Joyce had the responsibility for checking the effectiveness of the research steps that students took and how well they analyzed what they had done. She felt conferences with students were highly productive for this assessment. Joyce also wrote responses to students in their journals about their information-search strategies and use of information tools and resources. Her assessment of journal entries involved using Bloom's taxonomy to evaluate their level of thinking. Her purpose was to move students up the critical thinking hierarchy.

Teacher Observations

Martin and Joyce took considerable pride in their students' accomplishments with these papers and the succeeding oral reports. Joyce said that she would "never forget one of the kids who did his oral presentation. He said a couple of people who thought they knew more than he did kept asking questions and he knew all the answers. He was just so proud of himself...It was...because [the student became] the specialist."

The sophomores and juniors who had not been through the process seemed lost in their approach to the resources or what they needed to do during their term paper assignments. The ones who had done the I-search during their freshman year settled in immediately on finding a topic, focusing on the questions and locating resources.

Value of the I-Search

Martin considered the I-search approach as successful for students with lower academic abilities. She reported that they had more problems with the research process, library searching, topic selection and frustration levels. But they worked diligently. "They were actually reading something other than what the teacher assigned them to read and they were going to different sources, whether it be a CD-ROM, a periodical, a newspaper, or clippings...That taught them to understand their library. I'm hearing comments from sophomore teachers with these lower ability kids, 'Wow! They really know what to do, and they know how to get down to business and they can handle a project now. Before they just didn't do anything.'"

Other teachers in the building saw visible growth in the sophomores and juniors from their freshman I-search writing/research assignment. Students seemed to have higher self-esteem, a better grasp on their task management, better writing quality, more comfort in library research and a sense of expertise in their topic. A number of students appreciated the fact that the process made them think about their own opinions. They talked about working much harder on this assignment and were quite proud of what they had done.

The I-search appeared to prepare students for succeeding term papers and assignments requiring information problem solving. Through their reflections, students wrote about research strategies that were successful. They saw what steps they could easily transfer and reported feeling prepared and self-assured about their next project.

Martin and Joyce appreciated each other's contribution to the unit's success. Martin wanted the expertise of a teacher-librarian who knew what was in the library. She said, "When you're working with 27 students in one class and they're all doing a different subject, you've got to be able to pull information from all sources. Marilyn Joyce is tremendous in the informational skills area and the media skills area." Joyce reported that teaming with a process-oriented teacher was critical to the unit's success. Martin's enthusiasm for collaboration gave the unit time to mature over several years.

Recognition came from other faculty that students were developing more effective research strategies, participating more actively in classroom assignments requiring research and had better task-management skills. Martin and Joyce felt these points were a positive recognition of their success. They knew they had a strong start to a powerful research and writing component, exciting for their students, themselves and their teacher colleagues.

References

Macrorie, K. (1988). *The I-search paper.* (Revised edition of *Searching writing.*) Portsmouth, NH: Boynton/ Cook, Heinemann.

CHAPTER THIRTY

Designing Thematic Literature Units

Jean Donham van Deusen and Paula Brandt

The practice of incorporating trade books into the reading/language arts classroom has generated widespread enthusiasm for what are being called "thematic" units. As resident experts in children's literature, teacher-librarians can be important collaborators with teachers in developing thematic units. One potential benefit of thematic units is the opportunity to move students toward higher-order thinking in the discussion of the meaning in what they read. Achieving this benefit first requires some definition of "thematic units" and distinction from other kinds of literature units. Are all trade-book units thematic units? What is a theme anyway? Why is a theme an appropriate organizer for literature-based units?

Certainly, a reading program includes various types of units, but the thematic unit offers some opportunities for higher-order thinking beyond what the other types of trade units may elicit. A literary theme is defined as the central or dominating idea in a literary work (Handbook, 1960). A theme conveys a position or a perspective (Shanahan, 1995). Often, educators make no distinction between topical units and thematic units, but in fact there is a substantive difference

Categories of Units

Sippola (1993) suggests that there are several categories of units that bring together a variety of trade books:

- topic: focuses on a specific, concrete phenomenon, like bears, or the circus, or the rain forest, or habitats;
- form: focuses on a form or genre, like poetry, or tall tales, or fantasy;
- structure: focuses on literary structure, like trickster tales or the use of the number three in folktales;
- concept: emphasizes an abstract concept like change;
- author: focuses on the work of a particular author;
- picture book/novel: focuses on a single book;
- theme: focuses on an "underlying" idea.

between the two types. Because a theme is a complete thought, not just a topic or a concept, there is more meaning to reflect on and to discuss than a single word or concept might provide. A theme tends to offer a principle or a generalization about the human condition. A theme like "Celebrations bring families or communities together and provide memories that its members can share forever" offers more opportunities for in-depth conversation than a simple topic like birthdays. Stewig (1998) captures the significance of theme in the following statement:

> Specific details may set the story in the 16th or the 21st century; the main character may be a young woman or an old man; the environment may be here or in another world. But when these particulars are set aside the theme of two apparently diverse books may in fact be the same.

The distinction between topic and theme may at first seem a matter of semantics. The important point is that the unit center on an idea or generalization, not on a topic. In some settings, the word theme is used to refer to the general topic and the word generalization or the word focus is used to refer to the idea or focus of the unit. The terms are less important than that the unit's emphasis be on a complete thought or perspective or generalization as opposed to a concept or topic.

Why Thematic Units?

Themes offer opportunities for children to:

- analyze characters' motives or plot development by exploring the presentation of a theme in a variety of literary forms, e.g., narrative, poetry, essay, or drama;
- synthesize by comparing and contrasting situations, events, characters and outcomes among literary selections;
- evaluate literary selections, using comparisons among selections as well as explicit criteria to assess authenticity or morality of stories or characters.

Analyze, synthesize and evaluate are verbs at the high end of Bloom's taxonomy (1956). Moving students toward more complex thinking is one of the benefits of a thematic unit. A theme is an inherently meaningful, abstract generalization that encourages students to think inductively while they search for common patterns among the specific selections they read. The thematic unit comports with a constructivist approach to learning wherein new information becomes meaningful as it is integrated into existing schemata. Focusing on a theme enables students to develop complex webs of related ideas (Peters, 1995). Such webs are connected not merely by topic, but by principles, motives or generalizations. Students engage in constant comparison and contrast as they progress from one selection to the next in the quest for the common idea(s). In short, a thematic unit, as compared to the other types of literature units, offers opportunities for high level thinking and abstraction.

Constructing a Thematic Unit

Thematic units are challenging to develop, whereas topical units are fairly simple. The central task in developing a topical unit is assembling several selections about the same topic. Since it is merely a topic that holds the unit together, discussion and other activities tend to focus on each title individually, rather than on analyzing the subtle differences or similarities between selections.

The most common way to develop a thematic unit is to begin with a topic. Often, but not necessarily, the topic will come from the social studies or science curriculum for integration across the curriculum. There are many sources of topic ideas in professional journals such as *Book Links* or the index of *Horn Book Guide*, as well as teacher resource books and bibliographies from such publishers as the National Council of Teachers of English, Oryx Press, Scholastic, Christopher-Gordon and Libraries Unlimited/ Teacher Ideas Press. However, sometimes these resource books use the word theme in the title when the approach is really topical. Browsing through a standard reference source like *Best books for children* can also lead to topics. Once one has selected a topic—say, survival—the next step is to create a web that visually maps the different aspects of the topic. Here this might include survival involving mechanical accidents (airplane, ship), natural disasters (fire, earthquakes), human error/accidents (getting lost), serious illness/disabilities (cancer, visual impairments), survival in school (e.g., bullies), in families (e.g., abusive parents, abandonment), on the streets (homelessness), or war-related survival (refugees, Holocaust, nuclear aftermath).

Once one has narrowed the topic, viability becomes the next concern. The question for the teacher-librarian is, "Are there enough appropriate books available to support the topic?" Gathering books and skimming them is the next step. The skimming must be purposeful: in relation to the topic, what do these books have in common? What is unique about each one? For example, reading about earthquakes, fires and floods—fiction and nonfiction—a theme (i.e., pattern) may emerge: "Whether or not one survives a natural disaster is determined in part by luck, leadership, personal determination and the preparedness of individuals and agencies." This theme would connect books about the Johnstown Flood, Mt. St. Helens and Joe Cottonwood's Quake. Readers could focus their attention on why or how some people survived and some people didn't, and subsequently apply that knowledge to other situations.

When shifting our attention from examining topics of books to examining their themes, purposeful skimming becomes a way of reading. The purpose in skimming is to uncover underlying abstract ideas rather than state the obvious superficial ones such as, "This is a book about…." When the purpose of skimming changes, sometimes themes emerge when one least expects them. For example, we were recently reviewing books in picture book format that had as their subjects, historical figures—a topic. A pattern emerged among three titles—*Eleanor* by Barbara Cooney, *The bobbin girl* and *The ballot box battle*, both by Emily Arnold McCully—young girls' lives were changed by women who were not family members. This theme brought to mind other books where children were influenced—and sometimes saved—by other adults in their lives—books like Marie Bradby's *More than anything else*, Rachel Isadora's *Ben's trumpet*, Katherine Paterson's *Jip*, Kevin Henkes' *Lilly's purple plastic purse* and Roald Dahl's *Matilda*. A thematic unit

based on this idea could be limited to biography so that students read to discover who influenced famous people. Students could then interview community or family members to explore who outside their family influenced them and then write about a non-family member who is helping them grow as people. Or the unit could expand to include fictional characters. A stated theme might be: "While our families usually have the biggest influence on us, there is often a pivotal person outside of our family who changes our lives." By adjusting the way we were looking at the relationships among theme books from merely the topic of historical figures to a thematic perspective, the analysis grew more complex. This same increase in complexity will follow as we guide students' discussion of the books. If this had been a mere topical unit, the topic might have been "biography" or "mentors" or "growing up." But, by advancing to a thematic statement, the discussion has a tighter focus, students have more to look for in their reading and questions during discussion converge on the theme.

Sequencing

Once the titles have been selected, the next task is to decide how each title will be used. In some cases, one title works well to introduce a thematic unit and ought to be read aloud to all children. Here, a book becomes a foil against which all others will be compared. For example, consider a unit whose theme is, "We can help others overcome loneliness by reaching out to them." *Somebody loves you, Mr. Hatch* by Eileen Spinelli can work as such a foil. Questions can focus on motivation or on the effect of each character's actions on others. These issues may become key lines of questioning for all books in the unit and children will compare each future book to *Somebody loves you, Mr. Hatch*. Other titles then might include *One yellow daffodil; A Hanukkah story* by David Adler, *An angel for Solomon Singer* by Cynthia Rylant and *Train to somewhere* by Eve Bunting. Students will compare the Beckers, Angel and Mr. and Mrs. Book to Mr. Hatch's friends. The subsequent books can be read aloud to children, or they might each read one or two and then through discussion compare "their" stories to the common reading. Sometimes, all titles can be read by all children independently and sometimes the unit will have core titles accompanied by a selection of titles from which children can choose which they will read. The sequencing and assigning of readings will help guide the development of questions.

Key Questions

The next step in developing the unit is to determine the key discussion questions. Thematic units are inductive in their structure. Readers experience several examples that have a common theme; the intellectual task is to develop and refine a statement that ties all the books together. While the teacher knows the theme, children know the topic as they begin to read; it is their task to construct a thematic statement as they continue through various examples. This inductive approach facilitates children constructing their generalizations. Questioning helps lead them toward that generalization. For example, consider the theme, "We can help others overcome loneliness by reaching out to them." In *Train to somewhere*, the teacher might ask, "What are the risks for both Marianne and her new family as they reach out to one another?" In *An angel for Solomon Singer*, children can consider how to make friends out of strangers. In *One yellow daffodil*, readers might explore how the Becker family benefits from their friendship with Morris. And, in *Somebody loves you, Mr. Hatch,* a key question might focus on how one's actions can unintentionally discourage friendship. The power of the thematic unit is that these key questions can be posed in ways that ask children to compare and contrast each of these issues among all the books read in the unit. This process calls for children to infer meaning from the several examples they experienced to work at a cognitive level beyond what other types of units may demand. Children can best achieve that abstract thinking when they have key questions to help them focus their thoughts about what they read.

Factors to consider in examining the key questions include:

- Are student questions primarily literal comprehension questions? While some comprehension questions may be appropriate, the emphasis needs to be on those analytical questions that will help the child think about the theme.

- Are initiating questions helpful in focusing on the central theme or are they tangential? While the book may be about Christmas, for example, if the theme has to do with family celebrations, then initiating questions should be about family celebrations so that children have an appropriate set before experiencing the story.

- Do questions focus on higher order thinking: "What do you think about…? Why do you think that? How do you know that? How is that similar to or different from…? Why would he do that?"

- Do questions emphasize a holistic view of the work rather than isolated details? For each key question, consider whether it ties to the thematic statement that organizes the unit.

Culminating the Unit

Montgomery (1992) suggests that the thinking process for a thematic unit moves from concrete toward abstract. Indeed, if the culmination of the unit is to synthesize the meaning conveyed in the selections, then the structure is from concrete specific examples toward a generalization. That generalization is the theme.

Thematic units are perhaps the most difficult type of trade book unit to prepare. They require careful selection of titles that speak to the theme, development of key questions that will lead readers to generalizations about what they have read and thoughtful discussion to help students synthesize at the end. Are they worth it? Is a sentence better than a word? Thematic units consider the complexity of life situations in a way that topical units may not; they cause students to focus attention on the "big ideas" in their literature, moving them beyond literal comprehension to inferential thinking. Is that worth doing? We think so.

Resources

Books for Children

Angel for Solomon Singer. Cynthia Rylant. Illustrated by Peter Catalonotto. Orchard, 1992. 0-531-05978-2.

The ballot box battle. Emily Arnold McCully. Knopf, 1996. 0-679-87938-2.

Ben's trumpet. Rachel Isadora. Greenwillow, 1979. 0-688-80194-3.

The bobbin girl. Emily Arnold McCully. Dial, 1996. 0-803-71827-6.

Eleanor. Barbara Cooney. Viking, 1996. 0-670-86159-6.

Jip. Katherine Paterson. Lodestar, 1996. 0-525-67543-4.

Lilly's purple plastic purse. Kevin Henkes. Greenwillow, 1996. 0–688–12897–1.

Matilda. Roald Dahl. Viking, 1988. 0-670-82439-9.

More than anything else. Marie Bradby. Illustrated by Chris Soentpiet. Orchard, 1995. 0-531-09464-2.

One yellow daffodil; A Hanukkah story. David Adler. Illustrated by Lloyd Bloom. Gulliver, 1995. 0-152-00537-4.

Quake. Joe Cottonwood. Scholastic, 1995. 0-590-22232-5.

Somebody loves you, Mr. Hatch. Eileen Spinelli. Illustrated by Paul Yalowitz. Simon & Schuster, 1992. 0-027-86015-9.

Train to somewhere. Eve Bunting. Illustrated by Ronald Himler. Clarion, 1996. 0-395-71325-0.

Selected Topical/Thematic Sources

Book Links. American Library Association.

Horn Book Guide. The Horn Book.

Gillespie, J. *Best books for children: Preschool through grade 6.* New York: R. R. Bowker.

Irving, J. & Currie, R. (1993). *Straw into gold: Books and activities about folktales.* Englewood, CO: Libraries Unlimited/Teacher Ideas Press.

Jensen, J. & Roser, N. (Eds.). (1993). *Adventuring with books.* Urbana, IL: National Council of Teachers of English.

Lima, C. & Lima, J. (1993). *A to Zoo; subject access to children's picture books.* New York: R. R. Bowker.

Moir, H. (Ed.). (1992). *Collected perspectives: Choosing and using books for the classroom.* Boston: Christopher-Gordon.

Paulin, M. (1992). *More creative uses of children's literature.* Hamden, CT: Library Professional Publications.

References

Bloom, B. (1956). *Taxonomy of educational objectives: The classification of educational goals.* Handbook I: Cognitive domain. New York: David MacKay.

A handbook to literature. Theme. (1960). New York: Odyssey.

Montgomery, P. (1992). *Approaches to literature through theme.* Phoenix, AZ: Oryx.

Peters, T. et al. (1995). A thematic approach: Theory and practice at the Aleknagic School. *Phi Delta Kappan, 76,* 633–636.

Shanahan, T. et al. (1995). Avoiding some of the pitfalls of thematic units. *The Reading Teacher, 48,* 718–719.

Soppila, A. (1993). When thematic units are not thematic units. *Reading Horizons, 33 (3),* 215–223.

Stewig, J. (1998). *Children and literature.* Boston: Houghton Mifflin.

CHAPTER THIRTY ONE

What Do You Believe About How Culturally Diverse Students Learn?

Rita Dunn, Mark Beasley and Karen Buchanan

American schools mainstreamed and absorbed immigrants successfully when the latter comprised only a small percentage of the total population. However, as the birthrate among Caucasians declined, the proportion of minority children increased. By 1987, Edelman calculated that nearly one-quarter of all children under age 15 were black and Hispanic. That same year, Paulu (1987) reported that black and Hispanic students were more likely than others to perform poorly in school, become at risk and drop out.

Changing demographics in American schools show that, within the next five years, the current "minority" population will have become the majority population in 53 major United States cities (Rodriguez, 1988). Government and industry grants have provided extensive funding for a variety of new programs for underachieving minority students. Few of these programs have resulted in significantly improved, standardized achievement test scores among minority students (Alberg et al, 1992).

In schools that evidenced statistically higher achievement gains among black children, instruction had been changed to respond to how those students preferred to learn—their "learning styles" (Andrews, 1990, 1991; Bridge to Learning, 1993; Brunner & Majewski, 1990; Nganwa-Bagumah & Mwamenda, 1991; Perrin, 1990; Stone, 1992). For example, the Special Education Department of the Buffalo City Schools randomly selected and randomly assigned classified Learning Disabled (LD) and Emotionally Handicapped (EH) students (K–8) to two groups. Instruction for the Experimental Group was modified to accommodate students' learning style preferences. Instruction for the Control Group remained the traditional combination of methods the special education teachers had been using with the students. Between 1991–1993, the experimental group achieved statistically higher test scores than the control group in both reading and mathematics on two different standardized achievement tests— the Woodcock-Johnson and the California Tests

Table 31.1   Test Results

Report from the Independent Research Team from the University of Buffalo: Results of Standardized Achievement Test Scores in Reading and Mathematics for Students in the Buffalo City Schools' Learning Style Program (Experimental Group) in Contrast with the Results for Students in its Non-Learning Styles Program (Control Group) for the First Two Years of Program Implementation

Test Name	Group	Pre-Test	Post-Test	Net Difference
WJ * Reading	Experimental	72.38	79.1	+6.72
	Control	76.48	71.52	–4.96 (loss)
WJ * Math	Experimental	69.67	84.2	+14.53
	Control	73.52	69.09	–4.43
CTBS+ Reading	Experimental	18.76	31.33	+12.57
	Control	24.83	21.25	–3.58
CTBS+ Math	Experimental	15.83	18.61	+2.78
	Control	23.44	16.95	–6.49

* WJ: Woodcock-Johnson
+ CTBS: California Test of Basic Skills

of Basic Skills (CTBS). In contrast, the control group reported a loss between their pre-test and post-test scores (see Table 31.1).

Similar gains were reported for underachievers in Brightwood, a small town near Greensboro, North Carolina. In 1985 and 1986, Brightwood Elementary School students achieved in the 30th percentile on the CTBS. In 1987, after only one year of being taught with strategies that responded to their learning style preferences, students' test scores on the CTBS escalated to the 40th percentile. In 1988, after the second year of learning-styles-responsive instruction, the school's CTBS scores jumped to between the 74th and 76th percentile in reading and mathematics. In 1989, the third year of Brightwood's learning styles program, CTBS scores reached the 83rd percentile. One year later, they reached the 89th percentile.

Black children in the state of North Carolina consistently perform in the 20th–30th percentile range. In two North Carolina learning-styles schools, black students typically perform at the 70th percentile or better (Andrews, 1990, 1991; Stone, 1992).

Apparently, children whose learning styles do not respond to how their teachers teach learn significantly less well than children whose styles do. Neither financial support nor community involvement were factors contributing to improved test scores and behaviors. Rather, significantly higher test scores resulted from teaching directly to students' individual styles.

Before asking teachers to change how they teach, it is necessary for teachers to confront their beliefs about how students learn (see Table 31.2). If they believe that everyone learns identically, why change?

Answers to the Personal Belief/Bias Scale

1. *No.* Most people within each culture learn differently from other people of the same culture. There are as many different learning styles within a given culture as there are between various cultures (Dunn & Griggs, 1990).

2. *No.* Within every family in each culture, people learn differently from each other (Dunn & Griggs, 1990). Although significant differences do exist between how some people in different cultures learn, there are more differences among the people within a culture than there are between people in different cultures. Higher percentages of people with a specific trait live in one culture than in another, but the actual number of people who are very different from each other may be relatively few in comparison with the total group. For example, the percentage of Filipino students who are highly

Table 31.2   The Personal Belief/Bias Scale

Directions: Consider the following questions carefully. At the end of each sentence, check or write in what you believe is the most accurate answer. Leave blank what you cannot answer. After answering all the questions that you can, compare your answers with those at the end of the scale. The References list is the basis for the research findings. In this scale, "learning" refers to how individuals concentrate on, process and remember new and difficult information; "significantly" refers to statistically measurable differences.

Questions	Yes	No
1. Do most people in one culture learn differently from most people in another culture?	☐	☐
2. Do most people in the same culture learn in basically the same way?	☐	☐
3. Do most people who practice the same religion learn in basically the same way?	☐	☐
4. Do most people who practice different religions learn differently from each other?	☐	☐
5. Do most people of the same race learn in basically the same way?	☐	☐
6. Are certain learning style characteristics found to a greater extent in one race than in another?	☐	☐
7. Do boys and girls learn differently from each other?	☐	☐
8. Do high and low achievers learn differently from each other?	☐	☐
9. Is there a relationship between how someone learns and being gifted?	☐	☐
10. Does learning style contribute to underachievement?	☐	☐
11. Do children and adults learn differently?	☐	☐

12. Do the majority of students (K-12) learn best

	Yes	No
(a) by listening?	☐	☐
(b) by reading?	☐	☐
(c) by taking notes?	☐	☐
(d) by experiencing?	☐	☐

What is the modality through which the highest percentage of students learn best? _____

13. Can a majority of low/auditory and low/visual students become "A", "B+", or "B" students in conventional schools?	☐	☐

14. Do a majority of students (K-12) learn best through cooperative learning?   ☐ ☐
(a) Who does? _____
(b) Who doesn't? _____
(c) How do we know?_____

15. Do a majority of students learn best in early morning?   ☐ ☐
Of the following groups: (1) elementary students; (2) intermediate students; (3) adolescent students; and (4) adults,
(a) Who learns best in early morning? _____
(b) Who learns best at night? _____
(c) When is the best time to teach most young children to read? _____

16. Select the perceptual preferences most often found in: ☐ ☐

High Achievers	Low Achievers
☐ Visual	☐ Visual
☐ Auditory	☐ Auditory
☐ Tactual	☐ Tactual
☐ Kinesthetic	☐ Kinesthetic

17. Are the majority of students "analytic" (step-by-step sequential) learners?   ☐ ☐
(a) What is the opposite of being analytic? _____
(b) Do people with an analytical processing style tend to perform better on a typical IQ test (i.e., Stanford-Binet)   ☐ ☐
than those who do not have an analytic style?

18. Are the majority of teachers "analytic" (step-by-step sequential) instructors?   ☐ ☐
(a) Are the majority of adults analytic learners?   ☐ ☐
(b) Name a subject that tends to attract analytic teachers. _____
(c) Name a subject that tends to attract teachers with a processing style other than analytic. _____

19. Do people with one particular learning style perform better on a typical IQ test than people with another learning style?	☐	☐
20. Are there differences among cultures concerning attitudes toward school and teachers?	☐	☐
21. Does how a person learns (his/her "learning style") change over time?	☐	☐

From *Foundations for Effective School Library Media Programs*. © 1999 Ken Haycock. Libraries Unlimited (800) 237-6124.

parent motivated is significantly higher than the percentage of American students who are parent motivated. That is, more Filipinos than Americans achieve to please their parents, which is statistically significant because of large sample sizes. Thus, this is statistically interpretable, but its practical importance is questionable. In addition, percentages of learning-style traits fluctuate within each culture by age, gender and school achievement levels (Dunn & Griggs, 1990; Milgram, Dunn, & Price, 1993). For example, among those traits that are present to a lesser or greater extent in some cultures are differences in perceptual, time-of-day and motivational preferences and a proclivity for being more or less nonconforming. Chinese college students are significantly more auditory than Caucasian college students; Filipino gifted adolescents are significantly more parent motivated than gifted adolescents in Brazil, Canada, Egypt, Greece, Guatemala (Guatemalans and Mayans), Israel, Korea and the United States; and Israeli gifted students are more self-motivated than gifted students in Brazil, Canada, Egypt, Greece, Guatemala (Guatemalans and Mayans), Korea, the Philippines and the United States. However, there may only be a 5 percent difference in a specific learning style trait between any two cultures (Dunn & Dunn, 1992, 1993; Milgram, Dunn, & Price, 1993).

3. and 4. *No.*   Although no study of the learning styles of people who practice different religions is currently available, the differences between the styles of mothers and fathers, parents and their offspring, and siblings in most cultures suggest that styles differ to a greater extent among individuals than between groups (Dunn & Griggs, 1990).

5.   *No.* All learning style characteristics are present to a lesser or greater extent among the people of each race (Dunn & Griggs, 1990). Thus, within each race, different learning styles exist.

6.   *Yes.* The studies of learning style that compared specific racial groups revealed that specific traits are present in higher or lower percentages in some races than in others. Traits that appear to be present to a lesser or greater extent in some groups are differences in perceptual and motivational preferences and a proclivity for being more or less nonconforming. For example, African-American elementary students tend to be more tactual and kinesthetic than Caucasian elementary students (Jacobs, 1987; Sims, 1989). However, a few percentage points of variance from the norm may be "significant," which simply means that there are more students with this characteristic in one group than in another group (e.g., both groups may have many students with—and many students without—this particular trait). Thus, it is always important to assess each learner's individual learning style to determine the way the student/adult actually learns best (see Answer 2 for related information).

7.   *Yes.* Particularly during the primary school years, there are more differences between the learning styles of boys and girls than between the learning styles of people in different cultures. For example, girls develop comparatively strong auditory memory and small-motor coordination earlier than boys. Thus, they remember what they hear better and write more neatly than their male classmates. We rarely say to girls, "Why can't you remember?!" or "How many times must I tell you that?!" We frequently admonish boys for either forgetting, "not hearing," or not "concentrating"— because many of them cannot remember a great deal of what has been said to them. Girls also are better able to sit passively for a longer amount of time in conventional seats and desks, whereas most boys require mobility and an informal design significantly more than girls. This provides a potential explanation for why boys are reprimanded repeatedly for squirming in, or falling out of, their seats. Boys develop large-motor coordination earlier and excel in physical activities (e.g., most organized sports), in contrast with girls' ability to write more neatly, cut with a pair of scissors more precisely and draw within lines. Furthermore,

boys remain tactual and kinesthetic learners longer than girls. Girls are more authority oriented, whereas boys tend to become peer oriented earlier and remain that way longer. In addition, girls need significantly more quiet while learning, whereas boys tolerate noise in the environment better, i.e., few males are distracted by sound because most are not very aware of it (Pizzo, Dunn & Dunn, 1990).

8. *Yes.* The learning styles of high academic achievers and low academic achievers differ significantly. The former generally have preferences that respond to conventional schooling, e.g., they are (a) auditory or visual learners; (b) self-, parent, or authority motivated (rather than unmotivated or peer motivated); (c) not in need of mobility or food while learning; and (d) conforming rather than nonconforming. Underachievers tend to be tactual/kinesthetic learners who often require sound, soft lighting, an informal design, intake and mobility while learning. They often are peer motivated, or motivated only when interested in what they are learning. Underachievers also require a variety of resources, methods, or approaches while learning and become bored with routines. During a stage of nonconformity, both achievers and underachievers may be antiauthoritarian (Milgram, Dunn, & Price, 1993).

9. *Yes.* When students (a) are taught in ways that complement either their interests or natural talents; (b) feel a sense of accomplishment or pleasure; (c) reap benefits that respond to their emotionality; and (d) have the opportunity to engage in activities in which they can excel, over time their talent often develops into exceptional ability—which society views as giftedness (Dunn, Dunn, & Treffinger, 1992; Milgram, Dunn, & Price, 1993).

10. *Yes.* When children are not taught in their preferred style, they may not learn, and often give up, give in, or withdraw. These conditions may certainly increase poor achievement.

11. *Yes.* Many elements of style change as children grow older, mature and spend time in school. We do not know whether those changes are maturational or an outgrowth of students' ability to respond to conventional schooling. Elements that often change among individuals include responsiveness to sound, light, seating designs, motivational, responsibility (conformity/nonconformity), need for structure and intake, social groupings, perception and chrono-biological highs and lows (Price, 1980). Some elements change in some people and not in others (e.g., global versus analytic inclinations and motivation). Temperature preferences rarely change and persistence changes only slowly over time, if at all. Although some change can be predicated based on general patterns at various age levels, individual cycles are established because of biological and developmental uniqueness.

12. (a) *No.* Less than 30 percent of adults learn best aurally and, among K–3 children, the percentage is closer to 10–12 percent; (b) *No.* Visual learners comprise up to 40 percent of adults but many of those are graphic/photographic learners—among K–3 children, the percentage is closer to 15–20 percent, and it varies by gender and achievement; (c) *No.* Note takers tend to be visual/tactual students who cannot remember much of what they hear without writing it; (d) *No.* Kinesthetic learners master what they learn through experience, involvement and movement-while-learning—they often do not learn through someone else's experiences, or by listening or reading (Dunn & Dunn, 1992, 1993; Dunn, Dunn, & Perrin, 1994); (e) The percentage of modality preferences vary with age, gender and achievement, but there are more tactual and kinesthetic young learners than auditory learners everywhere we have tested students during the past quarter of a century.

13. *Yes.* Most students can learn anything when they (a) begin learning with their preferred processing style (global versus analytic); (b) are reinforced through their secondary or tertiary modality; and then (c) apply the new information they have been exposed to by

using it to develop a new instructional resource (e.g., explaining the information by writing a poem, creating a play, film, book, or game, or making a set of Task Cards, an Electroboard, a Pic-A-Hole, a Flip Chute, etc.). Furthermore, the ability to learn is based on individuals' interest in the topic/subject, which also affects their performance in school (Andrews, 1990, 1991; Bridges to Learning, 1993; Stone, 1992).

14. *No.* In the general population, approximately 13 percent of most students learn best alone; approximately 28 percent learn well with peers, but within that group are students who learn only with one classmate and others who learn in a small group. Another 28 percent need an adult; within that cluster are some who need a collegial adult and others who need an authoritative adult. Some can learn well in two or more groupings and many learn best only in one (Cholakis, 1986; DeBello, 1985; Dunn et al, 1990; Miles, 1987; Perrin, 1984). Those percentages, however, vary with academic achievement and age. For example, gifted adolescents in at least nine diverse nations strongly preferred to learn independently—by themselves. Their second most-preferred sociological preference was learning with an authoritative adult. Young gifted children also preferred learning alone, unless they could not complete their tasks alone, at which point they preferred learning with other gifted children (Perrin, 1984). In American schools, sociological preferences appear to be influenced substantially by age, grade and achievement levels (Dunn & Dunn, 1992, 1993; Dunn et al, 1994).

15. *No.* Time of day energy levels vary widely, particularly with age. Only 28 percent of elementary school children are most alert in the morning. A majority first "come alive" between 10:00 and 10:30 and their highest energy levels are between then and 2:00 p.m.—during which time we give them a one-hour lunch period. (a) Fifty-five percent of adults tend to learn best in the morning, while (b) only 28 percent of adults learn best

in the evening. This compares with only 13 percent of adolescents learning best in the evening. (c) The best time for most young children to learn to read is between 10:00 a.m. and 2:30 p.m. (Dunn & Dunn, 1992, 1993; Dunn, Dunn, Primavera, Sinatra, & Virostko, 1987).

16. Because most teachers teach either by talking (which requires students to learn well by listening) or by reading (which requires students to learn well by seeing), students who remember well by listening or seeing tend to become comparatively high achievers in school. Most young children are tactual and/or kinesthetic (Dunn, Dunn, & Perrin, 1994). When tactual or kinesthetic preferents are taught through lectures or readings, it is difficult for them to remember at least 75 percent of what they need to learn. When tactual and kinesthetic students are (a) introduced to difficult materials with tactual or kinesthetic instructional resources; (b) reinforced with a different modality resource; and (c) required to apply the new information creatively, they learn significantly more than when they are taught incorrectly (for them) (Andrews, 1990, 1991; Bridge to Learning, 1993; Carbo, 1980; Bauer, 1991; Ingham, 1991; Jarsonbeck, 1984; Martini, 1986; Thorpe-Garrett, 1991; Weinberg, 1983; Wheeler, 1980; Stone, 1992).

17. *No.* Based on correlations between at least three different instruments and learning style characteristics, the majority of young children and students who do not perform well in school appear to be (a) global (the opposite of analytic). Typically, global processors need to understand a concept before they can focus on the details, learn best when interested in the subject and often learn informally, with music, intake and others nearby. They may also learn better in soft light than in bright light and prefer to work on several tasks simultaneously rather than on one at a time. (b) People with an analytic processing style tend to perform better on a typical IQ test, because it is written in an analytic format and requires analytic

thinking to produce a single correct response (Cody, 1983; Brennan, 1984; Dunn, Bruno, Sklar, & Beaudry, 1990; Dunn, Cavanaugh, Eberle, & Zenhausern, 1982; Trautman, 1979).

18. *Yes.* Of the teachers we have tested during the past 20 years, 65 percent tend to be analytic, whereas, in the overall population, 55 percent of adults are global and only 28 percent of adults are analytic. In a study of gifted and talented adolescents in nine diverse cultures, 18 percent of the gifted students were analytic and 26 percent were global. Although analytic processors are found teaching all subjects offered in the K–12 curricula, math is nearly always taught by an analytic processor. Teachers who have a global processing style are more frequently found teaching art, music and physical education (Milgram, Dunn, & Price, 1993).

19. *No.* Students appear to be equally intelligent when they are taught in ways that respond to their learning style preferences. Cody (1983) found that, with an IQ of 125 and in the 94th percentile in reading or math, 8 of 10 students were analytic. With an IQ of 135, that statistic reversed, and 8 of 10 students were global. With an IQ of 145 or above, 9 of 10 students were global.

20. *Yes.* Different cultures express different values. A culture's values, the opportunities to which individuals are exposed, and each individual's interests, potential talents and learning style directs that person toward an area in which expertise can develop, mature and express itself (Milgram, Dunn, & Dunn, 1993).

21. *Yes.* The need for sound and intake can be observed by second or third grade, and for many it remains fairly consistent until about sixth grade, at which time the two preferences "explode." During adolescence, the need for sound and intake becomes even stronger. For many, at about ninth or tenth grade, the two elements begin to return to their previously "normal" intra-individual level (Price, 1980). The need for quiet appears to increase, and the need for intake appears to decrease, among adults over 60.

Temperature inclinations tend to remain the same throughout childhood and adulthood, but may gradually change toward needing more warmth among some—particularly among the aging.

Design preferences tend to remain the same during elementary school, gradually leaning toward becoming more informal as students reach adolescence and then may, or may not, change on an individual basis.

Responsibility tends to correlate with conformity versus nonconformity (Dunn, White, & Zenhausern, 1982). People tend to have three periods of nonconformity. The first occurs at approximately two years of age; the second during "adolescence"; and the third is sometimes called "mid-life crisis."

Motivation varies with interest and the degree to which the teaching matches the learning style preference.

Nothing holds true across the board, but persistence tends to be an analytic quality. Analytic processors, more than global processors, tend to "stay on task" while learning. Their global counterparts often require "breaks" for intake, interaction, changing focus and so forth.

The older students become, the less structure they need, although, under pressure (of exams or multiple study assignments), many college students require structure (Napolitano, 1985).

Sociologically, many young children come to school wanting to please the adults (parents and teachers) in their lives. Somewhere around third grade, many start becoming peer motivated. Students rarely used to become peer motivated before seventh or eight grade (Price, 1980). They have become peer motivated younger and younger during the past three decades.

Gifted children also come to school wanting to please the adults in their lives, but early, by first or second grade, most become learning-alone preferents and do not seem to experience a "peer" stage. Underachievers remain peer oriented longer than either gifted or "average" achievers. Usually, by ninth or tenth grade, most average students have emerged from wanting to learn with classmates and become self-motivated. At no time have we ever found more than 28 percent of students in the peer stage and, among that group, many learn better with just one other classmate than in a small group. Those students are "pair motivated," and often prevent a group from functioning when required to work in a group. Twenty-eight percent of most students are "adult motivated"; these need to learn with a teacher, but some need a collegial adult and others need an authoritative adult. In three studies of dropouts, at-risk students required a collegial adult, yet they had been assigned to an authoritative adult (Gadwa & Griggs, 1985; Johnson, 1984; Thrasher, 1984).

Perceptually, the younger the children, the more tactual and/or kinesthetic they are. In elementary school, less than 12 percent appear to be auditory (able to remember three-quarters of what they are taught through lecture or discussion), while 40 percent are visual (able to remember three-quarters of what they are taught through reading). The older children become, the more visual and, eventually, the more auditory they become. Females generally are more auditory than males, and males generally become more visual and tactual/kinesthetic and remain more tactual and kinesthetic than females.

Time of day preferences change with age (refer back to Answer 15 for a more thorough discussion of time of day). Many students require mobility and learn more efficiently when permitted to move *while* learning (Dunn, DellaValle et al, 1986; Miller, 1985).

Figure 31.1   Elements of Learning Styles

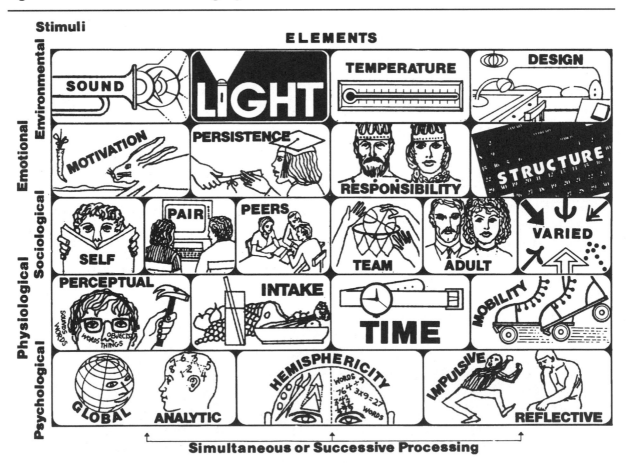

Learning Styles Model
Designed by Dr. Rita Dunn and Dr. Kenneth Dunn

From *Foundations for Effective School Library Media Programs.* © 1999 Ken Haycock. Libraries Unlimited (800) 237-6124.

References

Alberg, J., Cook, L., Fiore, T., Friend, M., Sano, S., et al. (1992). *Educational approaches and options for integrating students with disabilities: A decision tool.* Triangle Park, NC: Research Triangle Institute.

Andrews, R. (1990, July/September). The development of a learning styles program in a low socioeconomic, underachieving North Carolina elementary school. *Journal of Reading, Writing, and Learning Disabilities International, 6(3),* 307–314.

Andrews, R. (1991). Insights into education: An elementary principal's perspective. *Hands on approaches to learning styles: Practical approaches to successful schooling.* New Wilmington, PA: The Association for the Advancement of International Education.

Bauer, E. (1991). *The relationships between and among learning styles perceptual preferences, instructional strategies, mathematics achievement, and attitude toward mathematics of learning disabled and emotionally handicapped students in a suburban junior high school.* Unpublished doctoral dissertation, St. John's University, Jamaica, NY.

Bridge to learning. (1993). Videotape available from St. John's University's Center for the Learning Styles Network, Jamaica, NY.

Brunner, C., & Majewski, W. (1990, October). Mildly handicapped students can succeed with learning styles. *Educational Leadership, 48(2),* 21–23.

Carbo, M. (1980). An analysis of the relationship between the modality preferences of kindergartners and selected reading treatments as they affect the learning of a basic sight-word vocabulary. (Doctoral dissertation, St. John's University). *Dissertation Abstracts International, 41,* 1389A.

Cholakis, M. (1986). An experimental investigation of the relationships between and among sociological preferences, vocabulary instruction and achievement, and the attitudes of New York, urban, seventh and eighth grade underachievers. (Doctoral dissertation, St. John's University). *Dissertation Abstracts International, 47,* 4046A.

Cody, C. (1983). Learning styles, including hemispheric dominance: A comparative study of average, gifted, and highly gifted students in grades five through twelve. (Doctoral dissertation, Temple University, 1983). *Dissertation Abstracts International, 44,* 1631A.

DeBello, T. (1985). A critical analysis of the achievement and attitude effects of administrative assignments to social studies writing instruction based on identified eighth grade students' learning style preferences for learning alone, with peers, or with teachers. (Doctoral dissertation, St. John's University). *Dissertation Abstracts International, 47,* 68A.

Dunn, R., Bruno, J., Sklar, R., Zenhausern, R., Beaudry, J. (1990, May/June). Effects of matching and mismatching minority developmental college students' hemispheric preferences on mathematics scores. *Journal of Educational Research, 83(5),* 283–288.

Dunn, R., Cavanaugh, D., Eberle, B., & Zenhausern, R. (1982). Hemispheric preference: The newest element of learning style. *The American Biology Teacher, 44(5),* 291–294.

Dunn, R., DellaValle, J., Dunn, K., Geisert, G., Sinatra, R., & Zenhausern, R. (1986). The effects of matching and mismatching students' mobility preferences on recognition and memory tasks. *Journal of Educational Research, 79(5),* 267–272.

Dunn, R., & Dunn, K. (1992). *Teaching elementary students through their individual learning styles: Practical approaches for grades 3–6.* Boston: Allyn & Bacon.

Dunn, R., & Dunn, K. (1993). *Teaching secondary students through their individual learning styles: Practical approaches for grades 7–12.* Boston: Allyn & Bacon.

Dunn, R., Dunn, K., & and Perrin, J. (1994). *Teaching young children through their individual learning styles: Practical approaches for grades K–2.* Boston: Allyn & Bacon.

Dunn, R., Dunn, K., Primavera, L., Sinatra, R., & Virostko, J. (1987). A timely solution: A review of research on the effects of chronobiology on children's achievement and behavior. *The Clearing House, 61(1),* 5–8.

Dunn, R., Dunn, K., & Treffinger, D. (1992). *The giftedness in every child: A guide for parents.* New York: John Wiley & Sons.

Dunn, R., Giannitti, M., Murray, J., Geisert, G., Rossi, I., & Quinn, P. (1990, August). Grouping students for instruction: Effects of individual vs. group learning style on achievement and attitudes. *Journal of Social Psychology, 130(4),* 485–494.

Dunn, R., & Griggs, S. (1990). Research on the learning style characteristics of selected racial and ethnic groups. *Journal of Reading, Writing, and Learning Disabilities, 6(3),* 261–280.

Dunn, R., Griggs, S., & Price, G. (1993, October). Learning styles of Mexican-American and Anglo-American elementary school students. *Journal of Multicultural Counseling and Development, 21(4),* 237–247.

Dunn, R., Griggs, S., & Price, G. (1993). The learning styles of adolescents in the United States. In R. Milgram, R. Dunn, & G. Price (Eds.), *Teaching and Counseling Gifted and Talented Adolescents for Learning Style: An International Perspective.* (pp. 119–136). New York: Greenwood.

Dunn, R., White, R., & Zenhausern, R. (1982). An investigation of responsible versus less responsible students. *Illinois School Research and Development, 19(1),* 19–24.

Edelman, M. (1987). *The children's time*. Washington, DC: The Children's Defense Fund.

Elliot, I. (1991, November/December). The reading place. *Teaching K–8, 21(3)*, 30–34.

Gadwa, K., & Griggs, S. (1985). The school dropout: Implications for counselors. *The School Counselor, 33*, 9–17.

Ingham, J. (1991). Matching instruction with employee perceptual preference significantly increases training effectiveness. *Human Resource Development Quarterly, 2(1)*, 53–64.

Jacobs, R. (1987). An investigation of the learning style differences among Afro-American and Euro-American high, average, and low achievers. (Doctoral dissertation, George Peabody University, 1987). *Dissertation Abstracts International, 49(01)*, 39-A.

Jarsonbeck, S. (1984). The effects of a right-brain mathematics curriculum of low achieving, fourth grade students. (Doctoral dissertation, University of South Florida). *Dissertation Abstracts International, 45*, 2791A.

Johnson, C. (1984). Identifying potential school dropouts. (Doctoral dissertation, United States International University). *Dissertation Abstracts International, 45*, 2397A.

Martini, M. (1986). An analysis of the relationships between and among computer-assisted instruction, learning style perceptual preferences, attitudes, and the science achievement of seventh grade students in a suburban New York school district. (Doctoral dissertation, St. John's University). *Dissertation Abstracts International, 47*, 87A.

Milgram, R., Dunn, R., & Price, G. (Eds.). (1993). *Teaching and counseling gifted and talented adolescents for learning style: An international perspective*. Westport, CT: Praeger.

Miller, L. (1985). *Mobility as an element of learning style: The effect its inclusion or exclusion has on student performance in the standardized testing environment*. Unpublished master's thesis, University of North Florida.

Napolitano, R. (1986). An experimental investigation of the relationships among achievement, attitude scores, and traditionally, marginally, and underprepared college students enrolled in an introductory psychology course when they are matched and mismatched with their learning style preferences for the element of structure. (Doctoral dissertation, St. John's University). *Dissertation Abstracts International, 47*, 435A.

Nganwa-Bagumah, M., & Mwamenda, Tuntufye S. (1991). Effects on reading comprehension tests of matching and mismatching students' design preferences. *Perceptual and Motor Skills, 72(3, Pt. 1)*, 947–951.

Paulu, N. (1987). *Dealing with dropouts: The urban superintendent's call to action*. Washington, DC: U.S. Government Printing Office.

Perrin, J. (1984). An experimental investigation of the relationships among the learning style sociological preferences of gifted and non-gifted primary children, selected instructional strategies, attitudes, and achievement in problem solving and rote memorization. (Doctoral dissertation, St. John's University). *Dissertation Abstracts International, 46*, 342A.

Perrin, J. (1990, October). The learning styles project for potential dropouts. *Educational Leadership, 48(2)*, 23–24.

Price, G. (1980). Which learning style elements are stable and which tend to change over time? *Learning Style Network Newsletter, 1(3)*, 1.

Rodriguez, F. (1988). Minorities and the school system. In R. Gorton, G. Schneider, & J. Fisher (Eds.), *Encyclopedia of school administration and supervision* (pp. 172–173). New York: Oryx Press.

Sims, J. (1988). Learning styles: Should it be considered? *The Oregon Elementary Principal, 50(2)*, 28.

Stone, P. (1992, November). How we turned around a problem school. *The Principal, 71(2)*, 34–36.

Thrasher, R. (1984). *A study of the learning-style preferences of at-risk sixth and ninth graders*. Pompano Beach, Florida: Florida Association of Alternative School Educators.

Weinberg, F. (1983). An experimental investigation of the interaction between sensory modality preference and mode of presentation in the instruction of arithmetic concepts to third grade underachievers. (Doctoral dissertation, St. John's University). *Dissertation Abstracts International, 44*, 1740A.

Wheeler, R. (1980). An alternative to failure: Teaching reading according to students' perceptual strengths. *Kappa Delta Pi Record, 17(2)*, 59–63.

CHAPTER THIRTY TWO

Principals and Teacher-Librarians:
A Study and a Plan for Partnership

Patricia Wilson, Martha Blake and Josette Lyders

A 1990 article about teachers as professionals in *Phi Delta Kappan* declared: "Secretaries, librarians, and other ancillary staff will be subordinate to teachers in the line of command. Professional people don't wait on support people's pleasure for a photocopy or a needed document" (Swart, 1990). Needless to say, this article raised a furor among teacher-librarians. In letters to the editor, teacher-librarians called to the author's attention that while she was in the classroom busily checking her work sheets, other professionals were entering the information age (Dickinson, 1991).

On reading the article and rebuttals, we still were troubled by a nagging question: If this is how classroom teachers such as Swart view a teacher-librarian's role, how do administrators perceive this role?

Information power: Guidelines for school library media programs (AASL and AECT, 1988) is based on the premise that "teachers, principals and teacher-librarians must form a partnership and plan together to design and implement the program that best matches the instructional needs of the school." Teachers, principals and teacher-librarians become partners in a shared goal—providing successful learning experiences for all students. For this partnership to take place, it is necessary that principals understand the role of the teacher-librarian as well as the role of the library resource center within the total school program.

A National Survey

To determine principals' perceptions and knowledge of the role of teacher-librarians, Wilson and Blake conducted a national survey. Responses and comments by the 572 teacher-librarians and 423 principals who responded to the national survey indicate that the partnership idea outlined in *Information power* still has a long way to go. The survey was sent to a random sample of 1,000 principals and 1,000 teacher-librarians at elementary, middle school and high school levels. The survey included a 30 item questionnaire along with two questions and space for comments. A total of 572 (57.2%) of the teacher-librarians and 423 (42.3%) of the principals responded to the survey. The focus of this paper is on the two questions and the comments section of the survey.

The principals and teacher-librarians were asked to respond and offer comments to two questions. The first question investigated: "Are principals adequately trained regarding the management and function of school libraries?" Over 90% of the teacher-librarians responding agreed that principals were not adequately trained in the management and function of school library resource centers and felt principals needed more training. Over 68% of the principals responding felt they were not adequately trained in this area.

The second question asked: "Should the management and function of school libraries be a part of the principal's training?" In response to this question, an overwhelming 90% of the teacher-librarians agreed that part of the principal's training should focus upon library resource centers. Even more interesting, however, over 78% of the principals agreed that they should have more training in the functions of school library resource centers.

Prompted by comments from the participants, the authors developed a plan to help administrators become more aware of the role of the teacher-librarian and the management and functions of school library resource centers. The plan strengthens the teacher/teacher-librarian/administrator partnership and brings these professionals closer to the goals highlighted in *Information power*.

The plan focuses on three basic questions:

A. Why do principals need to know more about the function and management of school library resource centers?

B. What specifically do principals need to know concerning library resource centers?

C. How can principals become more familiar with the management and function of school library resource centers?

Why Principals Need To Be Better Informed

A: Why do principals need to know more about the function and management of school library resource centers?

1. To understand the responsibilities of a teacher-librarian.

2. To carry out performance evaluations.

3. To support resource center budgets.

4. To promote the role of the resource center in curriculum.

5. To ensure scheduling for optimum use of the resource center.

6. To better understand developments in information technology.

Comments received on the survey forms pointed to the above six reasons why principals need to become more familiar with library resource centers.

1. To understand the responsibilities of a teacher-librarian:

As mentioned previously, comments by many teacher-librarians highlighted their concern that principals do not understand their job or their role in the school. One teacher-librarian with 12 years' experience asked: "How can they oversee such an important part of a school as the resource center program if they don't understand it?" Another teacher-librarian summed up the feelings of many colleagues in her statement: "They often have no idea what goes on, so they try to use the library as a dumping ground for overcrowded study halls." Others went on to say that principals "don't understand the scope of the library beyond checking out books." Teacher-librarians from across the country pleaded for principals to become aware of everything they do during the day and not to view the library resource center as "a study hall," "part of teachers' planning time," "a meeting room," "a place to park the kids and give the teacher a break," or "a baby-sitting service." One principal with 11 years of experience commented: "Without a knowledge of the total job description, how can principals evaluate and hire teacher-librarians?"

2. To carry out performance evaluations:

A common comment concerning the need to understand the functions of school library resource centers focused upon the principal's role in evaluation. Teacher-librarians noted: "How can they evaluate us if they don't know what we do?" Others pointed out that "evaluation of teacher-librarians is based largely on the teaching role rather than the managing role." They went on to say that the principal only comes in to evaluate them when they are teaching—thus, reiterating the idea that principals do not understand the full role of teacher-librarians.

Principals indicated that evaluation of the teacher-librarian is an important part of their role because "how else will I know if my teacher-librarian is up to par?" Interestingly enough, even principals noted that they needed more knowledge because "if we are expected to evaluate, we need the training." One of the bright spots from the national survey came from teacher-librarians and administrators in Georgia, who praised their new instrument for evaluating teacher-librarians. Principals were required to attend seminars prior to using the instrument, and teacher-librarians and principals highlighted the fact that "principals came out of the seminars knowing a great deal more about school library resource centers."

3.   To support resource center budgets:

Principals and teacher-librarians noted the importance of principals' knowledge of school library resource centers for budgetary purposes. Knowledge concerning the high cost of books and audio-visual materials, as well as library technology, is important. At the same time, a principal who is knowledgeable concerning state and national standards for library resource centers is better able to understand the necessity for updating and adding to the collection. Knowledge of these standards gives both the principal and teacher-librarian a baseline by which to measure their own resource center and determine the amount of funding necessary to reach specific goals.

Teacher-librarians in the study noted that if principals had a better understanding of their job responsibilities, they might be more receptive to giving the library resource center a larger portion of the annual budget. By being acquainted with all a library resource center can have to offer—professional development for faculty, special programs to enrich the students' curriculum, workshops

on reading for parents, booktalks to encourage reading, training in information retrieval—principals may be more generous to the library resource center when it comes to planning next year's budget.

4.   To promote the role of the resource center in curriculum:

Teacher-librarians involved in the survey noted that their principals were unaware of the impact teacher-librarians can have on curriculum. By serving as a member of the curriculum planning and development team, the teacher-librarian becomes a valuable resource person to improve and enhance instruction. Knowing the needs of the teachers while curriculum documents are being written allows the teacher-librarian lead time to locate resources for enrichment, research, or possibly to assist in the integration of subject area content. They stated that principals need "to realize that the teacher-librarian is an integral part of the curriculum," and that part of the teacher-librarian's training emphasizes knowledge of specific curricular needs for all grade levels. For a true partnership to work, principals must "boost their understanding of the library throughout the entire curriculum and include the teacher-librarian in the curriculum decision-making."

Indeed, principals are quite knowledgeable concerning the basic school curriculum, but they also need exposure to the information retrieval curriculum that is an ongoing part of the library resource center program. With this knowledge, they can more fully understand the library resource center's impact on the total school curriculum.

5.   To ensure scheduling for optimum use of the resource center:

Teacher-librarian and principal comments indicate that by becoming more aware of the functions of school library resource centers, principals may better understand the need for flexible scheduling. Scheduling determines the use of and thereby the influence the library resource center will have upon the school, the curriculum and the student. It determines whether the materials are put to their optimal use by students and teachers. Unfortunately, as a library supervisor noted: "Many of the principals and teachers expect the library to be operated in the same manner as when they were students." In most cases, this results in traditional scheduling, whereby the classroom teachers bring their classes into the library resource center at least once a week to check out books and for skills. Since the students are admitted to the center only with their class, this form of scheduling is the least responsive to student and teacher needs.

On the other hand, flexible scheduling encourages students and classes to come into the resource center at times of particular need. Allowing this individualized daily access into the resource center to select and check out materials at all times promotes optimum learning. Class time in the resource center is directly related to teaching or reinforcing information skills and applying these skills to classroom work. Optimum learning occurs when there is an opportunity for practicing the newly acquired skill (Karpisek, 1989). With this in mind, principals and teacher-librarians must work together to develop flexible scheduling so that teachers can schedule classes according to project and unit needs rather than the availability of the teacher-librarian.

6.   To better understand developments in information technology:

Many principals are unfamiliar with the technological advances that have taken place in library resource centers in the past five years. Exposure to technology for the resource center should focus upon computerized cataloging systems for retrieving information about the collection, computerized management systems which enable efficient circulation and record keeping, and the new AV equipment and software available to support the curriculum. Several of the teacher-librarians in the study who commented that "principals need to keep up with the advances in information technology," added that this knowledge could result in their "allocating a larger budget to the library," as well as better "understanding the wide range of knowledge which teacher-librarians must have."

What Principals Need to Know

B. What specifically do principals need to know concerning library resource centers?

1.   The school library resource center standards and guidelines.

2.   The place of the resource center in the total school program.

3.   The available computer and AV technology in the resource center.

4.   Routine tasks performed daily by teacher-librarians.

5.   The certification requirements for teacher-librarians.

Comments by principals and teacher-librarians in the survey suggested that principals should become more knowledgeable concerning five major areas related to school library resource centers. A discussion based on the comments of these five areas follows:

1.   The school library resource center standards and guidelines:

Familiarity with *Information power: Guidelines for school library media programs* as well as the state and regional standards and guidelines for school library resource centers, will provide the principal with a means of comparing his or her school's resource center to others in the nation or state. At the same time, it gives the school a direction or plan to move toward in the future. Additionally, these standards and guidelines address the partnership idea and discuss the three basic roles of the teacher-librarian within the school: information specialist, teacher and instructional consultant. Such information will aid the principal in hiring teacher-librarians, as well as offering an effective evaluation procedure.

2.   The place of the resource center in the total school program:

One principal with 15 years' experience commented: "Principals need to realize the library of the late '80s and '90s is not what it was a decade ago." Another principal noted that a principal "must see how the learning resources center fits into the total school's program and the mission of the school." As mentioned earlier, however, comments by some teacher-librarians emphasized that they are not included in curriculum planning, and they stressed their desires for principals to recognize all they can do for the total school program.

Familiarity with the guidelines and standards, attendance at library conferences and discussions with teacher-librarians can help principals more fully recognize how the library resource center should fit into the total school program.

3. The available computer and AV technology in the resource center:

Computer and AV technology have resulted in many positive changes for the resource centers of the 1990s, but with these changes comes expense. Principals should become acquainted with the various computerized systems for managing a library, as well as the computerized catalog system. As principals examine the indexes and encyclopedias available on CD-ROM, they will come to realize the tremendous impact computers have on reference work. Even if funding is not available at this point for computerized systems, the principal will be familiar with the advantages and costs of such systems and can plan for the future.

The role of audiovisual technology in curriculum development cannot be overlooked. By becoming aware of the new software available to support and enrich the areas of science, math, social studies and English/language arts, principals can move toward higher level technology in their schools. This knowledge will aid in budgeting and planning for the future.

4. Routine tasks performed daily by teacher-librarians:

Principal and teacher-librarian comments indicate that principals expect teacher-librarians to teach information skills and to check out books. But what about all those other routine tasks that must take place in order for the resource center to operate efficiently? Teacher-librarians voiced their desire for principals to recognize the tasks they perform daily that go unnoticed, yet take up an enormous amount of time. Although principals recognize that part of a teacher-librarian's duty includes selecting and ordering books, teacher-librarians wonder if principals really realize the amount of time it takes for the teacher-librarian to keep up with the latest books through reading reviews and articles, and attending conferences and in-services; how much time is spent organizing files in which faculty and students have offered suggestions for needed books and materials; how much time is spent checking bibliographic data and completing order forms. Principals need to see what is involved in getting new materials onto the shelves and filing the catalog cards or entering them on the computer, managing the volunteer program, circulating and maintaining the materials, helping students select books to meet needs, working with teachers to identify materials for specific units, and programming special events. By having a general idea of the teacher-librarian's duties, the principal may be more receptive to a larger resource center budget and to hiring additional staff members.

5. The certification requirements for teacher-librarians:

Eighty-seven percent of the campuses surveyed indicated there was at least one full time teacher-librarian on staff. While this is an encouraging percentage, it is discouraging to note that the remainder of the campuses surveyed were staffed by part-time librarians, aides and volunteers. Schools served by such an arrangement clearly are not meeting the recommendations of *Information power.* Campuses that staff their library resource centers with volunteers and part-time assistants cannot be offering the maximum use of their library facilities.

While principals are familiar with the state certification requirements for teacher-librarians, many are unaware of the course work involved in their preparation. Most states require teacher-librarians to hold a teaching certificate and take graduate course work in literature, selection of materials, administration, audiovisual selection and production, reference, computers, cataloging, as well as the completion of an internship to obtain library certification. To prepare teacher-librarians for their roles as information specialist, teacher and instructional consultant, most universities include in their courses topics such as curriculum across grade levels, intellectual freedom, copyright laws, selecting good literature, teaching information retrieval skills and managing a resource center. Principals need to be familiar with the educational preparation a teacher-librarian brings to the job.

Furthering the Partnership

C. How can principals become more familiar with the management and function of school library resource centers?

Comments by principals and teacher-librarians to the second question in the survey provide ideas for practical steps in furthering the partnership between the two professionals. This second question asked both groups: "Should the management and function of school libraries be a part of the school principal's training?" An overwhelming 90% of the teacher-librarians agreed that it should be part of their training, and 78% of the principals also agreed that it should be a part of their training. The comments provide us with three alternatives for familiarizing principals with school library resource centers:

1.   During university course work.

2.   Through in-service, seminars and training at state or district level.

3.   Through actual on-job experience.

Based upon comments received on the survey forms, a discussion concerning each of these alternatives follows:

1.   During university course work:

The majority of the principals (78%) and teacher-librarians (90%) agreed that better training of principals at the university level concerning the school library resource center is a top priority. One principal states: "I can't remember any class in college that dealt with libraries and their management." Most principals and teacher-librarians agreed that the course work should not be in-depth. They went on to say that the principals' course work is already so heavy that the topic of school libraries does not warrant a whole

course. However, it could be integrated into several of the existing university courses for principals. Topics should include an overview of the activities that take place in the library resource center. Information on print and nonprint materials that are available to resource centers and their cost, state and national standards, AV technology, computer systems, the teacher-librarian's role—these are just a few of the topics respondents mentioned that could be integrated into university course work for principals.

Respondents to the survey offered three means of integrating school libraries into the university course work: integration into the administration class for principals, providing training during the principals' internship and imparting the knowledge at the teacher training level.

Information concerning school library resource centers would certainly fit into the administration course required for future principals. Respondents in the survey suggested several methods of integrating valuable knowledge of resource centers into this course. "During the course of their training principals should visit a number of school libraries at various levels." These field trips could be integrated into the administration course for future principals. Such on-site experiences will provide future principals with an opportunity to discuss topics of concern with teacher-librarians, examine the computer technology, become acquainted with various library philosophies and gain a better idea of how the library resource center fits into the total school. Exposure to library resource centers in a variety of settings, including exemplary schools, will help future principals set goals and realistic expectations for their own future library resource centers.

Respondents to the survey also suggested that perhaps a block of classes during administration courses could be devoted to school libraries. This could include at least six hours of class time focusing upon the teacher-librarian's role and how a library resource center should fit into the school program. This would be an ideal time to include visits by practicing teacher-librarians and perhaps their principals to answer any questions concerning school libraries.

Others involved in the survey suggested that the universities provide experience with school library resource centers during the internship for principals. In order "to get a feel for the wide range of duties a librarian has," future principals would find spending several days in a library resource center enlightening. This time could be spent on the job with the teacher-librarian, who could answer any questions and point out the difficulties encountered in the routine day.

Principalship seminars during the internship should include visits by teacher-librarians and representatives from computer, AV and trade book companies. Short presentations by teacher-librarians and material representatives can acquaint future principals with the role of the teacher-librarian, the way the learning resource center fits into the total school program, and the various print and nonprint materials and equipment available for the collection.

Other survey comments emphasized the importance for universities to impart the knowledge at the teacher training level. They pointed to the lack of library knowledge on the part of teachers as well as principals. "There is a need to train candidates for teaching degrees in using the school library. Colleges should place more emphasis on the library than they do." Additionally, another insightful teacher-librarian observed that "many principals begin as teachers, and there's little information given to teachers about school libraries." This appears to be an area in which all universities and schools of education fall short. Why not make certain all qualified teachers are knowledgeable concerning school library resource centers? Visits to school library resource centers, lectures on library resource centers and visits to education classes by teacher-librarians could be integrated into teacher training courses, particularly student teaching. The field experience for student teachers could consist of a required period in the library resource center to better understand the way a library resource center fits into the total program.

2.   Through in-service, seminars and training at state or district level:

Others responding to the survey noted that aside from university course work, principals can become more knowledgeable about library resource centers by attending workshops and in-services. For example, the state of Georgia requires that principals take a two-day training session. As mentioned earlier, the teacher-librarians and principals from Georgia who responded to the survey indicated that the training session was successful. Other states may want to consider this Georgia model. Some respondents noted that rather than being required by the state, workshop or in-service needs should be left up to the various school districts.

3.   Through actual on-job experience:

Several principals noted that "a person develops these skills with actual job knowledge." Yet, the comments from the teacher-librarians indicate that due to their heavy responsibilities, principals seldom have time to become acquainted with what really goes on in the resource center. Both principals and teacher-librarians involved in the study stressed that ideally the best way for principals to learn about school library resource centers is through their own teacher-librarians. As one principal aptly put it: "The librarian can communicate this expertise to the principal."

Many teacher-librarians involved in the study commented that they have been busy helping inform their principals. A teacher-librarian summed it all up in one sentence: "One of our primary responsibilities is to inform our principals of what a quality library needs to have and be." Another insightful teacher-librarian commented: "My principal has learned a great deal through my gentle informing." Others went on to say that even if universities assume the responsibility of educating the principals, teacher-librarians must continue to provide knowledge about the library and the teacher-librarian's role in the school.

A need for ongoing dialogue was emphasized by both groups of professionals. Given the limited amount of time available, the teacher-librarian and the principal must make a concerted effort to communicate on a regular basis as to the needs, activities and involvement of the library. This is where real change will take place.

Based on comments of both principals and teacher-librarians, the researchers found that principals need some background training in school libraries. If the partnership idea emphasized in

Comments from Teacher-Librarians Responding to Survey	Comments from Principals Responding to Survey
"All you need is good communication between the two parties."	"Too many principals delegate librarians to status of clerk."
"My principal has learned a great deal through my gentle informing."	"If we are expected to evaluate, we need the training."
"Principals don't have a clue as to what really goes on in a library."	"A principal must see how the learning resources center fits into the total school's program and the mission of the school."
"Greater knowledge in libraries may lead to greater support."	"No, I do not feel we have adequate knowledge of school libraries when leaving the university."
"They need to know what things we do."	"A person develops these skills with actual job knowledge."
"Until principals give us the respect we need, our roles in curriculum development and budget development will be nonexistent."	"I can't remember any class in college that dealt with libraries and their management."
"They have no idea of the responsibilities of a librarian or of the role in the school."	"If someone could develop a class that would be practical it would help the principal and his school."
"How can they oversee such an important part of a school as the library program if they don't understand it?"	"It always helps to hire a good librarian who can help guide the principal."
"Many principals begin as teachers, and there's little information given to teachers about school libraries."	"If librarians are properly trained, all this isn't necessary."
"I believe that until colleges and universities require their student teachers and principals to take some well-designed courses in their programs, an eternal battle for helping students will be fought. Teachers will not know how to use a library and principals will not see the need."	"I chose a good person and I feel comfortable in empowering her to do what she has professionalized herself to do."

Information power is to be attained, universities that train principals must take a leadership position in providing future administrators with that knowledge. Meanwhile, teacher-librarians must breach the communication barriers between teacher-librarians and administrators, and partially assume the training responsibilities.

The plan as derived from comments by both professional groups accomplishes this. Through emphasis upon school libraries during university course work, by attending workshops and in-services at state and local level, and by gaining knowledge from their own teacher-librarians, principals and teacher-librarians can move closer to the partnership envisioned in *Information power*.

References

American Association of School Librarians (AASL) and Association for Educational Communications Technology (AECT). (1988). *Information power: Guidelines for school library media programs.* Chicago: American Association of School Librarians and Association for Educational Communications Technology.

Dickinson, G. (1991). Look to the library. [Letter to the editor]. *Phi Delta Kappan, 72,* 644–645.

Karpisek, M. (1989). *Policymaking for school library media programs.* Chicago: American Library Association.

Swart, E. (1990). So, you want to be a professional? *Phi Delta Kappan, 72,* 318.

CHAPTER THIRTY THREE

Communication Skills and Strategies for Teacher-Librarians

Barbara Howlett

Cooperative program planning and teaching techniques between the classroom teacher and the teacher-librarian constitute an effective method for the teacher-librarian to be more directly involved in the instructional process. However, the professional literature reveals that teacher-librarians must overcome a variety of negative perceptions about their role before they can become completely accepted as professional teachers in their own right. Hambleton (1979) found, for example, that "the school library seems to play only a marginal role in the total education program, and that the low regard for the school librarian militates against a direct involvement in the instructional program of the school" (p. 5). Participants in a survey conducted by Casciano-Savignano (1976) identified several common impediments to cooperative relationships between teachers and teacher-librarians. These include lack of awareness of teacher-librarians in the school program, defensiveness by teacher-librarians regarding the use of the library, lack of understanding of the role of the teacher-librarian, and lack of frequent contact with the teacher-librarian. Suggestions made to remedy these problems almost all involved increased contact and improved communication between teachers and teacher-librarians.

It is evident that teacher-librarians must improve their image and the perception of their role within the school community. One way to accomplish this is to study different models of successful communication and to apply basic principles to develop better intraschool relations. There are several ways to facilitate communication between teachers and teacher-librarians which, in turn, should aid in developing more favorable relations and increased cooperation. These areas include those personality traits that lead to positive and effective communication, the development of improved interpersonal skills, and the cultivation of certain "selling skills" that help to promote services offered by the teacher-librarian.

Of primary importance to the teacher-librarian's success in promoting the resource center is a sense of confidence. It is essential that the teacher-librarian believe in the role of the teacher-librarian. Having confidence in the worth of the service will inspire the confidence of others; commitment will help sell it to the rest of the school. The confident teacher-librarian will make overtures, and will not be discouraged by rebuffs. It takes strength and a solid self-concept to survive the rejections that are experienced in approaching other teachers.

The teacher-librarian might also be less cautious in interaction with other staff members. Risks must be taken in introducing new ideas and concepts; the teacher-librarian must not be inhibited by any reticence or hesitation to "force" himself or herself on others. Both Hambleton (1979) and Blair (1978) comment on the effects of cautiousness in teacher-librarians. Hambleton states that "cautiousness may be partly responsible for the lack of cohesiveness within the library group...and the tendency to perform most often those tasks that relate to library expertise rather than those which involve the librarian in the teaching program" (p. 7). In her study she also found low cautiousness scores to be associated with high effectiveness scores. Blair notes that one of the best predictors of high circulation of materials is extroversion. One of the prime characteristics of extroversion is less cautiousness.

A third personality trait that makes for successful cooperative interaction is "communicativeness." The effective communicator is vocal, willing to speak up to convey ideas and attitudes, to support them, to see that they are carried out, and to advertise their eventual success. The teacher-librarian must also be proficient in organizing written communication, preparing briefs, articles and reports. Providing inservice programs is another important aspect of a teacher-librarian's communicativeness. Workshops and in-service sessions are essential in "getting the message across." As well, informed conversations over coffee provide a valuable means of communicating with teachers. Blair (1978) notes the great influence that such informal conversations have on teacher use of the library. Above all, effective communication necessitates being visible and getting involved!

The successful promotion of the resource center will also involve innovative programs and novel approaches which tend to capture the imagination of others, and often may succeed where other concerted, though perhaps less creative, efforts have failed. In seeking access to a teaching partnership, it is important to have fresh ideas and a diversity of interests to explore. Of interest here is Hambleton's (1979) observation that "school librarians rated high on both original thinking and cautiousness" (p. 7). Her hypothesis was that although teacher-librarians had original ideas, they were prevented from implementing them because of their extreme cautiousness. Clearly this is not the route to improved teacher/teacher-librarian cooperation.

A further characteristic which enhances the effectiveness of teacher-librarian interaction is determination or drive. A teacher-librarian may possess desirable personality traits, but unless he or she is persistent in practicing them, they will be of little benefit. It is difficult to overstate the importance of such assertiveness in the teacher-librarian's role. Although one must not, of course, become aggressive and hence offensive, to be determined in pursuing the goals of the program is both worthwhile and admirable.

In order to counteract low sociability, teacher-librarians must increase their efforts to be cheerful and friendly, to establish a pleasant and inviting atmosphere in their libraries, and to encourage teacher input in connection with both programs and facilities. Teacher-librarians should concentrate on being a part of the social aspect of school life and avoid sealing themselves off in isolation as too many seem prone to do.

Interpersonal Skills

Teacher-librarians tend to achieve low scores on measures of personal relations as compared to scores on other traits. A need, then, seems to exist for improved interpersonal relations between teacher-librarians and those with whom they interact. The very nature of the phrase "cooperative program planning and teaching" implies the use of interpersonal skills in the achievement of cooperation, as the essence of an interpersonal relationship involves "working cooperatively to achieve...goals" (Egan, 1976, p. 26). Egan goes on to say that "successful interaction requires the development of effective interpersonal skills" (p. 17). These skills are important in helping the individual to "develop feelings of interpersonal competence" and in enabling him or her to "establish effective working relationships."

Interpersonal skills may be roughly grouped into two areas—the skills of letting yourself be known, and the skills of responding. The former group involves the specific skills of self-disclosure, concreteness, and the expression of feeling; the latter encompasses listening and responding techniques, empathy, acceptance, warmth, and trust. Openness, spontaneity, and authenticity characterize both skills of expression and skills of response.

Self-disclosure involves revealing thoughts, attitudes, beliefs and feelings so that others may come to know us as we really are. The key to effective self-disclosure lies in not over-disclosing (talking too much about oneself, or talking too intimately in a casual situation), or underdisclosing (talking too little or not at all about oneself, even when the situation calls for it). The person who wishes to communicate effectively in a casual social setting with co-workers would be moderately self-disclosing, revealing enough to establish social relationships, but not enough to be threatening or offensive. Concreteness involves speaking about specific experiences and feelings rather than speaking vaguely or in abstractions. The latter creates distance between the speaker and the person with whom he or she is communicating. If self-disclosure is to be effective and immediate it must be concrete. Feelings and emotions arise in any interpersonal interaction and their proper expression must be considered. Interpersonal skills emphasize an open expression of honest feelings; they should not be disguised or repressed, but neither should they be manufactured for effect. Whether emotions are positive or negative, they can be expressed constructively, and although they are often difficult to verbalize (since their expression involves a degree of risk) emotional assertiveness "allows for emotional ventilation, (while leaving) the doors of communication open" (Egan, 1976, p. 75).

The skills of responding have a great effect on the success of interpersonal relationships. These involve practicing effective listening and responding techniques, and communicating empathy, acceptance, warmth and trust. The teacher-librarian who is skilled in these techniques will find it much easier to involve another teacher in an instructional partnership.

The aim of communicative interaction is to demonstrate understanding of the other. However, before this can occur, effective listening must have taken place. Effective listening involves attending to what is being said and not engaging in any peripheral activities. In demonstrating this attention, one adopts a posture of involvement, facing the speaker squarely, leaning towards him or her, maintaining eye contact, and above all, being relaxed. Such careful attention is far more likely to make an impact on the other person than a half-hearted attempt to listen. In effective listening, it is important to attend to both verbal and nonverbal behavior, for response must be to the words. Samovar states that "what a receiver sees guides his understanding of what he hears" and conversely, from the sender's viewpoint, "visual feedback clues sent by the receiver provide an invaluable index to the effect of the message" (quoted in Cathcart, 1970, p. 287).

Once effective listening has taken place, and understanding achieved, proper response techniques come into play. According to Barbour (1974), responses may be confirming or disconfirming. It is important, of course, to endeavor to provide confirming responses to someone who is communicating with you. Techniques of confirming include "direct acknowledgment, agreement about content, supportive responses, clarifying responses (those that elaborate on what has been said by asking for more information) and expressions of positive feeling" (pp. 32–33). To be avoided are such disconfirming reactions as impervious, irrelevant, impersonal, incoherent, or incongruous responses.

The communication of a listener's empathy, acceptance, warmth and eventual trust are all closely related responding skills. Empathy involves the listener's ability to understand another individual—to interpret correctly his or her feelings, beliefs, and attitudes. It gets at not only what another person states, but also what is implied or left unstated. To communicate empathy, one must create a climate of support, not feigning understanding, answering with a question or cliché, restating what the other person has said, or jumping in too quickly.

Leading from empathy, and essential to it, is acceptance. In addition to being understood, it is necessary for the speaker to feel accepted. If the speaker feels warmly regarded, he or she is much more likely to communicate with the listener in a genuine and relaxed manner. Acceptance and warmth gradually develop and eventually lead to trust, an essential ingredient in all interpersonal relationships. According to Griffin, a listener develops trust in a speaker according to his or her perception of the speaker's expertness, character, good will, dynamism, and personal attraction (quoted in Barbour, 1974, p. 29). Kaul and Schmidt found that "a person is trusted if he respects the needs and feelings of others, offers information and opinions for the benefit of others, generates feelings of comfort and willingness to confide, and is open and honest about his motives" (quoted in Egan, 1976, p. 139). Trust is such an essential ingredient in interpersonal relationships because in its absence very little communication will occur; no one is willing to take the risks involved. Clearly, if a teacher-librarian can communicate such empathy, acceptance, warmth and finally trust to another teacher, he or she is well on the way to achieving that elusive cooperative relationship.

Despite the best of intentions, and the most accomplished interpersonal communicative skills, occasions will arise where conflict and opposition will occur. The teacher-librarian must be aware of such problems, and be prepared to deal with them effectively. According to Robinson (1979), interpersonal conflict among coworkers often stems from jealousy, rivalry, or a personality conflict. He recommends approaching the problem positively, with the first step being to identify the source of the conflict. Try to operate from the other person's frame of reference to attempt to understand and resolve the negative aspects of the situation. Try to be constructive and positive, realizing that often it

is not necessarily a "bad" characteristic of the other person that is the source of the conflict, but how that person makes one feel—inadequate, awkward, etc.

Opposition to cooperative program planning and teaching is encountered by every teacher-librarian upon some occasion. A teacher may be reluctant to give up total control of students in order to create a team teaching relationship. Seyfarth (1978) found that "teachers moving from a self-contained into a team teaching situation...are attracted by the chance to take part in a new type of program...but at the same time they are reluctant to surrender the freedom of action inherent in the self-contained classroom" (p. 297). The teacher-librarian should try to anticipate problems with this type of attitude and endeavor to deal with them before attempting to implement a cooperative program. Teachers must be reassured that the teacher-librarian is sincerely interested in helping the classroom teacher to attain mutually agreed upon objectives, and not in taking control. Since the success of the entire cooperative teaching process depends upon the classroom teacher's favorable attitude, the importance of overcoming this kind of opposition cannot be overemphasized.

No one technique is likely to solve all conflicts, or counteract all the types of opposition that a teacher-librarian will come up against, but sensitivity combined with a knowledge of problem-solving techniques, and a competence in basic interpersonal communication skills will go a long way toward their resolution.

Selling the Service

A field much concerned with the presentation and promotion of products, ideas, and services is that of marketing. The teacher-librarian would do well to study sales techniques and incorporate them into efforts to "sell" a program of cooperative program planning and teaching to the classroom teacher. These include having a thorough knowledge of the product or service to be sold, using the tools of effective communication, being persuasive and knowing how to cope with resistance and objections.

In any sales presentation, good "product" knowledge is an indispensable asset. Only by being well prepared in advance, and having developed some expertise in the knowledge of the product or service to be sold, can a sales person expect to communicate its advantages. As well, the product must be explained in terms meaningful to potential customers. Most products and services have both features and benefits. A feature is "a desirable characteristic that is inherent in the product or in its performance" (Seng, 1977, p. 23). However, people don't buy a product for its features, rather they buy what the features of the product will do for them, or its benefits. A benefit is a "definable advantage, improvement, or satisfaction customers acquire or experience that derives from a feature of the product they buy" (Seng, 1977, p. 24). So it is the benefits to the customer that must be concentrated on in the acquisition of product knowledge. The teacher-librarian, in selling programs to the staff, must prepare a case well, and make sure that it is the advantages that accrue from cooperative program planning and teaching that are being emphasized.

Effective communication is as important a skill in sales as it is in interpersonal interaction. Sales communication, however, tends to emphasize the effective presentation of an idea, the communication of a message rather than concern itself primarily with the interpersonal aspects of a given situation. Of course, the interpersonal skills such as showing empathy, interest and listening attentively will come into play, but a salesperson is chiefly concerned with other aspects of communication such as presenting himself or herself and the product or service clearly, and using varied and effective selling tools—visual presentations—to reinforce the appeal of the product or service being offered. Certain principles of communication common in the establishment of good public sales relations are useful to anyone who is attempting to communicate the benefits of a service.

The audience should be preconditioned to receive favorably the service that is being promoted. As in the case of reassuring the classroom teacher who is reluctant to share control of the class, considerable advance groundwork promoting the benefits of the service will increase its chances of a favorable reception upon presentation. Once the audience has been prepared for the presentation, it is then important to tailor the message and the means of its communication to the predisposition of the intended audience. (The term "audience" as used here denotes any number of listeners from one to a large group.) The message should not be a one way outpouring of facts and information, but a two way communication with opportunities for audience interaction and participation. It should also stress positive benefits for the "customer," recognizing and dealing with the self-interest motive, the "what's in it for me?" attitude that is an essential and constructive component in selling a service. The presenter of the message must take care to speak the receiver's language, and to keep the presentation within the context of the interests and experience of those toward which it is directed.

Having devised an appropriate message and the means of delivering it, the next concern involves the audience to whom it should first be presented. It has been found effective in sales and public relations (Marston, 1979) to approach first those who are sympathetic to your views and who may be in a position to influence others. The satisfied customer is the greatest selling tool. The teacher-librarian who can reach and convince one or two key staff members probably won't have to sell others on the value of the program—they will do it. A final principle important in sales communication is that of repetition. It takes a long time for a message to get through to busy people who are involved with many different concerns. The message must be repeated often (in a variety of ways so as to avoid boredom or irritation) until it makes an impression on its intended audience. Sometimes the very repetition of a message creates a tendency toward belief—it gradually becomes accepted as true.

The art of being persuasive is inseparable from the art of selling. The whole sales "pitch"—the approach, the presentation, the close—is an act of persuading the prospect that a need exists and then motivating him or her to take action to fill that need. Learning certain principles of persuasion techniques will better equip teacher-librarians to convince other staff members of the value of their programs. It is important first to present the problem, then its solution. If this is done in the reverse order, it is not always easy to understand the solution's relevance because a need has not yet been established.

Studies in the art of persuasion have found that an audience is more receptive to the persuasive appeal if points that all agree upon are discussed first, before moving to any items of disagreement (Burgoon, 1974). Similarly, positive arguments can be discussed and refuted. "When people hear supporting arguments first, they become persuaded by those arguments and are, therefore, closer to the position of the source" (Burgoon, 1974, p. 57). One other variable that has been found to affect the persuasiveness of a message is the intensity of language used in its communication. For example, a program that will "drastically reduce" a teacher's marking load for an assignment sounds more appealing than one that will "decrease" or "cut down on" the marking load. Other ways of intensifying language are by inserting qualifiers such as "certainly," and by using metaphors to dramatize a description or comparison.

Like the salesperson who regularly comes up against resistance and objections, the teacher-librarian will also need to use good interpersonal skills and conflict management techniques to overcome opposition to innovations. There are also effective sales techniques that can overcome objections. First of all, however, it is worth noting that objections do not necessarily constitute a refusal to accept the proposal being offered. Often objections are to be welcomed, as they at least indicate that the proposal is being thought about, and provide feedback as to where, in the eyes of others, its potential problems lie.

In handling resistance, it is important to safeguard the other's pride, and exonerate him or her from any blame for expressing an objection. You might accept part of the objection, and make a concession before trying to overcome it. Most sources that deal with sales methods for overcoming resistance agree on some basic techniques. One tactic is to give validity to the objection but detract attention from it by pointing out other features or benefits of the proposal that offset or compensate for it. A variation of this technique is to agree, then convert the objection into a reason for accepting the proposal. Another suggestion is to treat the objection as a question, agreeing that it is a good question which should be dealt with. Sometimes it is possible to postpone answering an objection, or to avoid it entirely, especially if it is somewhat frivolous. Finally, it is even possible upon occasion to make a direct denial of an objection. This technique should be used with caution and usually only when the objection voiced is completely untrue, or is personally derogatory in some way.

In an effort to engage the classroom teacher in a teaching partnership or to maintain that partnership, the teacher-librarian can (if self-confident, creative, determined and skilled at communication and less cautious!) make use of an almost unlimited number of strategies. Some of these strategies reflect the acquisition of interpersonal communication skills, others, a mastery of sales techniques. Some are designed to advertise the library and improve public relations, others are specifically intended to demonstrate to the teacher that the teacher-librarian is willing and able to share in teaching. Some involve personal interaction; others are visual, oral and written. All will be useful in developing effective cooperative program planning and teaching programs with the classroom teacher.

Specific Suggestions

Blair (1978) found that at least three techniques, if practiced by the teacher-librarian, had a positive effect on the degree of resource center use. One of these strategies involves working with the teacher in cooperative curriculum planning (visiting classrooms, observing programs, assisting in curriculum development, providing consultative assistance for teachers, helping the teacher select materials, assisting in student assessment). Another practice is to provide in-service by disseminating information from professional journals, conducting orientation for new staff members, utilizing and producing instructional materials, and demonstrating the services and equipment that are available. A third method was to involve teachers in the selection and evaluation of resources.

Hoffman (1980), like Blair, recommends "encourag[ing] the interest, support and participation of others in the selection and use of materials" (p. 32). Also important in her eyes is the need to relate to students, fellow teachers, administrators, and parents by soliciting their suggestions, keeping them informed, and thanking them for their cooperation. Various methods of publicizing the library in the community include inviting school board members and parents to visit on special occasions, displaying student designed bookmarks in local bookstores, informing bookstore owners of popular titles so that they may be stocked, and offering information on activities to local newspapers. Hoffman (1980) suggests that it is important in successful library program promotion to "build your relationships long before you need them" (p. 35).

At a workshop on communication, members of the Ontario Library Association School Libraries Division (1973) made several recommendations. Personal techniques of communication involve the teacher-librarian being visible, available, having an open door policy, inviting teachers and parents to the library, holding staff meetings in the library, encouraging non-library happenings in the resource center, knowing key personnel, and participating in in-service presentations for staff. Further suggestions indicate that the teacher-librarian who wants to interact effectively with the school staff should smile (!), visit the staff room frequently, encourage social contact, invite feedback from teachers, and be positive. In connection with the teacher-librarian's instructional role, recommended practices include attending department meetings, keeping in touch with outside resources, visiting teachers in their classrooms, discussing new curricula, and offering one to one assistance to teachers.

The visual and aural strategies include displaying notices, posters or calendars of coming events, and graffiti boards, producing bulletin boards or displays in showcases, film festivals and slide/tape presentations of activities, showing new materials to departments and advertising positive results attained in library programs.

Graphic techniques of communication again chiefly promote the service offered by the library, only this time in written or pictorial form. Resource lists for staff and student handbooks, reports on service, letters to parents, surveys of student and teacher interest, and questionnaires to parents about library services are all suggested tactics for advertising some of the library's important functions.

Other miscellaneous methods of communication include having a coffee pot in the library to encourage informal visits and chats, installing a suggestion box in the library or staff room, getting involved with other programs in the school, planning wine and cheese or "coffee and goodie" meetings, displaying new resources, and holding orientations for new staff and students.

Teacher-librarians are bound to encounter conflict, resistance, and objections in their efforts to establish or improve communications with teachers. Various skills for countering such opposition have been suggested, and these will prove of value in coping with difficult encounters. However, more specific strategies to follow in dealing with unapproachable teachers may further clarify the steps to be taken. When having problems communicating with a teacher, it might prove useful to offer assistance in a concrete way by making your own suggestions. Sometimes an invitation to come in for coffee might have profitable dividends, or promoting materials to the students of the class might cause a difficult teacher to seek your aid. Ideal occasions to try some of these approaches occur in the staff room—informally, at the beginning of a new project, or after the receipt of particularly useful new materials. And remember at all times to be friendly, diplomatic and complimentary!

Only by striving to develop assertive personality traits, by learning and practicing effective interpersonal and sales communication techniques, and by employing specific strategies designed to facilitate teacher/teacher-librarian interaction, can the teacher-librarian hope to be successful in efforts to establish a meaningful and productive program of cooperative planning and teaching in the school. To quote Hambleton (1979) again, "Communication...will not take place...without a realization...that both teaching and learning go on in a school library, that the school librarian makes an important contribution to the intellectual and social growth of the student, and that this contribution is possible because of an expertise which effectively blends librarianship and teaching skills. This will be realized only when that expertise is both practiced and effectively communicated in such a way that it becomes recognized as a necessary part of the educational enterprise" (p. 7).

References

Barbour, A. (1974). *Interpersonal communication: Teaching strategies and resources.* Urbana, IL: ERIC Clearinghouse on Reading and Communication Skills.

Blair, S. (1978). Teachers and the school resource centre. *Canadian Library Journal, 35(2),* 93–100.

Burgoon, M., Heston, J. & McCroskey, J. (1974). *Small group communication: A functional approach.* New York: Holt, Reinhart and Winston.

Casciano-Savignano, C. (1976). Interpersonal relationships in secondary schools. *NASSP Bulletin. 60(399),* 26–30.

Cathcart, R. & Samovar, L. (Eds.). (1970). *Small group communication: A reader.* Dubuque, IA: Brown.

Egan, G. (1976). *Interpersonal living.* Monterey, CA: Brooks/Cole.

Hambleton, A. (1979). Static in the educational intercom: Conflict and the school librarian. *Emergency Librarian, 6(5–6),* 5–7.

Hoffman, E. P. (1980). The art of public relations. *School Media Quarterly 9(1),* 31–35.

Kinder, J. Jr., Kinder, G. & Staubach, R. (1981). *Winning strategies in selling.* Englewood Cliffs, NJ: Prentice-Hall.

Marston, J. (1979). *Modern public relations.* New York: McGraw-Hill.

Nbegan, M. (1979). Coping with conflict in educational circles. *Thrust for Educational Leadership, 9(2),* 25–27.

Ontario Library Association. School Libraries Division. (1973). *Communication with administration, teachers, students, and community.* Toronto: The Division.

Reid, A. (1975). *Modern applied salesmanship.* Pacific Palisades, CA: Goodyear.

Robinson, L. (1979). How to cope with people you dislike. *Ebony, XXXIV(5),* 135–44.

Seng, R. (1977). *The skills of selling.* New York: Amacom.

Seyfarth, J. & Canady, R. (1978). Assessing causes of teacher attitudes toward team teaching. *Education, 98(3),* 297–300.

Taylor, D. (1969). Cooperation: Teacher-librarian style. *Elementary English 46(1),* 66–68.

PART SEVEN

ACCOUNTABILITY

There are several elements to being accountable as a teacher-librarian. One is providing research evidence for the value and validity of one's program and services, particularly as they affect the quality of experiences that teachers and students have in schools and how they impact student achievement. Another is providing the tools necessary for the assessment of the program and thus of the contributions of each of the partners as well—school district, principal, teacher and teacher-librarian. Certainly the program is larger than the single teacher-librarian most often charged with its development and management. Having said that, however, it behooves the teacher-librarian to work with administrators to determine priorities for program delivery and perceptions of the degree of their implementation in the school.

As a district administrator, Bev Anderson was asked by a new superintendent how the library resource center program could be justified in tight economic times. Using attitude and skill measures, Anderson and her colleagues undertook a research project to determine baseline services in elementary, junior high and senior high school libraries and their impact on teaching and learning. The findings and conclusions supported the significance of the school library media program and a more coordinated and consistent approach across the school district. Although a dated study today, Anderson exemplifies the importance of undertaking school and district research and of letting others hear our success stories.

Doris Epler provides suggestions for aligning evaluation tools with national guidelines and standards to enable teacher-librarians and others to assess areas requiring attention and development. At the school level, Linda Rafuse and Ruth Law provide an approach based on levels of implementation of key factors for an effective program. Closer to our personal and professional role and responsibility is a model for the evaluation of the teacher-librarian using the school, district or state professional association's role description. Here the principal and teacher-librarian discuss relative priorities for time and attention and then examine how these priorities are translated into action. If nothing else, this instrument opens the door to improved and increased dialogue to ensure that administrators are aware of our work and its effect.

None of these approaches will be completely appropriate for your situation. They need to be revised and adapted so that they match your needs. However, the principles on which they are based and the approaches that are proposed have proven useful to hundreds of your colleagues and will support and enhance the implementation of *Information Power: Building Partnerships for Learning* (ALA, 1998). Similarly, Susan Casey closes by reminding us that the best of intentions need to be tempered by reality; in her case she undertook an examination of what she was doing and whether it met her expectations; from there, she could monitor and adjust and continue to improve, the best possible approach for a reflective practitioner and professional teacher-librarian.

CHAPTER THIRTY FOUR

School Libraries— Definitely Worth Their Keep

Bev Anderson

When dollars are devoted to school library services, is there corresponding value for students? An evaluation of school library programs in the Calgary (Alberta) Board of Education suggested that the answer is "Yes!" The evaluation project measured the extent of library service, the skill level and attitudes of students and the resource allocation and background characteristics of 65 sample schools. Findings indicated that when there was sufficient staff time and resource budget, teacher-librarians performed a role of school-based consultant and were able to provide audio-visual services. When this expanded role occurred, there was corresponding increase in student skills, positive student attitudes and assistance for teachers (Calgary Board of Education, 1981).

Background

In 1977, the Chief Superintendent of the Calgary Board of Education commissioned an evaluation of school library/resource center programs. The purpose of this evaluation was to investigate the question "Is the Board receiving sufficient value for the dollars that are/have been devoted to school resource services?" Specific direction was provided to include qualitative and quantitative data regarding the effects of resource services upon students. Rather than circulation statistics or reading preferences, the evaluation was to assess the relationship between provision of library service and learning outcomes for students.

The first phase of the evaluation was to establish baseline information about resource center programs. The second phase was to examine variations among programs and to assess their relative impact on schools. When dollars are devoted to school library services, is there corresponding value for students? There were two areas to explore: the role of teacher-librarians and the skill level and attitudes of students. To address the first area, a committee composed of the school principal, teacher-librarian, and two teachers in each school responded to the Liesener Inventory of Services (Liesener, 1973, 1974, 1976).

The Liesener inventory was selected not only because it has been extensively field tested, but also because it stands as a major authoritative instrument in school library evaluation. This inventory is a refinement of the Gaver inventory administered in Calgary in 1971 (Gaver, 1971). The inventory was used to describe the breadth of the resource center program through a description of its events. District staff personally administered each inventory to ensure consistent interpretation at a regularly controlled pace.

A locally developed attitude measure was designed to determine students' feelings about their resource centers through response to items such as:

Item 14: The library is a favorite place of mine in the school.

An elementary school research skills test was developed locally, based on the district's scope and sequence research chart. It was subsequently pilot tested in two elementary schools that were not to be participants in the project. A senior high school research skills test was based on one developed and field tested by a committee of school and district personnel.

For both attitude and skill measures, two Year Six classes and two Year Twelve classes were tested in each school, except in small elementary schools where there was only one Year Six class available. In each case, the tests were administered by district staff.

The above measures were used to gather quantitative data, which were then coupled with qualitative data gleaned from all of the schools sampled. This was done through detailed observation in a wide variety of school resource centers using goal-free observation techniques such as those described by Barry Macdonald (1974) at the University of East Anglia and Elliot Eisner (1973). An important consideration was that the past observations of the library media consultants could not be relied upon because those observations tended to be biased, as visits usually occurred on an individual basis.

Each case study involved a two-day observation period using unobtrusive observational techniques and interviews with students, classroom teachers, library media staff and administrators. As the case studies progressed, it became obvious that background variables other than those described in the Liesener inventory needed to be taken into account. These variables might enable, or limit, the capacity of the resource center to provide the services listed in the Liesener inventory.

The Liesener Inventory of Library Services includes items related to the existence of various types of library material, access to production services, in-library instruction services and consulting services, contribution to school curriculum and teacher instruction.

Student skills and attitudes include library access skills, general book knowledge, instrumental value of the library to school work and positive sentiment towards the library.

Background characteristics include personal qualifications of the teacher-librarian, size of the library program, size of the school, consultant visits, educational ability and others such as seniority of the principal and age of the school.

Analysis of the extensive data collected was directed by Dr. W. J. Reeves of the University of Calgary Department of Sociology. His involvement as a methodologist was crucial to the project. A multivariate regression analysis was conducted to determine relationships between the objective data and background characteristics. With a possibility of approximately 30,000 correlations, only those findings that could be confirmed in both statistical and observational data are reported and, of these, only findings which can be supported by correlation of .6 and more are included.

Findings

At the first level of research findings, this study has confirmed what resource centers in Calgary look like. It is now known that even the basic core services offer support for teachers, opportunities for students and a variety of general services including instruction for children. These "baseline library services" do not, in and of themselves, represent an ideal nor complete program. What is amazing, however, is that in spite of dramatically different conditions in schools, resource centers are able to offer a broad list of common services.

When a service was offered in all or almost all schools, it was considered a program norm or part of a core of services offered throughout the district. Approximately fifty-five baseline services were offered by all resource centers. In addition, approximately thirty baseline services were offered by all or almost all elementary schools. Similarly, approximately thirty different baseline services were unique to senior high school resource centers.

Table 34.1   Baseline library services

Elementary Schools	High Schools
The Child's Domain	Individual Instruction for Students
Reference Service for Individual Teachers	Group Instruction of Students
	Teacher Services
General Use Services	Library Administration

Core services were clustered into four areas (see Table 34.1). Because the configuration was different at the elementary level and senior high level, they were labeled differently. The similarity of focus is, however, readily apparent.

In the elementary school, the child's domain encompassed a variety of awareness and guidance services regarding resources.

Students had a wide variety of materials to choose from, in a variety of locations, and they were also alerted by the resource center staff to materials and services in the library. Once students were cognizant of the existence of materials, they also received assistance from the teacher-librarian in locating and selecting materials most appropriate to their interests and needs. Renewal procedures were available in all elementary schools, should the student require this service. It was apparent that individuals and small groups of students used the library if the need arose in the classroom; in fact, small groups were regularly sent to the library to work with the teacher-librarian on assignments. Audio-visual equipment was available as required.

Student instruction occupied a large amount of resource center staff time. Formal instructional program activities were evident in all elementary libraries. Individual instruction and guidance was offered to all students in all elementary schools, on request. This instruction occurred in the areas of reference material and skills, research skills and the use and handling of audio-visual equipment.

Services clustered under the label "general use" in the elementary school centered around management of the library facility, collection and equipment, and awareness activities directed towards special events such as Book Week.

In the senior high schools, library administration was directed toward improving access to materials, including reservation systems and interlibrary loans.

Having identified the constants regarding school library programs in the district, it was noted that the role of school librarian as teacher and resource specialist was implicit. At this stage of the analysis only those items that varied in the sample (that is, where approximately half of the sampled schools said "Yes!" and half said "No!" to the item) were investigated. Given the theoretical model of the research, it was important to know if it made a difference to the students whether the school had a particular library service or not—were the students in approximately half the schools who said "yes" to a Liesener item more skillful or more positive than the students in the other schools who said "no." From another perspective, was the existence or absence of a library service determined in any way by the background characteristics of the librarian, library or school?

Examination of services which were found to be provided in some schools, and not in others, revealed an expanded role for the teacher-librarian. This role is one of the school-based consultant, with an additional program component dealing with audio-visual services. These two elements of consultation and audio-visual service manifest themselves differently at the elementary and senior high school levels. Nevertheless, the pattern of development relative to individual schools and the district at large was remarkably consistent.

Elementary Schools

Initially, cooperation between teachers and teacher-librarians led to the selection of resources for teacher use or to extend and enrich experiences of students. At the next level, both these elements were present. A further stage of development was found when classroom teachers and the teacher-librarian engaged in a form of team teaching. In this case, the approach was frequently a division of labor, with the teacher-librarian entering the instructional sequence based on expertise. For example, instruction in the use of biographical reference works might be designed into a social studies unit. Fully developed consultation occurred when classroom teachers and teacher-librarians planned an instructional sequence, conducted instruction cooperatively and shared in student and program evaluation. Approximately 20 percent of the schools exhibited this level of development.

Consultation Index Level

Consultation leading to team lesson planning and teaching cooperatively	5
Consultation leading to team teaching with classroom teacher	4
Consultation leading to selection of resources for teacher use and for enrichment of student programs	3
Consultation leading to selection of resources for teacher or for enrichment of student programs	2
No consultation with teams of teachers	—

Along with the consultative role of the teacher-librarian the production of instructional materials was found to be a critical variable. This service element was not, at the time of the study, well developed. Typically, the library staff provided a video tape dubbing service for teachers.

It was important to consider what characteristics were related to whether or not the expanded role of the school library was present in elementary schools. Those with background and experience in libraries will not be surprised that the relationship was one of time and money. What was gratifying about this finding was the strength of the relationship and the precision with which we could establish cut points regarding variables. Because there was not a perfect relationship between school size and the amount of teacher-librarian time, some relatively small schools were able to exhibit the two variables and some large schools did not. Systematically, however, in small schools with less than half-time teacher-librarians and larger schools with less than two thirds of the teacher-librarian's time deployed to the program, the consultative role and production service was absent. Admittedly, "small" and "larger" applied to school size are defined differently. At the time of the study, 14 elementary schools had enrollments of fewer than 150 students and the average size of the school was nine classrooms. In addition, every school library has clerical staff and is supported by centralized ordering, cataloguing, processing, and a variety of school-directed services.

Similarly, data analysis revealed that, in terms of 1978 dollars, any school library budget which was less than $2,500 for materials, systematically exhibited no consultative or production role. Of particular interest was a further systematic relationship between the amount of time devoted to the school by central office library media consultants and production. When there had been five or more visits to the school, there was a strong positive relationship to the presence of the expanded role. This finding inspires much speculation and is deserving of more attention than can be paid in this paper.

What about student outcomes in terms of skills and attitudes? Certainly, there were some items that stood out as bearing a strong relationship to the sentiments and skill development of children. For example, there was a .8 correlation between the housing of photographs in the library and children declaring that the library was the most interesting place in the school. An interesting phenomenon, but hardly a significant one in the overall scheme of things. An equally strong relationship was one of socio-economic status (SES) of the neighborhood to the importance of which students assigned to the library. In lower

SES schools, children systematically indicated that the library was important to their success in school. The reverse was also true; and this phenomenon was also related to the way the library was scheduled and the specific skills that were acquired.

The observational data collected during the case studies, together with the strong results regarding consultation, confirmed that the "first clients" of the elementary school library were the teachers who, in turn, sponsored children individually or in small and large groups to go to the library. Because the library program does not, nor can be expected to, have a mandated curriculum, the inconclusive results were not surprising. There was, however, strong positive effect upon students' attitudes when teacher-librarians performed a consultative role with teachers. When this full partnership occurred, as was the case in five of the sampled schools, there was an obvious coordination and integration of the library program with classroom activities. Typically, the teacher-librarians in these schools were involved at the initial planning stages of the project, took part in cooperative or team teaching activities as the project progressed, and were certainly engaged in evaluation and follow-up at the project's conclusion.

In regard to the testing procedures, no attempt was made to test for library skill ability in subject areas, nor was performance testing carried out due to constraints of time. What is known, however, is that in schools where consultation did occur, library skills per se were not generally taught as a separate curriculum area, but instruction appeared to be given as the need arose in the classroom and after careful consultation between teacher and teacher-librarian. Furthermore, because only grade six students were tested and knowing that teachers sponsor their classes to the library, it was not possible that the classes tested had not yet been sponsored for instruction in the skills that were being tested. Ideally, the entire school population should have been tested and those results examined in light of students being sponsored or non-sponsored to the library. The effects of the library program upon students is indirect, and is dependent upon teachers sponsoring student use of the services and resources that are resident in the resource program.

Senior High Schools

Relationships between school library program development and student outcomes was more conclusive at the senior high school level. In the area of extended library services, the elementary beginnings come to fruition at the secondary level. The continued importance of time in regards to consultation between teacher and teacher-librarian is, further, more specifically identifiable at high school to include the effects of specific kinds of consultation on student skills and attitudes.

Similarly, the audio-visual component which has its beginnings in the expanded teacher-librarian role at the elementary level, through the production of instructional materials for teachers, matures at the secondary level through more extensive audio-visual services.

In senior high, the expanded role can be obtained only when there is an adequate library budget and adequate clerical time which in turn manifests itself in two major areas inside the expanded role: the audio-visual component and differentiated consultative services. The audio-visual component, which includes services such as photography, has a significant impact on student attitudes.

At the secondary level, the existence and type of consultation are heavily dependent on how much clerical time is resident in the program. Since all senior high teacher-librarians work on a full time basis, the operant variable, therefore, became the number of clerical staff and/or the amount of time spent in the program by the clerical assistants. This was a refinement in terms of the elementary program where not every teacher-librarian was able to devote full-time to the library program and his or her time became the operant variable. In addition, at the secondary level, given an adequate number of clerical assistants, the resources center was able to act as a media clearinghouse, and became involved in student-oriented consultation as well as in specific classroom projects.

Consultation was manifested in different ways, each of these having a strong positive relationship to specific student skills and sentiment. For example, when a classroom teacher and teacher-librarian cooperatively developed alternative learning situations for students, the students systematically responded that the library staff was helpful and that the library was the most interesting place in the school. When team teaching occurred as a result of consultation, student reference skills were high. In the case of these items, the range of student scores by school was 30 percent to 78 percent on the administered skills test.

High scoring schools typically exhibited team teaching consultative behaviors. The range of student scores in the area of research skills, that is knowledge of how to begin a research project, was 47 percent to 80 percent. High scoring schools typically provided audio-visual services and the teacher-librarian was involved in developing and implementing class projects.

When school libraries provided extended audio-visual services, including listing, stocking and evaluating nonprint materials, and provision for photography, students systematically reported positive sentiments toward the library. These were manifested in students declaring that the school library was important to their success in school, that they used the library outside of class time, and that they used the library even when this was not required for assignments.

The presence of the audio-visual component was, as one might expect, strongly related to significantly higher expenditure on nonprint materials. In these schools, students placed more instructional value on the school library and exhibited higher scores in research skills. Interestingly, the presence of selection services in the area of nonprint was related to significantly higher expenditure on periodicals.

Consultation, particularly with regard to team teaching and the presence of a clearinghouse function, dealing with the widest range of school resources, was related to higher expenditure on books and the presence of two or more clerks. The number of clerks required to have an impact on this type of consultation varied directly with the size of the school.

Leading Edge Services

When a service was offered by only a few schools, this service was at the "leading edge." These program elements are considered to be important in the field of school librarianship and may be common in other districts, but at this time, in Calgary schools, represented program extensions.

Examples of leading edge services included computer applications, identification of student learning styles and cooperatively developed resource center goal and budget statements. However, this role was not well-defined at the time of the study. It is hoped that as programs progress, there will be a "collapsing toward the middle" whereby those services presently considered leading edge will move into the area of variable services and some of the variable services will shift into the area of core services. There had been some confirmation in this regard, available only one year later, in the area of microcomputers.

The overall finding that important program elements have direct positive impact upon the students and that sufficient resources must be present in order for this to occur, will be no surprise to those familiar with school libraries. As is always the case, the process of data gathering and analysis was, in itself, beneficial and stimulated some important activities. The Chief Superintendent accepted the conclusion that the Calgary Board of Education was receiving value for dollar in the areas of teacher support and positive student outcomes.

It is said that good research raises more questions than it provides answers. Many surprises were found and those bear further scrutiny. Among these are:

1. The training background of the teacher-librarian was unrelated to the extent of the program or to student outcomes.

2. Verbal ability of students and socio-economic status of the neighborhood was not related to the presence of extended services or positive student outcomes.

3. The Liesener inventory is based on the assumption that "more is better." There are, clearly, some services that are more important than others. Indeed, the provision of some services was found to have a negative correlation with student outcomes.

Conclusions

Analysis of the findings yielded four major conclusions:

1. Library programs are an integrative resource in schools. Successful programs involve the teaching staff, school administrators, and central office functions.

2. The inconsistent deployment of staff time and materials budgets results in uneven program implementation from school to school. It appears that this inconsistency is related to administrative support and the teaching styles prevalent within the school.

3. The resource center program is unlike a curriculum. Rather it is a service that must be entrenched in the total school program if students and teachers are to receive maximum benefits. When the program is dealt with as a residual of school resources, there is little provided that is meaningful for its clients.

4. Some schools do not have the necessary resources to support quality library programs without severely penalizing a curriculum area.

References

Calgary Board of Education. Office of the Chief Superintendent (1981). *School library program evaluation.* Calgary: Author.

Eisner, E. (1973, March). *The perceptive eye: Toward the reformation of educational evaluation.* Paper presented at the meeting of the American Educational Research Association Division B, Curriculum and Objectives, Washington, DC.

Gaver, M. (1971). *Services of secondary school media centers: Evaluation and development.* Chicago: American Library Association.

Liesener, J. (1973). The development of a planning process for media programs. *School Media Quarterly, I,* 278–287.

Liesener, J. (1974). *Planning instruments for school library media programs.* Chicago: American Library Association.

Liesener, J. (1976). *A systematic process for planning media programs.* Chicago: American Library Association.

Macdonald, B. (1974). *Evaluation and the control of education.* Ford Foundation Safari Project. University of East Anglia: Center for Applied Research in Education (mimeographed).

CHAPTER THIRTY FIVE

Using Evaluation to Bring School Library Resource Center Programs into Closer Alliance with *Information Power*

Doris Epler

To conduct an evaluation of any program, one must first understand its mission. The mission of the school library resource center is to ensure that students are lifelong users of ideas and information for education and pleasure (AASL/AECT, 1988).

Evaluation of school library resource center programs is a topic that is currently under discussion in many arenas. But why should school library resource center programs be evaluated in the "real" world and how should they be performed?

The school library resource center program must be evaluated systematically in order to review overall goals and objectives in relation to user and instructional needs, and to assess the efficiency and effectiveness of specific activities. Regular and systematic evaluation provides the basis for decisions regarding the development, continuation, modification, or elimination of policies and procedures, activities, and services,

and begins anew the planning process (AASL/AECT, 1988).

Evaluation must be an ongoing process. The program must not only permit the achievement of the school's current goals and objectives, but it must also be flexible enough to respond to the new and emerging technologies which may have an impact on its future. Data generated from an evaluation, combined with projections for future needs, can then be translated into a written plan which adheres to the recommendations indicated in *Information Power*, the national guidelines established by the American Association of School Librarians (AASL) and the Association for Educational Communications Technology (AECT). (This approach also reflects the 1998 revision, *Information Power: Building Partnerships for Learning*.)

Procedures for evaluation can range from those which are extremely complex to those which employ simple strategies. The more complex procedures produce large quantities of data but also require a great deal of time to conduct the evaluation and to analyze the results. The key here seems to be the focus of the evaluation. For instance, the objective of the evaluation is to take a broad look at the library's program for the purpose of selecting a few areas for enhancement, then it appears to be best to choose a simple, rather than a complex, format. If, however, the objective is to delve deeply into a specific area, then a more complex strategy should be employed to ensure that enough detailed data will result.

Teacher-librarians need evaluative data to keep the school library resource center on target. But, most need a process that is easy to implement, relatively quick to analyze, and very cost effective; that is, they cannot spend a great deal of time or money on the process.

Development Process

In 1980, AASL published a small booklet entitled "Evaluating the school library media program: A working bibliography" prepared for the building-level media specialist. This fourteen page publication provided annotated citations about articles and books that dealt with the topic of evaluating school library media programs.

During 1987, AASL formed a new subcommittee entitled Evaluating School Library Media Programs. This group received the following function statement:

> To improve the effectiveness of school library media programs by promoting the need for research to define more clearly their essential elements, identifying areas which need study, and serving as a clearinghouse for information on evaluation instruments and activities which demonstrate that effective school library media programs have a positive impact on student learning.

The subcommittee struggled for several months to narrow its focus. It was felt that most teacher-librarians needed an instrument that would help them to evaluate their programs quickly and efficiently rather than some type of research report.

Through informal contacts with their colleagues, the subcommittee members felt that whatever they produced had to be designed in such a way that would generate information that would enable the teacher-librarian to bring about desired change. Therefore, a decision was made not to produce another bibliography, but to develop an evaluative instrument—one that teacher-librarians could implement on their own to assess the school library resource center program.

The committee began their work by reviewing various evaluation instruments from across the nation and analyzing what elements of the school library resource center program were targeted for evaluation. One of the first problems that had to be overcome was that of language. Different terms were being used to describe the same situation so terms had to be specified carefully.

The second step involved looking at the different strategies for rating the elements under evaluation. Some forms that were reviewed used rating criteria such as "definitely true, mostly true, mostly untrue, and definitely untrue." Several formats employed a rating scale of "essential, important, minimal" while others used "fully operational, partially operational, and non-operational." Many other rating scales were investigated by the subcommittee.

Evaluation forms that are designed for analyzing the current status of a program against predetermined criteria can use a variety of rating scales and rating terms. It is obvious, however, that criteria and rating scales cannot be developed until the objective of the evaluation has been clearly defined. Therefore, the committee developed the following objective for their work:

> To develop an instrument that will enable the building level school library media specialist to conduct an evaluation of the school library media center program in such a manner as to produce the information necessary to bring about desired change.

The committee then began to analyze the major components of an effective resource center program as identified in *Information Power* and these elements were grouped into categories.

In analyzing who should be involved in the evaluation process, the subcommittee focused on six different groups: (1) teacher-librarians, (2) district or regional library directors, (3) teachers, (4) administrators, (5) parents, and (6) legislators. A separate checklist was developed for each group. Elements of effective school library resource center programs were chosen from the list prepared, and used to determine how much each target group knew about their school library resource center program. Some of the items on the checklists were similar so that the responses from two or more target groups could be compared.

The six checklists were field tested in Dallas, Texas, at the 1989 conference of the American Library Association (ALA). Checklists were given to a group of 220 teacher-librarians from across the United States for their review and comments. In addition, each of the committee members field tested the checklists in their own areas. All recommendations were carefully considered and the checklists were refined.

A workshop on how to use the six checklists, as well as how to develop action plans from the results obtained, was presented at Salt Lake City in 1989 at the AASL Conference. The more than 300 participants were very enthusiastic about the usefulness of the checklists and integration with the change process.

Teacher-librarians are encouraged to use all the checklists when conducting an evaluation. However, the lists were designed to stand alone for times when just one target group needs to be surveyed. The checklists are also adaptable for gathering evaluation data about local or state specific school library resource center elements.

Six Checklists

1. Teacher-Librarian Checklist

This checklist is intended to be a starting point for the teacher-librarian to discover where their school library resource center program stands in relation to *Information Power.*

The checklist includes criteria covering six major areas: (1) personnel, (2) library resource center instructional program partnerships, (3) information/access skills program, (4) facilities, (5) resources and equipment, and (6) professional development.

A five point rating scale is used on this checklist:
0 = not at all and no planning under way,
1 = mostly,
4 = totally.

Teacher-librarians are asked to rate how well their school library resource center meets each of the 30 criteria presented. Teacher-librarians are encouraged to provide the leadership necessary to conduct the evaluation. This includes disseminating and collecting the completed forms from the targeted groups, as well as forming a committee to analyze the results and to plan for bringing about the desired changes in the program. A sample from this checklist is:

- The information skills curriculum is integrated with classroom instruction.

2. School Administrator Checklist

This checklist is intended to be a starting point for the administrator to discover where the school library resource center program stands in relation to *Information Power.* Included are 26 criteria covering five major areas: (1) personnel, (2) facilities, (3) resources and equipment, (4) program, and (5) professional development. And once again, a five point rating scale was applied. A great deal of thought went into the selection of the criteria used on this checklist. It is anticipated that many of the elements will cause the administrator to learn more about the school library resource center program and to become aware of the importance of each of the five areas listed. A sample from this checklist is:

- Funding is available for continuing professional education activities for the school library resource center.

3. District and Regional Library Directors' Checklist

This checklist has a different focus. Four areas are presented: (1) leadership, (2) communication, (3) coordination, and (4) administration. Using the same five point rating scale, the directors are asked to rate how well they feel they are currently providing support for each of the 28 items presented. A sample from this checklist is:

- Do you share current information on research, technology, and instructional strategies with teacher-librarians, principals, and other district administrators?

4. Teacher Checklist

This checklist is intended to be a starting point for the teacher to discover where the school library resource center program stands in relation to *Information Power*. They are asked to rate how well they feel their school library resource center meets each of the 20 criteria identified in four major areas, (1) personnel, (2) facilities, (3) resources and equipment, and (4) program. In addition to the five point rating scale used in the other forms, a "Don't Know" category is included. Teacher-librarians will glean valuable information from the teachers' responses around which they can plan training sessions or in-service presentations. A sample from this checklist is:

- The teacher-librarian works closely with the faculty and staff in planning, implementing, and evaluating instruction.

5. Parent Checklist

This form uses 16 criteria elements that are presented as a straight list rather than categorized into major areas. Parents are asked to indicate their knowledge of whether or not the item is being provided in their child's school library media program by checking either "yes," "no," or "don't know."

Parents are also encouraged to arrange meetings with school administrators and the school library resource center staff and, working as a partnership, help to develop long range plans for improving the program in their child's school. A sample from this checklist is:

- Does your child's school provide encouragement for students to use resources beyond those provided by the school library resource center?

6. Legislator Checklist

If excellence in school library resource center programs is to be achieved, strong partnerships must exist among the state department of education, state legislative bodies, and local school districts.

This checklist was designed to help legislators determine whether their state provides the key elements necessary to achieve excellence in school library resource center programs. They are asked to indicate their knowledge about 13 items by checking "yes," "no," or "don't know." They are also encouraged to investigate all the items they checked as "don't know' to determine if the items are being provided. Then they can change any "don't knows" to either yes or no. A suggestion is made for the legislator to consider analyzing all the items remaining "no" and establish a priority list for improving library resource center programs and services for educational reform in their state. A sample from this checklist is:

- Does your state include school library resource centers in the program funded by Library Services and Construction Act monies?

After the checklists have been completed, responses can be analyzed and the Action Plan Worksheet form provided in the AASL document "A planning guide for *Information Power*," can be used to develop long range plans to bring about change. The action plan worksheet addresses the goal, the objective, the plan of action, and also provides space to indicate action steps, resources needed, individual or group responsible, time frame, and measure of success.

If many of the items are identified as not satisfactory, there is a tendency to become overwhelmed. Therefore, concentrating on no more than three elements and by developing their action plans change becomes more realistic and within reach.

The checklists that the AASL subcommittee developed, attempt to measure school library resource center program excellence, as defined by AASL and AECT in *Information Power*. Teacher-librarians may use these approaches and materials and make any modifications they deem necessary to reflect current standards and guidelines.

References

American Association of School Librarians (AASL) and Association for Educational Communications and Technology (AECT). (1988). *Information power: Guidelines for school media programs*. Chicago: American Library Association.

CHAPTER THIRTY SIX

Evaluation: The Key to Growth

Linda Rafuse and Ruth Law

Although school libraries have operated for many years, their role has changed dramatically. From keepers of books, teacher-librarians have evolved into specialists who have expertise in a number of areas. The role has expanded from providing services for curriculum support to being involved in curriculum development and implementation. The teacher-librarian is a partner in the planning and execution of educational programs.

With the increased significance of school library resource centers and the current emphasis on effective schools, evaluation of the school library resource center program assumes new importance and serves several purposes. In general, such an evaluation is a means of measuring the degree to which objectives have been achieved and of setting further goals. It increases the visibility of the library and the teacher-librarian and gives direction for professional development programs. Evaluation tools give hard facts to support the philosophy of cooperative planning and the teaching of resource-based programs.

In many jurisdictions policy guidelines have been developed which outline the responsibilities of the teacher-librarian, including AASL's *Information power*. From these policy statements, evaluative tools can be developed. The implementation profile described here is adapted from *Implementing innovations in schools: A concerns-based approach* (Loucks & Hall, 1980) and *Partners in action* (Ontario Ministry of Education, 1982). Figure 36.1 is the profile.

For each critical component of the library program there are four levels of implementation. These levels are defined as follows:

Awareness

The teacher may be aware of the requirements of the innovation but demonstrates few of the desired behaviors.

Mechanical

The teacher is using parts of the innovation but in a disjointed fashion. Some changes have been made but these tend to benefit the teacher rather than the student.

Routine

All parts of the innovation are in place; the teacher is able to anticipate short problems. Very few changes are being planned.

Refined

The innovation is working well. The teacher is beginning to make changes which have impact on the students. Integration between subjects and with other teachers is taking place.

Teacher-librarians and administrators use the school library resource center program checklist to record the school's stage of implementation for each component of the program. This profile is then used to assess the degree to which the various components of an ideal program have been implemented. An invaluable by-product of using such a device is the communication that occurs between the administration and teacher-librarian. With their differing experience and perspectives, a more comprehensive plan to equip students with the needed skills for the future is possible.

References

Loucks, S. & Hall, G. (1980). *Implementing innovations in schools: A concerns-based approach*. Austin: University of Texas Research and Development Center for Teacher Education.

Ontario Ministry of Education (1982). *Partners in action: The resource centre in the school curriculum*. Toronto: Ontario Ministry of Education.

Figure 36.1 Cooperative Program Planning and Teaching Implementation Profile

Critical Components	1. Awareness	2. Mechanical	3. Routine	4. Refined
Advocacy and Philosophy	The teacher-librarian:	The teacher-librarian:	The teacher-librarian:	The teacher-librarian:
1. Concept	and/or principal are cognizant of the concept of cooperative program planning and teaching	and principal are beginning to informally promote the concept of cooperative program planning and teaching with some teachers	and principal utilize staff and department meetings to develop a positive image of the concept of cooperative program planning and teaching	and the principal regularly utilize staff meetings, formal and informal communication channels to develop a positive image of the cooperative program planning and teaching concept
2. Communication	and/or principal is beginning to provide information about cooperative program planning and teaching	with the support of the principal, is beginning to provide information about cooperative program planning and teaching and demonstrates some strategies for its implementation	with the support of the principal, regularly communicates with teachers, encouraging implementation of cooperative program planning and teaching	with the support of the principal, provides on-going in-service for teachers. Articulates to parents and community the role of the library resource center in the school program
3. Professional Development	is aware of professional development opportunities in librarianship and participates in some available activities	often participates in library and extra-curricular professional development activities	uses a process and self-assessment to select appropriate professional development experiences. Joins professional organizations	frequently seeks opportunities for professional growth in librarianship and assumes a leadership role at the school, area and regional levels
Curriculum	The teacher-librarian:	The teacher-librarian:	The teacher-librarian:	The teacher-librarian:
1. Cooperative Planning	independently plans information skills activities which may or may not relate to classroom objectives	occasionally plans with some teachers, units which integrate library activities with classroom objectives	regularly meets with the majority of teachers to cooperatively plan units of study which integrate information skills with the classroom program	meets with the majority of teachers to cooperatively review and refine specific learning outcomes and related information skills
2. Curriculum Development	houses curriculum documents in the library and provides resource lists for teachers	occasionally works with teachers to develop a unit of study	often participates with staff as a team in the development, implementation, and evaluation of school curricula	always participates as a valued member of the school's curriculum team. Seeks opportunities to be involved in regional curriculum activities

Figure 36.1 Cooperative Program Planning and Teaching Implementation Profile (continued)

Critical Components	1. Awareness	2. Mechanical	3. Routine	4. Refined
Selection of Resources	The teacher-librarian:	The teacher-librarian:	The teacher-librarian:	The teacher-librarian:
1. Policy	is aware that the board has a policy for selection of learning resources	begins to use the criteria in the board policy when selecting or developing a rationale for learning resources	with input from staff and students, regularly selects learning resources appropriate for the subject area and for the age, emotional development, ability level, learning styles, and social environment of the students	involves staff in developing school policy for the selection of learning resources
2. Consideration	is aware that a variety of selection aids could be accessed to assist in selection of materials, e.g., displays, curriculum, in-service, periodicals, reviews, state/provincial publications, teachers and resource staff	makes some use of available aids to review, evaluate and select learning resources	regularly uses a consideration file, arranges in-school displays, and relies on a variety of other selection aids to maintain a relevant, up-to-date collection	in consultation with the principal and staff, develops a long-range plan for building an up-to-date collection relevant to the school's curriculum directions, and ensuring the most cost-efficient use of the allocated budget
3. Acquisition	provides learning resources after informal consultation with staff	increases the range of learning resources following consultation with staff	provides a wide range of learning resources to reflect needs of current curricula, individual students and staff	in consultation with staff and students, provides a wide variety of resources to support cooperatively planned curricula and to meet students' individual learning needs
Consultation	The teacher-librarian:	The teacher-librarian:	The teacher-librarian:	The teacher-librarian:
1. Implementation Support	lends some support in curriculum development	collaborates with teachers and support staff in the implementation of curricula	suggests a variety of learning strategies to support effective implementation of curricula	functions as an in-school resource person for curriculum implementation and modification
Management	The teacher-librarian:	The teacher-librarian:	The teacher-librarian:	The teacher-librarian:
1. Organization of Learning Resources	has developed a system of organizing and circulating learning materials and audio visual equipment without communicating procedures to staff	communicates library resource policies and procedures regarding organization and circulation to staff and students on request	ensures that all learning materials as well as audio visual equipment are processed, filed and organized for efficient access and maximum circulation. Policies and procedures are disseminated to staff and students as needed.	utilizes input from staff and students to maintain an effective, organized system which reflects the changing needs of the school

Figure continues

Figure 36.1   Cooperative Program Planning and Teaching Implementation Profile   (continued)

Critical Components	1. Awareness	2. Mechanical	3. Routine	4. Refined
2. Human Resources	makes limited use of clerical staff as well as student and adult volunteers where available	recruits volunteer help and uses clerical and technical help where available	expands the effective use of support staff, including clerical and volunteer assistants, and professional media and library personnel	plans for the efficient utilization of all support staff
3. Budget	spends the allocated budget with little concern for its appropriate distribution	begins to consider the needs of the library resource center and tries to distribute the funds accordingly	regularly assesses the needs of the library resource center, sets priorities, and allocates appropriate budget	depending on availability of funds, consistently manages a library resource center budget which provides for curriculum needs of students and staff, reflecting the educational goals of the school
4. Timetabling	specifies a fixed schedule for each class to have access to the library resource center	schedules some class visits, leaving some periods open for planning and group work	regularly operates the library resource center on an open, flexible schedule	in an ongoing consultation with staff, arranges an open, flexible library timetable to meet the learning needs of all students and the planning and program needs of staff
Instruction	The teacher-librarian:	The teacher-librarian:	The teacher-librarian:	The teacher-librarian:
1. Finding and Using Information	teaches information skills independently from classroom programs	teaches some information skills as part of cooperatively planned learning activities	regularly collaborates with teachers to develop information skills as part of cooperatively planned learning activities	and the teachers provide frequent opportunities for students to develop skills characteristic of the independent learner
2. Appreciation of Literature	(a) exposes students to a variety of literature, print and non-print	begins to offer opportunities for students to hear and respond to a range of literature	collaborates with the teacher to provide opportunities for students to hear and respond critically to a variety of literary experiences	with staff, fosters the appreciation of literature by providing a variety of enriching experiences, e.g., authors' visits, publishing and recognizing student authors, young authors' conferences
	(b) provides books that are appropriate to the age and interest of the students	occasionally provides and recommends resources which expand the students' spectrum of literature	regularly recommends to students and teachers relevant theme-related literature to encourage personal reading	ongoing with the classroom teacher, provides a variety of literature for everyone to continue to grow as literate, thinking people
3. Media Literacy	suggests some media resources and new technology to staff	begins to provide some inservice to staff on the use of new learning resources and technology	with staff, provides opportunities for students to use, appreciate, and critically respond to a variety of media	with staff, demonstrates expertise in developing appreciation and modeling effective use of media resources

CHAPTER THIRTY SEVEN

Evaluation of the Teacher-Librarian: A Discussion Guide

Ken Haycock

Evaluation: The Person or the Program?

Evaluation of the teacher-librarian (TL) is a difficult area for many school administrators. Too often it is confused with evaluation of the "library program" itself, which is a much larger and more complex matter. In working with principals, teachers and teacher-librarians, it is often useful to separate the evaluation of the TL from the program. Curiously, though, many TLs see the program as the TL alone—carrying both the total responsibility of one person and the accountability therein. This is not only foolhardy—why be accountable for a lack of district support?—but also egocentric in the extreme—how do you develop an effective program without administrator and teacher commitment?

Evaluation of the program involves two significant components—quantitative measures together with a variety of qualitative contributions.

Quantitatively, the TL does not determine the amount of time allocated to the position, does not decide on the level of clerical support, does not single-handedly build the facility for effective use, does not prescribe the nature and delivery of district consultative and management services, does not write the budget figures, does not make purchasing policy, and so on. Others make these decisions and others must be accountable for them since they all, each and every one of them, have an enormous impact on the effect of the program.

Qualitatively, the program is a partnership of the teacher, teacher-librarian, principal and school district. Each of the partners has an essential role to play in the development and implementation of a high quality, integrated program of resource-based teaching and learning. Certainly, the teacher-librarian is a key player, but not a solitary one. Each of the partners has specific skills, experiences, resources and responsibilities which bear on the nature and extent of the program.

The evaluation of the teacher-librarian, then, is one ingredient and only one ingredient in the mix. Nevertheless, having stated these parameters the evaluation of the teacher-librarian should be a critical force in the ongoing professional development of both principal and teacher-librarian. Two issues arise here, however. Many principals are uncertain of criteria for the evaluation of teacher-librarians and find contractual criteria and obligations very limiting for those in non-classroom teaching positions. Many teacher-librarians, on the other hand, are concerned about knowledgeable principals since the role description of the TL can be so broad and encompassing as to make it nearly impossible to achieve a level of success and job satisfaction.

This brief guide attempts to address both of these concerns. It is by no means perfect, since only a locally developed instrument can reach that lofty ideal. It does, however, provide a vehicle for the education of principals in the role of the TL and it likewise does provide a vehicle for the TL and principal to establish priorities together and assess the extent of implementation together. In this supervisory cycle the TL has much to gain from the professional insight of the administrator.

Two factors are necessary to guarantee a mutually rewarding experience: discussion of relative priorities and discussion of degree of implementation. It is not possible that everything be a high priority, nor is it possible that everything be well-implemented; program development is, after all, an ongoing activity.

As professional teachers, however, TLs must demonstrate the skills necessary to work with teacher colleagues to diagnose learning needs, jointly prescribe and develop programs to address those needs, and assess the extent to which the program has been successful in addressing the needs determined. The principal will want to examine three major areas: observation of the TL in planning sessions with colleagues, observation of the TL actually teaching, and observation of the management of the resource center itself. Too often we have focused on the latter to the detriment of this unique teaching role.

A Framework

During the past two decades, schools have been struggling to adapt to the changing needs of society. What has emerged is an institution which focuses on the development of individuals who are prepared to think rationally and logically for

themselves and to assume responsibilities. To develop students of this type has meant that schools have had to emphasize learner-oriented methods such as guided discovery and inquiry as well as traditional teacher-oriented methods.

This broadening of educational methodology has had a great impact on school libraries. Many teacher-librarians have been leaders in understanding and focusing on the expanding variety of teaching approaches and student experiences which the changing needs of society require. It is fact, however, that the inclusion of inquiry, individualization and independent study programs has placed many additional demands on the library and on the librarian. The need today is for the teacher-librarian to be a highly skilled teacher, able to function on the school team as a professional with competencies from teacher education and classroom experience as well as competencies from school librarianship and media services. Similarly, the library has moved from being a subject and merely a place, to a service and a concept, a learning resource center for teachers and students.

Expectations for teacher-librarians are very high. It is expected that a TL will be in the forefront of curriculum and professional development services, will be familiar with the full range of instructional strategies and learning styles, will be able to organize time, personnel and materials to maximize utilization of each and will be active in professional concerns within the school and the district.

For the TL to achieve these expectations, adequate support staff is essential to free the professional from clerical and technical tasks. School districts must recognize this need if the potential of the teacher-librarian and resource center is to be realized.

It should be noted that successful completion of formal course work will not guarantee success as a teacher-librarian. Personality factors, interpersonal relations skills, creativity, flexibility, professional commitment and willingness to participate in continuing education, should be major factors in evaluating a teacher-librarian.

Recent advances in education make it essential that the teacher-librarian demonstrate the competencies outlined to the degree possible if the resource center is to offer an educational service which is vital to the school's instructional program.

General Considerations

1. There is a written role description for the teacher-librarian; minimum academic qualifications have been specified and are in place.

2. The program is viewed as a partnership of district, principal, classroom teacher and teacher-librarian. Each has a defined role in program development and is accountable for its implementation.

3. The resource center is flexibly scheduled after planning between the classroom teacher and teacher-librarian.

4. A school-based continuum of research and study skills has been developed by the staff and is used as a framework for cooperative program planning and teaching.

5. The following allocations are provided to the fullest extent possible: teacher-librarian time; paid clerical assistance; budget for materials; physical facilities.

For quantitative guidelines refer to state/provincial and school district standards.

The Role of the Teacher-Librarian: Nine Areas of Competence

Although teacher-librarians have competence in the areas listed, services are offered on the basis of the school program and the availability of personnel, materials and facilities. Priorities are determined by the individual school since not all services will be offered in every school or to the same extent in all schools. Different approaches to evaluation are available to administrators, school staffs and teacher-librarians and several of these have been outlined in the profession literature and by professional associations.

1. *Administration* includes the ability to manage resource center programs, services and staff in order that these services may contribute to the stated educational goals of the school.

2. *The selection of learning resources* includes the ability to apply basic principles of evaluating learning resources for the purpose of developing a collection which will support the instructional program in the school.

3. *The acquisition, organization and circulation of learning resources* includes the professional tasks of classifying and cataloguing information and of organizing circulation procedures and the supervision of efficient and systematic technical and clerical support services.

4. *Guidance in reading, listening and viewing* includes the ability to assess student needs and interests and to provide resources which satisfy a given situation. Through this guidance students develop attitudes, appreciations and skills that motivate and stimulate the improved selection of appropriate learning resources.

5. *The design and production of learning resources* includes the ability to plan, design and produce materials for a specific instructional purpose, such as to improve communication effectiveness skills, where appropriate commercial materials are not available.

6. *Information services* includes the ability to use reference materials in seeking answers to questions. The teacher-librarian also acts as a liaison between the resource center/school and outside agencies for information services and resources.

7. *The promotion of the effective use of learning resources and services* includes the ability to alert users to the full range of available resources.

8. *Cooperative program planning and teaching* includes the ability to participate as a teaching partner in the accomplishment of identified learning objectives through a knowledge of recommended resources and appropriate teaching/learning strategies.

9. *Professionalism and leadership* includes the ability to develop and promote the use of the human and material resources of the school resource center and its facilities through cooperative professional activities.

Cooperative Use of the Instrument

This instrument (Figure 37.1) has been developed as a relatively simple means of communication between the school principal and the teacher-librarian. Other instruments and measurement devices have been prepared to assess the needs and satisfaction of teachers, students and the community; these will be available from the district office and professional associations. As part of the supervisory cycle, however, principal and teacher-librarian can begin with discussion of services and perceptions of their relative priority and implementation. This instrument is designed to facilitate that discussion—it does not remove the critical components of principal observation of the teacher-librarian, planning with classroom teachers and team teaching, and of evaluation of the effective management of the resource center.

It is recommended that each partner, principal and teacher-librarian complete the document separately, indicating the degree of priority for the school program and degree of implementation on a high, medium and low scale. Not every item can be a high priority; try to aim for approximately a third being a high priority, a third being a medium priority and a third being a low priority. Where an area of competence is essential, but a low priority, provide an explanatory note in the comments section. Comments might also include further elaboration, suggestions for improvement (including alternatives to "more") and recommendations for improvement.

Each partner might then review his or her own assessment, together with the other's, in confidence, and meet to discuss areas of agreement, disagreement and uncertainty. This should be a positive, professionally renewing activity with an emphasis on the teacher-librarian providing information and knowledge for the administrator who in turn can provide useful insights to the library program.

Figure 37.1   The Role of the Teacher-Librarian—Nine Areas of Competence

Priority			Administration of the Learning Resource Program	Implementation		
H	M	L		H	M	L
			Establish rapport with school staff, students and community.			
			Establish short and long range goals in terms of district guidelines and school objectives.			
			Select, supervise and plan for the effective use of resource center staff.			
			Recruit, select, train and motivate adult and student volunteers.			
			Invite and accept suggestions from teaching staff about the services the program provides.			
			Develop resource center facilities to support the objectives of the instructional program.			
			Plan for efficient use of space and equipment and for appropriate security for learning resources.			
			Plan and manage a flexible budget which reflects the instructional program.			
			Organize and develop staff, collections, budget, facilities and services to achieve objectives.			
			Maintain an inventory of materials and equipment.			
			Prepare oral and written reports on the resource center program.			
			Provide an environment conducive to learning.			
			Apply technological advances such as automation to resource center services.			
			Involve school staff in the evaluation of the effectiveness of resource center programs in terms of district guidelines and school objectives.			
Comments:						

Figure 37.1   The Role of the Teacher-Librarian—Nine Areas of Competence (continued)

Priority			Selection of Learning Resources	Implementation		
H	M	L		H	M	L
			Develop and implement criteria for the evaluation and selection of a wide range of resources.			
			Develop policies and procedures for the selection of learning resources which meet curricular, informational and recreational needs.			
			Build a collection of bibliographic and evaluative sources to provide current information about learning resources and equipment.			
			Organize teacher involvement in the preview, evaluation and selection of learning resources.			
			Develop extensive "consideration for purchase" files of book and nonbook media.			
Comments:						

Priority			Acquisition, Organization and Circulation of Learning Resources	Implementation		
H	M	L		H	M	L
			Implement procedures for ordering, receiving and processing learning resources.			
			Classify and catalog learning resources as necessary and according to accepted standards.			
			Maintain an accurate catalog according to established rules.			
			Develop an efficient system for lending, renewing, reserving and recalling resources and equipment.			
			Route curriculum resources and professional materials.			
			Establish procedures for, and encourage use of, interlibrary loans.			
			Select commercial cataloging services appropriate to school needs.			
Comments:						

Priority			Reading, Listening and Viewing Guidance	Implementation		
H	M	L		H	M	L
			Work with individuals and groups of students to provide direction, improve selection and develop critical thinking.			
			Provide guidance for students and teachers during the school day and before and after school.			
			Share with students and teachers the joy of reading.			
			Promote appreciation and interest in the use of learning resources by giving book/media talks.			
			Develop storytelling, storyreading and other resource-centered programs for language development.			
			Assist students and teachers in the effective use of media.			
			Recommend to teachers learning resources in various formats which may assist in the accomplishment of specific learning objectives.			
			Advise teachers of "medium appropriateness" for particular instructional purposes.			
Comments:						

Figure continues

Figure 37.1   The Role of the Teacher-Librarian—Nine Areas of Competence (continued)

Priority			Design and Production of Learning Resources	Implementation		
H	M	L		H	M	L
			Advise students and teachers in media design and production through instruction and in-service programs.			
			Supervise the production of materials such as cassettes, slides, transparencies, talking books, video and slide/tape presentations.			
			Assist in the evaluation of media produced.			
Comments:						

Priority			Information and Reference Services	Implementation		
H	M	L		H	M	L
			Answer, or obtain answers to, questions from teachers and students.			
			Provide guidance to teachers and students on locating information.			
			Develop a working relationship with public libraries, specialized libraries, other resource centers, community organizations, resource people and district resource services.			
			Locate specific information and resources found outside the school.			
			Participate in cooperative and coordinated projects within the district which involve the sharing of ideas, experiences and learning resources.			
Comments:						

Priority			Promotion of the Effective Use of Learning Resources and Services	Implementation		
H	M	L		H	M	L
			Communicate effectively with teachers and administrators.			
			Develop an informational and public relations program for staff, students and the community.			
			Capitalize on themes through special promotions and media celebrations.			
			Develop bulletin boards, displays, and other publicity materials.			
Comments:						

From *Foundations for Effective School Library Media Programs.* © 1999 Ken Haycock. Libraries Unlimited (800) 237-6124.

Figure 37.1   The Role of the Teacher-Librarian—Nine Areas of Competence (continued)

Priority			Cooperative Program Planning and Teaching	Implementation		
H	M	L		H	M	L
			Develop cooperatively with teachers a sequential list of media, research and study skills for cross-grade and cross-subject implementation.			
			Plan and develop units of work with teachers from the setting of objectives to evaluation.			
			Integrate media, research and study skills with classroom instruction for independent and continued learning.			
			Pre-plan with teachers and teach skills integrated with classroom instruction to large and small groups and individuals.			
			Integrate the planned use of learning resources with the educational program.			
			Provide leadership to develop programs which integrate the promotion of reading with the total school program and with individual teacher programs.			
			Initiate specific teaching units to encourage the acquisition of skills and the effective use of learning resources.			
			Provide curriculum-related book and nonbook media talks and celebrations.			
			Compile bibliographies, resource lists and book and nonbook media lists as needed.			
Comments:						

Priority			Professionalism and Leadership	Implementation		
H	M	L		H	M	L
			Develop a strong team approach with other teachers.			
			Lead in-service education programs on the effective use of the resource center: criteria for the selection of materials; designing resource-based units of study; using audio-visual equipment; promoting voluntary reading; media, research and study skill development; cooperative teaching; community resources.			
			Share techniques and strategies for using learning resources.			
			Involve students and staff in establishing learning resources policy and service guidelines.			
			Plan strategies for developing, presenting and securing support for learning resource services.			
			Serve on local and district curriculum committees.			
			Keep abreast of current developments in school librarianship, library and information science, media services and related fields.			
			Participate in the school's educational program by serving on advisory groups and committees and working with the student extracurricular program.			
			Take advantage of opportunities for continuing education and professional development.			
			Apply specific research findings and the principles of research to the development and improvement of resource center services.			
			Maintain membership and participate in professional education and library associations at the local, provincial and national levels.			
Comments:						

Documentation for the particular content of this instrument is based on the work of two committees chaired by the author: one to develop a role description for the teacher-librarian in an urban school district and the second to define competencies for the "qualified" teacher-librarian for the Canadian School Library Association. The framework is taken from the resulting CSLA document *The Qualifications of School Librarians.*

CHAPTER THIRTY EIGHT

Theory—Where Is My Reality?

Susan Casey

I had always been interested in cooperative program planning—it seemed to me to be the major goal of a school library program. However, from practice I knew it was not in place as widely as I felt it should be—including in my own resource center. At the time that this study was completed, I was a teacher-librarian in a grades 6–9 open area school. I was convinced cooperative program planning and teaching, or curriculum development at the school level, as the process is often referred to in the literature, was an important part of my role, but how did I "measure up?" The literature made the process sound widespread—was I falling below the mark? How much was I already doing? How could I increase the amount of time I spent in this activity, and where would the time come from in an already hectic schedule? I decided I needed to examine how I was currently spending my time—both at school and at home—on those activities that related to my role as teacher-librarian.

I am assuming that most teacher-librarians are the "already converted," and believe, as I do, that cooperative program planning (CPP) should be the major focus of the teacher-librarian role—but the more I talk with practising "in-the-field" teacher-librarians, the more I am convinced that CPP is not as extensively practiced as the literature would suggest. The most common problem for teacher-librarians wanting to engage in CPP is the lack of time.

Role Clarification

I began by examining the role of the teacher-librarian as a whole—what aspects make up this role that is a combination of teacher and librarian? This was a difficult process, but by becoming actively involved in examining what it is that I do, I came to a much clearer understanding of my role. It became much easier for me to set priorities for my time, increased my feelings of professionalism, and above all else had an extremely positive impact on my job and satisfaction by allowing me more time to do what is important—CPP. It also increased my awareness of the role, and has allowed me to speak with more conviction to the administration and teachers at my school.

How did I arrive at these results? I have had the following quotation on my bulletin board for years:

If you don't know what is important,

→ then everything is important.

If everything is important,

→ then you try to do everything.

If you are attempting to do everything,

→ then people expect you to do everything.

And in trying to please everyone.

→ you don't have enough time to find out what's important.

I originally stuck it up because I thought it was funny, but one day in the middle of this study, it jumped out at me, and since then it has become my creed. I willingly share it with those of you who find the element of truth in the statement!

I also realized my own perceptions were a combination of what I believed, and the often deflating perceptions of friends and colleagues. When someone very close to you asks you why you need a master's degree just to stamp out books to kids, it can have a rather depressing effect on your professional ego. It seemed I was always justifying my role, and I was beginning to wonder about it myself. Teacher-librarians are continually fighting the battle to be recognized as the professionals they are, and not just as clerical staff. Unfortunately, most school systems do not provide enough clerical assistance to school libraries, and the teacher-librarian often must perform clerical duties. As a result of the examination of my role I found that I was doing fewer clerical tasks than I originally believed. I think this was because I always felt guilty—clerical tasks were not a good use of my time and so they frustrated me. My attitude has changed in the last year as a result of the study. First, the strictly clerical duties I must do—for example, maintaining the catalogue—I try to do when no one is watching. I have become a "closet cleric" if you will! Perceptions of others are often based on stereotypes, but those perceptions can be effectively altered if reality does not support them. I now do these unavoidable clerical tasks before the resource center opens, or after it closes. No one

sees me doing them and I'm not resentful of the time because I "should" be working with kids or teachers. I think it is extremely important that the teacher-librarian stop and examine the role being perpetuated in the school.

Of course there are always some clerical tasks that must be done by the teacher-librarian during the course of the day. I found that by recognizing these activities and stretching the role beyond the clerical task, I can intensify my impact, perpetuate my role as a professional, and increase the job satisfaction I feel. (And the term clerical is not meant to be derogatory. I have been extremely fortunate to have had highly competent clerical assistants. By the term clerical I am referring to those aspects which are not of a professional nature—enough on that point.)

Let me share with you an example. I'm sure many of you have experienced the frustration of dealing with a teacher whom you have not been able to reach with the virtues of CPP. After five years he still asks you to pull all the books on a certain topic for his grade 9 social studies class, and send them all to his room on a shelf! I find these requests to be exceedingly frustrating for a number of reasons, the main one being that I am not given the opportunity to help teach the process of information search, identification and synthesis. I feel as if I am spoon feeding, rather than working toward one of my main goals which is the creation of independent learners. The concentration on product, rather than process, goes against my fundamental educational beliefs. Until I completed this study, I would have tried to convince him of the positive benefits that could result for his students if we cooperatively planned an integrated unit using the resource center as a resource base for the students. He would have politely listened, and then reiterated his request, insisting that he didn't have time for such "frills," and I would have gone and pulled the books, all the while muttering under my breath about the lost teaching opportunity, and the poor use of my time which didn't call on any of my specializations as I perceived them. This year, however, I was ready! The conversation began in much the same way—up to the point where I would give in because "he has so much to cover before exams"—a legitimate concern on his part no matter how frustrating for me! I compromised, I let him know that with my clerical assistant's time cut in half this year, I was also short on time, and could he please send three or four students to help pull the books—a legitimate concern for me. I also requested that the entire class come in for one period following the initial search to identify their specific needs. The four students came in, and received some intensive search strategy instruction from me while we pulled the materials. They were also able to assist me when the rest of their class came into the resource center. Those four students had obtained ownership of their problem, had a more positive attitude toward the resource center, and I had changed a clerical task of pulling books into a teaching function that had very positive side benefits. In addition I was no longer frustrated—better four students than none! All of these positive results merely by a creative stretching of the clerical role, and only possible because I had taken the time to examine what I was doing.

This is just one simple example of how examining my role has led to positive changes in my performance of the teacher-librarian role. The process I went through was exceedingly helpful to me, and I'd like to outline it briefly to you.

Time: Analysis and Management

First of all, it is important to discern the goals and objectives of your school's curriculum, and the philosophy of the school. Next, the teacher-librarian needs to carefully think through goals and objectives for the library program. I went through this goal setting and objective stating process under protest. I found it both a more difficult process than I had anticipated and a more useful one than I had expected. I always knew I had my objectives "in my bones"—I knew what I was doing "instinctively." However, the process of thinking through my feelings, precisely wording my ideas, and committing them both to paper was extremely useful, and I would recommend it to those of you who, like me, are content to leave them unstated. I had to focus my ideas and, in the process, where I was headed with the

library program became much clearer. It also gave me something concrete to discuss with my administration and staff. This was the next step, discussion with the rest of the staff. As well as opening discussion and allowing for school ownership of the resource center, looking at the goals and objectives provided an excellent introduction to the uninitiated staff members as to what the resource center could do. The goals were no longer my hidden agenda. They belonged to the school. It became our resource center, and I could work with staff members as a partner in the learning process.

It is important for the teacher-librarian and the administration to realize that the process of becoming a partner in the integration of classroom and library programs is a slow one. Gains will be small at first but a commitment to a school library program that supports all areas of the curriculum and development of the student, will have significant educational results. Small, solid steps, based on research, and an understanding of goals and objectives, are much better than huge leaps and bounds that ultimately result in a fall.

Becoming a full partner in curriculum development at the school level is a process of evolution, not creation. Where you begin the evolution will determine your success.

I was, at this point, even more committed to the idea of CPP, but I still didn't know where I would find the time. I decided to complete a five week study on myself as a teacher-librarian. Very real terror struck! What if it turned out I do nothing more than the clerical aspect, and somebody in power finds out, and I lose my job! Some research project! After being reassured that the results could not possibly measure up to my wildest nightmares, I began the time study.

I examined the role of the teacher-librarian, and attempted to divide it into various aspects, or functions of the role. I read a great deal of literature on the topic, and finally chose the following functions as the focus for the study:

Administrative/Managerial—those activities which ensure the effective running of the physical plant;

Reference—those activities whose end product is information for its own sake, quick response items;

Clerical—those activities of a non-professional, or secretarial nature;

Teaching—this function was split into three categories: A. non-library related teaching; B. teaching which is directly library-related; C. non-directive teaching such as casual discussion with student "guidance";

Professional—activities which keep the teacher-librarian current in both the educational field and the field of school librarianship;

Cooperative Program Planning—those activities which draw on the unique expertise of the teacher-librarian in bringing students and resources together in the learning process.

This is a very brief outline of the six functions I used for the purpose of analyzing my time. I carefully thought through each of the functions, and made the description of each specific task, with examples. In this way I had clearly delineated for myself the areas each of these functions encompassed.

I set up the study using a tape recorder and a pad of paper to note down everything I did during the day and madly transcribed both every night onto a data sheet. From there I was able to figure the amount of time spent in each function, and arrive at daily, weekly and complete five week percentages for each of the six functions. I decided to keep track of the number of interruptions I received—that lasted for the first part of the first day. I quit counting when the total was over one hundred interruptions, and it wasn't even near lunch! I began to realize why I felt frustrated because I wasn't getting anything accomplished! Few teacher-librarians just sit and wait for questions and therefore much of our role involves interruptions. I am now more realistic in my planning, realizing that interruptions are merely opportunities in a strange disguise. I find my frustration level to be much lower, and many of those "interruptions" lead to exciting opportunities for CPP and real teachable moments.

The study was successful in that it fulfilled the initial purposes I had set out, but also had many side benefits, a few of which I have attempted to illustrate in the above discussion.

My first purpose was to find out how I was spending my time in each of the six functions at the time of the study. The chart fulfills that purpose in a very narrow manner. The results are neither right, nor wrong. They are merely mine and reflect how my time was spent during that five week period only. In no way do they reflect my average day, or week, nor are they able to be generalized to the way anyone else spends a "typical" day. They are, however, extremely useful when interpreted. They gave me a graphical representation of not only how I spent my time, but also the total time I spent—an average of 55 hours per week at work, or at home doing some work-related activities. No attempt was made to account for every minute spent at work, yet I was really amazed at the number of hours I put in. I think other teacher-librarians would find they have much the same results as far as the amount of time spent is concerned. It can give you a real boost when you wonder why you are so tired!

The results also led me to examine my yearly plan. I chose the particular time of year for the study because it was a traditionally low use time in our school library and I knew I would have the extra hours necessary to complete the type of introspection I knew would occur. Ideally, I would have had an impartial observer follow me around and note how I was spending my time, but I am not sure that would have been as productive a learning situation as this was for me.

The high result in the category of Administrative/Managerial activities was, at first, upsetting. Then I realized that as I had identified the time period as one of low use, I naturally left such activities as weeding, paperback purchasing and so on until that point in the year.

Figure 38.1 shows the final percentages for the five week study in each function.

By taking a look at pattern of use, I was able to identify other traditionally low use times during the year, and was then able to begin slotting some new CPP units into these low use time frames. I also developed a large "year at a glance" chart

Figure 38.1   Final Percentages

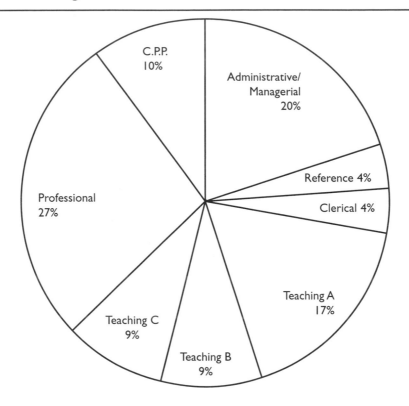

where I mapped out all of the yearly type projects, like a grade 7 CPP orientation to the library/social studies project for the last two weeks of September. This chart I have found to be invaluable for a number of reasons. It is visible and allows teachers to see what units I am involved with in the school as a whole. It allows for more effective use of the resource center and its resources (including me!) by creating a realistic timetable for units across the subject areas. I can also determine activities which should be delegated to the clerical assistant, volunteers, or student aides. Some of the things I was doing were just not a productive use of my time. I now find myself being much more aware of the activities I choose to do and those I choose to delegate. If there is someone else who can effectively do the task I am doing, it frees me to complete activities that I am specially trained to do.

In the year since I completed the study, my time spent in the clerical function has increased. This is entirely the result of the administration's

decision to cut my assistant's time from full to half. I know I now spend less time in some of the other functions, but I have kept this frustration to a minimum by stretching the clerical function at every opportunity. I am more aware of the clerical functions I choose to perform and make sure they involve a reasonably effective use of my time. I have also become much more aware of the role description I wish to perpetuate and keep the visibility of the clerical function to a minimum.

This chart does not make a distinction between the time spent during and after school hours in the professional function. When I examined the data to discover the breakdown of time in this function, I found that 70% of this time was spent outside of school hours. Evenings and weekends I spent a great deal of time attending workshops, reading and pursuing other professional activities. I no longer feel guilty when I see another teacher or staff taking home a huge pile of marking. Teacher-librarians do their share of after-hours work—and I have the statistics to prove it!

Shifting Focus

At first glance, I felt the percentage of time spent in the Cooperative Program Planning function was low. After reflecting on the data, I realized that this included planning time only, and that once a unit is moved from the planning stage to the teaching stage, the time spent became part of the Teaching B function. As a result of examining my time, I was also able to include two new units of CPP in that time slot in the next year.

My second purpose was to determine which functions were basic to my role, and had to be in place before the other functions could occur. Through the course of the study it became obvious that the Administrative/Managerial function is fundamental. It must be in place and operating smoothly before CPP can occur, otherwise there just isn't time. Similarly, classroom teaching assignments of a non-library related nature severely handicap the effectiveness of the implementation of CPP in an integrated teaching situation. The more flexibility that is lost in the teacher-librarian's daily schedule, the more difficult it is to implement a successful CPP philosophy.

I discovered how much CPP I was doing, and, when I reflected on the results, it was much more than I had anticipated. I had taken a great deal of the cooperative program planning that I do for granted, not realizing that CPP was just a term for much of the work I was already doing with teachers on my staff. I also found ways of restructuring and prioritizing my time which allows for more integrated unit planning and cooperative teaching this past year and so my third purpose was realized.

My fourth purpose was an examination of my own working habits. The study was a process of reflection and so many of the results are not transferable to other teacher-librarians, but I believe the process I went through may be of benefit to others.

I have been able to incorporate some time management skills and as a result I now have more direction. I have come to understand the need for quiet reflective time to set priorities and directions. Time to assess where I've been, what I have accomplished, and what is the next direction has become a priority.

My fifth purpose was to discover the impact I had on the school, both within and outside the curriculum. I found I had worked with over three-quarters of the staff during the five week study at some level of CPP. This was the area that was the real confidence booster. The extent of the guidance function I performed really surprised me—a great deal of my time is spent talking with students, something that we, as teachers, often forget to count as an important part of our day.

I have learned to concentrate on what I did accomplish on any given day, rather than focusing on the seemingly ever increasing pile of things that I didn't manage to get to. My goals are stated, realistic and therefore attainable. I've come to understand the necessity of reflective time. I now take the time to find out what is important, rather than trying to do everything because I thought it was all important.

So how does this relate to the title "Theory—Where is my reality?" I found out what my reality was by stepping back and analyzing it with as much objectivity as I could muster. In doing so I realized that the theory must become the goal. It is a goal that can be reached if it is backed up by introspection and the examination of where you are and where you want to be. It is a goal that I have not fully achieved as yet. I don't engage in as much cooperative program planning as I would like to—but I am doing more than I used to and I'm continually working towards that theory becoming my reality.

Index

About the Editor

Ken Haycock is professor and director of the graduate School of Library, Archival, and Information Studies at The University of British Columbia in Vancouver. Dr. Haycock began his career as a teacher and teacher-librarian before becoming a media consultant and coordinator of library media services for a large urban school board; he has taught graduate courses at several universities and has led hundreds of staff development programs for school and library systems, associations and government agencies. He was also an elementary school principal of a school of 500 students. As director of program services with the Vancouver (British Columbia) School Board from 1985 to 1992 his responsibilities included program development and implementation, the management of resources and technologies, and professional and staff development and training for more than 7,000 staff in 110 schools.

Ken Haycock has been honored by Phi Delta Kappa as one of the leading young educators in North America and received the Queen Elizabeth II Silver Jubilee Medal for contributions to Canadian society. He was elected president of the Canadian School Library Association (CSLA) at age 26 and became president of the Canadian Library Association (CLA) three years later. For his work in education and librarianship he has received distinguished service awards from several associations, including the Canadian Library Association in 1992 and the American Association of School Librarians in 1996.

In 1993 Dr. Haycock was named a Fellow of the Canadian College of Teachers, one of only ten active in Canada, and was elected as a school board member in the West Vancouver (British Columbia) School District; in 1994 he was elected Chairperson of the Board. In 1996 he was named executive director of the International Association of School Librarianship.

Ken Haycock is president of the American Association of School Librarians and chairs the association's task force on implementation of national guidelines and standards for school library media programs.